THE MAKING OF
AMERICAN RESORTS

D1523020

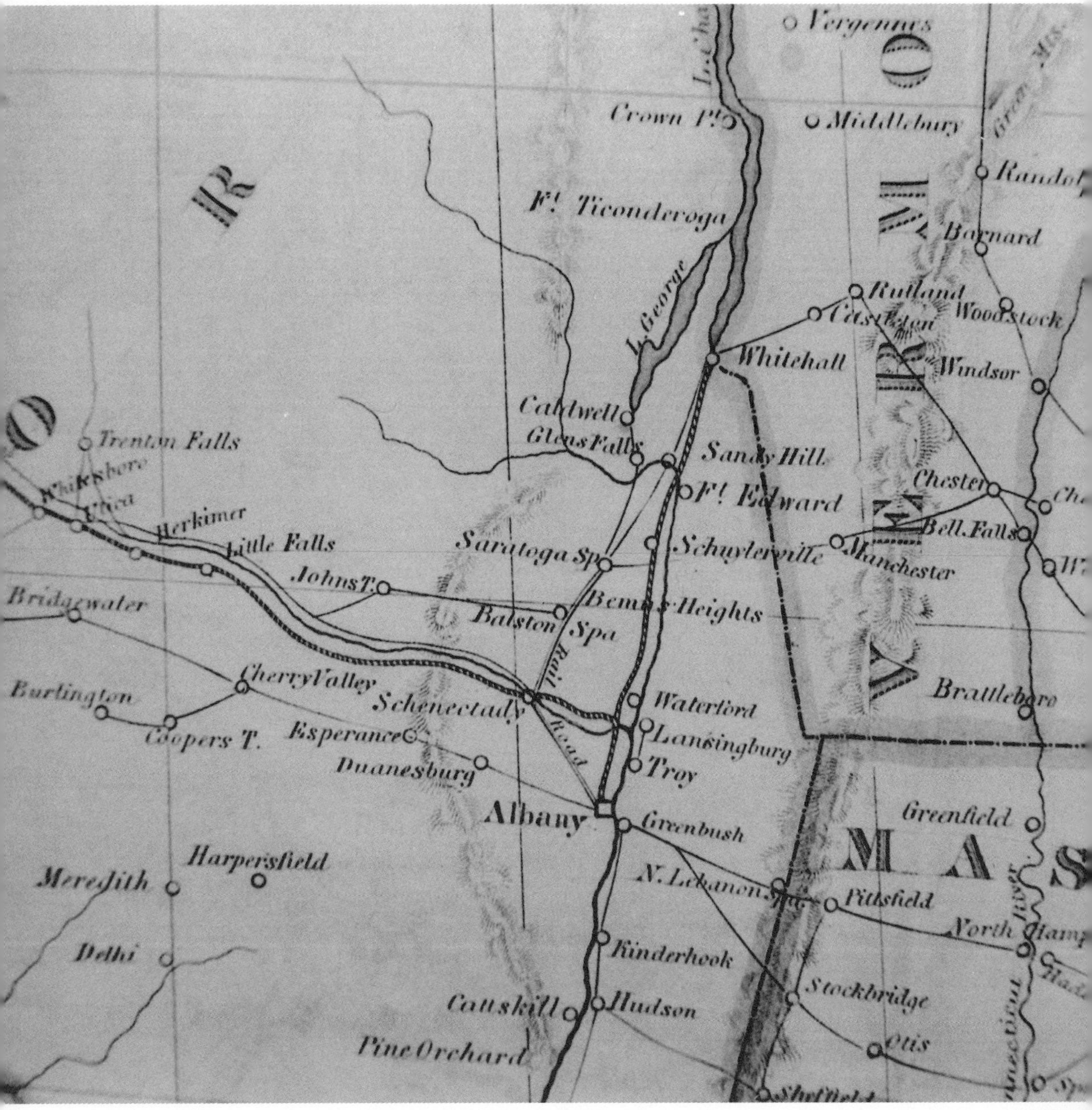

Vergennes
Crown Pt.
Middlebury
Ft. Ticonderoga
Barnard
L. George
Rutland
Castleton
Woodstock
Whitehall
Windsor
Caldwell
Trenton Falls
Glens Falls
Sandy Hill
Ft. Edward
Whitesboro
Utica
Herkimer
Little Falls
Chester
Saratoga Sp.
Schuylerville
Bell. Falls
Manchester
Johns T.
Bridgewater
Bemus Heights
Balston Spa
Rail Road
Cherry Valley
Burlington
Schenectady
Waterford
Brattleboro
Coopers T.
Esperance
Lansingburg
Duanesburg
Troy
Albany
Greenbush
Greenfield
MAS
Harpersfield
Meredith
N. Lebanon Spa
Pittsfield
Delhi
Kinderhook
Stockbridge
Cattskill
Hudson
Otis
Pine Orchard

THE MAKING OF AMERICAN RESORTS

Saratoga Springs, Ballston Spa, Lake George

❦

THEODORE CORBETT

RUTGERS UNIVERSITY PRESS

New Brunswick, New Jersey, and London

Library of Congress Cataloging-in-Publication Data

Corbett, Theodore, 1941–
    The making of American resorts : Saratoga Springs, Ballston Spa, Lake George /
Theodore Corbett.
        p. cm.
    Includes bibliographical references and index.
    ISBN 0-8135-2841-0 (cloth : acid-free paper) — ISBN 0-8135-2842-9 (pbk.: acid-free paper)
    1. Resorts.   I. Title.

    TX907 .C67 2000
    647.94747'01—dc21

                                                                                    00-028074

British Cataloging-in-Publication data for this book is available from the British Library

Frontispiece: The Caldwell–Saratoga Springs–Ballston Spa area. (*Routes and Tables of
Distances Embraced in the Traveller's Guide through the Northern and Middle States and the
Canada's,* published by G. M. Davidson, Saratoga Springs, N.Y., 1833.)

Designed by John Romer
Typeset by G & S Typesetters, Austin, Texas

Manufactured in the United States of America

To my mother,
MARION CORBETT DOME

Contents

Illustrations

❧ ❦

Tables

Preface

❦ ❧

T he idea for this book developed in the summer of 1989, when I received a National Endowment for the Humanities Fellowship to study American history with Kenneth Jackson and a dozen scholars at Columbia University. It was here that I first viewed resorts as a particular type of community, one devoted to leisure and pleasure rather than to industry and commerce.

This book was originally conceived of as a study of material culture, with the emphasis on architecture and planning. However, it increasingly became a social history of resort communities as I discovered the crucial role of ethnic and racial groups. I wrote two seminal articles for the Saratoga County History Center, Ballston Spa, one on African Americans in Saratoga County and the other on women visitors to the spas. The book was perfected each time I did a project, each time I gave a presentation or walking tour, and each time I held a class. Gathering illustrations required creation of an exhibit catalogue because I wanted them to support and be fully integrated into the text. I thank the institutions that have generously allowed me to use images from their collections.

In the last stages of writing the book my true colors as a historic preservationist appeared. Two Saratoga Springs structures that were vital to my account were demolished, even though both were on the National Register of Historic Places and had had their fate reviewed by the city's Design Review Commission. The Pitney House Hotel and the Flanigan house were judged to lack economic viability, and many neighbors considered them eyesores. I came into this controversy late, probably too late, but I did want to be certain that every effort was made to give these buildings a chance for renovation. Saratoga Springs was New York State's first certified local government in that it met all requirements for protecting its historic resources, and it was known for the preservation of its heritage. Some like-minded individuals and I formed a friends-of-historic-buildings group to spearhead the effort to save the two buildings, and I want thank them for fighting a good fight even though we lost. Yes, even in a community where historic preservation has been pioneered and has contributed to the revitalization of the economy, progress can outweigh historical and architectural integrity. In any case, I hope this book will preserve the memory of what has been lost in the built environment as well as contribute to the growing body of scholarship on resort communities.

Acknowledgments

❧ ❧

I am particularly indebted to two colleagues who have served as co-authors of two of the book's chapters. Without John Cromie's enthusiasm for Ballston Spa, both past and present, my knowledge of that community would never have been enhanced. He shared his copies of the Low papers, which he had painstakingly extracted on visits to the Library of Congress, as well as discussing with me the intricacies of the earliest spa's past. Without Reid Larson, formerly director of the Essex County Historical Society, the chapter on the planned alleys in Saratoga Springs would not be as comprehensive or as rigorous as it is, nor would it meet the highest standards for studies of vernacular architecture and planning. We walked the city's alleys separately and together, discovering significant structures and discussing the fine points necessary to make sense of the built environment.

I am also indebted to colleagues whose contributions were more sporadic but equally intense. Sonia Taub has made Solomon Northup her subject and has been unselfish in keeping me abreast of developments in this growing field of interest. Saratoga Springs City Historians Bea Sweeney and, currently, Martha Stonequiest always smoothed the path to locating information. At the Saratoga Room in the Saratoga Springs Public Library, Ellen deLalla, Saratoga Room coordinator, and Jean Stamm, assistant director of the library, were ever helpful and encouraging. Holly Schwartz-Lawton, director of the Saratoga Springs Urban Heritage Area, has followed every aspect of this project, offering me opportunities for presentations and exhibits. Issues relating to the city's historic resources often brought me in contact with the always helpful Geoff Bournam, Saratoga Springs city planner. Doris Lamont, the Historical Society of Saratoga Springs librarian, went out of her way to make available the society's collection of hotel registers. Faye Dudden at Union College read an early draft and made helpful comments. Throughout the project, Kate O'Connell, who worked with me at the Saratoga Springs Preservation Foundation, has been a supportive friend and source of information on how Saratoga Springs really works.

In looking at Caldwell, no one can possibly start without consulting Pam Vogel, former Warren County historian and now Warren County records manager, and her able assistant Thomas Lynch. In Ballston Spa, I have been aided at Brookside, the Saratoga County History Center, by the former director, David Mitchell, and by the former dedicated board member Fran Finkbiner.

I also owe a profound debt to the students in my local-history courses at Adirondack Community College, Glens Falls, New York. They have contributed to this book through their original research, their spirited questioning, and their effort to make a difference in their communities.

Encountering the world of publishing was also an eye-opening experience for me. I am pleased that Rutgers University Press was enthusiastic about adding the book to its list. Leslie Mitchner, associate director and editor-in-chief, wanted to publish this book from the beginning and brought her enthusiasm and dedication to the project. She and her staff have guided me through the intricate editorial process. I commend the press for its groundbreaking series on resort and tourism history.

Finally, I must acknowledge a debt to those who have attended my public programs or viewed my exhibitions, especially the participants in my walking tours. I am grateful for the underwriting of these activities, chiefly from the New York Council for the Humanities in 1989, 1991, 1996, 1997, 1998, and 1999. This book grew out of such experiences, and it is profoundly richer because of these opportunities.

THE MAKING OF
AMERICAN RESORTS

Introduction
The Creation of Resorts

Betweeen the end of the American Revolution and the centennial of the new republic, the United States experienced a birth that has been neglected by historians. Resort life emerged in upstate New York, where three communities—Ballston Spa, Caldwell at Lake George, and Saratoga Springs—were developed chiefly because of their ability to attract visitors. This book concerns the environment and the amenities that these resorts offered visitors, placing the emphasis on those who were most responsible for the resort experience, the "hosts"—that is, the workers and the citizens in these communities. The book shows that the resort business developed from within a community in order to entertain a captive audience of visitors. The hosts created the facilities and services that formed a resort infrastructure—from full-service hotels, the anchors of the hospitality industry, to the elegant Casino in Saratoga Springs, the personification of exclusive hedonism. Yet the resorts also harnessed nineteenth-century religious fervor through the construction of large churches that accommodated the needs of the faithful. To explain these contrasts, no effort will be spared in getting under the skin of the resort community to see how it functioned and led the way in making vacations an accepted experience in the United States.

My own experience with these three communities shows how far the resort industry has come since the early years. About the time of World War I, my family acquired an 1885 Adirondack camp that it still owns; in my youth I spent two weeks of every summer at this Queen Anne log cottage on Lake George. Surrounded by the woods that I glimpsed through the chinks in the logs, with a central stone fireplace to gather around on rainy days, the cottage is the most vivid feature of my vacation memories. At this family vacation spot, I could greet my relatives from all over the country, without even remembering their names, by simply saying, "How are you, cousin?" And if things became a bit dull, there was always the village, Lake George that is, where all kinds of entertainment and recreation were possible. Our parents did say the village was getting "to be like Coney Island," but we didn't care because it offered an opportunity to play miniature golf and meet the opposite sex. An occasional place to visit was Saratoga Springs because of "the track," its thoroughbred racecourse. The formality of the "spa" contrasted with the casualness of the camp; to enter the grandstand I had to improvise the required coat and tie. Most of the Saratoga crowd stayed in hotels on Broadway, where they spent the day socializing on the porches or studying the racing forms to handicap the meet. To me, Saratoga represented an exotic urbanity; it was far too much like New York City for a summer retreat. As for Ballston Spa, I remember scarcely anything; at best it was a crossroads factory town that I had to drive through.

The three communities lay north of New York City, two hundred miles inland, and belong to a region that stretches along both sides of the Hudson River, bounded on the south by Albany and on the north by the Adirondack mountains. The area's history put it on the map, for it had been marked by great eighteenth-century conflicts among Native Americans, Europeans, French Canadians, and British Americans. The culmination of these rivalries came in 1777 at the decisive Battle of Saratoga; on the west bank of the Hudson River, the site of the American victory would later be visited as hallowed ground. In the 1790s, military action was a distant memory, but visiting the famous battlefields became a pleasurable pastime, with local people acting as guides. To the west of the site of the Battle of Saratoga were the region's emerging mineral springs, Ballston and Saratoga, only six miles apart. The region also had scenic wonders. Lake George's fabled crystalline water was already sought by visitors, who would eventually gather in the Greek Revival village of Caldwell to enjoy the scenery and catch the abundant fish. This was the village that a century later my parents would warn me was turning into Coney Island.

Like many a visitor, I became interested in the history of the Saratoga–Lake George region. The early military campaigns had been widely popularized by the nineteenth-century writers James Fenimore Cooper and Francis Parkman. I read all their books and explored the sites that inspired some of the country's best historical writing. In the process, I came to realize that these writers were, in fact, visitors who helped to create a tourist industry for the region. My annual trek to the family camp, however, did not resemble the experience of visitors like Cooper or Parkman. In the first half of the nineteenth century they had come under far different conditions. They visited Lake George singly or with a comrade, finding the experience far too arduous to bring their families. The journey by railroad and stagecoach was time consuming, taking them from Albany to Ballston Spa and then to Saratoga Springs in order to reach Lake George. Moreover, in the 1790s, the "summer place to be" was the surprisingly popular Ballston Spa. Even when Saratoga Springs became Ballston's rival and eclipsed it, it was not because of the thoroughbred track, for it was not yet established. Thus I suspected my need to wear that sport coat to the spa had much deeper roots than the appearance of the track. And when visitors got to Lake George, there were no summer cottages and scarcely any hotels; Parkman, acting as a young bohemian, had to camp on the lake's islands, an activity so popular today it requires a reservation months in advance. The world of tourism that Parkman and Cooper knew had clearly evolved into something quite different by the time I was visiting the same places.

My early pleasure with history grew, and I took a Ph.D. in the subject, with my interests gravitating toward social history. Looking into the region's colonial history, I found an abundance of sources and monographs, for Parkman had many imitators, and multivolume sets of the correspondence of the chief players in the colonial wars and the Revolutionary War had been published. However, when I sought sources from after the Revolution and especially those involving the resort era, I came upon a conspicuous abyss. True, there were early guidebooks to the region, and many of the twentieth-century ones were still using tales and material from them. But there was little else, principally because resort life was not deemed an important enough topic for serious historians to investigate. Early resort communities did not fit easily into academic accounts of the nineteenth century. Without the requisite manufacturing base and an industrial working class on the road to self-consciousness, the resort was far from being a typical product of the Industrial Revolution. Instead, resorts depended on a market that originated chiefly outside the community, and an overabundance of public spaces and amenities were required to attract those visitors. Because of these conditions, sources on resort life were geographically diverse and fragmentary, a pitfall savvy historians avoid. In formulating a history of the three resorts, I found myself on my own, searching in unusual ways and places for material that might provide insight into these communities' development.

One of the unusual ways included my special relationship with Saratoga Springs. In 1984, I moved to Saratoga Springs to became director of its preservation foundation, the organization charged with protecting and enhancing the city's built and landscaped environment. Here, as what you might call a "participant observer," I acquired a new perspective on a community with more than two million annual visitors, the mainstay of the city's economy. I not only promoted cultural tourism but profited from it. My circa 1840 Greek Revival house contained a small apartment that during July and August commanded a rent four times the usual amount. Of course, I had to spruce up the apartment, emphasizing its location near Broadway, as well as provide air conditioning and cable. In those two months, however, I was transformed into an entrepreneur, contributing to the resort infrastructure, just like so many of the figures in the coming pages. Thus I experienced firsthand the need for a resort community to provide comfort and services to draw visitors.

Combining my personal experience with my research, I became convinced that resorts attracted visitors through their own initiative, that there was no such thing as a resort made by its visitors. To prove this theory, a historian would have to dispose of the thesis of the most widely read book on Saratoga Springs history, in which the author, George Waller, claimed the spa's success depended on the appearance of certain visitors.[1] He portrayed the development of resort communities in the following way. The rich and famous of a nearby city invite their friends to spend free time at these charming places. Their demands on the local inhabitants force the creation of services and accommodations. Some visitors like it so much they return annually and eventually establish their own cottages. Thus is born a resort. In other words, Waller argues that great and gracious visitors created a resort; no matter what the area offered in scenic wonders or comforts, where fashionable people went, the public was sure to follow. He assumed that well-defined social activities, as established by well-to-do visitors, played the dominant role in the success of resorts. In sum, Waller portrayed Saratoga Springs as the result of these social conditions and also offered them as a standard explanation for the rise of other successful resorts.

It is possible, however, to view these communities in another way, in terms of what can be called resort infrastructure. Infrastructure is born out of the creation of public spaces like streets, alleys, squares, public buildings, open spaces, and neighborhoods. These spaces are charged with social symbols that derive from concrete changes in architectural, landscape, or residential conditions. To find these meanings I had to search for patterns in the way that streets were laid out in various communities. Focal points around which communities clustered—

such as hotels, retail establishments, churches, railroad depots, pleasure grounds, and assembly halls—had to be identified. Behind these focal points were alleys and the structures that lined them, crucial, if less apparent, public spaces whose role in the development of resorts requires a detailed explanation.

Because public places were so important for the success of a resort, I had to use images to trace their development. Here my work at the Saratoga Springs Preservation Foundation was helpful, as field observation of existing spaces, based on National Register of Historic Places survey techniques, made buildings into documents.[2] Above-ground archeology confirmed or rejected the written trail offered by estate records, family papers, and archival sources. Maps, sculptures, buildings, and popular prints provided important evidence that sustained an argument rather than merely decorating a presentation. Tracing growth through public planning and the private development of streets, alleys, and gathering places required close scrutiny of maps. Structures and landscapes were examined as to their placement, design, decoration, and popularity. Analysis of vernacular architecture was useful because it explained the significance of the overlooked porch, the forgotten stable, the neglected landscape. Additionally, popular visuals such as Currier and Ives prints told me about nineteenth-century visitors, especially their religious convictions and gender roles. Photographs were also important because they were one of the few sources in which visitors were caught practicing the social art of "seeing and being seen."

With public buildings, the Saratoga–Lake George region had an important first, for it was here that the full-service hotel was introduced as the chief magnet for tourism. In 1804, the nation's largest hotel appeared at Ballston Spa, not New York, Philadelphia, or Boston as one might expect. Moreover, Saratoga Springs was never a single-hotel resort; from early on it spawned a plethora of hotels and respectable boarding houses to serve every taste and pocketbook. In 1855, Saratoga Springs had twenty-two hotels, twice as many as the rising resort community of Niagara Falls.[3] More than other resorts, Saratoga Springs became and continued to be a resort of hotels and boarding houses, while other destinations preferred the row house, cottage, camp, or suburban estate. Hotels became social melting pots because they offered no reliable index of social status, allowing any social misfit with cash or credit to stay and put on a stylish show. Thus the numerous hotels in Saratoga Springs made money as respectable as breeding in setting the standards for resort society. In fact, because of their enormous size and uniquely American effort to provide all services under one roof, the spa's hotels represented the entrepreneurial spirit of the hosts. In these three communities the need to attract visitors led entrepreneurs to erect hotels, which were the beginning of a resort infrastructure.

To establish the presence of a resort infrastructure, the labor force needs to be defined and quantified. Women were the largest segment of it; they catered to visitors by practicing public domesticity—managing boarding houses and hotels, providing entertainment, and serving as domestics. The initial clue to a community's seriousness as a resort was that its population had a considerable surplus of females over males. In 1855 at Saratoga Springs, for instance, females constituted more than 53 percent of the population, while in contrast at Niagara Falls they were only 47 percent.[4] Usually the surplus was created by single women who had to work for a living. The resort workforce also included those existing on the edge of U.S. society, like Native Americans. They left their reservations to work at resorts, where they provided glimpses of their culture to visitors by selling birch-bark sewing baskets to ladies as souvenirs or guiding gentlemen through the wilderness to obtain hunting and fishing trophies.

The women who provided the bulk of the services at resorts came largely from two groups: African Americans and the Irish. The place of blacks in the resort community has long been recognized, but they have been seen much more as examples of a "buffoon" or "Sambo" mentality than as an essential part of the workforce. Blacks were relegated to the lowest echelons of resort services and had little opportunity beyond that; often in their declining years they left the region or eked out their existence on isolated farms. Even in domestic service they had competition from whites, especially after the 1840s, when large numbers of Irish immigrants arrived. The Irish were able both to support extended families in Ireland and to marry in the resort. Yet the Irish "micks" suffered from the same subtle yet virulent northern discrimination as blacks, although they were able ultimately to overcome most of the barriers. In domestic service, groups of single Irish women, often sisters, pushed black women aside and took over the role of being the largest segment of the resort workforce. In Saratoga Springs the Irish were still symbolically separated from the rest of the community, however, in Greenridge Cemetery, where they were allotted the flat and unlandscaped plots below the ridges dominated by the haughty Protestants. Evidence of changes such as these in the resort infrastructure contributes to the growing fields of African American and ethnic history.

In creating a resort infrastructure, commercialization is crucial. To make resorts accessible, entertaining, and, most important, profitable, development was necessary. It was not enough to simply attract the proper visitors to a scenic or healthful place; promotion and financial investment were required for communities to make a living from tourism.[5] The timing and extent of commercialization determined the success or failure of the resort community. Commercialization created tension between cultural leaders, who saw the pristine state of natural wonders as the chief attraction, and developers, who saw these wonders as places to be organized for profit. Americans were proud of their scenic spots, and so it was near them that they placed their resorts and inevitably commercialized them. Hotels such as the Catskill Mountain House, which opened in 1823 on a spectacular mountaintop site, served the broad public, who felt that natural beauty was spiritually uplifting. The development of natural wonders as popular as Niagara Falls improved the experience, as entrepreneurs sought to create an infrastructure that would help people enjoy them. An excursion to Niagara Falls came to be a visit not only to the falls but, as perfected by promoters, to Termination Rock, to the Cave of the Winds, to Terrapin Tower at the edge of the falls, or for a cruise on the famous *Maid of the Mist.* One historian feels that the souvenirs purchased at Niagara Falls were a means of educating middle-class visitors about the value of nature, a way of explaining such phenomena to a broad section of U.S. society.[6]

Debates over scenic wonders overshadowed the fact that urban wonders were an attraction of almost equal popularity. From the beginning they were commercial ventures, so there was no need to discuss their compatibility with nature. In fact, the ability of Americans to mold their environment was as admired as was the hand of God in creating scenic wonders. The Lowell mills, the prisons at Auburn and Philadelphia, the state hospital at Utica, the shops of New York City stimulated pride in the new nation's urban achievements. The spas served as a bridge between the urban experience and the scenic experience because they combined the health-giving qualities of mineral springs with an expansive infrastructure. They contributed civilizing functions like bringing the visitor and the Native American Indian peacefully together; visitors could appreciate another culture, and Native Americans could earn money from selling crafts and teaching traditional skills. Saratoga Springs was uniquely able to bring the city and the countryside successfully together and mute the debates over the degree of commercialization.

The ability to commercialize to a moderate and tasteful extent lay in the hands of resort leadership. Developers were divided along various lines. They disagreed over the advantages of investing in private cottages and homes or in public amenities like hotels and boarding houses. Resort entrepreneurs were also divided between those who fostered community prosperity through emphasis on the public good and those who starkly put their individual interests first, seeking a quick return on their investment. In fact, most nineteenth-century businessmen chose manufacturing over resort investment because returns were faster and more substantial. Among resort entrepreneurs, outsiders generally had investments in several areas that they judged against each other within their financial empires — a situation in which resort enterprises were at a disadvantage. Resident developers, however, were usually more altruistic; they introduced permanent improvements and were concerned with freedom of access to amenities and the enhancement of their fellow citizens' quality of life.

Commercialization of the upstate New York resorts was dominated by entrepreneurs from New York City and the state capital, Albany.[7] The state's peculiar institution, the control of property by landlords through leases, gave them exceptional control over their investments. Like the resources of the English aristocracy they sought to emulate, their wealth was based on landed estates, and at first their resorts attracted aristocrats of similar temperament. In Saratoga Springs and Ballston Spa, landlord influence was always present but never all-pervasive, and it eroded rapidly in the 1820s. At Lake George, however, it survived in its most virulent Hudson Valley form until the death in 1848 of the lake's landlord, William Caldwell. Although the aristocratic demeanor of the early resorts continued until the end of the century, it became an ideal more than a reality. New York's aristocracy was as open as possible; it constantly absorbed new blood from the middle class and even lower classes, serving as a clearing-house for the nouveau riche, who on vacation sought to create the impression that their families had long been related to English gentry.

Some historians are convinced that hedonism was the key to a resort's ability to flourish. Waller insists, for example, that a resort needed wickedness to succeed. He argues that when Saratoga Springs was tolerant, bohemian, and fun-loving, it flourished, but when it became puritanical and moralistic, it declined.[8] The durability of masculine pastimes like drinking, gambling, and horse racing made it a great resort. He establishes temperance and evangelical religion as a cause of either the spa's difficulties or its outright depression. In essence, according to this theory, the most flamboyant, free-thinking, and theatrical visitors created a successful resort and made it a place in which to see and to be seen, the key to a resort's commercial success. Thus Waller sees tourism expanding as Americans put aside puritan values, and he views those places in the forefront of this movement as most successful. Waller may draw his interpretation too starkly, but it is evident that he feels religion had a negative effect on the life of a successful resort.

To settle this controversy, the nature of pleasure has to be probed far more deeply than Waller did. Some resorts flourished on the emotional appeal of religious revivals and changing nineteenth-century middle-class morality. In the 1830s and 1840s, certain resorts that were founded with a religious purpose were open to all who practiced revival spiritualism but were definitely avoided by those who rejected such enthusiasms. These resorts sprang up in rustic areas, largely in the form of tent camps. After the Civil War they became permanent, as they were transformed into cottage villages. Specifically, in the 1830s the Methodist camp meetings on Martha's Vineyard moved from tent cities into newly built cottages, creating a "spiritual Newport."[9] By the Civil War era, the cottage communities of Wesleyan Grove and its commercial extension in 1867, Oak Bluffs, were places with a special environment: they combined the spiritual bonding of the revival with respect for the material accomplishments of the faithful, exemplified by their cottage homes. Overarched by oak trees, the community appeared to be set in untrammeled nature. Yet the two-story Gothic gingerbread cottages were purposely crowded on narrow lots, forming a tightly packed "heavenly city," pervaded by Christian values. The open double doors of the cottages derived from the original revival tents, ensuring a total lack of privacy for the spiritual families. Boarding houses were also common and added to the public and urban aspect. The cottages and the families who summered in them became an open spectacle, an object of tourism, because of the picturesque sanctity of the place. In the 1870s the spectacle included summering visitors like Harriet Beecher Stowe and President Ulysses S. Grant. For the religiously inclined and those looking for an aesthetic experience, the cottage communities of Wesleyan Grove and Oak Bluffs were at first glance a holy alternative to the worldly spas like Saratoga Springs. Still, the religious villages shared with the spas a concern to offer visitors the buildings, design, and amenities of a sophisticated urban neighborhood.

Were the Martha's Vineyard resorts exceptional? The fact that medieval European tourism was based on the spiritual renewal of the pilgrimage shows that a close and positive relationship had existed between tourism and religion. Certainly the shrines and monasteries along the pilgrimage routes were places "to get away from it all" and enrich oneself spiritually. The Saratoga region was the center of age-old religious controversies, some dating from seventeenth-century England, which supported radical nineteenth-century religious revival in the surrounding countryside. However, the zealots soon turned to Saratoga Springs as a potential heavenly city on earth. The spa was split over temperance and other conduct issues between sober puritans and fun-loving Episcopalians. The village fathers were aware of how to turn religious fervor into profit, catering to American pilgrims just as shrines and monasteries had catered to religious travelers in the Middle Ages. Famous preachers were invited to expound on temperance in order to attract crowds to the spa. The region's grandest churches were erected to hold and entertain the faithful and thereby expand the spa's visitor amenities. Simultaneously, however, local temperance legislation was avoided so that all visitors could enjoy themselves, and thus the spa stopped short of becoming a heavenly city. Saratoga Springs had the amenities and the tolerance to hold both the spiritual and the epicurean visitor.

The hedonism question leads me to ask who visited the spas in both quantitative and qualitative terms. Historians have begun to explore this issue, providing more background than on the previous topics. One helpful authority, Neil Harris, finds two eras of nineteenth-century vacationing, based on work, demography, and income distribution. In the first, pre–Civil War era, he argues, "the power to take time off for parts of the year, or to send one's family on trips for health and recreation, belonged almost exclusively to the wealthier classes." They sought to get away from summer heat and to avoid their urban workers, whom they derided as "civic scum." Thus U.S. resorts followed the tradition of eighteenth-century English spas, enclaves of the upper class. In the second, post–Civil War era, Harris claims this exclusivity began to wane, and the rest of the century saw the dominance of "the Commercialized Vacation." The numbers of vacationers increased drastically because of the appearance of a new urban middle class, made up of salaried clerical and bureaucratic workers who wanted to enjoy a vacation. Expanding railroad transportation made it easier to travel, and railroad companies began to promote inexpensive vacation destinations that had not existed in the past. Travel agencies such as Britain's Thomas Cook appeared, and by the 1870s vacations could be cheap excursions, open to more Americans than ever before. The vacation was now viewed "not as a luxury but as a necessity for anyone who aimed to do a large amount of high-grade work." Harris attributes this opening of resorts to the middle class to two aristocratic attitudes: the acceptance of the English notion of the healthful and educational value of a vacation and the decline of the traditional puritan ethic and its replacement with a nineteenth-century derivative, the idea that a vacation strengthened one's ability to cope with work and family life.[10]

Although Harris is a useful starting point, visitation is a complex issue. Resort exclusivity declined in the face of commercialism well before the Civil War, when Harris claimed it did; in some places this decline began as early as the 1820s. Furthermore, the middle class penetrated U.S. resorts and society at different rates, making its appearance a crucial but uneven moment in the evolution of resorts. For instance, tourism in New York State, not just aristocratic traveling, commenced in the early nineteenth century with the publication of guidebooks for the grand tour up the Hudson River, then northward to Ballston Spa and Saratoga Springs and westward to Niagara. This profusion of published guidebooks democratized travel because these once-exclusive itineraries for the well-bred were now open to anyone who could afford the trip. Additionally, steamboats plying the Hudson River to resort destinations forced visitors to mingle with a variety of travelers, regardless of social class, a situation that made prerailroad transportation a leveling force.[11]

Explanations of visitation are complex also because the development of communities as resorts was uneven, and their fame was not equally lasting. Ballston Spa had ceased to be a resort by 1850, while at that time Lake George's Caldwell was just beginning reluctantly to develop a tourist trade. The story of these two villages is typical because most communities could not economically sustain themselves as resorts for long. Uniquely Saratoga Springs would always settle its public and economic disputes by deciding what was good for a diverse clientele; this pattern enabled it to become the region's leading and most long-lived resort as well as its largest community. Of the three, although Saratoga Springs did undergo Harris's middle-class revolution, Ballston Spa never experienced it, and Caldwell held it off until the 1950s.

There is another problem with Harris's view that the vacation was democratized by making it available to the middle class: women were left out of the visitor mix. The hotel registers of Ballston Spa and Saratoga Springs testify to a gender gap, regardless of social class, in favor of men. Before 1880, vacations were a masculine rather than a feminine or familial preserve in the United States. Early vacations were oriented around hunting, fishing, camping, or tramping over historical battlefields, activities from which women and children were usually excluded. Even with the advent of the hotel, male occupants were twice as numerous as females, and activities such as billiards, gambling, and horse racing, which attracted men, were off limits to most women. The conduct of young women on a visit to the spas was more restricted than that of young men, women being treated as if they belonged to a secluded Arabian culture. True, as the century advanced, women did stay at resorts in parties of their own sex, ignoring the need for male chaperones, and they may have had more freedom than before to walk about. Women's role at most resorts was not based on their significant position as wife or mother. Even if they came with their husbands, their role was minimal because their children and domestics were not there, the exception being at the family camps and cottages of post–Civil War Lake George and similar resorts. Women could, however, become aggressive in practicing the arts of seeing and being seen; they provided an air of gentility, eventually helping to create the social season journalists so minutely scrutinized and reported on to the outside world.

Resorts leaders could choose to attract an exclusive or an expansive crowd, a decision that contributed to their long-term success. Some resorts followed a trend toward diversity and democratization of clientele, but others, such as White Sulphur Springs (West Virginia), Newport (Rhode Island), and Ballston Spa, stubbornly held on to the early ideal of an elite society. Looking at a different section of the nation, the South, rather than the Northeast or the Middle West, we find that a decidedly different time line and perspective emerges than the one outlined by Harris. In the South, resorts were built and sustained by the select good company that Waller emphasizes, and the aristocratic demeanor of the southern resorts was prolonged well beyond the Civil War. After all, the South had only muted participation in nineteenth-century urban industrial expansion and in the rise of the middle class or the salaried bureaucrat.

White Sulphur Springs, for instance, remained the epitome of resort exclusiveness. It was the private investment of Baltimore merchant James Calwill. Bankrupted and forced to leave the Chesapeake city, he exploited springs in the Blue Ridge Mountains of Virginia on property he had inherited from his wife.[12] Around an ordinary tavern and spring house, he built log cabins to accommodate his guests; the cabins were ultimately replaced by row houses and a few private cottages. Although the mountain air was cool in the summer and the white classical buildings of his plantation inviting, it was the presence of the flower of southern aristocracy that drew visitors such as President Martin Van Buren. The atmosphere was exclusive; facilities on the self-sufficient plantation were limited, so even members of the best Yankee families were turned away for lack of room. The family-run enterprise was undercapitalized, and amenities were delayed; no hotel appeared until 1858, and the railroad did not arrive until 1869. The likes of Robert E. Lee and "southern belles" were the spa's leading post–Civil War guests, as it continued to draw visitors from the same prewar pool. Even if the grounds were a bit shabby, it radiated southern gentility; the best southern families returned annually and renewed their acquaintances. Here was a tradition of aristocratic exclusiveness, even when amenities were lacking, that does not fit the northern trend of developing a resort infrastructure and offering the vacation to a widening middle class.

Politics also played a role in the popularity of vacation destinations, a fact that Harris neglects. Northern resorts had competed with White Sulphur Springs but began to lose their aristocratic southern constituency in the 1850s as a result of the antislavery movement and recognition by southerners that they had been squandering their wealth in the North to their own economy's detriment.[13] The northern press had dutifully reported that southerners were still coming to the North in order to encourage their presence, but in fact southerners had defected. The president's wife, Mary Todd Lincoln, and her son Tad made a journey to stay at the very Vermont resorts, including the Equinox House in Manchester, that had suffered from the southern exodus. The presence of the ailing members of the president's family, who were cured by rest at a northern resort, successfully attracted large segments of the Yankee middle class. In contrast to the southerners, they brought no servants but were pleased that hotels now had immigrant white Irish girls replacing black help. In this patriotic climate the bulk of Americans above the Mason-Dixon Line were encouraged to take a vacation at a northern resort, and at most northern resorts the aristocracy had to vacation alongside the middle class.

After 1876, a few exceptional resorts benefited from an aristocratic reaction to expanding middle-class tourism. Many of the old-money families abandoned hotels and public resorts for the privacy of their seaside or lakeside cottages, which they supplied with the same conveniences and servants that hotels had. In established cities like Newport, they added a "suburban" enclave to entertain a restricted company of their equals, as in the early days of resorts, by building clusters of cottages in pastoral, lakeside, or ocean settings, away from the main street of the spa or religious village. This was when Mrs. Gates of Philadelphia chose to build the log cottage two miles from the village on forested Lake George that my family later purchased. The exclusive tradition of the English and early U.S. spas thus survived in the North in suburban form; this tradition was maintained whenever a resort sought to replace hotels with private mansions and retreats.

At the same time, the working class made its first appearance as guests at resorts, chiefly in rustic areas near major metropolitan centers, where cheap accommodations could be found that held an extended family. To the north of New York City, the Catskill region became the most accessible to working-class immigrants as it developed into "an escape from the city, and a preventive medicine as well as a cure."[14] The Catskills provided luxury for wealthy visitors who alone, as couples, or with friends stayed at hotels without their children. After the U.S. centennial, although most immigrants could not afford or were discriminated against at hotels, they could rent a room in a farm or accept the responsibilities of a cook-your-own-food place, where even an extended family was welcome. Thus the Catskills contrasted with Newport, White Sulphur Springs, or even Saratoga Springs because they had a range of accommodations for every class of visitor, including recently arrived immigrants. Here is a final example of the changing complexity of the visitor mix.

Popular perceptions of life in resorts also do not acknowledge the complex reasons for their success. The tendency has been to treat the story of resorts as lightweight history, with facile, one-dimensional explanations for a resort's achievements. It is an exaggeration to reduce certain resorts to little more than the site of horse racing, gambling, and alcoholism. Before 1880, the vast majority of visitors to Saratoga Springs did not attend the meets, did not gamble at a casino or in a back room, and did not frequent the makeshift bars and taverns that radiated along and from the main streets. They were too genteel to engage in these activities, and risqué attractions were restricted largely to males anyway. This restriction kept these activities outside the important social rituals that were supported by women and that were held in the resort's public spaces. In an effort to sell newspapers, journalists sought to portray spas as far more exotic and displaced from the norm of U.S. society than they were. The reporters' accounts bear little resemblance to reality, and their veracity should be regarded in the same way that today we accept the word of the *National Enquirer*. In making judgments about conduct, one must assume that nineteenth-century Americans were far more earnest than we are today. The major concern of nineteenth-century resort hosts was to provide not the pleasures mentioned above but rather a restful, healthful, and entertaining experience that would appeal to the broadest respectable public.

Could it be that the hosts, not the visitors, created resorts? Obviously, this would be going too far, but certainly both have to be covered and shown to interact in explaining the dynamics of resort life, which is what I hope to do in the rest of this book. As each of the three communities is described, the focus will be on the hosts, who provided the visitor with an entertaining and healthful environment long before the word *vacation* came into common usage. I will probe Ballston Spa, Saratoga Springs, and Caldwell to see how their entrepreneurs and proprietors succeeded in developing the required resort infrastructure. I also give the visitors their due by looking at the composition of parties that stayed at hotels, their origins, and the gender gap that favored males. Social rituals are scrutinized in order to show how they were established through the combined efforts of visiting women, respectable hosts, and exaggerating journalists. In every facet, the process was new to the United States but not to Europe. Therefore we begin by looking backward, evaluating the eighteenth-century English resorts that set the standards by being the first communities devoted chiefly to entertaining visitors.

PART ONE

Early Resorts

CHAPTER 1

The Tradition of the English Spa

The origin of Saratoga's spas and the nearby lake resorts can be found as much in England as in the forests that surrounded the mineral springs. In the early nineteenth century, the influence of the English motherland was strongly felt in the infant United States. England and the United States remained each other's chief trading partners, a fact that united merchants on both sides of the Atlantic. A pro-English stance identified one of the young nation's two emerging political parties, the Federalist, based as it was on a political agenda that would enhance commercial development and new manufactures. The party was centered in New York State and New York City, where its leader, Alexander Hamilton, resided. On the West Indies island of St. Croix, he had served as a teenage agent for the New York City merchant family of Nicholas Cruger, and was connected to the Saratoga region through his Albany patrician father-in-law, Philip Schuyler. These U.S. leaders were fond of old England, its benevolent aristocracy, its commercial power, its culture, and its pleasures, and they modeled themselves on English gentlemen. A French visitor to New York City in 1788 was surprised at the city's lack of republican simplicity, instead noting the "English luxury" of manners, clothing styles, architecture, and retinues of servants.[1] Young men from wealthy New York families visited and carried out business in the British Isles as part of their education, taking back to their homes a respect for English institutions. Americans returning from England were supposedly smuggling knowledge of English technology to create U.S. factories, but of more significance for this history of resort life was the impression they carried back of what it took to make an English spa.

England's role in pioneering the idea of whole cities devoted to pleasure was based on acceptance of the idea that pleasure included the enhancement of health.[2] In 1800 Americans had numerous English spa towns to visit. Among them, six had come or were coming to the forefront: Tunbridge Wells, Buxton, Cheltenham, Harrogate, Royal Leamington Spa, and, the most renowned, Bath. Except for Bath, spas were sophisticated country towns, located in rugged and undeveloped terrain, and they were spread throughout England, so that many regions could claim a local watering spot. Spa communities flourished or declined depending on the popularity of their springs and the pleasure afforded by their visitor amenities. There were alternative resort areas such as the English Lake District, northwest of Liverpool, where from its discovery in 1769 visitors enjoyed the natural beauty of sixteen lakes and 180 peaks. Still, the rustic villages of the Lake District never possessed the combination of urban sophistication and rural charms that distinguished the spas. As places where leisure was conspicuously spent, the spas also contrasted with industrial cities, where business was organized around the clock, so that no productive moment would be lost.³ Although urban, spas sought to negate the effects of industrial routine, offering instead amenities and amusements to pass the day.

A few Englishmen settled in spas in the United States, but the transfer of European ideas was most likely carried out by Americans who had visited the English spas. For instance, Washington Irving, the romantic writer who believed in the enriching value of travel, spent a good deal of his life in England. At the age of only twenty-two he made his first visit to the motherland, which included in the next year a sojourn at Bath. He was back in the British Isles in 1815 for a seventeen-year period, reputedly to save his family's trading interests but also to serve his native country as a minor diplomat and to sell his novels in the English market. In 1831, as secretary to the U.S. ministry in London, he entertained the new minister designate, Martin Van Buren, by taking him on a tour of England, which included Bath and Buxton. The future president of the United States would adopt the habit of visiting watering places and would frequent both Saratoga Springs and White Sulphur Springs during his administration. Twice more, in 1842 and 1846, Irving was in England. He was among the first to note that taking the waters at a spa was a social as much as a healthful experience; for him the spa was a great laboratory in which to study all elements of society with their moral and physical problems. He noted, "At a watering place like Buxton where people really resort for health, you see the great tendency of the English to run into excrescences."⁴ His pen would be just as penetrating in describing Americans at their own resorts.

Irving had gone to England as a young man to gain seasoning and learn business affairs, a popular form of education among the New York patricians. Earlier, in 1761 and 1762, twenty-eight-year-old Philip Schuyler spent nineteen months in the motherland, taking in the sites of London and investigating aspects of the countryside, from the production of hemp and flax to the functioning of England's canal system. When he later came to name springs near his Saratoga estate, he designated them Chalybeate, the term used by most English spas to designate their iron-impregnated springs. His son-in-law Stephen Van Rensselaer was also impressed by spas on his visits to England following his graduation from Harvard in 1782. In 1790, at the age of thirty-six, he marshaled his resources to create a spa across from Albany, which he pretentiously dubbed Bath. His surveyor for the project, Elkanah Watson, had taken the waters at England's Bath and spurred his employer on to create the spa. And although Ballston Spa's developer, Nicholas Low, did not get to England, his business partner, William Wallace, often did. In October 1801, he wrote from England to Low that to cure his wife's headaches "we gave Cheltenham waters a fair trial but I much fear they will not have the desired effect."⁵

Other Americans did more than visit England for extended durations. Although born in America in 1768, Saratoga's Henry Walton was a thorough Englishman. The Waltons and the related Crugers were among New York City's preeminent merchant families and included leading loyalists among their ranks. From 1778 to 1788, Walton was educated in England, where he studied law. During the American Revolution, ten-year-old Walton went to England with Peter Van Schaak as his guardian. Well connected to wealthy rebel leaders such as John Jay, Van Schaak was an attorney whose loyalist convictions were strong enough that he was forced to leave New York. After landing in Bristol, Van Schaak took his pupil to Bath, which impressed the attorney because "the houses are grand, magnificent and uniform, more especially those of the Circus, Crescent and Parades, and the pavements of flat stones are like floors. The rooms are large and superb."[6] By 1785, Van Schaak had had enough of England and decided to return to New York and the American republic, while Henry continued to enjoy England.

On his return from England after the fury of the Revolution had abated, Henry Walton found his family's landed interests intact, and he was able to develop those in distant Saratoga County. In 1799, Henry Walton married his first cousin, Matilda Cruger, who had been born in England the year of the Declaration of Independence and raised as the daughter of the mayor of Bristol. At Ballston and Saratoga Springs, their memories of England were strong as they brought up their five offspring.[7] At Saratoga Springs, Henry designed the Georgian Pavilion Hotel, laid out Regent's Park, and planned squares like those in Bath. More of an English gentleman than any his contemporaries, he took the radical step of leaving his comfortable home on Broadway in 1823 and establishing a country house and modest estate to the northwest of the village on the road to Greenfield. Here he played the English gentleman at his seat, with a main house, stables, gardens, orchard, and a romantic grove. Certainly the English experience with spas and country living impressed this gentleman.

What made these English spas successful resorts? If we look at them as a group, we can isolate six factors necessary for the establishment of a successful resort community: entrepreneurial leadership in the creation of amenities and accommodations; public spaces that combined the luxury of the city with the charm of the countryside; the cleanliness of the infrastructure, especially of the back streets; the attraction of a workforce to provide the necessary service and construction skills; the solicitation of visitors through public entertainment and order; and religious piety to temper the worldly diversions of a spa. As we will see, these issues remain of constant concern in the creation of resorts in the United States as well as in England.

Resorts were unique among communities because they had to continuously attract visitors and residents to be successful. An important provision of a successful spa was the organization of sophisticated public entertainment. Visitors wanted to escape from the tension of urban living and yet enjoy a certain measure of urban sophistication while they savored the healthful benefits of the springs. For instance, Charles Dickens was a three-time visitor to Leamington spa from 1858 to 1862, doing public readings from *A Christmas Carol* and *David Copperfield.* Dickens saw his visit as a way of making extra cash, being entertained by society, and gauging which of his works were most popular. The spas attracted not just visitors but a permanent population that enjoyed the quality of life. When Jane Austen's father retired from the ministry in 1801, the family moved to Bath to enjoy its now-faded reputation as a center of health and social display. They stayed until 1807, when they moved back to quiet Hampshire, Jane having gained new material for the novels that she had yet to publish. A spinster, she was fascinated by the delicate business of providing husbands for marriageable daughters, a business that still flourished at spas like Bath. She ridiculed the silly, affected, and stupid rituals of spa society, showing that there was no consensus on how society should conduct itself.[8]

To smooth over such problems for visitors and newcomers, the position of master of ceremonies was created. The duties of such a person were to organize the activities of an assembly room or pump room and to orchestrate events that would encompass all segments of society. Not every spa had a master of ceremonies to match Bath's Richard (Beau) Nash, who combined

a love of social gatherings and gambling with a reputation for fair dealing and democratic treatment. He had written rules on dress and social decorum, but he enforced them informally so
that people were willing to conform.[9] This arrangement avoided embarrassment and created
the genteel atmosphere necessary for the performance of social rituals. However, the position
required a salary and skills at promoting social and cultural activities, the advantages not always outweighing the expense. Hotel proprietors and women of influential social standing
could perform the duties at no expense, and thus the position was far from universal.

Entrepreneurial activities were also needed for success, especially by people who were
convinced that long-term investment in resorts would eventually be as profitable as manufacturing. Spa development was a real estate enterprise that attracted only the most experienced
and well-to-do capitalists. Projects had to be innovative and unusually attractive, and this requirement caused exceptional expense for land acquisition, architectural fees, and construction. Rather than offering the opportunity for a quick return, a wide promenade, an elegant
assembly room, or a choice accommodation took years to plan and build. Those who failed to
comprehend these limitations faced the strong possibility of bankruptcy.

In Bath the sophisticated entrepreneurial system worked as follows.[10] In 1700, when it
was still a medieval town, agrarian capitalists owned much of the land around the city's walls
and were interested in maximizing their assets. Their aim was to reparcel their holdings, dis-
persing them on long and profitable leases to speculators and builders, who in turn were eager
to improve them for the growing market in fashionable housing and public spaces. One of
Bath's leading speculators was architect John Wood Sr. He leased land from the agrarian capitalists, subdivided it into house lots, and then subleased the lots to builders. Wood designed
his tracts according to high standards of taste, laying out streets, specifying the details of building facades, designing the site plan, and providing the water and sewage lines. Individual
builders assumed responsibility for the construction of buildings, using mortgage money they
had raised and accepting Wood's supervision on the construction of facades. To gain capital
for such enterprises, his son, John Wood, raised project capital by collecting it in tontine. In
this system the shares of those who died were added to those of the surviving investors so that
the last survivor inherited all. By this method in 1769 seventy shares were sold to produce the
New Assembly Rooms. The shareholders then served on committees to furnish and choose
the management for the Assembly Rooms.

In a few projects a speculator attempted to combine several activities, from raising the
capital to planting the gardens. This course was much riskier, as seen in the case of Cheltenham's Pittville development.[11] In 1800, as Cheltenham began to expand as a spa, Joseph Pitt acquired marshland on the outskirts of the town from the Earl of Essex. Having embarked on a
career as an attorney twenty years earlier, Pitt now had capital to invest in banking and land,
which in 1807 also included a countryseat, Eastcourt House in Whitshire. Until the 1820s his
Cheltenham purchase remained farmland, but then Pitt decided to create a new spa and town
on the edge of the city, which he modestly named Pittville. He raised money to begin his enterprise through a series of bank loans.

Pitt's 1824 plans called for a site of a hundred acres, crossed by several miles of tree-
lined walks and rides, on which lots for six hundred houses were laid out. A lake, a church, and

an assembly place over the mineral spring—the Pittville Pump Room—were to be the town's focal points. A local architect, John Forbes, was initially in charge of the design and building, while Richard Ware, a nurseryman, oversaw the landscape. Forbes created the pump room, a monumental two-story classical structure. On its ground floor it had a great central hall leading on the north side to the pump room. Placed inside was a marble and scagliola pump by which the healthful spring water was extracted from the ground. Forbes devoted the rest of the pump room to a card room, a billiard room, a library, and a reading room. The building was crowned with a dome whose interior was decorated with fine plasterwork. Almost five years were necessary to complete Pitt's elaborate centerpiece, which was a beacon for social display and entertainment.

As the sole sponsor of the enterprise, Pitt soon ran out of money, and although he could raise more, the delays in construction caused by cash-flow problems meant that he was unable to realize profits from the development. The leased pump room did bring in revenue in the 1830s, but after that it had difficulty competing with similar facilities in the center of Cheltenham. A recession caused housing construction to come to a standstill in 1826, and as late as 1850 only two hundred of the six hundred lots had houses on them. When the pleasure gardens were laid out in 1827, they included a long graveled walk with trees and shrubs on either side, two broad lawns south of the lake known as the Long Gardens, and ornamental bridges at either end of the lake (Figure 1). But no entrance or enclosure was erected to mark the gardens, and the design for a church was eventually discarded, as efforts were made to reduce the scope of the original plans. Driven by his noble scheme, Pitt sank deeply into debt, so that at his death in 1842 he owed creditors £150,000. His property was sold in the following years to pay his debt. In 1890, the Corporation of Cheltenham purchased the pump room and gardens, and they became part of the municipal public parks system. To judge from Pitt's experience, even a well-planned and lavish spa neighborhood was not a guaranteed success if the real estate market was weak or the competition was strong. Nevertheless, Pitt was the type of visionary entrepreneur needed to convert farmland into a sophisticated resort; such a person would also be necessary for resort development in the United States.

Despite Pitt's failure, the idea of developing a resort with housing lots around public spaces as focal points had wide success in England and the United States. Spas required the most elegant urban amenities, even in the smallest and most remote places such as Buxton. Spas also required that the built-up area harmonize with the countryside, that urban luxury blend with pristine landscape. A spa's urban amenities could not have the negative aspects of a Victorian city—crime, overcrowding, dirt, foul air, and poverty. This combination of urbanity in the midst of natural beauty was a hallmark of the English spa.

At the top of the list of requisite spa amenities were public spaces that would serve as an elegant background for leisure activities. These spaces had to be open and socially neutral, so that a wide spectrum of society could congregate to watch and be watched. All entertaining had to be done in public; the most negative situation would be one involving a private party. Public spaces included pleasure gardens, parks, promenades and parades, assembly rooms and pump rooms, and residential squares. Comfortable inns and hotels were also in this category, especially after hotels became popular in the early nineteenth century.

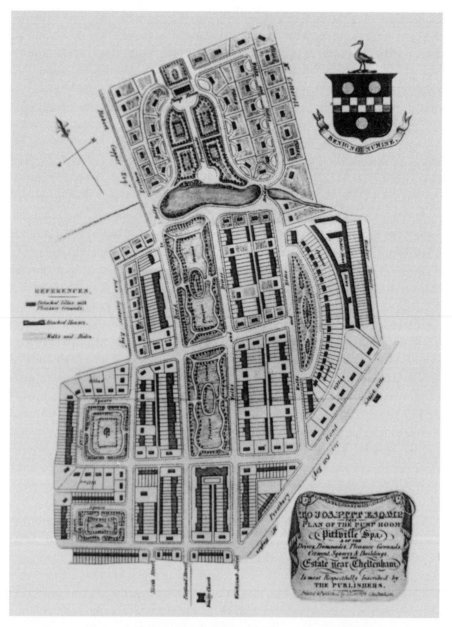

FIGURE 1. "Plan of the Pittville Estate 1826"; Pitt's proposed layout of Pittville Spa.
(Cheltenham Library, Cheltenham, U.K.)

Amenities also included municipal improvements such as paved and clean streets, street lighting, public fountains, and sewage disposal. Bath's Corporation Act of 1709 provided for stone paving, lighting, and a water-cleaning system, which created the best streets to be found in any English city.[12] The vast cobblestone spaces of Bath's Circus and South Parade were ideal for public gatherings. The fact that today the spaces have been relegated to parking lots or filled with gardens shows that in the age of the automobile we put a high priority on privacy and no longer have the same desire to gather in these spaces.

There was a need for multipurpose public spaces, best exemplified by Bath's New Assembly Rooms and Cheltenham's Assembly Rooms. In Bath, John Wood Jr. designed and built the commodious rooms from 1769 to 1771 to provide facilities that traditionally had required separate buildings.[13] The New Assembly Rooms had a tearoom for refreshments and concerts, a ballroom that held twelve hundred for dancing, and an elegantly appointed card room. The combination of gaming with food and dancing attracted both sexes, a mixture necessary for social success. The Assembly Rooms were meant to bring audiences to a variety of scheduled functions, from elaborate cotillion balls to country dances, from ridotto masquerades to revelries known as "riots." With its diverse entertainment, the structure fulfilled the need for pleasure, so that no visitor should ever want for diversions.

In Cheltenham, the Assembly Rooms were one of many private rooms competing with the Pittville Pump Room and the city's four other mineral-water facilities, which were dispersed throughout the city. The structure was erected in 1815–1816 at the cost of more than £60,000.[14] The portico of the Assembly Rooms sprawled along the entire walk that fronted the structure, enticing visitors to use its ornamental forty-foot-high ballroom and its refreshment, card, billiard, and club rooms. The upper rooms were devoted to meetings of the Cheltenham and Gloustershire Clubs. A private body of seven gentlemen, the Committee of Public Amusements, supervised the structure. By 1845, it was the property of a joint stock company that leased it to a manager, who was responsible for attracting an audience to guarantee its financial success.

Ultimately, the ideal multipurpose public space was the full-service hotel, which combined a wide array of entertainment and services. Such hotels were rarer in England than in the eastern United States, where by the mid-nineteenth century even the most insignificant villages had one.[15] The English hotel had evolved under more competitive conditions; it was not the only source of lodging and entertainment. Since the sixteenth century, the English had chains of posting inns, as close as every ten miles, where food, lodging, and fresh horses could be obtained.[16] If the object were speed at no expense, one could obtain a fresh mount or team every ten miles, and as a result it took one only an hour to cover the ten miles. Most English inns were built with transportation in mind; they were erected around an enclosed courtyard with galleried porches through which one entered the chambers. The bulk of the courtyard was devoted to stables for the post horses and coaches. The courtyard served occasionally as a stage for troops of traveling actors, whose performances kept the guests up to all hours of the night. In fact, inns changed their clientele nightly, often taking better care of their horses than their guests, and they were definitely not the place to spend an extended period of leisure time.

Similar inns and lodging houses abounded at English spas, and some were upgraded in the eighteenth century to the level of hotels. In Cheltenham, the centrally located Plough Hotel had originally been a country inn that expanded as the city grew.[17] Other hotels appeared as part of broader projects such as Buxton's Crescent, which had several separate establishments and staffs within its expansive walls, of which only one was a hotel (Figure 2).[18] The full-scale hotel facility that would become so popular in the United States was not as needed at English spas because inns provided overnight accommodations for travelers and because existing

FIGURE 2. "The Crescent at Buxton, designed by John Carr," c. 1800. The Crescent was a combined hotel, assembly room, ballroom, and local government office.
*(*The Illustrated London News, *August 26, 1854.)*

assembly rooms, pump rooms, and tearooms already provided public social facilities. Additionally, most wealthy English visitors preferred to rent private quarters during the long social season. The tendency in the United States to concentrate facilities under one hotel roof resulted from the fact that no other tourist services were available in resort communities.

In England hotels were built for uses far beyond simple accommodations. In Stamford, Lincolnshire, the grand Stamford Hotel was constructed in 1810 as a political center, a Whig counterweight to the political influence of the Cecil family.[19] They treated the town as a pocket borough, and the hotel was thus a meeting place and power base for an opposition party. Still, in spas the quality of the services for visitors was paramount. If we generalize from 1845 advertisements for Cheltenham, we see that hotels succeeded by attracting the right clientele. Many hotels advertised themselves as being especially for families, with all the comforts of home, or conversely for "commercial gentlemen," clearly traveling businesspeople. Amenities were also crucial. Most hotels emphasized the quietness and airiness of their apartments, and many had rear gardens. The best hotels were distinguished from ordinary establishments by their wine cellars and cooking staffs. A manager who was also a wine merchant ran the Belle Vue Hotel, while the Lamb Inn and Commercial Hotel advertised their wine cellars and cuisine. Facilities for transportation were also crucial. The George and Fleece hotels had coaching departments, and the Royal Hotel had a commercial room and coach office attached to it. The top of the line in Cheltenham, the Queens Hotel, claimed to have the city's best family suites, offices, kitchens, wine cellars, and stable with a carriage department.[20] Here were the services necessary for the success of an English hotel.

The problems of spa sanitation were usually caused by the dirt created by animals. Although occasionally visitors favored keeping their horses and equipage in the same building in which they lodged, the more genteel and the sick sought to put a distance between themselves and their animals. Yet the crush of horses and carriages at a spa was excessive because of the number of wealthy visitors, the need for display, and the popularity of riding as an exercise. Elaborate and separate facilities for horses and livestock were necessary because no one on holiday wanted to be reminded of the stench and filth of farmyards. In Cheltenham, liveries and stables were placed behind the main building in mewses, where one could rent a "lock-up coach house" and could choose to rent or purchase a variety of carriages, including "flys, phaetons, gigs, post and job horses, good hunters, and hacks."[21]

To eliminate unhealthful stables that were in proximity to visitors, the Duke of Devonshire had Buxton's Great Stables constructed from 1787 to 1789.[22] They served those who lodged at the Crescent, but they were located more than one thousand feet from it, a location that ensured that guests could enjoy the fresh mountain air. The coach houses were arranged in a bank attached to a vast octagonal space reserved for protected riding. This octagonal building was eighty feet in diameter, covered by a domed ceiling twenty-eight-feet high, supported by an interior Doric colonnade, and decorated with plasterwork. The octagonal ceiling was open to the air in the center, but one could reputedly ride in the space for the equivalent of twenty miles and always be partially protected from rain. The attached coach houses could hold up to 120 horses, with additional space for grooms and carriages. This grand structure carried the desire for amenities to an extreme, but it enhanced Buxton's reputation for cleanliness and order and helped to make it an attractive resort.

Extensive staffing was required to create diverse and separate public spaces, from tearooms and coffeehouses to assembly rooms, inns, and full-service hotels. This specialization of English accommodations and entertainment in many establishments was possible because of the numerous skilled workers in personal and domestic service. In 1831, service to households, both great and small, employed more people in England than any sector of the economy, save agriculture. The demand increased in the eighteenth century, as servants were regarded not only as a necessity but also as a sign of having arrived in society.[23] They ranged from highly skilled stewards, who ran the great country houses, to the most menial scullery maid. Because of the demand, they could change positions often—a leading complaint of their employers. They received not only a contractual wage but board or, instead of it, board wages, the cost of livery, and the right to used clothes and household items from the master, plus customary tips such as vails. They also had the presumed advantages of having lived with their betters and of having seen some of the world in an urban or country house. Thus, one authority claims that "we may confidently list them [household servants] among the more favored groups whose standards [of consumption of food and dress] improved on average slightly during the Industrial Revolution."[24]

Many left service—for they did not regard work in resorts as being traditional service—and managed or worked in the public houses, inns, and hotels that were the basis of the hospitality trade. A career in service often made it possible to accumulate the capital necessary to go into this trade. For instance, John Williams and his wife, Sarah, who had previously served as the butler and housekeeper of a local landowner, established Leamington's famed Regent Hotel in 1819. At the same spa in 1851, occupations in the service sector by percentage were as follows: lodging housekeepers 5 percent, female servants and maids 57 percent, male servants 19 percent, cooks 8 percent, housekeepers 6 percent, nurses 3 percent, errand boys and girls 3 percent. Not only in Leamington but in other resorts, women in service or working as lodging housekeepers made up a higher percentage of the workforce than they did in other communities.[25] Although women did outnumber men in English towns, in spas such as Bath the figure was exceptionally high; women constituted 61 percent of the population in 1801. Employment was seasonal, however, so that service workers attempted to extract exorbitant wages during a limited time to tide themselves over for the rest of the year.

The other important source of resort employment was the building trades, the crucial workforce that erected the spa's accommodations and public spaces. In 1831, the number of people in the building trades was second only to the number in domestic service; building trades accounted for perhaps four hundred thousand of England's men and boys.[26] They were divided between those who catered to the luxury trade of hotels, assembly rooms, and expansive developments of flats, and those small jobbers who were responsible for working-class housing. Working-class housing was necessary at the spas for sedan chairmen, laundresses, and wigmakers. Plain rows of tiny dwellings for the working class were built behind the elegant villas in Cheltenham's Tivoli section.[27] In addition, the trade was divided between those in the smaller towns, who depended on the craft tradition and custom of set prices, and those in the cities, who had moved into the realm of the wage contract and bottom-line management. Because imported materials such as Baltic timber, bricks, tiles, and slate added to the expense of a structure, the wise builder used local materials, especially English building stone, to keep costs down. Spas such as Buxton and Cheltenham had nearby quarries that provided employment and the stone for their construction expansion.[28] Craft specialization such as practiced by Regency Cheltenham's metalworkers led to lacelike canopies and balconies for buildings, pieces that the city's Vulcan Ironworks eventually supplied to the world. Beyond skilled craftsmen, Irish workers, "intensive in labor, but boisterous in relaxation," entered the trades as helpers at the lowest level, attending masons, bricklayers, and plasters in their most messy tasks.[29] The building trades held on to the craft system longer than other trades because their work was largely outdoors; they depended on individual skills rather than on factory organization and production.

English spas reflected the same tension between pleasure and piety that would haunt U.S. spas, the central question being whether pleasure was so excessive as to exclude piety. The debate often focused on the consumption of alcoholic spirits and the corresponding neglect of the crucial mineral waters. In 1845, Cheltenham had seven wine merchants and five beer brewers but only five outlets for its renowned mineral waters. Wine shops were respectable establishments patronized by royalty; one designated itself as "Wine and Spirit Merchant to Her Majesty," while another claimed it served as wine merchant "to their Royal Highnesses the Duke and Prince George of Cambridge." Cheltenham's spirit retailers were often found next to or within hotels, and proximity to their shops was a leading attraction for a hotel's clientele. Most carried more than wine; the Royal Cambridge and the Belle Vue's wine and spirit vaults held bottled ale, cider, and Porter stocks, Schweppes seltzer and soda water, and lemonade. As for breweries, they targeted their advertising to families. The Albion Brewery asserted that "for supply of good family beverage equal to home brewed" they had "attained a celebrity as ancient as Cheltenham itself."[30] Guidebooks like the *Illustrated Cheltenham Guide* emphasized that if taken moderately, spirits and beer were healthful and an important part of the overall spa experience.

Yet the consumption of alcoholic spirits did not go uncontested. Because the need for religion was especially acute among the sick, who sought spiritual and physical cures, Cheltenham had seventeen religious establishments, which outnumbered the wine shops and breweries combined. Seven of these, 40 percent, were Anglican, and there also were a Roman Catholic chapel and a Jewish synagogue. Still, most of the churches belonged to dissenting Protestants, the chapels—as they were called to separate them from the established Anglican churches. The Methodists were most numerous, with Wesley Chapel seating an incredible one thousand, while Baptists, Unitarians, and Quakers also had a significant presence.[31] As a result, visitors of every persuasion might find a place to worship. Ultimately, churches and preachers vied to attract visitors to their worship services.

The leading light of Cheltenham's preachers was Reverend Francis Close, the curate of Holy Trinity Church, which had been established to hold the overflow from the prestigious Anglican parish church.[32] This preacher exemplified Victorian earnestness and found much to criticize in the Regency town's uninhibited materialism. Cheltenham's new churches charged a shilling entrance fee at the door, which was no barrier to wealthy visitors but definitely one to the working class. Thus Close built a church with no admission, the Free Church of St. Paul, to attract the spa workforce. Next he railed against thoroughbred racing; in 1829 his followers disrupted the races, and a year later the grandstand mysteriously burned to the ground. Still, he failed to get the racecourse abolished, but he was able to do away with the notoriously ribald race-week fair. He also opposed the theater and Sunday trains, and his efforts delayed the building of a rail connection between Cheltenham and London. By the 1840s, the influence of his middle-class values was so pervasive that Cheltenham was described as "a polka, parson worshiping place of which Francis Close is Pope."[33] No doubt, Close's actions lessened Cheltenham's appeal to aristocratic visitors, but the church-oriented environment he created attracted the more puritanical middle class. Close's Protestant reforms would have had the same appeal in the United States, where piety and temperance were the convictions of the majority and the pleasures of the English spa seemed more hedonistic than redeeming.

English spas thus had much to offer as models for Americans interested in the development of resorts. The crucial role of entrepreneurial investors, from the Duke of Devonshire to Joseph Pitt, was evident. These investors had to be inspired not only by the profit motive but also by the belief that they were creating communities that were exceptionally attractive and functional. Additionally, spas pioneered the development of public spaces, ranging from parades and squares to assembly rooms, pump rooms, tearooms, and hotels. Such spaces had to be elegantly designed to serve as a backdrop for the resort ritual of seeing and being seen. Furthermore, spas attempted to set the standard for cleanliness and sanitation; they forced stables and noisome activities to the back of a lot, away from the living quarters and served from the outside by an alley. Spas also created a service workforce of skilled and presentable operatives. The English had an advantage over Americans in the form of an already trained servant class in the homes of its nobility and gentry; this workforce could be drawn on for the hospitality business. Of these workers, a high percentage was women, who found many employment opportunities at resorts. Additionally, resorts succeeded by encouraging visitors to participate in public activities, to become active members of resort society. Because spa visitors had diverse backgrounds and often did not stay in hotels, resort society had to be unified through rules that social leaders enforced. Enforcement was the responsibility of a master of ceremonies, a position that would rarely appear in the United States. Finally, English spas responded to the age-old conflict between pleasure and pain. In both England and the United States, puritanism still influenced the leadership of most communities, and these puritans viewed leisure time as a danger that undermined the moral fiber of society, especially causing intemperance among all the lower classes. At the English spas, with their healthful waters, most visitors also came for pleasure, and thus the resorts could be regarded as a threat to the work ethic. As a result of the puritan ethic in both England and the United States, it would be decades before the captains of industry could bring themselves to relax.

CHAPTER 2

The Rise and Fall of Ballston Spa as a Resort

*I*t was neither to Saratoga Springs nor to Lake George that visitors first flocked to pass their leisure time. This honor belonged to the now forgotten Ballston Spa. The rustic village north of Schenectady and southwest of Saratoga Springs quickly forged ahead of its rivals and overnight grew to become the leading resort in the United States. The key to this meteoric success was the enterprise of the community's landlord, Nicholas Low, together with the ingenuity of the series of overseers who represented him at the spa. Within Low's "Estate at Ballston Springs," he constructed the nation's largest hotel, laid out lots and streets to create a village and connect the springs, and fostered all manner of economic enterprise. As a result, from 1794 to 1830, Ballston Spa was a resort with a clientele from every part of the Union and from foreign countries, a spot where the best of society gathered for health and relaxation.

Previous Area Spas

Ballston Spa did not have the resort field to itself. In the late 1700s several rival spas in the Albany area were devoted to the water cure and a rudimentary measure of pleasure. These early efforts would set a pattern for future resort development. Although resorts flourished momentarily after the Revolution, most enjoyed only fleeting popularity and failed to become population centers. Because they lacked the permanent public spaces and the skilled service workers needed for an enduring resort, many faded or were forced to turn to other forms of enterprise for economic survival. To the east of Albany in Columbia County, Caleb Hull cautiously expanded the rustic facilities at Lebanon Springs. At High Rock Spring to the north of Ballston, we know that Philip Schuyler had pitched a marquee by the springs, while his son-in-law Stephen Van Rensselaer created Bath, a modest spa across the Hudson River from Albany.

The early spa at Lebanon Springs was a full day's journey east of Albany near the Massachusetts border. Discovered in 1756 by Captain Jonathan Hitchcock, the medicinal powers of Lebanon Springs had supposedly been secretly known to Native Americans. In 1771, a small bathhouse was attached to a settler's home and used by Hitchcock. After seven years, the site was leased to Hitchcock for the "love of God, the public good," and "the miraculous virtues of the water."[1] Here he remained until 1806, charging occasional visitors for the use of his springs and a tiny bathhouse. Caleb Hull ran a modest hotel near the spring, and in 1818 he purchased the springs including the cover that had been erected over them in 1794. He built a complex, the Columbia Hotel, with bathhouses, which eventually accommodated three hundred guests. Visitors included the Hudson Valley's influential Livingston family. By the 1830s, however, the luster of this most rustic mountain spa had begun to fade. Its location in the Taconic Mountains made it inaccessible to travelers traveling from New York City up the Hudson River to Albany, the chief route of the "grand tour." Its single hotel remained the only amenity, and it failed to become a center of style. For the rest of the nineteenth century, this early spa remained as isolated as it had been when it was established.

To the north, Philip Schuyler was a casual spa developer, concerned mainly with his family's health. In 1783, the Albany patrician landlord and former Revolutionary War general built a road from his estate at the confluence of the Hudson River and Fish Creek to mineral springs inland thirteen miles to the west.[2] These waters were Saratoga's as yet undeveloped High Rock Springs. For the next four years, Schuyler and his wife, Catherine Van Rensselaer, spent their summers taking the waters in a marquee on the site of the springs. Schuyler was a rich and influential man—a friend of George Washington—yet he was willing to live in a tent to gratify his desire for the waters. Finally, in 1787, the military tent was put aside and replaced by a small frame house. An engraved view of the springs shows this lonely structure and identifies the spot as Chalybeate Springs (Figure 3). At this time, the site of Saratoga Springs was essentially wilderness, without any amenities, but Schuyler's effort was the beginning of a resort that would eventually have many of the advantages of English spas.

FIGURE 3. Chalybeate Spring, 1787; the earliest view of High Rock Springs,
the first developed in Saratoga Springs.
("Description of the Chalybeate Spring, near Saratoga, with a perspective view of the main spring,"
The Columbian Magazine of Monthly Miscellany, *Philadelphia, March 1787; copy in the Saratoga Room,*
Saratoga Springs Public Library, Saratoga Springs, N.Y.)

As befitting gentry, Philip Schuyler's family continued his interest in the Albany region's mineral springs. His eldest son, John Bradstreet, developed his Saratoga estate until his untimely death in 1795, and another son, Rensselaer, would be a regular at social events held in Ballston Spa hotels in the early 1800s. The most active member of Schuyler's extended family in spa development was Stephen Van Rensselaer, who had married his daughter Margaret.[3] Van Rensselaer's delicate heath was in need of the medicinal powers of mineral springs.

Van Rensselaer was landlord of the vast Van Rensselaer Manor, south of Saratoga and surrounding Albany. Popularly know as "the Patroon," he was born to a princely fortune and high social station and was a Federalist admirer of his brother-in-law, Alexander Hamilton. He espoused Hamilton's support for commercial improvements, including resort communities, which he had seen on several visits to England. Van Rensselaer had a characteristic of a few future spa developers. He was a temperance man, avoiding the consumption of alcoholic spirits, an attitude exemplified by his spartan life style and expressed in his ideas about reforming the lower classes.[4] He believed that strong drink was ruining the stability of the lower orders, causing them to waste their money on spirits, money that should have been used for his rents, and leading them to the extravagant hope of obtaining the franchise. He promoted the idea that mineral waters could not only improve the health of an individual but also reform a person morally. Such a view was not universally held by his class, but as in England it encouraged the consumption of mineral waters and the popularity of U.S. spas.

As noted, Van Rensselaer had sought in 1790 to lay out a settlement across the Hudson River from Albany that was similar in conception, if not scope, to that of Joseph Pitt's development at Cheltenham. Encouraged by Elkanah Watson's surveyor report on the value of the iron springs at this location, Van Rensselaer called his new settlement Bath in honor of England's foremost spa.[5] It was designed in four blocks with complementary streets along the river, the chief of which was Mineral Street. Two houses were to be built at the landlord's expense and leased. From this beginning, by the early 1800s there were thirty houses. In Bath's early years, a public bath at the end of Mineral Street covered the medicinal springs and provided bathing facilities. In the 1790s, the springs rivaled those of Ballston Spa, with the advantage that Bath's ferry landing provided immediate access to and from Albany. Because it was a quick excursion, no hotel was thought to be necessary, and by the time one was built, the springs had passed their prime. After only a decade of operation, the springs were shut up and neglected, evidently the victims of pollution. Moreover, residents complained of annoying springs in their cellars. Bath's role as a ferry crossing to Albany with highway and eventually railroad connections would provide it with a future, while its springs languished.

Despite his wealth and vision, Van Rensselaer could not sustain Bath as a spa into the nineteenth century. Ranged against his belief in mineral springs, his wealth, and his entrepreneurial spirit were the difficulties of making the spa a going concern: the declining quality of the waters, the lack of accommodations, the very proximity of the location to travelers. In addition, as a landlord Van Rensselaer held the leases to the properties in the spa and thereby prevented ownership. Van Rensselaer was the first to fail in such an enterprise, and his example became a warning to other spa investors. Nevertheless, he believed in the curative powers of mineral waters. After the failure of his spa, in 1794, he bought a lot from Nicholas Low at Ballston Spa, and in the early 1800s he became a regular visitor.[6]

Of primary importance in the growth of the region's tourism was the willingness of de-velopers like Van Rensselaer to invest their time and capital in enterprises and amenities for leisure enjoyment. The presence or lack of such investors ultimately caused resorts to swell with visitors or to be abandoned by the crowd. In the middle of the nineteenth century, best-selling accounts of fictional resorts such as Glauber Spa made it seem as if a popular spa could be manufactured from a mere farmyard well if a self-serving physician had the audacity to pro-mote the spring's supposed qualities.[7] In fact, a substantial commitment of resources was nec-essary to create a spa, and although some developers came from the region, the effort usually required the capital and imagination that could be found only in urban centers such as New York City.

In that metropolis, entrepreneurs were experienced in those real estate investments that could produce a handsome rental income.[8] In contrast to local landlords in the Hudson Valley, Manhattan investors showed more flexibility in the terms offered to renters, reacting quickly to market conditions and producing a variety of lease and sale agreements.[9] New York City in-vestors were among the first to surmise that significant profits could be made by entertaining visitors in the region north of Albany. There was, however, a negative side to their interest: compared with local entrepreneurs, investors from New York City not only had more capital to invest but could also more easily walk away from an enterprise that turned sour.

The Development of Public Space

As the proprietor of much but not all of the land at Ballston Spa, New York City's Nicholas Low would be the resort's chief landlord-developer: he dominated the community for more than three decades and was responsible for its success as a resort. He began to subdivide his Kayaderosseras Patent property in 1790. His New York–area family had owned the vacant land since the 1770s, but it was he who eventually decided to concentrate his wealth and influence on the creation of a spa, officially purchasing his "Estate at Ballston Springs" from the estate of his deceased father, Cornelius, in 1793.[10] Nicholas Low was an active member of the Federalist Party, supporting the improvement of commerce and transportation. Like other local Federalists—the Schuylers, Van Rensselaers, Gansevoorts, and Caldwells—he was a landlord-developer who sought to improve the community in order to rent out the already im-proved land that commanded the highest fees.

Ballston Spa had advantages before Low paid attention to it. Before 1800, the village had the best accommodations in the region. The earliest hotel was built on the banks of Gor-don Creek on land to the west of and adjacent to Low's property. In 1787, Benjamin Douglas had established this log hotel near the Iron Railing Spring. Five years later he built a Federal-style frame house near the Iron Railing Spring, part of which still exists today (Figure 4).[11] The house-hotel passed to Joseph Westcort, who died in 1795. His widow married Joshua Al-dridge a year later, and Aldridge became the hotel proprietor, running it as a family business in which his two youngest daughters served as chambermaids. To supply fresh vegetables for his guests and family, Aldridge cultivated a garden adjacent to the hotel. In 1800, he added a sixty-foot-long dining room, a rear kitchen, and nine lodging rooms "for gentlemen." Even with his expansion, Aldridge's Hotel was suddenly eclipsed by Nicholas Low's project at the opposite end of what would become Front Street.

Figure 4. Aldridge's Hotel (now the Brookside Museum), Ballston Spa. Built 1792. One of the earliest hotels in the region, it overlooked the Iron Railing Spring and Gordon Creek, the banks of which became a fashionable promenade.
(Photo, Theodore Corbett.)

At the time Douglas was building his frame house, Low began to take an interest in his family's property, countering Douglas by building a substantial home on his property, just east of the Iron Railing Spring.[12] Low, however, immediately leased the house to other parties because he needed accommodations only on his brief annual visits. In 1794, he had a wharf built on Gordon Creek in front of his house and a bath and shower house constructed near his valuable mineral spring, in which he installed bathtubs in time for the summer season. A bathhouse was also located at a bend in Gordon Creek, where the grassed space was improved to become the "Bathing Green." Across from the green and facing the rival Aldridge House, he constructed in 1793 his first hotel, the McMaster House, which would be his chief resort investment until 1803. Gordon Creek roughly followed the fault line on which the springs were secured. Low channeled it in 1804, making the banks of the creek a popular promenade for visitors, a minor scenic attraction, although the open sewer from his next hotel and its stables ran into it.

Low's greatest enterprise began in 1803, when he had New York City builder Joseph Newton design a hotel and send the architectural plans to his Ballston agent, George White. James Hawkins, a Ballston master carpenter, lost the first copy of these plans, but with a fresh copy he continued the construction of the Sans Souci Hotel in the spring of 1804.[13] The hotel was named for the palace that Frederick the Great of Prussia had constructed from 1745 to 1747 and then occupied for the next forty years. Americans considered Frederick to have been an "enlightened despot," a designation he achieved when he invited the French philosophe Voltaire to live and dispute with him at Sans Souci. The palace had contained every imaginable facility for enlightened life, including a landscaped park, a library, public galleries lined with works of art, an orangery, plus spectacular fountains. Low audaciously hoped his guests would be able to duplicate Frederick the Great's life style at Ballston Spa.

In 1803 the Sans Souci's foundations were laid, and Hawkins erected the wood-frame structure and piazza over them.[14] Two years later, an addition with fifteen servants' rooms, a gaming room, and a tavern was completed. The resultant hotel was 160 feet long in front, with two 153-foot-long wings at each end, in the form of a U. Green shutters at each window accented its white painted exterior. There were a hundred chambers, for which board in 1811 was $10 a week or $2 a day, children under twelve and servants being charged only half price. The hotel had a drawing room set aside for the ladies where no smoking or drinking was allowed, these vices being relegated to the tavern. Balls were held in the front hall, which was hung with elegant chandeliers and where live music was provided for cotillions and quadrilles. Outside, gravel walks enclosed with shrubbery led the visitors to the hotel's private mineral springs. To the west of the hotel were the gardens, which eventually were shaded by elm trees.

Several outbuildings were required to support the Sans Souci. These included a laundry house, bakehouse, woodhouse, workshop, icehouse, coach house, and stables (Figure 5).[15] These outbuildings gave the hotel a degree of self-sufficiency, allowing it to be managed much like a country estate. However, the expense of maintaining the hotel beyond the summer sea-

FIGURE 5. Doubleday House, Ballston Spa. Built 1804. This wash (laundry) house is the only structure remaining from the Sans Souci complex. After only a year as a wash house, it was turned into a duplex residence, with one apartment available for Low's agent.
(Photo, Theodore Corbett.)

son was excessive, and thus it was closed for most the year. Low's house continued to be rented to the managers of the Sans Souci or to others who maintained a smaller separate hotel, the Ballston House, which could be open in the winter, when the Sans Souci was closed. In the winter, management of the Sans Souci and Low's property proceeded more quietly.

During the summer the Sans Souci's table d'hôte was spread in the dining room, which could seat one hundred guests of all classes. There were two meal schedules, one for servants and the other for regular guests.[16] Ladies and gentlemen were requested not to enter the dining room while the tables were being set. When the doors were opened, one needed a certain aggressiveness to get a seat. Although the food was well prepared, it was often scarce because it disappeared quickly. Waiters took orders for liquor once the patrons had penciled in their choice on cards. For refreshment, the Sans Souci stocked old Madeira, sherry, claret, burgundy, Holland gin, brandy, and brown stout; it was definitely not a temperance house.

Low's Other Economic Enterprises

Low did not view Ballston Spa as only a resort; he was willing to enhance the community by any means that would produce economic prosperity. In 1816, fire destroyed the Saratoga County courthouse in the town of Ballston, and his reaction was to provide a choice village site on the hill overlooking Front Street for a new one. A struggle ensued with other Saratoga County villages to capture the prize of the courthouse and the business that derived from its activities. Low was successful, and the courthouse was moved from Ballston Centre to the town of Milton and placed in Ballston Spa, thus making it the political hub of the county.[17]

Low had other budding interests. He conceived of building a cotton mill in Ballston Spa as early as 1812, but he could not gain control of the water rights to the swirling Kayaderosseras Creek.[18] Thus in 1814 he had a steam-powered mill constructed alongside more sluggish Gordon Creek. Operations were to begin that August, but after only a few minutes of operation a large summer beam and short shaft broke. Taking the engine apart and transporting the pieces to a place where they could be fixed and then returning them was deemed economically unfeasible, and the factory was forced to shut down. The Ballston Spa Company continued to hold the assets and to exist on paper, and Low leased his new brick factory for other uses, but for much of its history the building was empty. Still, it demonstrated that Low regarded manufactures as an additional source of income and that his cotton factory was meant to be as crucial to the village's prosperity as the Sans Souci Hotel.

To enhance his landholdings, Low placed the Sans Souci on the far side of his property.[19] The village sat in a basin surrounded by hills, the basin floor dissected by the meandering Gordon and Kayaderosseras creeks. From 1792 to 1819 Low laid out a more than sixty-six-foot-wide village main street, Front Street, and then a series of streets parallel to or crossing Front Street.[20] Ballston was thus centered on its linear main street, which ran essentially from the Sans Souci to Aldridge's Hotel. Ballston Spa was the area's first planned main street–centered village, a distinction that would soon apply to Saratoga Springs and Caldwell on Lake George as well. Low's most ambitious scheme for the Front Street area appeared in 1805: a proposal for uniform building lots on the north side of the street, backed by Chestnut Street—which at twenty feet in width was in practice a planned alley (Figure 6).[21] The lots were to have small twenty-five-foot frontages and fifty-two-foot depths. On Front Street's south

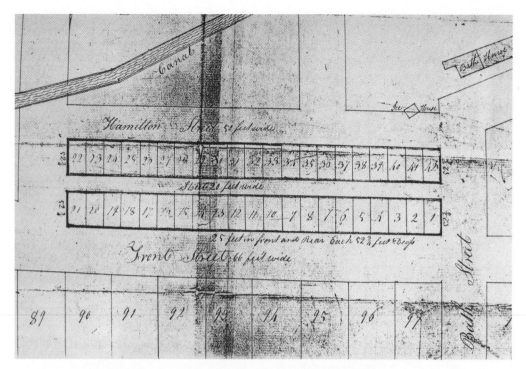

FIGURE 6. "Map and Survey of 42 Building Lots near Ballston Springs the Property of Nicholas Low . . .
November 15, 1805"; the urban design of Low's proposed development on the north side
of Front Street, Ballston Spa's chief street.
(Collections of the Manuscript Division of the Library of Congress, Washington, D.C.)

side he retained his earlier plan for larger lots at sixty-six feet in width, because he was able to
sell many of them. The project was difficult to carry out because it was located on a steep hill,
and as a result Chestnut Street was never realized. However, the small properties on the north
side remained a feature of Front Street, while on the south side most properties were larger, the
place for the village's best houses and shops. This pattern still held in 1853, although some of
the large lots on the south side were eventually subdivided.

Low's policy was to divide his property into the smallest possible parcels. He had been
offering such parcels near the Iron Railing Spring since at least 1794, when he had sold parcels
of one-fifth of an acre at relatively affordable prices. He assumed that by controlling prime locations like the land near the Iron Railing Spring and around the Sans Souci Hotel, he could
charge high rents for numerous small properties on or near Front Street. This was a technique
that worked well in densely populated New York City, but in Ballston Spa, even at its center,
the real estate market was not competitive.

To Low's disappointment, village lots did not sell immediately; in 1796 the heart of
the village was still undeveloped and covered with young pine trees. Low's agent suggested it
remain unimproved for three years until the pines had reached substantial growth and could
be harvested, judging the lumber to be more valuable than the proceeds from cultivating the
land.[22] After the pines were cut, only telltale stumps in the midst of the village showed that timber was still more profitable than retail or commercial enterprise.

By 1810, several Front Street business leaders were complaining to Low about the "very limited encouragement . . . given to applicants for lots." [23] There were problems with the smallness of the lots, which meant that they were "without any room for conveniences"; with the limit of the lease, which was only seven years; with the fixed rate, which remained even if the property "lessened in value"; and with the discouragement of improvements, as the lots were selling now "for less than half the prime cost." They noted that already the "crowd of visitants which used to flock here have deserted us." Moreover, people of substance and potential shop proprietors could find properties just beyond those held by Low that were larger and less expensive, and they could develop an enterprise or their own country estate on them. One could also find lots that were larger with much more favorable terms in nearby Saratoga Springs.

Low's Front Street achievements did stimulate his competition. As early as 1806, Joshua Aldridge surveyed the land around his hotel and divided it into building lots for sale or lease. They were taken up along Gordon Creek by a blacksmith, a bakehouse, and other shops.[24] The Sans Souci's presence attracted other hotels, especially on Front Street. These included the Mansion House, Clark's Hotel, and the Village Hotel. This last, constructed in 1804 on one of Low's larger lots at the corner of Front and Spring streets, was a ponderous four-story structure that included a basement built into the hillside (Figure 7). A less expensive inn, the

FIGURE 7. The Village Hotel (later Medbery Hotel), north side of Front Street, Ballston Spa. Built c. 1804. Right portion built in 1804, later additions in 1824 and c. 1840. Low's real estate policies inadvertently fostered the development of inexpensive hotels, such this one, that offered an alternative to the Sans Souci.
(Photo, Theodore Corbett.)

Village Hotel catered to those who could not afford the Sans Souci. This tactic proved profitable, and the hotel was expanded in 1824 and again in the 1840s. In 1847, Stephen Medbery purchased it and turned it into a temperance house, which attracted a different clientele than its larger rival did.

Ballston Spa's population growth was modest, especially during Low's patronage. By 1818 the village had 614 inhabitants and 112 houses, while ten years later—the year of Low's death—it had modestly reached 800 inhabitants.[25] Its growth did not keep pace with that of Saratoga Springs, which gradually moved ahead of it. In the 1820s, Ballston Spa was the center of the most populous town; in the 1830s this distinction was shared with Saratoga Springs, and in 1840 Saratoga Springs surpassed Ballston Spa. From then on Saratoga Springs increased its population until by 1875 it was twice as populous as Ballston, 10,775 to 5,277.

Such figures support the prediction of Ballston business leaders in 1810, who concurred that "within seven miles of us another village rises in proportions to our decline and we feel that the time is not far off when Saratoga Springs will be the general resort and Ballston Spa viewed only at a distance like the ruins of a moldering convent."[26] After 1830 Ballston Spa prospered as an industrial community, not a tourist destination.

Low did not witness the transformation of Ballston Spa to an industrial center, for the Sans Souci and the rest of his holdings—with the exception of the cotton-factory lot—were sold in 1823 to Harvey Loomis, an early partner in a Ballston Spa harness shop. Low was uninterested in nurturing investments that did not show an immediate return, and Ballston Spa was soon classified among those enterprises that were flagging. He was then able to concentrate on his other New York State properties, and five years later he died. Loomis sold his investment in 1835 to George Hill, who was acting for General John Fenwick, a federal army officer. By 1849, even the Sans Souci was forced to close its doors as a hotel and to reopen as an educational institution, the State and National Law School.[27] It would return to taking guests in later years, but its fate was sealed; in 1887 the grand building was demolished. Ironically, Low's greatest investment and ornament for the spa disappeared just as Saratoga Springs was becoming the country's favorite Victorian resort.

Low's Workforce

Because Low was rarely present in the village, he was dependent on agents to do his bidding; these agents ran his day-to-day operations.[28] The job of these local magnates was to supervise improvements of the village's infrastructure, to extract rents and fees on time, and to pay Low's local taxes. Some also operated a small sheep farm for Low. Low's rents came from the lots improved by the lessees, who built homes, shops, and hotels. A reservoir that Low had constructed was also a source of revenue because each resident was charged for the water supply. The agents also had more mundane duties such as supplying Low's New York City residence with bottles of Ballston Spa mineral water.

As a separate enterprise, Low leased the Sans Souci and its stables and billiard rooms on a year-to-year basis to a manager, who attempted to make a profit.[29] The managers hoped to attract a first-class clientele by offering various amenities. The staff was mainly free New York City blacks, and at the chief meals these handsomely attired servants were plentiful—a sign that no expense was spared on service. Although local free blacks were numerous, the hotel managers assumed that most were farmers or field hands who lacked skill in the genteel arts of serving meals and providing comfort.

Reasons for Decline

As both a spa and the seat of county government, Ballston Spa should have attracted gentlemen and merchants to build townhouses and seats in which to reside year-round. In this it failed, except for those who built on a few large lots on the south side of Front Street. In 1810, Ballston Spa's shopkeepers complained that as "gentlemen make such short visits" they could not make a living on Front Street. Low himself was absent much of the year, visiting Ballston Spa three times annually: to open for the season in the spring, during the summer season, and to close in the fall. He did not bring his family; they remained in New York. Because he rented his house year-round and had leased the Sans Souci, he had to pay for accommodations at the Sans Souci during his stays.[30]

Indeed, members of the gentry chose to reside away from Front Street in the countryside. There they could develop their own estates rather than becoming one of Low's tenants. Take, for example, Henry Walton, mentioned in Chapter 1, whose New York City family and shipping interests were already known by Low.[31] After completing his legal studies in England and New York, in 1790 Walton moved to family property near Ballston Centre, five miles southeast of Ballston Spa. Here he developed a country estate on the English model; it consisted of a fully staffed house with a coachman, cook, gardener, and servants. He farmed the land, diversifying his production among grain, cattle, and apple orchards. In 1808, family interests called Walton back to New York, and when he returned in 1815, he sold his farm and moved to Ballston's emerging rival Saratoga Springs. Evidently there was neither opportunity nor interest for Walton in Low's Ballston Spa, and he was but one of many gentlemen who would choose to leave Ballston Spa and reside in Saratoga Springs.

Low was also indifferent to religion. In contrast to many Federalist landlords, he made no effort to promote the establishment of churches in Ballston Spa, and he did not join one after they were formed. Resident families in the resort business such as the Aldridges and Medberys were active in the earliest Episcopal church.[32] Most churches were established in the area around the spa and then ultimately moved their existing buildings from the countryside to the village. In general, visitors were left to their own devices for religious services on Sundays. Clearly, religious institutions were not viewed by Low as an amenity and were not part of his plans for making Ballston Spa a resort or viable community.

Ballston Spa had only a modest number of mineral springs for those visitors who believed in their powers. Most were located along the margins of and were often flooded by Gordon Creek, the stream that meandered through the center of the village until Low channeled it in 1804.[33] In 1792, Beriah Palmer wrote to Low, his employer, that one of his lots contained a newly discovered mineral or salt spring, which made the lot more valuable and therefore able to command a greater price.[34] This discovery stimulated a rush to control Ballston's springs. Ballston Spa village records, which begin in 1807, when the village was incorporated, are full of ordinances to protect, maintain, and beautify the often-flooded springs.

After 1807, Low had two or three other springs drilled on the grounds of the Sans Souci Hotel, but they failed to flow consistently. In 1813, a Philadelphia visitor commented that Ballston's waters were not so powerful as those at Saratoga Springs, and they "decrease in strength every year."[35] Four years later four additional springs were found in the former bed of Gordon Creek, but they proved difficult to control. The Iron Railing Spring remained the village's chief attraction until 1824, when a second spring was discovered 100 feet from it; the new spring was named for Lafayette, who had visited the area. The proximity of the two springs caused difficulty; the Iron Railing Spring's flow and therefore its use were cut back. Later the Washington Spring was drilled 237 feet into slate in the continuing effort to provide the village with another mineral spring. Despite these gallant efforts, by the 1830s none of Ballston's springs was consistently flowing to the surface. Overall, nature had dealt Ballston Spa a weak hand: the waters at the early spa would never match the freely flowing waters at Saratoga Springs.

An absentee landlord like Low could not solve Ballston Spa's numerous long-term problems. The limited season, the lack of an extensive local service workforce, the failure to attract the gentry permanently, the scarcity of churches, and the erratic springs contributed to Ballston's failure as a resort. Low's manufacturing failure with the cotton mill, however, did not slow Ballston Spa's gradual evolution from a resort into a manufacturing community.

The Saratoga and Schenectady Railroad was chartered in 1831 by the New York State legislature, with Ballston Spa the destination of the first leg of tracks leaving Schenectady; passengers had to get off in Ballston Spa and take a second train to Saratoga Springs.[36] Elaborate embankments were planned to carry the rail line through the Ballston basin, over Front Street, and on to Saratoga Springs. Ballston Spa's remaining tourism enterprise was supposed to benefit from the influx of visitors who came by railroad, but in fact the visitors did not stay, going on instead to Saratoga Springs. Thus Ballston's tourism suffered another blow. Yet, Ballston profited from the railroad: on November 21, 1833, the first load of anthracite coal was carried from Albany to Schenectady and then to Ballston by railroad, an impetus for the spa to become a manufacturing center. The railroad connected Ballston Spa to the outside world, offering it marketing opportunities for its manufactures and allowing the village to change the basis of its economy from tourism to manufacturing.

By 1844, two cotton mills were in existence. In 1839 the Ballston Spa National Bank, the county's first permanently operating bank, purchased a home on Front Street and converted it into its headquarters.[37] The brick gabled building, built a decade before, was, among other fine buildings, finally giving Front Street the year-round commercial prestige that Low had never achieved for it. Boarding houses once meant for visitors were converted to cater to single men who worked in the mills. Women who had once served at the hotels also found work in the cotton mills. The streams that flowed into Ballston Spa's basin were channeled into a canal-like system that provided waterpower to the factories, and working-class housing appeared along their banks.

Why had Ballston Spa failed to sustain its early success as a spa on the English model? Low was a superb businessman but was not the right kind of entrepreneur for a resort. For every dollar he invested he expected an immediate return. In addition, he failed to spend enough time at the spa, treating it as but one of his many upstate New York enterprises. The Sans Souci's limited season, the lack of tenant incentives on Front Street, and the failure of the cotton mill left a bitter taste in Low's mouth. His monopolistic landlordism also prevented others from participating in the village's growth. In addition, the early village lacked symbols of community permanence such as churches. Finally, even the springs did not have the flow necessary to attract visitors. Ballston Spa succeeded by losing its landlord in 1823 and through local effort becoming a thriving manufacturing center.

As an alternative resort the Ballston Spa of 1800 was able to eclipse its rival resorts not because of Low's Sans Souci Hotel, its scenic beauty, or the purity of its springs, bur rather because of the fame of its stylish company. Thus, Ballston Spa began as an exclusive resort for a narrowly fashionable clientele, but the village found it was risky to put its future in the hands of visitors who were capricious in their loyalty.

CHAPTER 3

The Reluctant Resort
Caldwell on Lake George

Lake George, only thirty-two miles to the northeast of Ballston Spa, is nestled in the Adirondack Mountains. It beckoned visitors as early as the 1780s and 1790s, when the trek to the lake became a favorite trip from Ballston Spa or Saratoga Springs. Excursions followed the trails to Jessup's Landing on the Hudson, then to Hadley-Luzerne, and finally north to the head of Lake George. Lake George's natural beauty and historical memories also attracted later visitors, who made it a required stop on nineteenth-century grand tours. In the nineteenth century, the settlement at the south end of Lake George was open to a variety of economic and political possibilities; it emerged only reluctantly as a resort, more by chance than by design, after its landlord had experimented with commercial and manufacturing alternatives. Before the appearance of the village of Caldwell in the 1820s, accommodations at the head of the lake were most primitive. The way to see Lake George was by canoe excursion, which proceeded from campsite to campsite on the numerous islands.[1] In 1800, a party of both sexes from Aldridge's Hotel in Ballston Spa conducted its visit by tenting on the islands. Although hotels would appear in the next half-century, a visit to Caldwell remained a rustic experience; it was not the kind of place that attracted visitors accustomed to sophisticated amenities, those who wished to see and to be seen.

A Family of Landlord-Developers

The overriding factor in Caldwell's early development was that it was the estate of a family that sought to control the development of the region by creating modest amenities designed to ensure prosperity. The Caldwells recruited tenants to cultivate the land, to cut timber and run their sawmill, and to manage their shops and their enterprises, which eventually included a hotel that had once been their house. They sought to make Caldwell into an English country town. Such a paternalistic system, with a landlord who did not see the development of tourism as a priority, limited the community's first efforts to become a resort. Instead, the Caldwell family controlled one of the first great Adirondack forest estates and sought to exploit it by extracting natural resources, earning income from leases, and establishing manufacturing. Although they generously lavished their resources and time on Lake George, family members were interested only occasionally in Caldwell's role as a resort. After the death of the founders of the Caldwell dynasty, the village was opened to other resort interests, but, with picturesque hotels and summer cottages, it remained a place for only the upper classes.

James Caldwell, an Ulster Irishman, settled in 1774 in Albany, where he operated a grocery store.[2] Over the next thirty-five years, Caldwell prospered to become one of Albany's richest and most innovative merchants; his enterprises included a store, a distillery, a glassworks, and a mill complex. The jewel of Caldwell's early commercial empire was a refining complex on Mill Creek, a stream located on the edge of eighteenth-century Albany, which today is part of Albany's industrial north end (Figure 8). Lying within the Van Rensselaer Manor, the land was leased from Stephen Van Rensselaer and the complex was located 400 yards to the west of the Patroon's Watervliet manor house. The buildings included quarters for Caldwell, so the structures served the dual purpose of being both a country house and a factory. Constructed about 1785 by Boston architect Christopher Batterman, the complex was regarded by a Connecticut visitor as "the most extensive collection of manufactures which I have seen in the possession of a single man."[3] It contained at least three mills run by waterpower, as well as kilns and storehouses for drying tobacco (even at this early date all were run by machinery). The complex's principal function was to refine imported products such as chocolate, snuff, tobacco, and mustard; it also could hull barley, split peas, and process flour to make hair powder and starch. In turn, these products were sold in Caldwell's Albany shop. The complex employed forty to sixty persons, in English fashion mainly boys, who earned what was considered then a good wage. The mills were such a community asset that when they were destroyed by fire in 1794, Caldwell's friends loaned him $20,000 and the New York State Legislature matched the sum, making it possible to reconstruct the mills in only eleven months.

Caldwell wanted to be an Albany patrician, a member of that aristocracy of families of Dutch descent that dominated Albany's economic and political life.[4] He bought land from the patricians, held a household slave in 1790, and branded his furniture with his name or initials just as they did in order to ensure the continuity of pieces within the family. But he had two strikes against him: his differing religious background and political convictions. First, he was a Scotch-Irishman and leader of the Presbyterian meeting, not the patricians' Dutch Reformed Church. Second, while the patricians were staunch Revolutionary patriots, Caldwell was suspected of being a loyalist. From 1778 to 1780 he posted bail for five alleged Albany loyalists who were under investigation by Albany's Commission for Detecting and Defeating Conspiracies. Apparently he cleared himself, but his support for the Revolutionary cause was certainly lukewarm.

A Caldwell pattern of business and family ties to the British and their Iroquois allies became more open after the Revolutionary War. As a merchant, James had business connections in the Indian trade, an enterprise that tied him closely to the Iroquois and to British merchants in Montreal. After the war, some of his children would be educated in Canada and marry Canadians, while his son Edwin sought to join the British army in Montreal when the War of 1812 broke out. James also served as the Albany agent for the Iroquois leader Joseph Brant and in 1806 entertained the Native American loyalist at his home, even paying Ezra Ames to paint Brant's portrait.[5] Revolutionary patriots regarded Brant as an unforgivable enemy because of his staunch support for George III and his supposedly ruthless plundering of the Mohawk Valley during the Revolutionary War.

FIGURE 8. "The property of Mr. James Caldwell of the City of Albany, Merchant,
with a distant Prospect of Hudsons River and the Seat of Stephen Van Rensselaer Esquire,"
c. 1790; the properties of two of the region's leading developers,
who were instrumental in the creation of resorts.
(Joel Munsell, The Annals of Albany, *Albany, N.Y., 1850–1859.)*

Mending his loyalist ways in the postwar era, Caldwell became increasingly like the patriot Schuylers or Gansevoorts. Following the Schuylers he became a Federalist, supporting the adoption of the federal Constitution and Hamilton's fiscal policies. He shared their ambition by becoming a landlord-developer, opening frontier territory to be settled by tenants. He was aware of the Schuylers' enterprise on the Fish Kill and the Gansevoorts' efforts along the Snook Kill, enterprises that had created the communities of Schuylerville and Gansevoort.[6]

In the 1780s, Caldwell made a commitment north of Albany by purchasing a lot close to the Sans Souci Hotel in Ballston Spa, and in 1797 he built a substantial federal-style summer house, which he designated Mount Merino (Figure 9).[7] He now controlled the land to the east of Front Street, a fact that cannot have escaped the notice of Nicholas Low. The construction of homes by ambitious and wealthy persons at watering places could be regarded as a threat to the interests of Ballston's primary landlord. But nothing further came of Caldwell's investment, for he soon turned away from Ballston and pursued opportunities further north at Lake George; this move allowed him to be the exclusive developer of his own estate.

In 1787 Caldwell purchased the patent from Udney Hay for 1,595 acres at the southwestern end of Lake George, which made him the area's chief landowner and real estate developer. His patent centered on the southern end of the lake, including the present site of the village as well as the Garrison Grounds, which held the ruins of Fort William Henry and Fort George. Over the next twenty-three years, although he did not improve his land, he added to it. By 1810, when he decided to make his first effort to settle the land, he had acquired a total of 7,000 acres around or near Lake George, a modest forest estate. And he did not stop there; eight years later, he acquired 1,811 acres on the east side of the lake.[8] Caldwell would continue to be driven to acquire undeveloped land until his death in 1829 brought a conclusion to his purchases.

FIGURE 9. "Mount Marino Summer House Adjoining the Sans Souci Hotel at Ballston Spa," 1807.
The house belonged to James Caldwell, who sold it about 1810 in order to develop an estate
at the south end of Lake George.
(Courtesy of the Brookside Museum, Saratoga County Historical Society, Ballston Spa, N.Y.)

In 1803 Caldwell had Caldwell village laid out on the west side along the lakeshore.[9] The street village was centered on a main thoroughfare running north and south; appropriately, it was named Canada Street, for the future lay with commercial relations in Montreal. Lots on the lakeside had one-hundred-foot frontages, while those on the far side had only fifty. Along the lakeside of Canada Street Caldwell built a courthouse, a stone store, and a large home overlooking the lake next to the courthouse. In contrast, he left the west side of Canada Street undeveloped in these early years, and it probably served in 1820 as the common for grazing hogs with the required yoke around their necks. In 1813, Warren County was carved out of Washington County, and James Caldwell began four years of lobbying to designate Caldwell village as the county seat. From 1810 to 1817, court was already held in Caldwell at his Lake George Coffee House. Concerned with making the village a proper government seat, in 1817 Caldwell designated the lake-front lot on Canada Street on which the first courthouse was built "for the sole use and a benefit of the inhabitants of Warren County."[10] This donation centered the village on the courthouse; the smaller lots across from it on the west side had alleys to serve them, a sign that it was the center of town.

Caldwell's early commercial efforts focused on the streams that flowed into the head of the lake. Following his experience with his Albany mills, he attempted to establish sawmills and gristmills on the tributaries, but the flow proved too sporadic to be a dependable source of waterpower. As a result, the timber he cut was floated north toward Ticonderoga's sawmills. By 1832, however, the Feeder Canal in Glens Falls diverted the log-shipping business to the Hudson River, and it became cheaper to drag logs to the sawmills at Glens Falls; this development diminished the family's hold over the lake's lumber business. Caldwell was more successful with navigation. In 1817 he established the Lake George Steamboat Company, which constructed the lake's first steamboat at Caldwell. Equipped with third-hand boilers, the eighty-foot vessel was appropriately named the *James Caldwell.* It plied the lake for four years before it accidentally burned at its dock.[11]

By the late 1820s, an English visitor confirmed that Caldwell was the local center, "a recently built county town of public buildings," including a jail, newspaper office, and hotel from which to fish or see the lake.[12] The English and Irish country towns familiar to Caldwell were centers for the exchange of goods, news, legal transactions, and entertainment. Their major function was to be markets and processing centers for commodities produced in the hinterlands. Coffeehouses and taverns served as centers of business; there, transactions could be carried out with a degree of privacy. The ultimate goal of such a town was to have shops on the main street—that is, places with glass windows for display that were devoted to retail sales as much as to the making of goods. Overall, such a place depended on good transportation for carrying out these activities. As we will see, Caldwell's village was able to meet some of these requirements but not all of them.

The extent of the Caldwells' proprietary power over the estate was unusual. Unlike other area landlords, James Caldwell and his son William were determined to retain their unaltered leases, rather than offering ownership opportunities or leases with options to buy. This contrasted with the practice of Saratoga Springs's leading landlord, Henry Walton, who was usually willing to change tenure obligations from those of tenant to those of landholder.[13] We know about Caldwell's tenantry from reading an inventory, made near the time of his death, covering the period from 1819 to 1828. His landed estate was based on leases that were long-term or "forever" in nature, so that they could be and were in practice sold. He also loaned mortgage money for purchasing his leases or developing his land, and this practice provided him with a substantial interest income. Caldwell sold leases for village lots on the west side of the lake; he sold leases for lots in the Garrison Grounds around the ruins of Fort George; he sold leases for timberland in the surrounding Kennedy Patent and Luzerne Tract. Many of the lots he leased were already developed, either by himself or by a previous tenant. These improved lots included not just wood-frame dwellings, and in one case a stone house, but also a lime kiln, a printing office, a coffeehouse, a grocery store, the remains of Fort George, the ruins of Fort William Henry, and the Lake House, the community's only emerging hotel. Caldwell was often paid in kind for rent, the most popular items being cattle and rye, evidence of farming in the area. How thoroughly the landlord dominated politics in the Town of Caldwell is difficult surmise, but at least two of his tenants were among the members of the original 1810 town board, although he himself was not. Increasingly, it was his retentive control of leases that gave Caldwell his greatest return and his considerable influence over the town.

Visitors Popularize the Resort

James Caldwell's role in the development of Caldwell as a popular tourist destination was limited, for he saw it as only one avenue for securing the village's growth. He admitted to running on "so extravagantly in praise" of the beauty of the lake that in 1810 he obtained a prepublication description of it, written for *Spafford's Gazetteer,* to be certain that its account of the lake

FIGURE 10. Ezra Ames, *A View of Lake George & Caldwell Village,* c. 1812. Commissioned
by James Caldwell, this is the earliest landscape depicting Lake George as a scenic wonder.
(Historic Hudson Valley, Tarrytown, N.Y.)

was glowing. To his credit, James Caldwell was the first patron of the arts to focus attention on
Lake George as a worthy subject for painting on canvas. The family portraits resulting from
commissions given to Ezra Ames, the Albany portrait painter, have not survived, but Caldwell
also requested two or perhaps three landscapes of Lake George, which still exist. Ames painted
the scenes only at the bidding of his patron, for he was not inclined to do landscapes. The inscription written by William Caldwell on the back of one painting reads, "Taken by Ezra Ames
from Fort George by request of my father who took him to the lake to make this view" (Figure 10).[14] Ames's own account book shows that the year was 1812, two years after Caldwell
began development of the village. Ten years later, Ames modified one of the copies when he
painted out Fort George. The early date and the primitive quality of these landscapes, painted
before the lake became a favorite subject of the Hudson River romantic painters such as Thomas
Cole, ensured that they would remain Caldwell family heirlooms rather than being devoted to
promoting the lake.

  The inspiration for the growing popularity of Lake George in the 1820s would come
not from James Caldwell but from the works of two famous visitors: James Fenimore Cooper
and his acquaintance Thomas Cole, who both explored Lake George in the mid-1820s. Their

artistic efforts gave natural wonders and historic sites in the United States the type of exposure that only European destinations had previously enjoyed. In 1824 and 1825, Cooper visited Caldwell village and traveled the lake on the steamboat *James Caldwell,* gathering material for his *Leatherstocking Tales.*[15] Cooper was upset that a utilitarian cornfield was growing in the ruins of Fort William Henry and that they had not been preserved in their romantic splendor. Published a year later, *The Last of the Mohicans* ignored the reality the author had seen at Caldwell; the romantic novel was set at Lake George during the French and Indian War and featured the siege, capture of, and massacre at Fort William Henry.

After being contacted by several patrons who wished to have scenes on their walls taken from Cooper's bestseller, Thomas Cole visited the lake.[16] From 1826 to 1827 Cole worked on at least four paintings set in the area. Cole produced three versions that did depict a scene from *The Last of the Mohicans;* in it one of the heroines, Cora, kneels before a circle of unbending Native Americans, who have her life in their hands. Another Cole painting related to Cooper's novel is entitled *Gelyna* and consists of a view of the rugged heights commanding Lake George with two tiny British officers in the foreground (Figure 11). The subject is based on a roman-

FIGURE 11. Thomas Cole, *Gelyna (View near Ticonderoga),* 1826. Visiting Lake George in 1826, Cole made sketches for *The Last of the Mohicans* and this legendary story about a British officer who died tragically in Abercrombie's fatal attack on Ticonderoga.
(Fort Ticonderoga Museum, Fort Ticonderoga, N.Y.)

tic tale concerning an officer in Abercrombie's 1758 expedition who was mortally wounded in the battle at Ticonderoga.

Although neither the artist nor the writer meant to promote the lake as a tourist attraction, the works of Cole and Cooper instilled Lake George in the minds of the well-educated public, convincing them to add its history and beauty to their summer itineraries. As a result, the village of Caldwell began to prosper from tourism in the late 1820s. By 1802 a tavern existed ten miles to the north at Bolton Landing, and the Trout Pavilion entertained fishing parties on the east side at Van Wormer's Bay as early as 1810, but Caldwell's Lake House was the first place on the lake to claim the distinction of being a hotel, even though it was not built as one. In 1808, James Caldwell had erected a substantial federal-style home on a choice Canada Street lot near the courthouse.[17] A decade later it was described as a house that also had accommodations for visitors. By 1828, Caldwell had allowed it to be converted into a hotel named the Lake House. His son William would expand the Lake House, but for the moment even James Caldwell seemed willing to accommodate the influx of visitors whose trips Cooper and Cole had inspired. Thus, the village's first hotel was the landlord's converted home, evidence that he was willing to try options other than manufacturing to make his village prosper.

James Caldwell died on February 1, 1829, only a few months after the death of Ballston developer Nicholas Low; his death ended efforts to create an enterprising English country town. His funeral was held in Albany, but he was buried at the family plot in Caldwell. Although his attitude toward tourists had remained ambivalent, he had fostered a respect for the beauty of Lake George among his now influential and broadly extended family. Today the best place to get a sense of the extent of his respected clan is at the family plot, now the Lake George Village Cemetery. The Caldwell family plot in the southwest corner is where James and Elizabeth Caldwell, five of their seven daughters, three of their four sons, and members the marriage-related Beck family are memorialized in stone, despite the fact that some of them are buried elsewhere. The Caldwell plot tells us about the contrasting personalities of James and his eldest son, William. Although elevated on marble supports, James's stone is a simple undecorated slab that is shared with his consort, Elizabeth. In contrast, William's stone is a fashionably carved, upright Gothic tablet (Figure 12). Four marble posts once supported a cast iron chain that surrounded it. The epitaph boldly defines William as "the second proprietor of this estate," a landed pretension that his father did not publicly share. There is no inscription or stone for the mother of his daughter, Eliza.

William Caldwell played the role of landlord more intensely than his father did. A visitor in 1833 reflected Caldwell's view of his position by referring to the village at the south end of the lake as "Caldwells Manor." William was born in Albany in 1776, not long after his father had set up his grocery business. In 1802, William was given responsibility for the family store, so that his father could pursue other interests. In the early 1800s, William also was a state auctioneer.[18] William was not interested in extending his career as a shopkeeper or auctioneer. In 1821, he gave up the management of family enterprises in order to spend time following pursuits suitable for an English gentleman. He could well afford to do so, for the Caldwells were by now extremely rich. His passions included champagne breakfasts, and his gifts to New York

FIGURE 12. Burial stone of William Caldwell, c. 1848,
Lake George Village Cemetery, Lake George, N.Y. The
stone proclaims that he was "the second proprietor of
this estate." Such titles were becoming increasingly
archaic as a result of the Anti-Rent Wars.
(Photo, Theodore Corbett.)

City acquaintances included such luxuries as saddles of venison and pineapple cheeses. He owned Japanese porcelain that was imported via Newport, Rhode Island, as well as a gold snuff-box, a gold watch, and a silver shaving box. In the fifteen years after his father died, William contributed $200 so that the Albany Institute could complete its mineralogical collection, endowed a prize at the Albany Academy for the best scholar in mathematics and natural philosophy, and, closer to Caldwell, was a founding trustee of the Glens Falls Academy.[19]

At Lake George, William maintained the policies of his father, although he did make a greater effort to provide more comfort for visitors. To visit Caldwell in June 1835, he needed several days on the road, traveling from Albany to Schenectady by coach, then from Schenectady to Saratoga Springs by railroad, where he spent two days at a hotel and then renewed his journey by stage to Lake George.[20] This was the same complicated route that tourists would have to follow, and so it was crucial that the village of Caldwell be worthy of the journey. From 1830 to 1832, he expanded his father's Lake House Hotel, adding a long wing, three stories high, with half the rooms overlooking the lake; the addition made it possible to lodge a hundred persons. Added along the lakeshore were a bathhouse and wharf, where the lake steamboat *Mountaineer* landed. The addition was successful, as ten years later the hotel was filled in the summer with fashionable New Yorkers.

Although homeless as a result of continued development of the Lake House, William did not suffer; he built a substantial country home, the Mansion House, a complex of barns, separate cottages, and a boat house, immediately to the north of Caldwell village.[21] From its completion until 1845, the Mansion House was rented to village resident Seth Baldwin, county judge and Caldwell supervisor, for Caldwell occupied it only seasonally. The home was renovated in 1846 with the addition of an icehouse, a stable, and a new well, but from then on it was rented on an annual basis to outside parties, much as one might rent a summer cottage to strangers. William also had a stone office built on Canada Street to administer his property. From 1830 to 1837, he continued his father's effort to purchase parcels of land along the lake, although many were repurchases from settlers who had evidently given up their leases.

The Caldwell Workforce, Population Decline, and Landlordism

To make a workforce, the Caldwells recruited proprietors, mechanics, and workers from Albany and the area around Caldwell. Few resided in Caldwell for more than a year or two. The Caldwells' earliest enterprise, the Lake George Coffee House, was run by the former proprietor of Albany's Northern Hotel, Samuel Prayn, while being owned by landlord Caldwell.[22] In 1823, the coffeehouse lease was purchased by John Baird, Caldwell now holding the mortgage and serving as the recipient of the property's insurance policy. Prayn went on to do other work for the Caldwells, building and running the original Lake House Hotel. John Sherrill was the proprietor of the coffeehouse in 1830. When William Caldwell expanded the hotel in the 1830s, the Goodmans, a family of carpenters from Bolton, were contracted to construct an extensive Greek Revival–style wing. Like his father, Caldwell financed the expansion and then recruited others, William Sherrill and later his son-in-law Fred G. Tucker, to manage the establishment. The Caldwells were able to find local masons and carpenters like Halsey Rogers and Daniel Furguson, who built the Caldwell's stone store in 1819. Frederick B. Hubbell began his career as a carpenter working on Caldwell's Mansion House; he later became a contractor, mill owner, and one of the Lake's most prominent politicians.

Despite the Caldwells' efforts at building and recruitment, they were unable to keep businesses in the village and attract a permanent workforce. By 1830, there were only two stores on Canada Street. One was Hiram Hawley's shoemaking establishment; he was a leading citizen and owner of lots throughout the town. However, from 1830 to 1837, he sold most of the lots back to William Caldwell. Ultimately, in 1841, Hawley sold his shoemaking business to his apprentice, Samuel R. Archibald.[23] Archibald survived in the 1840s and 1850s by a running a tannery as well, an indication that a businessman had to do more than retail to prosper in Caldwell. Other businessmen did not stick it out. The earliest blacksmith, Daniel Nichols, soon left Caldwell, moving to western New York State. Keeping businesses in the village remained a problem for unswerving landlords like the Caldwells, whose lease tenure was detrimental to the community's growth. After 1820, the population of the town of Caldwell fell while the that in the rest of Warren County grew. From 1825 to 1835, Caldwell's population declined by 28 percent; this loss of 245 out of 885 inhabitants was a sign that the tenant system was failing to hold settlers.[24] The village of 200 souls in 1813 had at mid-century a population of only 350, and a decade later it had fallen to 250. Not until 1860 would the town's population return to its 1820 level, a decline that was unique to Caldwell and not reflected elsewhere in growing Warren County.

Indeed, this was not an ideal time to be a landlord, for a strong antirent sentiment was sweeping New York. Warren County had sent no representatives to the state convention of 1821, which had been called together in Albany to draft a new constitution, including a review of landlord privileges. Instead delegates from neighboring Washington County represented it, chiefly Melanchton Wheeler.[25] Like Caldwell, he was a man of property, owning sawmills in Fort Edward and agricultural enterprises in Whitehall. He defended these rights in Albany, urging that suffrage be restricted to those "entitled to vote" through ownership of property. As a result of his opinion and that of like-minded landlords, the New York constitution of 1821 continued to give landlords considerable power over tenants and encouraged the maintenance of the rental system. The constitution listed the obligations of tenants to their landlords: providing labor, grinding their grain at the landlord's mill, and giving the landlord the right of first refusal in selling crops. Hence, tenanted land carried obligations, even if it had the advantage of being already developed. In 1839, conflict over landlord-tenant issues broke out to the south, in the Van Rensselaer Manor. As a result, the new state constitution of 1846 abolished the last vestiges of landlordism, and this abolition, combined with William Caldwell's death, helped to revive the town's population. Still, at Lake George as late as 1899, an untested law required property owners whose land had been purchased from James Caldwell to make an annual rent payment of a shilling an acre. At the end of the century, the Caldwell heirs were still attempting to enforce this outdated tenant obligation.

William Caldwell also attempted to extend his powers as a landlord by gaining control over Lake George's numerous islands, creating in the process one of the earliest forest preserves in the Adirondacks. In January 1840, he owned only undeveloped Tea Island, which was adjacent to his Kennedy Patent, but he was so unsettled by fear of outside island developers that he asked New York State for the privilege of purchasing all the lake's islands, including two already in private hands. He also requested that the state grant him the title of superintendent of the islands. His petitioning supporters claimed that he would maintain the islands in their natural state, a condition that was "a great inducement for wealthy individuals and parties to visit the Lake and dispose of their time and money among the inhabitants of the vicinity."[26] The state compromised; it would not sell the islands, but it did recognize Caldwell as superintendent. Here, Caldwell and his friends foresaw the economic importance of the lake's natural beauty to the village. They fostered tourism, but it was limited to the rich and aristocratic. William Caldwell assumed the pose of an early conservationist to ensure the natural beauty of the lake, thus placing the economic value of respectable visitors over the profits to be made from lumbering or farming. He had a parallel desire to protect historic monuments such as Fort George from being quarried for building stone. Such efforts, however, cannot have endeared him to local people who wished to open the lake to a wider spectrum of visitors and economic developers.

William was observed in 1842 at the height of his influence, when young Francis Parkman visited the lake. A Bostonian with a mistrust of New Yorkers, Parkman failed to see Caldwell as the benevolent landlord or English gentlemen that he aspired to be. He described Caldwell as a "great Nabob," lounging on his barge as he traveled the lake, flags prow and stern flanking a huge box of wines. As he moved down the lake, settlers saluted the proprietor in deference to his position. Parkman found this show distasteful and called Caldwell "a consummate tyrant and fool" who "treats the townsmen, his vassals, with favor or the contrary according as they yield him due reverence." The New Englander observed correctly that Caldwell's property came entirely from his father, who was "an Irish emigrant who built himself a fortune by trading in Albany."[27] Here was a classic example of the clash of temperament between the Yankee descendant of Puritans and the pleasure-loving Yorker.

After the Proprietor: The Opening of the Resort to Outsiders

William Caldwell died in 1848. Three years later, a New York City visitor, George William Curtis, summed up Caldwell's legacy in these words: Caldwell was "an eccentric gentleman . . . who owned the whole region, built a hotel on the wrong spot, determined that no one else should build anywhere, and ardently desired that no more people settle in the neighborhood."[28] The visitor was concerned that the Lake House looked toward the east side rather than north up the lake, a more spectacular view, not realizing that the hotel had originally been built as a home. Curtis admitted, however, that despite the faults of location and size, the Lake House was "kept admirably" by a courteous and able host; but he also observed that Caldwell village had become completely dependent for its livelihood on the inadequate Lake House. William Caldwell left his Warren County property to three women heirs: his daughter, Eliza, wife of John McGillis; and his sister's daughters, Helen Louisa Beck and Catherine Elizabeth Beck, whose father was the famous scholar Theodore Romeyn Beck.[29] Residents of St. Johns, Lower Canada, Eliza and her husband received the Mansion House and Lake House properties, as well as Green Island and Caldwell's Lake George skiff, the *Emerald*. Caldwell wanted the rest of his Warren County property split equally among the three heirs, a wish that was fulfilled only by a settlement signed on September 2, 1852. The property of Catherine and Helen would include Tea Island and the sites of Fort William Henry and Fort George. Nevertheless, the two Beck daughters did not accept their uncle's will. For the next forty years Eliza's more extensive portion would be contested by the two American heirs because she was a resident of Canada. This legal battle continued to cloud land-title issues, although pieces of the estate were sold to outside parties.

William Caldwell's restrictive policies could not survive his death because of the lake's increasing popularity. The year of Caldwell's death a plank road was built from Glens Falls to Caldwell, making Lake George more accessible to visitors than before. Furthermore, from 1848 to 1854 Caldwell's heirs parted with some of the choicest portions of his estate, which were freed from most of the tenancy obligations, although the lion's share of the property as late as 1885 was still in their hands. The parcels were sold mainly in the Kennedy Patent to local surveyor and sometimes lumberman John H. Smith of Caldwell and to lumbermen Rufus Anderson of Bolton and Frederick B. Hubbell of Caldwell, who were interested in doing what James Caldwell had been unable to do, establishing a profitable sawmill at the south end of the lake. In 1876 Hubbell built immediately north of Caldwell village a fifty-horsepower steam mill, which included a dock on the lake for shipping and receiving logs.[30] The mill, with its circle and gang saws, planing mill and lathe, and fancy molding saw, provided jobs for up to thirty men. Although Hubbell would clear-cut the timber on his new property, leaving the lake's mountainsides denuded, his lumbering inadvertently created open spaces along the shoreline and provided the building materials for the elegant summer cottages constructed there. The death of the proprietor thus opened Caldwell and Lake George to the expansion of lumbering and tourism.

Outside investors, particularly from New York City, began to construct extensive luxury hotels, and soon the village took on some of the characteristics of a resort community like Saratoga Springs. In 1853, Daremus and Dixon of New York City erected the United States Hotel on the east side of the lake facing Caldwell village. Greek Revival in style, it had the latest conveniences, including bells and baths, and in answer to critics of the Lake House a better view of the lake.[31]

Only a year later, ground was broken for an even larger hotel on the south edge of the village, near the ruins of Fort William Henry. The hotel, to be named for the fort immortalized by James Fenimore Cooper, was financed by a joint stock company headed by Thomas Thomas of New York City. His son, Thomas, was the builder. When it opened the same year, the Fort William Henry Hotel had a two hundred-foot-long facade, a rear wing, and a basement, and it accommodated over 150 guests (Figure 13). On the north front facing the lake a

FIGURE 13. Fort William Henry Hotel of 1855, Caldwell. The first of several great hotels by that name on a location near where the fort once stood.
(Nelson's Guide to Lake George and Lake Champlain, Nelson & Sons, 1859.)

grand piazza covered two of the structure's four stories. The overall form of the building was eighteen-century Georgian because it had a central, pedimented projecting pavilion, but the decoration acknowledged the more fashionable Italianate mode. The new hotel was so successful that it put the United States Hotel out of business within a year. Its popularity continued, and in 1856 an addition extended the length of its facade by 134 feet. The hotel attracted the 1860 presidential candidate Stephen Douglas for a stay, even though few votes were to be gained in the village. In 1865, the Fort William Henry Hotel was sold. The new owners expanded the structure further with the addition of a fifth floor and a mansard roof. Until the arrival of the railroad in 1882, the hotel's success was based on its position as a hub for the stagecoaches that traveled the plank road to the lake.[32] Thus, in the 1850s, the village's elegant and extensive accommodations made it a destination that travelers eagerly sought.

In 1866 a visitor described Caldwell as containing "two churches (Presbyterian and Episcopal), a court-house, a jail, and a number of elegant private residences." Clearly the village had made a comeback; a decade later its population was slightly more than it had been in James Caldwell's time. Moreover, the village had realized its original design, focusing on amenities that encouraged visitors to stay. Canada Street was now a broad and straight thoroughfare, at least in the four blocks between the entrance to the Fort William Henry Hotel grounds and the courthouse (Figure 14).[33] On the west side of Canada Street, the two blocks closest to the courthouse had been designed with rear access through a system of alleys lined with stables. These alleys were now filled with businesses and houses. The oldest and previously the only hotel, the Lake House, kept its livery stable on one of the alleys. In addition to the livery stable, the Lake House had extensive pleasure grounds as well as its own steamboat landing. On the hotel's Canada Street side, there was a walkway and a mall planted with grass and lined with trees, marked here and there by tethering posts, much as could be found on Broadway, the contemporary main street in Saratoga Springs. The proprietor of the Lake House was now the widow of Fred G. Tucker, a man who had obtained his original lease from William Caldwell. Across from the Lake House was another hotel, the Central House, which had grown from a tavern and which was rebuilt in 1875 to be open year-round. Farther to the south on the west side of Canada Street, accommodations were available at the Carpenter House. Beyond it was the entrance to the elaborate grounds of the Fort William Henry Hotel, which included fountains, a bowling alley, and the hotel's own steamboat landing. On the west side of Canada Street, in proximity to the Fort William Henry Hotel, a hamlet developed in support of the hotel.

Scattered around aptly named Mohican Street was a new diversion for visitors familiar with Cooper's *Leatherstocking Tales:* an Indian encampment, where they might sample Native American culture. Beginning in the 1870s, the Indians came yearly by canoe from Canada for the summer season, raising this temporary village, hunting and fishing in their traditional lake hunting grounds, and selling their crafts to visitors. The Indians interviewed by S. R. Stoddard about 1880 resided at Canada's St. Francis Mission; they were descendants of those Catholic converts who had made war in the eighteenth century against the New England borderland and whose village had been sacked in 1759 by the New England brush fighter Robert Rogers. The St. Francis Indians were now an attraction, testing visitors in their ability to master the skills of archery.[34]

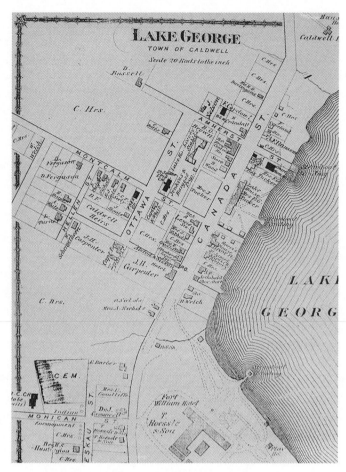

FIGURE 14. "Lake George Town
of Caldwell." Map showing
Canada Street, Lake House,
Fort William Henry Hotel,
and the Indian encampment.
(F. W. Beers, County Atlas of Warren
County, New York, *New York, 1876.)*

Less than thirty years after the death of William Caldwell, the village had passed from
the paternal dominance of a single family to become a summer resort with a variety of hotel,
lumbering, and family interests, a resort community that began to resemble the present and
popular Lake George Village. Grand lakeshore cottages began to appear, the earliest development of this type in the Adirondacks. However, on his property, among the summer places,
Hubbell's steam mill continued to operate until it burned in 1890.[35] Hubbell's own house was
in a practical location for his economic interests, up the mountainside on the Bolton Road, signifying the role of Adirondack lumbering in providing year-round employment. How the owners of the cottages reacted to the belching mill in the midst of the lake's natural beauty is not
recorded. They may honestly have found it to be picturesque, as painters of the Hudson Valley School had come to include manufactories in their expansive views of nature.

As the nineteenth century came to an end, a new public enterprise appeared, signifying
the distance the village of Caldwell had come since it was laid out in 1802. Around the ruins of
Fort George and the garrison grounds a historical attraction was proposed, a commemorative
battleground and a wooded park that would eventually hold a series of monuments and ruins

dedicated to the combatants of the Battle of Lake George in 1755. From 1897 to 1900, working with members of the State Senate, the newly formed Society of Colonial Wars was able to convince the New York State legislature to appropriate money to purchase land from the heirs of the Caldwells.[36] To facilitate the transaction, the Caldwell Village Improvement Association was established. It gave way to the Lake George Historical Association and then in 1899 to the New York State Historical Association, which was designated the caretaker for the new park. Thus was born a new historical society and the idea of a battlefield park to match those that were being widely established to commemorate the Civil War. But Caldwell's resources remained slender because of its tiny population, and the creation of the battleground was largely the effort of summer residents rather than of its permanent community.

Nineteenth-century Caldwell and Ballston Spa have much to tell us about the history of resort life and the development of the New York frontier. Both were the creation of a single landlord-developer in the patrician tradition of the Schuylers, Van Rensselaers, and Gansevoorts. The leadership of Low and the Caldwells provided a variety of schemes to establish a community on a sound economic basis, including manufacturing experiments, the prestige of being county seats, and, often as an afterthought, tourism. There was an important distinction in the timing of these efforts: Caldwell began as a manufacturing community in the early 1800s, the very time when Ballston was at its peak as a resort; after 1840, as Ballston became a manufacturing center, Caldwell shed its early economic interests and gradually became a resort. Ultimately, both towns lost the paternalism of their great patron. Low left in 1823 because he found his investment was not providing high enough returns. In contrast, William Caldwell was more of a leisured gentleman who retained control of the estate until his death in 1848 because he enjoyed the prestige of being the proprietary landlord. Regardless of these differences in personality, both villages prospered more after the landlords left than they had when their founders were present, for they began to provide diverse opportunities for different investors, many of whom resided in the community. After 1848, William Caldwell's descendants eased restrictions, opening Lake George to lumber and hotel developers, who were driven by the need to make quick profits (in the case of hotels from an increasing volume of visitors during the short summer season). Nearby, another community was forming that would be more successful than either Ballston Spa or Caldwell, and its success was based exclusively on an enduring resort economy.

PART TWO

The
Establishment
of
Saratoga Springs
as the
Leading Resort

CHAPTER 4

The Development of Public Spaces

The precarious nature of the nineteenth-century resort economy was demonstrated by numerous failures. The conditions that forced Ballston Spa to abandon resort life were common. After success as a spa in the eighteenth and early nineteenth centuries, Stafford Springs, Connecticut, lost its popularity and put aside its resort economy for one based on woolen-goods manufacture, pearl-button making, and the mining and processing of iron. By the post–Civil War era, another resort, Clarendon Springs, Vermont, was on its way to becoming a ghost town. The construction of hotels would save Caldwell and White Sulphur Springs in Virginia as resorts, but many others would not survive the nineteenth century.

The key to both survival and success for a nineteenth-century resort was the creation of public spaces where a visitor could see and be seen. These spaces included not only accommodations with public rooms (which will be discussed in the next chapter) but also parks, walks, squares, spring pavilions, outdoor sculpture, pleasure gardens, and even cemeteries. These amenities were organized to combine visitors' respect for natural beauty with the need to have sophisticated entertainment; they allowed the spa to the bridge the gap between natural and urban wonders. By the 1840s, Saratoga Springs had all these amenities, a remarkable feat for a village two hundred miles inland from New York City. As a result, the spa was a pioneer in the planning and construction of public space—what Saratogians thought of as providing amenities that would attract visitors. And it provided these spaces with the slender resources of a country village at the edge of the wilderness; as a resort, it, by definition, lacked the traditional source of urban productivity, manufacturing establishments. Saratoga Springs was thus the first village in the nation to base its continuous prosperity and growth on its ability to become a center of entertainment.

From 1780 to 1880, population growth in Saratoga Springs showed that a community could prosper as a resort. The growth followed an upward trend in four periods, two of them times of boom and two them eras of modest increases. Our knowledge of growth in the first period, before 1830, is based on slender documentation, but it appears that the early spa grew slowly. Saratoga Springs failed to become a county seat like Ballston Spa or Caldwell, and not until 1826, two decades after its rival Ballston Spa, did the village government have a charter. In 1820, the village had a population of eleven hundred and the town a population of under two thousand, figures not decisively larger than those for Ballston Spa or Caldwell.[1] The second period, from 1830 to 1845, was one of booming expansion brought about by the influx of visitors and freight carried on the railroad, which appeared in 1832. If we ignore the effects of the Panic of 1837, we find that in the decade from 1835 to 1845 the town's population almost doubled, from 2,438 to 4,276; the village around the main street, Broadway, accounted for about two-thirds of those figures. The third period, from 1845 to 1868, was one of slower growth, as the gains of the previous decades were consolidated. During the Civil War, 1861 to 1865, the town lost population, a sign that the war interrupted the flow of visitors to the spa. Still, in 1859 the village built-up area was expanding beyond Broadway, and the construction business was providing housing for the population and meeting the need to accommodate visitors. In this era Irish immigrants arrived in the greatest numbers to take jobs in the resort, and most of the modest growth must be attributed to them. By 1850, village dwellings, with 6.4 persons each, a figure that included a conjugal family and an additional person, were more crowded than those in the surrounding countryside. In the fourth period, from 1868 to 1880, the village again experienced a boom. In 1875 the town's population surpassed ten thousand and continued to expand to the level of fourteen thousand by 1880, a figure close to the city's 1970 population.

By 1880, the influx of Irish immigrants had subsided, so that the increase had come by natural growth and the arrival of native New Yorkers and New Englanders to work or retire at the spa. The built-up area of the village continued to spread beyond the Broadway nucleus to reach to Nelson and East Avenues and Ludlow Street on the East Side and to Grand Avenue and Walnut Street on the West Side. Lincoln Avenue was the southern limit of the populated area, while in the north North Broadway now extended to the open fields at the Greenfield town line. (For streets in Saratoga Springs, see Figure 15.) At this time numerous structures appeared in alleys, which were often used for housing or commercial purposes, a sign of shortages of both types of space. As Saratoga Springs approached the turn of the century, it had passed through four periods that had raised its population fourfold, and it was taking on the appearance of an urban place, but one that was based uniquely on an economy that catered to tourists.

Civic-Minded Leadership

The responsibility for the growth of Saratoga Springs lay immediately in the hands of a few entrepreneurial families. Although the municipal government did supply some important services such as licenses for the sale of alcoholic beverages starting in 1826, a municipal water system and street lighting and cleaning in 1844, and fire protection in 1857, it was swayed by influential community leaders and forced into action by volunteer organizations.[2] The village depended on civic-minded citizens. Its first police force, the Association for the Detection of Horse Thieves and Burglars, was chartered in 1823 as a volunteer organization without municipal financial support. It was dependent on membership dues to prevent petty crime, which was caused mainly by the influx of summer visitors. In another instance, the village's first water system was established and maintained from 1832 as a public-spirited act by developer John Clarke. His death in 1843 forced the village to take over responsibility for the water system.

Real power remained in the hands of a few wealthy and civic-minded families. At the top of everyone's list were Henry Walton (literally at the top of the membership list of the horse thieves' detection association) and John Clarke, followed by James and Thomas Marvin, Samuel Freeman, and Judiah Ellsworth. In the middle of the list were the printer-journalist Gideon

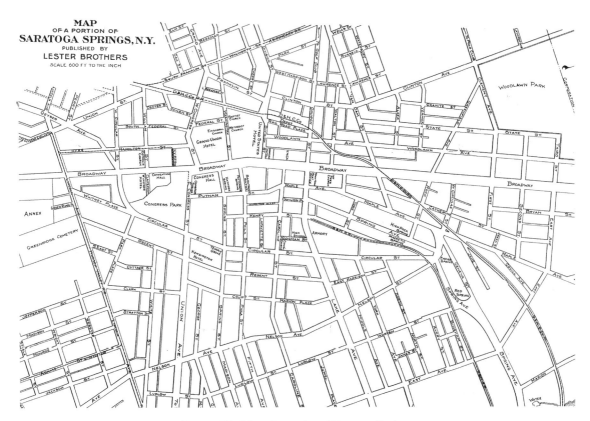

FIGURE 15. Map of a portion of Saratoga Springs.
(Published by Lester Brothers, copyright 1903 by Willard Lester.)

Davidson, the master builder Runion Martin, and the furniture maker Ransom Cook. Gideon Putnam also played a role, but he died in 1812, just as his resources were being marshaled for developmental purposes, and hence it was his descendants, like Rockwell Putnam, who made a difference. Unlike Ballston Spa or Caldwell, where a single all-powerful individual dominated the early years, Saratoga Springs had a cooperative expansion effort, with several families sharing the credit for making it the country's leading spa. As a group, these leaders were often trained in the law and either ran for or obtained judgeships.[3] Thanks to Reuben Hyde Walworth, the New York State Court of Chancery operated in Saratoga Springs from 1833 to 1848, creating an atmosphere in which legal minds flourished. Many developers were attorneys, including Henry Walton, Judiah Ellsworth, and Thomas Marvin. In 1841, in a crisis over freedom of access to the springs, a hotel proprietor was forced to change his policies in the face of popular opposition led by attorneys. The civic leaders who persuaded the proprietor to back down were three attorneys (two would become judges), two newspaper publishers, a physician, and the furniture maker Ransom Cook. Clearly men of the law or professions had become the community's natural leaders.

The Layout and Planning of the Village

The original focal points of the community were two settlements that had grown up as crossroads around separate sets of springs, roughly at each end of Broadway. In the 1790s and

1800s the upper and lower villages had been established around High Rock and Congress springs, respectively. Henry Walton developed High Rock Spring, while Gideon and Doanda Putnam and their children exploited Congress Spring. The springs were the natural resource that most spurred the development of the resort. As the springs were exploited, a pavilion, bathhouse, or nearby hotel appeared, and ultimately a following of devotees. Thus tubed and accessible springs provided for the village's expansion.

Saratoga Springs was created by connecting the two early settlements together along the edge of the escarpment that marked the presence of the mineral springs. Saratoga Springs emerged in the early nineteenth century as a linear street village centered on Broadway. On the west side of Broadway, building foundations were relatively level, while on the east side foundations were built into the side of the escarpment, requiring additional floors under the street level. Streets and alleys were laid out parallel to Broadway, so that it became the spine of a network that spread west and east. Broadway first appears on a map of Gideon Putnam's property in 1810, where it was located below Division Street. Three years later it is evident on a map of Henry Walton's property, where it was shown above Division Street.[4] The main street was wide and perfectly straight with one exception, a bend at Division Street where Putnam's and Walton's properties met. An 1825 street view made by Henry Walton Jr. shows Broadway flanked by wood-frame structures fronted by Lombardy poplars but without sidewalks or other indications of the street's future amenities (Figure 16). Sidewalks appeared in the 1830s, but they were made of packed sand, clay, or loam until Miles Beach had placed in front of his Broadway shop a walk made of stone, which he replaced with brick a few years later.

FIGURE 16. Henry Walton, del., "Saratoga Springs," c. 1825. One of the earliest views of Broadway.
(Pendleton Lithograph, from Gideon M. Davison's Fashionable Tour, Saratoga Springs, N.Y., 1822.)

The Putnam family established one of the original settlements. In 1804 Gideon Putnam leased land south of today's Division Street from Henry Walton, who claimed an annual rent and dower rights over the property. However, only three years later Walton released Putnam from these obligations so that he in effect held freehold title. Walton evidently was secure after three years that his tenant would not default or engage in his own petty speculation. The Putnam family's plan for the development of their Saratoga Springs land, the lower village, was produced in 1825 by Gideon's heirs, thirteen years after his death, although it was supposedly based on a survey done in April 1810.[5] The survey shows a property running from Franklin Street on the west to Putnam Street on the east, north beyond Washington Street, but short of Division Street, and south to Congress Street. It was a relatively compact parcel that contained the crossroads for the lower village. The focus of the property was understandably Broadway at Congress Street, where Putnam's Congress Hall Hotel stood on the east side and the boarding house, later the Grand Union Hotel, on the west. Although a few structures appear on Broadway and on Washington and Congress streets near Broadway, it is clear that most of the lots went unsold in the years after Putnam's death. Thus the plan represents a future that would not be realized until the 1830s. It included a square set aside for a meeting house, where the First Baptist Church was eventually built on Washington Street, a lot for a school, and a space for the burying ground that became the Gideon Putnam Burial Yard. Overall, the Putnam family parcel was important, but it covered only a fraction of the village that would be built in the first half of the nineteenth century.

The other original settlement was the result of the efforts of Henry Walton, who, as we have seen, was familiar with English spas. Walton's father, Jacob, owned much of the land on which Saratoga Springs was built. After living in Ballston, New York City, and Albany, Henry settled permanently at the spa in 1815–1816.[6] From his New York experience, he knew how to encourage the rapid turnover of urban lots (whether through lease or sale), to stimulate investment and reinvestment in village property, and to promote the erection of buildings on that property. In Saratoga Springs he sold the land he held below Division Street to Gideon Putnam and John Clarke, and from 1813 to the 1840s he developed his remaining property, plotting rectangular lots on both sides of Broadway and providing free lots for desirable structures such as churches and schools. He constructed a substantial home and then a hotel on Broadway and also tubed Flat Rock Spring. In 1839, he laid out a grassy space, between Van Dam and Church streets, which he called Regents Park, in an abortive effort to establish the village's first municipal park. As a planner, architect, and entrepreneur, Walton was more responsible for the creation of the spa than any of his colleagues.

Like Walton, John Clarke was familiar with English spas because he was a native of Yorkshire, England, the provenance of Harrogate spa. He emigrated to Manhattan, where in 1819 he opened the city's first soda fountain. He came to Saratoga Springs in 1823 and purchased the Putnams' springs; two years later he built a successful bottling facility east of Congress Spring in order to distribute the mineral waters beyond the village.[7] In 1824 he laid out Circular Street above Congress Park, where eight years later he built his own home (Figure 17). This was the first effort to expand the village beyond Broadway, and as it evolved Circular Street became an upper-class enclave of fine residences within easy walking distance of the main street. The design of Circular Street along the curvature of the escarpment was innovative because

FIGURE 17. John Clarke House, Circular Street, Saratoga Springs. Built 1832. When constructed, this Greek Revival house stood alone on Circular Street overlooking Congress Park and Clarke's bottling plant. *(Photo, Theodore Corbett.)*

street planning in the United States generally followed a strict grid pattern. Keen to beautify the village, in 1827 Clarke convinced the village trustees to reduce the highway taxes of any property owner who planted trees along the street. This was evidently a problem, as we learn from a comment made by a visitor in 1820 that Saratoga Springs looked "more destitute of ornamental trees" than its rival Ballston Spa. Like Walton, Clarke had a vision of the public places in English spas, where visitors could walk and enjoy natural and cultural beauty.

Clarke divided his extensive acreage into lots, although he does not appear to have sold many in his lifetime. His land was adjacent to those prime amenities Congress Park and Circular Street; it ran south from Spring Street, past Union Avenue and Park Place to today's Lincoln Avenue. At his death in 1843, there was only a scattering of houses along Circular and Regent streets, while the bulk of his land beyond these streets consisted of empty lots. It appears that the terms he offered were costly and that the village's population did not include enough wealthy members to take up his offer.[8] Although his property crossed Broadway to the west, it was still not developed much beyond Regent Street in 1854, when his heirs had it surveyed. Clearly Broadway was still a magnet for the well-to-do, which prevented the development of upper- and middle-class residential areas beyond the main street. This propensity is demonstrated by the fact that the wealthiest resident of Circular Street, Madame Jumel, took her main meals daily by traveling in her carriage to a Broadway hotel.

After Clarke's death in 1854, Amos S. Maxwell, a member of the Clarke family through marriage and a village trustee, had the rest of Clarke's property platted, focusing on Congress Street, which was renamed Union Avenue (Figure 18).[9] Maxwell's design treated the Congress Street trail to Saratoga Lake as the village's first boulevard, or straight artery along which great houses could be built. At the same time, realizing Clarke's problems in selling lots, Maxwell decided to limit expensive properties to Union Avenue and divide the rest of the tract for more modest middle- and laboring-class housing. Maxwell provided Union Avenue with support alleys and enormous lots of 100-foot frontages and 240-foot depths. On parallel White Street the lot sizes fell to 50-foot frontages with 150-foot depths. Farther south the lots became even smaller, and no alleys were planned. Clearly, Maxwell aimed at setting a range of prices depending on the lot size and the presence of alleys. The lots designed in the 1854 plan were laid out, but, as with Clarke's earlier lots, housing construction remained minimal in this parcel

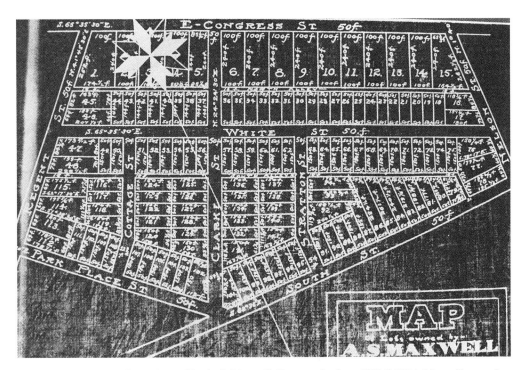

FIGURE 18. "Map of Lots Owned by A. S. Maxwell, Saratoga Springs, N.Y.," 1854. Maxwell created a spectrum of properties by varying the size of lots, providing the best parcels with alleys.
(Saratoga County Clerk, Ballston Spa, N.Y.)

until the boom of the early 1870s and the establishment of the thoroughbred track at the end of Union Avenue.

Two other early developers, Judiah Ellsworth and Samuel Freeman, had more success as landlords than Clarke and his heirs precisely because they marketed smaller and less costly lots to the middle and laboring classes. These developers fostered residential growth on the West Side, the most extensive development beyond Broadway. In 1838, five years after he purchased the land adjacent to the west side of the Putnam property, Judiah Ellsworth, a successful Saratoga Springs attorney and village postmaster from 1841 to 1843, laid out a compact model neighborhood.[10] An examiner in chancery, Ellsworth had leading attorneys Esek Cowen and Augustus Bockes for protégés and is the village's best example of an attorney-developer. From 1848, he resided with his mother and sister at the Pitney House hotel, from which he could oversee the development of his adjacent tract. He arranged his tract in uniform rectangular blocks, each bisected by rear alleys, the epitome of a classical design and the closest the spa would come to a utopian ideal (Figure 19). The scale was, however, smaller than that found elsewhere in the village; as a result smaller structures were built and smaller alleys were laid out,

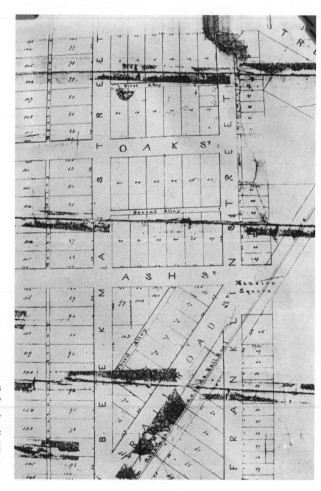

FIGURE 19. "Map of Village Lots Surveyed for J. Ellsworth, Esq.," 3 June 1838. These uniformly designed streets and alleys were the most classically inspired in Saratoga Springs.
(Saratoga County Clerk, Ballston Spa, N.Y.)

a typical street being only 50 feet wide. Lots uniformly had 50-foot frontages, but varied in length from 120 to 144 feet; this was the first documented attempt to market lots in the same development to the laboring and middle class. Over the years, the area's smaller and less expensive lots attracted successful immigrants, especially the Irish, and thus it became known as Dublin.

In 1841, Henry Walton sold an extensive tract of land on the West Side to Samuel Freeman, a Ballston Spa resident and physician who in 1837 was elected sheriff of Saratoga County. Three years later Freeman found a buyer for his Ballston practice and was permanently settled in Saratoga Springs by 1845. Six years before, Walton had designated the area as Regents Park, but he abandoned the idea and sold the property to Freeman, who laid out lots meant for middle-class residents with an alley system from Church Street north to Van Dam Street (Figure 20).[11] Freeman was acquainted with John Clarke, as they both were Whigs, and he joined other Whigs in attending Bethesda Episcopal Church, where he was a warden. From 1856 to 1870 Freeman, with his partner Thomas Marvin, marketed additional lots on the West Side, and Freeman became president of the Marvin-controlled First National Bank of Saratoga Springs. Within a decade Freeman's lots were filled with houses, making him the equal of Ellsworth and more successful than the Clarke family in real estate projects.

Freeman in partnership with James and Thomas Marvin continued to develop his tract and the land around Franklin Square in the 1850s and 1860s.[12] They acquired three additional lots on the north side of Division Street. The successful development of Franklin and Clinton streets was a logical outcome of the Marvins' original interest in developing a residential square with proximity to Broadway, and the West Side's Franklin Square was their private enterprise. They had moved from the Malta countryside to the spa, investing in the United States Hotel and the nearby railroad depot. The depot was a major undertaking in 1843; it included a 160-foot-long station with two tracks entering it through arched doorways and a brick machine shop.[13] An uncle had opened the United States Hotel in 1824, and James Marvin became its proprietor by 1830. He was also a Whig Congressman, a vestryman of the emerging Bethesda Episcopal Church, a director of the Schenectady and Saratoga Railroad, and a leader in the movement to improve Greenridge Cemetery. In 1842, his brother Thomas joined him as an owner of the hotel, a situation that continued until his death in 1852. In the 1840s, the brothers built their Greek Revival homes along Franklin Square, on which three more houses of similar style were constructed to create a residential ensemble (Figure 21). With Walton and Clarke, these brothers would be leaders in making Saratoga Springs into a resort. At the time, the Marvin homes and a few others on the square made that space the most prestigious residential area in the village. Franklin Square was fashionable because it was adjacent to two of the Marvins' prime facilities: the Schenectady and Saratoga Railroad Station and the rear of the United States Hotel.

Created in the 1840s, Franklin Square remained an unfinished residential enclave for about thirty years, with the houses covering only two sides of a grassy space. After the Civil War it lost part of its original configuration. In 1866, a short-lived fountain appeared in the middle of one of its side streets, and four years later the grassy space at the center became the site of a new residence. This ostentatious home, erected for wealthy lumber baron George Harvey in flamboyant French Renaissance style, was built on land that had been set aside as the

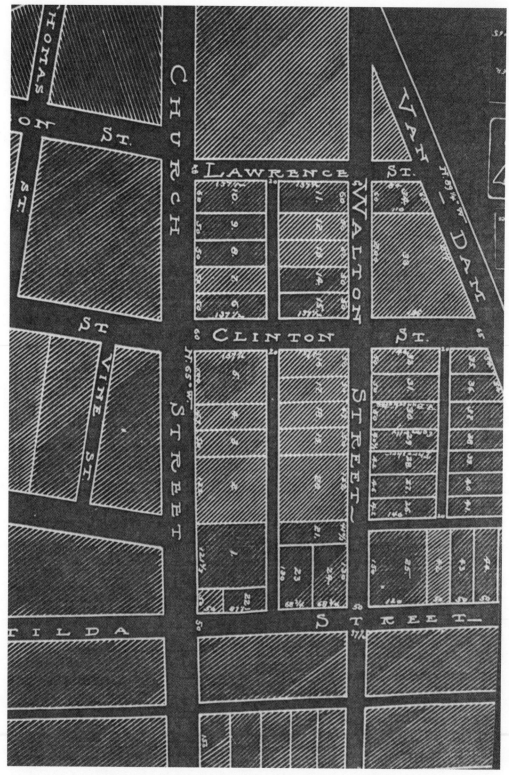

FIGURE 20. "Map of Property at Saratoga Springs Owned by Dr. S. Freeman," 1841; the streets
supported by alleys that Freeman laid out in the vicinity of Walton Street.
(Saratoga County Clerk, Ballston Spa, N.Y.)

FIGURE 21. Thomas Marvin House, 4 Franklin Square, Saratoga Springs. Built in the early 1840s.
(Photo, Philip Haggerty.)

center of the residential square. He sold the home in the 1870s, after only a few years' occupancy, and it became a cure institute and boarding house; this transformation allowed for the commercialization of the square. The reduction of the residential aspect of the square and the fact that the new intersection of streets became a traffic meeting point diminished the square's desirability as a residential address.

Saratoga Springs weathered the depression of the Civil War era and was prepared to participate in the post–Civil War boom. This expansion involved not so much the initiation of new projects as it did the development of existing sites with new houses and outbuildings. Residential enclaves that offered housing for all classes now surrounded Broadway. The construction of elegant summer cottages in areas beyond Broadway meant that the main street was no longer the only center of fashion. The development of two broad, straight boulevards, Union and Grand avenues, characterized the expansion of the 1870s; they were lined exclusively with substantial residential properties of the type that Maxwell had hoped to introduce on Union Avenue. The creation of Union Avenue was an example of private initiative. The Union Avenue Association was formed in 1865, and it spent the next three or four years developing Union Avenue as the connection between the village and Saratoga Lake; the avenue also passed the racecourse that had been established in 1863. The Association's board had the authority to issue bonds, erect tollbooths, and construct and maintain "a macadamised or turnpike avenue one hundred feet wide." The board, with members like Leonard Jerome and William Travers, included considerable New York City money. It also claimed those with an interest in Saratoga Lake, notably Cary Moon, proprietor of the famous Lake House, and Frank Leslie, a publisher

Figure 22. Cavalcade of fashionable equipages passing Morrissey's Club House on Congress Street
on their way to the track in 1873.
(Frank Leslie's Illustrated Newspaper, New York City, 1873.)

with the most expansive villa on the lake. The Association was dissolved in 1870, when its powers were taken over by the town's Street and Avenue Commission. The activities of the board
illustrate again how private concern forced the village to take action. Ultimately, Union Avenue
in the village became the most successful residential avenue because it was an important corridor for horse-drawn and foot traffic from Congress Park and the Casino on East Congress Street
to the thoroughbred track and Saratoga Lake (Figure 22). Grand Avenue on the West Side, a
wide street that began at the Pitney House hotel and dwindled into a minor country road, had
only a few substantial properties along it. New homes were built on both boulevards in the High
Victorian style's Italian, Second Empire, French Renaissance, and Victorian Gothic modes.[14]
By 1880, although partially settled, neither of the boulevards was fully developed, and many
open lots remained between the houses, a sign that the summer cottage in a semisuburban setting was still not the Saratoga ideal.

It took three stages of development to make North Broadway into a boulevard. North
Broadway usually is designated as the area above the Saratoga and Washington Railroad, which
bisected the city's main street in 1846. However, for the next twenty years, North Broadway
was indistinguishable from the rest of Broadway as houses, hotels, and boarding houses clustered on either side of the railway tracks in long narrow lots that were typical of the rest of the
village. The road to Greenfield, which doglegged to the left and carried traffic out of the village,

defined North Broadway's first terminus. North of this intersection the village stopped, and maps show numerous empty lots that the Bryan family had plotted but was unable to sell.

After the Civil War, North Broadway grew into a boulevard as it expanded northward, with many of its lots occupied by houses. The limits of this second expansion were the two blocks between North Circular Street and Second Street. The lots were enormous compared with those below the Greenfield road, and there were no alleys to break into lots to back them up, for Matilda and Bryan streets served that function. These houses were built in the Italianate or the latest Second Empire styles; these styles had evolved in urban settings, so they looked quite out of place in the middle of expansive lawns. Influential families like the Fullers and the Roots from Troy, the industrial city across the Hudson from Albany, built homes in which to enjoy the summer season.[15] At the end of North Broadway, the Glen Mitchell Hotel, in colonial–Second Empire style, offered a range of entertainment, from a driving park to a trotting racecourse to a rifle range. It was a terminus to compete with the thoroughbred track at the end of Union Avenue.

After 1880, in the third stage of North Broadway development, housing appeared further north, covering the next two blocks of North Broadway to Fourth Street, an area of Queen Anne–style houses, which looked ideally situated on the village's largest lots. However, the appearance of these houses did not prevent the demise of the Glen Mitchell, which was sold in 1886 to become a college. Despite its expansive prospect, therefore, North Broadway was left without a terminus and thus did not meet the need of a boulevard to have a destination. This furthest development from the town center was totally isolated from the hubbub of downtown Broadway; it thus was an ideal place for peaceful repose but not an ideal boulevard.

In fact, Broadway's business district still attracted elegant new homes, as witnessed by the construction from 1870 to 1872 of Dr. Lewis Whiting's and Dr. Tabor Reynolds's separate, four-storied, double townhouses, which, with mansard roofs and porch networks, looked as though they belonged in New York City or Philadelphia (Figure 23). Reynolds, Saratoga County's most successful physician, could think of no better place for his retirement.[16] The urban attractions of Broadway would continue to counteract the demand for suburban homes and summer cottages.

Broadway in the era of the U.S. centennial was a magical place, to be enjoyed by visitors and citizens alike. Novelist Marietta Holley introduced the pleasures of Broadway through her characters Samantha and Josiah Allen, country bumpkins who came to the spa to cure Josiah's annoying toe corns. The 1887 bestseller *Samantha at Saratoga* described how the couple, walking at night, found Broadway to be a "scene of enchantment," "a land of perfect beauty and delight."[17] Their momentary fear of numerous "perfect strangers" whose "motives and weapons" were concealed was allayed by the presence of a soldier, elevated above the throng. Ironically, the bright lights had seduced the couple, for the soldier turned out to be a piece of bronze sculpture, a tribute to the spa's Civil War veterans (Figure 24). The nightly illuminated effect was the result of technology from three sources: Chinese lanterns hung from trees, gaslight street fixtures, and after 1879, when they were first introduced, electric lights, most popular in strings of different colors.

Broadway remained both a commercial and a residential center even as late as the 1880s, and a geographical division into gender spheres failed to appear. In New York City, men

FIGURE 23. Residence of
Dr. T. B. Reynolds, Saratoga
Springs. Built c. 1872. This
Second Empire residence was
erected for Reynolds's retirement;
it is an example of homes that
were still being constructed in the
Broadway business district
in the 1870s.
(Nathaniel Bartlett Sylvester,
History of Saratoga County,
Philadelphia, 1878.)

dominated the commercial sphere at the center, while women, both domestics and their mistresses, ruled the outer, more suburban sphere of residences.[18] Instead, on Broadway in Saratoga Springs male hotel proprietors worked closely with female housekeepers, cooks, and armies of other domestic workers. The presence of so many hotels as well as residences on and around Broadway meant the commercial and domestic spheres continued to mix rather than becoming separate. This disregard for the spheres, widened by the development of boarding

FIGURE 24. "Way up over all our heads stood a big straight soldier volunteerin' to see to the hull crew of 'em below"; the effect of the new lighting systems on visitors, who viewed Broadway as being enchanted.
(Frederick Opper, illustration for Marietta Holley, Samantha at Saratoga, *Philadelphia, 1887.)*

houses run by women and cure institutes in the neighborhoods, brought the commerce of Broadway to the sanctified residential areas.

In Saratoga Springs, the stratification of neighborhoods exclusively for one class, be it rich or poor, was muted. True, the laboring class gravitated to Dublin and the village's many alleys, while Franklin Square, then Union and Grand avenues, and finally upper North Broadway were marketed for the rich. The inability to sell expensive residential lots and housing, however, modified the developments, making them available to the middle class as well, a condition Maxwell's 1854 Union Avenue development took into account. Blurring social barriers, the alleys allowed the laboring class to live in the rear of well-to-do households. Of all the residential areas, only upper North Broadway was able to sustain a suburban ideal without alleys and with the type of exclusivity that would appeal to the summer rich.

The Public Landscapes: Pleasure Gardens, Parks, and Cemeteries

One of the reasons for the spa's exceptional social patterns was the overabundance of public spaces. Within the spa's street layout, public spaces served as places for people to meet and to be entertained. Such spaces included Franklin Square, the three boulevards, several pleasure grounds or parks, a theater and an auditorium, racecourses, Native American encampments, and a cemetery.

Walton and Clarke derived the idea for pleasure parks from their experience with the picturesque gardens that had been introduced on English estates in the 1720s. At the same time, the English landscape tradition was being commercially exploited for a broad public through the creation of pleasure gardens, which became miniature resorts. Combining gardens with theatrical and flimsy pavilions and displays, the pleasure garden took the private picturesque English garden and opened it to a broad public. The most famous of England's pleasure grounds, ultimately named Vauxhall Gardens, operated from 1661 to 1859.[19] It started with a simple design for straight, tree-lined promenades, the Italian walks, and then expanded. First, the promenades were improved by a covering of triumphal arches. Then, formal groves were added as a focal point; they contained the orchestra rotunda and the Prince of Wales pavilion, which signified the importance of music and royal patronage to the attraction's success. Later improvements included supper boxes about the grove, new pavilions in "Chinese Gothic" style, and numerous illuminated trompe l'oeil paintings of leisure activities and didactic scenes. Interspersed was sculpture, ranging from renowned works such as Louis-François Roubiliac's *Handel as Apollo* to a lead cast of John Milton. Landscape had become entertaining not just for the gentry but for anyone who could gain admission.

Picturesque landscapes later appeared in U.S. urban residential squares and parks. They could be found in New York City in the 1820s and 1830s; speculative residential squares like Washington, Gramercy, and Union were successful developments because the green space attracted wealthy residents.[20] The chief advocate of English gardens in the United States was landscape designer Andrew Jackson Downing, whose 1841 *Treatise on the Theory and Practice of Landscape Gardening* began to popularize the pleasure garden for middle-class cottages. Histories of public landscaping in the United States usually begin by discussing the work of Frederick Law Olmsted and his municipal creation, New York's Central Park in 1857. Olmsted had discovered the English natural park on a visit to Liverpool in 1850, and for the next seven years, until construction began, he and his supporters urged the city to create a park with a uniform English design that artfully combined natural surroundings with a high degree of regulation. Such regulation was crucial because although the park was officially to be open to the working class, they were to be discouraged from certain types of behavior such as drinking alcohol, gambling, dancing, or listening to raucous music.

By the time Downing and Olmsted started planning such spaces, Saratoga Springs already had several pleasure grounds, most having been established when Downing was a mere

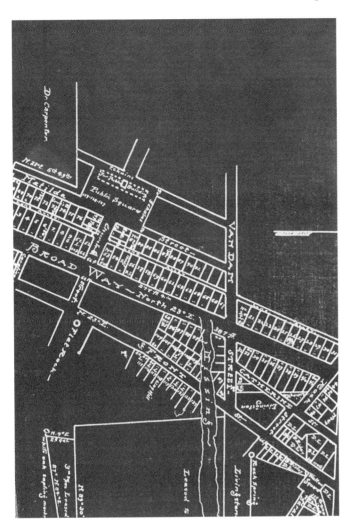

FIGURE 25. "Map of Lands Belonging to Henry Walton at the Village of Saratoga Springs, in December, 1813"; Broadway at Van Dam Street. *(Saratoga County Clerk, Ballston Spa, N.Y.)*

boy. The spa needed such amenities in order to cater to visitors. The resort's entrepreneurs believed that amenities such as a square or green space would set off a development, enriching a community's beauty and providing visitors with a focus of attention. Walton laid out two public squares in 1813.[21] One overlooked High Rock Spring, connecting the upper village to the spring below the escarpment; this square he named for himself (lower left corner of Figure 25). The other square began at the corner of Matilda (now Woodlawn) and Church streets, one block west of Broadway ("Public Square" in Figure 25). It was designed as an extensive open space surrounded by public buildings. Although neither of these squares was realized, Walton partially fulfilled his scheme for a downtown public square by encouraging the erection of the Presbyterian and the Universalist churches there in 1816 and 1825, respectively. However, no government seat was ever erected in the area. In 1813, Walton also laid out Regents Park in line with his desire to give the spa an expansive public landscape, although as with his other plans the proposed park was ultimately split into streets and housing lots. In 1839

Walton planned two additional public squares, Flat Rock, around the spring of that name, one block east of Broadway, and Hanover, where the Greenfield road joined upper North Broadway. Again, these squares were not realized.

The pleasure garden was the first form of U.S. park when it appeared at Saratoga Springs in 1819 adjacent to hotels. The history of hotel pleasure grounds in Saratoga Springs begins with their private development for the sake of guests (although such grounds had no admission charge and were usually accessible to the entire visiting public). In 1819, the Pavilion was the first hotel to have extensive pleasure grounds; they were located to the side and rear of the structure.[22] Twenty years later, its grounds had come to occupy an area to the north of the hotel along Broadway, a rectangular space five hundred feet by two hundred feet. In these pleasure grounds, Daniel McLaren constructed an elegant theater, the Covent Garden House, named after the theater district in London. As the focal point of the gardens, the theater was appropriately the site on July 15, 1841, of one of the spa's early charitable events, a Ladies Fair, in which funds were raised to furnish the new Presbyterian church.

By then the Pavilion was not alone. The United States Hotel had five acres of trees, shrubs, flowers, and lawn, where a band played in the season. Between the hotel's wings were a "well-rolled and well-mowed lawn, and clean gravel sidewalks." Trees were planted in the center, and a picket fence with an elaborate, classical-style entrance closed the rear to outsiders and provided access for guests to the train station.[23] By 1843, its rival, the neighboring Union Hall, had three and a half acres of gardens and pleasure grounds. These hotel pleasure grounds were designed with the geometric beds of the French parterre style, but the plantings and trees were informally arranged according to English ideals.

Next, to improve the site of his bottling plant, Clarke, who knew about pleasure grounds without, like Olmsted, having to visit England, matched the hotel pleasure grounds by creating, between 1823 and 1826, a crescent-shaped pleasure ground that became still-existing Congress Park. The lawn was enhanced with spring pavilions and embellishments. Although it was his private development, Clarke opened the park free to the public.[24] It covered his property from Circular Street to Congress Street and had a narrow entrance directly on Broadway. Except on the edge of the escarpment along Circular Street, the park was on swampy ground through which flowed the village brook; the park contained two of the most renowned springs, Congress and Columbian. The creation of the crescent-shaped lawn was no easy matter in a swamp and in an age when the lawn mower had yet to be invented. First, the land was drained, filled, and rolled to create a flat surface. Then, local farmers were employed to skillfully cut the grass with their razor-sharp scythes early in the morning when the grass was still damp and soft. Finally, the cuttings had to be swept up.

In the 1830s, Clarke erected a Greek temple supported by ten massive Doric columns above the Congress Spring.[25] An arbor led southward to a domed circular temple that covered the Columbian Spring (Figure 26). There was also a sixty-foot high water tower camouflaged to look like an Egyptian obelisk. Cast-iron planters in the form of Grecian vases were placed in the park in the 1830s and removed seasonally, making them early examples of public sculpture. Reliefs appeared on two of the vases, which were inspired by the Danish neoclassical sculptor Albert Bertal Thorvaldsen and designed by one of the American students who had studied with him in Europe (Figure 27). An elaborate system of graveled paths transversed the

FIGURE 26. Congress Park, Saratoga Springs, 1843. The pavilions for the Congress Spring (left)
and the Columbian Spring (right) and John Clarke's house overlooking the park.
(Lithograph by George Endicott.)

fenced-in space. Groves of ancient pines, elms, and oaks grew throughout the space, from
which walkers could look down on reflecting pools.

By mid-century, Clarke's pleasure-garden design had been expanded and changed, as
eclectic and popular novelties appeared, similar to those in England. A circular railway amused
visitors by taking them on a short ride in a grove at the southeast corner of the park. In the
1870s, at least two ponds surrounded by cast-iron fences were placed at the confluence of several paths. By 1878 a rustic cottage, designated the Deer Lodge, served as a shelter for animals.
When Samantha and Josiah Allen made their fictitious visit to the park in the 1880s, they en-
countered sculptured figures in its glades and wooded spaces, including the nude figure of a
woman, which embarrassed Josiah because he thought it was alive.[26] Congress Park had become the greatest pleasure ground in Saratoga Springs, a combination of natural beauty, classical embellishments, and, after the middle of the century, entertainment. Crucially, the park
remained free to the public, ensuring that it would continue to serve a diverse audience.

Although the largest and most permanent, Congress Park was not the only public pleasure ground divorced from a hotel. On the west side of Broadway, across from Congress Park,
a short distance below the Union and Congress Hall hotels, was the Washington Gardens or
Grove. On its undulating ground in the 1840s were a fine grove of trees, a flower garden, and
a pond adjacent to the Washington Spring. Attractions included arbors, walks, and, for recreation, bowling alleys, this last being private so that "ladies or gentlemen might exercise in

FIGURE 27. Thorvaldsen
Vase, Congress Park, Saratoga
Springs. Placed in the park
c. 1830. Probably created by a
Thorvaldsen student following his
designs, these vases were the
earliest pieces of sculpture
in Congress Park.
(Photo, Theodore Corbett.)

perfect seclusion." No gambling was allowed, and admission was charged to screen the clientele because the gardens were "designed particularly for select parties and those who wish to avoid the annoyance of a promiscuous crowd." Although exclusiveness might have succeeded elsewhere, charging admission to a public space was rare in Saratoga Springs, and it did not bring long-term success. The Washington Gardens disappeared as an enterprise by 1860, when the Clarendon Hotel was built at the location. Still, the existing gardens survived as the new hotel's grounds, which were advertised as the "beautiful promenade grounds in which is the famous Washington Spring." [27]

The example of Clarke's Congress Park was irresistible to developers, who saw how he combined a mundane bottling works with a visitors' park and then with the development of the real estate adjacent to the park. In 1858, at the same time that New York's Central Park was being established, New Yorker H. H. Lawrence purchased at tract of twenty-five acres on the northeast edge of the village, over a mile to the east of Broadway. [28] Here he drilled fifty-six feet, retubed an existing spring, which he dubbed Excelsior, and began to bottle the water. His son, A. R., took over the growing business after the Civil War, erecting by 1873 an Italianate-style bottling plant and a classical pavilion over the spring. He developed the adjacent grounds as a woodland park to draw visitors from Broadway who sought the exercise of a lengthy walk or carriage ride. He established the park in a valley created by the Loughberry Brook, which flowed out of the lake by the same name. Along it, ten springs were designated, hence the park's early name, the Valley of the Ten Springs. However, maintaining ten springs was no easy feat, and the woodland soon became more readily known as Excelsior Park. Beyond the managing the bottling plant and the tourist services in the valley, the Lawrence family also laid out lots on the ridge to the north to encourage the building of cottages, and after the Civil War they erected their own hotel, the Mansion House. As a result, picturesque Gothic and Italianate cottages were built on the edge of the ridge so that their back windows had views of the scenic springs. The family exploited this property to the fullest and succeeded in creating a suburban attraction that was close enough to draw visitors from Broadway.

Unlike Congress Park, Washington Gardens, and Excelsior Park, a fourth early green space was not constructed as a pleasure garden or park, although it served the same purpose because its grounds and monuments became a favorite place to promenade. This was the Greenridge Rural Cemetery, which was planned by private investors in 1843.[29] It was the result of a northeastern urban reform movement that lasted from the 1830s until the Civil War; as part of it, new places of burial were planned at the edge of town and became known as rural cemeteries. In the nineteenth century the term *cemetery,* meaning sleeping chamber, was revived as sounding more up-to-date than the earlier *burial yard.* The object of rural cemeteries was to create an environment in which the living might cope with the loss of loved ones. Instead of being spoken of as buried, the dead were said to be laid to rest, in an effort to alleviate the pain caused by death. The cemeteries were designed to be places of beauty, with the type of landscaping found in pleasure gardens, in contrast to the austerity of traditional burial yards. This movement was associated with the idea of mourning as a public social activity.

These new cemeteries were formally planned landscapes, the result of extensive investment in design and plantings by private investors who saw cemeteries as self-supporting and even profitable enterprises. The rural cemetery movement originated in New England, spreading from there to New York City, Albany, and Saratoga Springs.[30] Saratoga's Greenridge had its first burial in 1844, the same year that Albany Rural Cemetery was consecrated, and thus it shares the honor with Albany of being one of the oldest rural cemeteries in New York State.

The idea for Greenridge Rural Cemetery arose because the village's Gideon Putnam and Sadler burial grounds were overcrowded and, according to critics, unsanitary.[31] Burial was a burden, for the village had to provide not only for its own dead but also for gravely ill visitors who died while taking the cure. On March 4, 1843, a law was enacted that made the village trustees responsible for a new rural cemetery, obligating them to repay private investors who advanced the initial funds to improve the grounds, to convey lots to purchasers, and to preserve and protect the grounds. The Village of Saratoga Springs thus became a party to the Greenridge Cemetery, and today the city is still partial owner of this public-private enterprise.

Saratoga Springs was unique in that it already had an example of natural landscaping from which to copy, namely its hotel pleasure grounds and Congress Park. Land for Greenridge Cemetery was purchased on the southeastern edge of the village. Not yet twenty-five, Joseph D. Briggs was employed to survey and design the new cemetery. His planned landscape provided a natural setting for elaborate tombs and memorials. It was laid out with curving paths and avenues that directed visitors along the undulating ridge overlooking Broadway and then returned them to the entrance fronting on South (today's Lincoln) Street (Figure 28).[32] At least

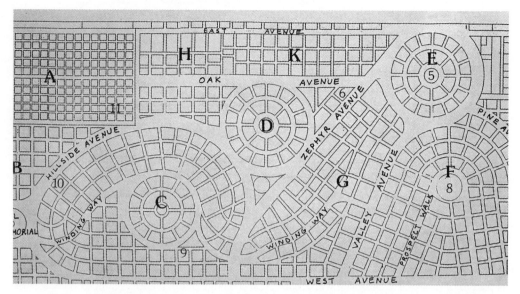

FIGURE 28. "Map of Old Portion of Greenridge Cemetery," 1844. The cemetery was designed by
Joseph D. Briggs to fit the contours of the ridge so that it was integrated into its natural surroundings.
(Greenridge Cemetery Association, Saratoga Springs, N.Y.)

four circular focal points, similar to culs-de-sac, were laid out on the ridge; burial lots were
grouped around these centers, which were themselves choice burial sites. The original cemetery fronted along Lincoln Avenue for some 340 to 400 feet, but the bulk of the landscaped area
stretched over a five-acre rectangle to the south and was protected from intrusion by the fact
that were only one or two adjacent houses. By 1876, the patronage of James Marvin further
protected the cemetery from intrusive development because he owned most of the neighboring property. Private effort and the sporadic support of municipal government were thus combined to give the village an additional amenity, not unlike Congress Park.

Racecourses also became important public spaces, although their facilities were nowhere
near as elegant as those of the pleasure grounds or the rural cemetery. The courses consisted
of four components: the dirt or grass track, a grandstand for spectators, barns to stable the animals for the meet, and a temporary blacksmith shop. Early racing at Saratoga involved trotters,
not thoroughbreds. The 1847 trotting meet, a part of the New York State Fair, was held on
grounds along Union Avenue on the Maxwell-Clarke lands, which had yet to be laid out in housing lots.[33] The boundaries of the fairgrounds were Phila Street on the north, Regent Street on
the west, and Nelson Avenue on the east, with Union Avenue on the south.

A racecourse later was laid out on the north side of Union Avenue where it meets East
Avenue. It was operating in 1859 when two famous trotters, Flora Temple and Princess, were
raced in a duel, which Flora Temple won. This dirt track was of oval shape, large enough to
encompass the required distance and completely fenced, but narrow in width so that the field
had to be restricted.[34] The grandstand was flimsy and was meant to accommodate only a small
portion of the crowd. People who wanted to create a spectacle did so with elegant open carriages from which they watched the race. Betting was handled by individual bookies, who set

up shop under a tree. An irregular complex of board-and-batten barns was constructed on the west end of the track in the 1860s to house horses, along with their trainers and hands, who slept in the hay.

This track was purchased in 1863 by the newly founded Saratoga Racing Association, making it the forerunner of the famous thoroughbred track that exists today. The Association was the brainchild of John Morrissey, the New York City casino builder, who encouraged three of his New York City friends, William Travers, Leonard Jerome, and John Hunter, to formally establish it. Initially there were only four days of racing with two races each day, but the success of this modest venture led to the construction of a larger track immediately across Union Avenue, which opened in 1864. Thus, a private venture of New York City investors produced a racecourse; but it was not yet the showplace it would become by the turn of the century.

Although the village government was never very powerful, it had been pulled into involvement with Greenridge Cemetery, and it continued in its modest efforts to provide an infrastructure for the community, activities that finally culminated in the erection of the community's first major governmental building, the Town Hall. Although an English market hall had been proposed as the design for a seat of village government in 1847, in 1871 the village put the old plan aside and designed a structure that was not so much a seat of government as it was a convention center with a theater (Figure 29).[35] Such a space would offer complete

FIGURE 29. Town Hall, Broadway, Saratoga Springs. Built 1871. Instead of a market hall, the village fathers chose to erect this palazzo style structure, whose principal feature was an auditorium for conventions. At the spa the demands of tourism took precedence over the need to hold markets.
(Photo, Theodore Corbett.)

protection from the elements as well as allow the city fathers to regulate the quality of programs and entertainment.

The Town Hall was constructed by the Troy firm of Cummings and Burt in High Victorian Italianate in style.[36] The large two-story theater filled the entire back half of the building. The stage measured thirty-four by thirty feet, and a gallery increased seating in the room. Four crystal chandeliers hung from the ceiling. The theater was not only for political meetings but also for conventions and theatrical performances. The second-floor courtrooms in the building were the site of the formation of societies such as the American Banker's Association in 1875 and three years later the American Bar Association. The building was a grand gesture, a bit too expensive for the small municipality to completely carry through (New York State was forced to intervene to cover the final debts), but it did provide the spa with a needed public space that enhanced its role as a resort.

Saratoga Springs succeeded because it had several public-spirited entrepreneurs who were willing to invest their resources in projects without immediate return. Walton, the Putnam family, Clarke, the Marvin brothers, Ellsworth, and Freeman planned the village in sections, established its first water system, planted and constructed its earliest tree-lined sidewalks, opened innovative pleasure grounds, organized one of New York State's first rural cemeteries, and promoted a town hall that was in reality a convention hall. Saratoga Springs had several founding fathers and mothers who made their homes permanently in Saratoga, while in Ballston and Caldwell a powerful absentee landlord controlled development from afar. Nicholas Low gave Ballston Spa the Sans Souci Hotel, developed the springs, and experimented with manufacturing; but his bottom line was profit, and when his investments ceased to be lucrative, he lost interest in Ballston. The Caldwells were less concerned with money but more enamored of their position as proprietors of the estate. James Caldwell envisioned Caldwell as a prosperous county town and had little interest in tourism, while his son William wanted visitors limited to the rich and well-bred, with whom he could socialize. Of the leadership in the three resorts, the diverse leadership of Saratoga Springs succeeded, while the solitary landlord-developer was only as effective as his interest in the community—and this involvement was often fleeting or misguided.

CHAPTER 5

Accommodations
Private Spaces for the Public

Stimulating the growth of Saratoga Springs was the need to provide accommodations for visitors during the summer season. They could be found everywhere in the community. Often single-family homes were converted into boarding houses, cure institutes, or small hotels. In season, almost every dwelling had the potential of being rented to visitors. In the early 1820s, the famous French traveler Jacques Gerard Milbert could find accommodations only in a private home, where he had to share a room with three strangers and "get up, dress, and go to bed without appearing to notice" that he was "surrounded by people" he did not "know."[1] As noted, the hospitality business was not limited to the Broadway area but extended into the residential areas, so even the most private areas were caught up in catering to tourists. In the 1830s, large parties of county visitors could practice "house room boarding" off Broadway. Here they paid a shilling a day to place their own bedding in a room for sleeping and to use the family fireplace to cook their own provisions. Nineteenth-century distinctions between private family residences and public accommodations were therefore not clearly drawn, and the blurring of this line inhibited the rise of a domestic sphere for middle-class women or the suburban ideal of a single-family home with private yard as a refuge from the business world. Using one's domestic skills to run a boarding house or hotel became an accepted role, even for married women. Although substantial homes were eventually built, the bulk were domiciles for residents, not visitors. Saratoga Springs continued to encourage accommodations on Broadway and beyond.

Women in the Accommodations Business

Women found special opportunities in the development of accommodations. From mid-century on the spa's middle-class white women ran boarding houses or hotels on the basis of their respectability and housewifery skills and in this way made a living to support a family. This opportunity was in direct contrast to the tradition in New York City, where boarding houses catered to undisciplined, single young artisans, who gave them a sordid reputation.[2] The appearance of hotels in the 1820s in New York State's rising cities usually meant a decline in the number of boarding houses because such sordid places could not compete with a first-class establishment.

In 1828, Ballston Spa was the location of Mrs. Macmaster's boarding house, which English visitors praised for the quality of its coffee and poultry. She managed it with her daughters and a young female servant. At the same time in Saratoga Springs women and a few self-styled deacons or preachers established boarding houses or small hotels; visitors were attracted by their moral and familial respectability.[3] Such establishments began when a woman, especially a widow, started taking in a few lodgers. A fifty-eight-year-old widow, Marcia Chase, ran a boarding house on Division Street that was highly respectable, as indicated by the names of her permanent boarders. In 1860, these boarders included the family of a manufacturer and the family of Augustus Bockes, the established lawyer and temperance leader, plus a sprinkling of singles such as attorney George Batcheller, who would later build one of the spa's most substantial residences. Such was the quality of her establishment that her house was usually full, and she could take only an occasional visitor.

Housewifery was expanded from the residence to the boarding-house enterprise and thus came to cover both the domestic and the commercial spheres. It included not only cleaning, laundering, and mending, but also setting a good table. The board, the quality of the scheduled meals, established the reputation of a boarding house. The back yards of most spa homes were in practice urban farms, where the owners raised vegetables and kept poultry and cows for fresh eggs, meat, and milk. Staff consisted of family and household members. In 1860, Chase ran her fifteen-room boarding house with her eighteen-year-old son and a single female servant. Even the managers of the most refined households needed skill in preparing meals and servant support to compete in the growing enterprise of running a boarding house.

At the spa, women had the opportunity to graduate from being the proprietress of a boarding house to running a hotel, a top-of-the-line position in the resort business. In 1860, one fifty-two-year-old Irish native of the expansive Dinnen clan, Mary Dinnen, was the proprietor of a hotel. With this precedent, women could do what long-time Saratoga Springs resident Mrs. Mary L. Weston did in 1887 and open a high-class hotel on Broadway, where she charged the highest rates.[4] She managed the Columbian Place, at an ideal location just opposite the Town Hall. The hotel operated in a portion of the Ainsworth Building, so that Mrs. Weston was free of the burden of maintaining the building. Catering to families, it had twenty-seven rooms for forty guests, a reputation for a fine spread at meal times, and steam heat, so that it could be open year-round.

Hotels

Although many nineteenth-century U.S. communities had a hotel, in resorts they were exceptionally large and numerous. Most visitors agreed that the best accommodations were to be found in hotels. By definition a hotel was a large commercial accommodation offering a variety of services: lodging, an extensive menu, entertainment, cleaning of clothes and shoes, and spaces for meetings and socializing. Originally, hotels were the most respectable accommodations; they regulated their clientele by the prices they charged and the rules they set, and they offered the latest domestic conveniences and comforts, ranging from plumbing to elegant furnishings. Such services were for only the upper class in 1800, but by the middle of the nineteenth century Webster's dictionary affirmed that although hotels had "formerly" been "a house for genteel strangers or lodgers, . . . the name is now given to any inn."[5] Thus, many types of accommodations strove to be called hotels, even if they did not provide the services of one, and the growth in their numbers, to the point where every community had one, diluted the quality of their services. Still, as the epitome of a resort public space that catered to the visitor's comfort and also provided the village with an amenity, the hotel deserves special attention.

Resorts could exist without hotels as their chief accommodation, although the lack of a hotel limited visitation and made it inevitable that the resort would be exclusive rather than open. For instance, the cottage was more popular than the hotel at White Sulphur Springs, Newport, and Lake George. In White Sulphur Springs, accommodations were mainly row cottages; they were built by the spa's owner, attached to each other, and leased by a private party for a season or more. These cottages were modest wood-frame structures, large enough for a family with servants; they attracted the same families year after year. Richard Singleton's family from South Carolina, for example, used one annually for twenty-eight consecutive years.[6] Beyond the cottages, the plantation resort contained only a tavern, which was so modest that visitors commented that the facilities did not attract them as much as the "very agreeable company." From the 1870s, at Newport and Lake George, the exclusive resort was carried a step further: "cottages" there were privately constructed and privately owned homes; in reality, they were mansions, as fashionable as and more private than hotels.

The exteriors of hotels looked like anything from domestic residences to pretentious monoliths. Early hotels were designed as large houses with a modest number of spare rooms. Architecturally, they were indistinguishable from the typical Federal home. They were conservatively embellished, in step with but not ahead of the popular taste of their time. The spa's first large hotel, the United States, was an architectural derivative of a step-gabled townhouse, in appearance a vastly expanded home. On Broadway, these Federal-style hotels mixed easily with similar residences. Only two of Saratoga's hotels were truly of some architectural distinction: the Pavilion of Henry Walton with its Georgian-inspired elements (1819) and the Adelphi of William McCaffrey in the Lombard style, with elegant supports for a second-level porch that had no access from the street (1877). Run like large households, hotels had utilitarian porches and grounds; the grounds contained outbuildings and were run like self-sufficient farms. Some of the outbuildings, such as stables, were on separate sites. The floor plans of the hotels formed an L, a U, or a T; the encompassed outdoor space was landscaped. Separate farms were later established for the largest hotels.

Hotel interiors consisted of two distinct spaces: the public rooms and the private sleeping chambers. This layout created the conflict between the public and private nature of the hotel. Public rooms could be lavish, whereas sleeping areas were usually spartan. The entire first floor of a hotel was given over to public rooms, while the chambers, sandwiched into upper floors, were often no larger than a closet. In 1828, English visitors complained that their chambers in Saratoga's Congress Hall Hotel were small, fourteen feet by ten feet, had no carpeting, and had windows that could not be opened and that let in the cold.[7] There was no bell for a chambermaid, but that hardly mattered: the quality of service was dreadful because the maids were burdened with an excessive number of duties and chambers. Only in smaller establishments such as the cure institutes was there some luxury in furnishings and service within the chambers, which gave these places a deserved reputation for exclusivity.

In Saratoga Springs, the number, quality, and size of hotels grew progressively, a fact that did not please all visitors. New York City attorney George Templeton Strong came to Saratoga Springs in 1841 and swore he would never come back because the spa was "a mean little country town," with "an immense wilderness of hotels — like stray cabbages in a potato patch" and "such confusion as would be thought wholly unendurable in town."[8] He was not the first to complain about the spa's hotels, but his comment does demonstrate that they were numerous. This situation began modestly in 1802, when Gideon Putnam completed work on a "great house" to lodge visitors at the south end of undeveloped Broadway. This three-story tavern and boarding house, the largest of its kind in the village, was so pretentious it was called "Putnam's Folly." As a tavern it served food to travelers. But it was exceptional in having extensive accommodations. As a boarding house it offered visitors the possibility of renting rooms for long periods with meals on a regular basis. Thus, Putnam catered to both brief and long-term guests. His great house was also his home, the center of family enterprises, which included the farming and lumbering that took most of his time; catering to visitors fell mostly to his wife, Doanda.

By 1811, Putnam's Tavern and Boarding House had become prosperous enough for Gideon Putnam to consider establishing a hotel across Broadway. However, he did not see it completed, for he died as the result of a fall while constructing it.[9] Without her husband, his widow wisely chose not to maintain both establishments; she sold the new hotel in 1812 to Gradus Van Schoonhoven, who named it Congress Hall after the nearby spring. Doanda continued the boarding house under her family's management for the next half century as the Union Hall, and it was expanded to become a full-service hotel (Figure 30). By 1843, Union Hall had a 240-foot front on Broadway with 160-foot wings on the north and south, and the columns of the piazzas on both the front and the rear were hung with garlands. There were small balconies on the side of the structure. The public drawing room was seventy feet by thirty-six feet and was arranged so that part of it could be shut off by folding doors to form a ladies' parlor. There were thirty private parlors and two hundred lodging rooms; the dining room held three hundred guests. By 1864, when the family sold its remaining interest in the business, Union Hall had become one of the foremost hotels in Saratoga Springs.

In 1828, English visitors described the Congress Hall Hotel as immense, given its 120 beds and large and handsome public rooms. A visitor in 1833 commented on its spacious hall, which opened by means of folding doors into a splendid saloon, ornamented with paintings and a large lamp. Other doors led to the dining room, which was decorated with engravings of scenes from Sir Walter Scott's chivalric romance *Ivanhoe.* The most renowned feature of the hotel was its piazza, which extended the full length of its Broadway front, an ideal space in which visitors could promenade. Contemporary lithographs of the expansive porch were even produced in Europe, where its height, reached from the street by eleven steps, was shown in exaggerated dimensions (Figure 31). But although Congress Hall's public spaces were elegant and commodious, the bedrooms of this most fashionable hotel left much to be desired,

FIGURE 30. Union Hall, Saratoga Springs, c. 1843. This was the original tavern and boarding house that Gideon Putnam established in 1802; by 1843, when this view was made, it was the much expanded Union Hall, run by his sons Rockwell and Washington Putnam.
(Lithograph by George Endicott.)

and English tourists also complained that the season was short, for the hotel closed on September 15. Characteristically, the Congress Hall emphasized its public rooms at the expense of its sleeping chambers.[10]

After the Putnam and Congress Hall enterprises, the next early accommodation was the Pavilion Hotel, constructed from 1818 to 1819.[11] While residing in Albany in 1815, Henry Walton had served on the building committee for the Albany Academy, which had chosen architect Philip Hooker's Federal design for the new school. Hooker's drawings as well as Walton's own experience led him to build a Federally inspired structure for his hotel; it included piazzas and superb grounds, which covered one hundred thousand square feet (Figure 32). Built on Broadway by Nathan Lewis, the village's first recorded master carpenter, the structure was two and half stories on Broadway and three to four stories to the rear because it was close to the edge of the escarpment. The piazza that eventually covered three sides and the open space underneath the porch were enclosed with a delicate lattice. The early hotel was built in the shape of a T, with the kitchens stretching to the back. Outbuildings in the rear included an icehouse and a wash house. In front, a line of Lombardy poplars and a picket fence protected the front porch from the street because as yet there were no sidewalks. Inside, the ladies' parlor was twice the size of the men's parlor—an indication of which sex was more likely to use a parlor. Eventually, with twenty-two private parlors and two hundred lodging rooms, the facility could hold three hundred visitors. In sum, the Pavilion looked like an English gentleman's country house.

FIGURE 31. Colonnade of Congress
Hall, Saratoga Springs, 1837. The long
colonnaded porch, decorated with
garlands, attained an international
reputation as a place for walking.
*(W. H. Bartlett, American Scenery,
London, 1839.)*

By 1841 Daniel McLaren owned the Pavilion, and he caused a stir by attempting to
charge a fee for visiting the adjacent Pavilion Spring, which his workers had excavated. At a
public meeting of citizens and visitors held on July 12, with Thomas Marvin presiding, the as-
semblage resolved "not to visit the springs [the Pavilion Spring] . . . or drink the waters until the restrictions [are] removed; and the obnoxious regulations abandoned; and we pledge

FIGURE 32. Pavilion Hotel, Saratoga Springs. Built c. 1825. Henry Walton designed and Nathan Lewis
built this Federal-inspired structure. A later owner, Daniel McLaren, attempted to charge a fee for use
of the nearby Pavilion Spring but withdrew his plans in the face of strong opposition
from village political leaders and visitors.
(Rawdon, Clark & Co., Albany, N.Y.)

ourselves that we will use our utmost exertions to prevent this imposition from being inflicted
upon the public." [12] A committee, which included Samuel Freeman and Gideon Davidson, was
designated to approach McLaren and Henry Walton about their concerns. The public reaction was so negative that McLaren abandoned the project, and two years later he sold the hotel for $18,000. The next season the hotel opened with a full staff of cooks and assistants and
with the added attraction of half price for guests' servants and children. However, the structure
caught fire at the end of the 1843 season; arson was suspected. The damage ended the existence of one of the village's most elegant hotels. The possibility of arson reflected the difficulty
that the early modest-sized hotels faced in making a profit with such a short season. More significant, however, was the public meeting in which the public good and the freedom of the
springs were placed above the concerns of an individual hotel owner. The controversial issue
of public access to springs and amenities would often divide resort communities, but in Saratoga Springs public access inevitably triumphed.

In the 1820s, fashionable brick step-gabled residences and shops appeared on Broadway; this regional style had been imported from Waterford, a nearby village where there were
many examples of it. [13] The stepped gable had substantial brick extensions beyond the gables
at the sides of the building. The extensions held two to four chimneys, making it unnecessary
to cut back the brick to follow the roofline. The extensions were formed into a pattern of steps,
therefore the name. In 1841, construction of the step-gabled townhouse of Judge Nicholas Doe
at the corner of Broadway and Walton streets was completed; it is still a residential presence on

Figure 33. Doe House, Broadway, Saratoga
Springs. Built between 1834 and 1840. The step
gables of this home were similar to those of the United
States Hotel, built in 1824.
(Photo, Theodore Corbett.)

the city's main commercial artery (Figure 33). It was raised high above the street level by a cellar story to allow for a kitchen, and the first floor doorway was accessible by an elevated stoop. The effect was to create the same entrance barrier as the hotel porch.

The Doe house gives clues about the appearance of the first of a long line of hotels named for the new nation. The earliest United States Hotel was the first step-gabled building on Broadway and the village's largest public structure in the first half of the nineteenth century.[14] In 1824, Elias Benedict purchased twenty-five acres on Broadway between Washington and Division streets and built the United States Hotel. Originally, it consisted of an exceptional four stories with accommodations for four hundred; by 1843 there were twenty private parlors and 230 bedrooms for five hundred guests. Built in an L shape, it faced Broadway, while a north wing ran roughly along today's Division Street. Behind it were gardens and pleasure grounds, which were fenced. By 1843, an additional wing of 220 feet on the south made a complex U shape, and it was tied together by an eight-hundred-foot continuous piazza that in the front and rear had two stories. There were three stepped gables, one at the end of each rectangular wing and one where the two wings joined. A small classical cupola surmounted the middle of the Broadway block. The windows of the entire structure were shuttered, and there were elliptical windows in the stepped gables.

Despite its refined architecture, some complained when the United States Hotel first opened; visitor Caroline Gilman claimed that it lacked public rooms comparable with those of its competition and that it was "raised so high from the street as not to be convenient of access."[15] The observer went on to note that some preferred it that way because a barrier was needed between the porch and the street. Besides, to the hotel owners, the height was necessary to allow for space under the porch that was attractive for retail shops and ideal for the hotel's kitchens and workrooms.

As business grew, so did the services of the United States Hotel. In 1839, its great dining room was decorated with flowers and festoons of evergreens to greet eight hundred guests at a meal to honor Henry Clay, and its great salon provided entertainment for the president of the United States, Martin Van Buren. Four years later, it advertised that its grounds and buildings covered five acres and included the innovation of three private cottages. The cottages were designed as up-to-date residences; they looked like Greek Revival–inspired temples, lined together on the south side of the rear grounds. A guest in a cottage reported that his family had "a suite of two parlors and four bedrooms in the delightful south wing."[16] A large clubhouse was added to the north wing, and two more cottages were constructed. An indication of the amount of the investment is the $350,000 insurance estimate of its value when the hotel was destroyed by fire in 1865.

By mid-century two more hotels had been constructed that still stand today. Conservative structures, their architecture was still Federal, not reflecting the latest Greek Revival or Italianate style. The existing Rip Van Dam Hotel dates from 1840, when George Wilcox built it on Broadway as the American Hotel. Its narrow lot extended deep to the rear to form an L shape that touched the property of the United States Hotel. It served as Wilcox's home; he lived there with his family until after 1850.[17] It resembled an enlarged Federal-style townhouse, a style compatible with the earlier United States Hotel (Figure 34). Although the existing porch is not original, it is in the same location as the first one, and, in contrast to the United States Hotel, it was low enough to be easily accessible from the street. It was an ideal place to sit in order to see and to be seen. From 1841, the hotel's basement story housed the village's post office, an important amenity that ensured year-round business. As a result, the American could set a standard in 1868 by being the first hotel to stay open year-round. An addition to the rear of the structure, the demise of the second United States Hotel in 1870, and a delay in constructing new hotels briefly made the 450-bed American the village's largest hotel in 1873.

The hospitality business was beginning to stretch away from Broadway and appear in the residential neighborhoods. The first neighborhood hotel, which emerged in 1848, was the one-hundred-bed Pitney House, on the edge of Ellsworth's West Side development. It may have been the extension of buildings that had been the home of Nathaniel Waterbury, a Revolutionary War veteran; the buildings also were occupied by the artist-craftsman Ransom Cook (Figure 35).[18] The wood-frame structure was constructed in the now old-fashioned Federal style. Before long it consisted of two wings that came together on its west side to form an L, the point of juncture producing a two-story facade decorated by lines of six-over-six paned sash windows, which were spaced to form a balanced rhythm. The centered front door had sidelights flanked by four pilasters, or decorative columns, which were thinly cut to reflect the

FIGURE 34. American Hotel (now the Rip Van Dam Hotel), Broadway, Saratoga Springs.
Built c. 1840. Erected by proprietor George Wilcox, it housed the village's post office,
and in 1868 it became the first hotel to stay open year-round.
(Photo, Philip Haggerty.)

Federal style. The hotel's public rooms were off the recessed porch at the building's corner;
one of these expansive rooms was heated by a north-wall fireplace, which welcomed visitors
and local neighborhood people. A basement cistern was the source of the hotel's water supply.
The roof on the corner had a wide overhang characteristic of Greek Revival buildings. The
rest of the space was devoted to corridors of bedchambers. In the rear the structure's cellar had
a full entrance, which created another floor that must have included kitchens and service areas.
In the early 1870s, the structure was expanded to the east; the elegant mansard-roofed addition was protected from the original hotel by a brick firewall. This roof was covered with expensive red-slate scallops, which were pierced by decorative dormer windows. Despite its later
construction, the addition balanced the Federal style block at the opposite end, forming a surprisingly unified whole.

The Pitney family ran their hotel and boarding house along with a construction business. At mid-century the Pitneys' hotel was an extended family enterprise, which had been established at the spa by carpenter Jacob Pitney in the late 1820s.[19] His sons conceived of the
hotel and put together the property for it. Son Jonathan purchased the first lot between 1844
and 1846 and became the Pitney House proprietor; twenty-four-year-old son Jacob Jr., the

FIGURE 35. Rear view, Pitney House, Grand Avenue, Saratoga Springs. Built c. 1850. The house was constructed by carpenter Jacob Pitney, who ran the hotel and boarding house along with his carpentry trade. The top floor is a later addition.
(Photo, Theodore Corbett.)

chief builder, purchased the adjacent lot in 1847. By 1860, Jonathan's wife, Betsey, was running the hotel with the help of their son, Jerome, who was the hotel's clerk, and eight years later the twenty-eight-year-old replaced his father as the proprietor. Jonathan had become interested in a nearby farm, which supplied the hotel with fresh vegetables, milk, and cream. Pitney House was now advertising that it had in its landscaped yard cottages that were attached to the hotel, similar to such amenities on Broadway.[20] The Pitney House was run as a first-class boarding house until the early 1880s; at that time Betsey died and Jerome moved to Kansas, so the family gave up their interest. By then only one member of the Pitney family was still a carpenter.

The number of hotels continued to increase—from nine in 1850 to twenty-six in 1870. Typical of these Civil War–era hotels was the Continental Hotel (Figure 36).[21] It had been built originally as the Bedortha Water Cure in 1866, and in the 1870s it became the Continental Hotel. An L-shaped, three-story brick building, the hotel was a utilitarian establishment whose major attraction was its proximity to the railroad station. In the rear the Continental had an extensive network of wooden porches and stairs that provided access to the three floors. The adjacent chimney indicates the fireplaces that provided heating for the three floors. The

FIGURE 36. Continental Hotel, Washington Street, Saratoga Springs. Built 1866. Known for its
proximity to the railroad tracks and station, the hotel employed blacks as cooks and domestics,
including Emma Waite (see Chapter 8).
(Photo, Theodore Corbett.)

Continental was decorated with brownstone window lintels and sills; those in the front were
stepped and then flared at the top, while those in the rear were plain. Its overall design was conventional, but it attracted a special clientele: women and religious groups.

    A few structures, such as the High Victorian Lombard-style Adelphi, were built as
smaller, intimate hotels to cater to the affluent. Constructed in 1877, six years later the Adelphi could hold only 150 guests, at that time a size that appealed to an exclusive clientele (Figure 37). The Lombard style was adopted from that of northern Italian builders, famous in the
Middle Ages for their ornamental structures. The Adelphi had Gothic piers, thin elegant supports for the porch, which covered the entire expanse of the facade, while pointed arches and
brackets with hanging pendants completed the Gothic effect. Together with the Grand Union
Hotel to the south, the Adelphi was one of the first hotels to restrict access from the street to
its main piazza, which was placed on the second floor, a full story above that of its neighbor,
the American Hotel. Although the Grand Union Hotel's porch was at the same level, it was
broken in several places by stairs for access, but the facade of the smaller Adelphi was too narrow to allow such access. In 1883, a wing and an additional story were added without altering
the basic proportions of the structure. William McCaffrey, a conductor on the Rensselaer and
Saratoga Railroad, had inherited the hotel site through marriage and became the proprietor in
1877.[22] John Morrissey, the colorful politician who built the village's first formal casino, chose

FIGURE 37. Adelphi Hotel, Broadway, Saratoga Springs. Built 1877. The Adelphi was the spa's most
exclusive small hotel; in 1878 John Morrissey died here of a stroke.
(Photo, Philip Haggerty.)

the exclusive hotel as a refuge the year after it opened; here he died in his room at the untimely
age of forty-seven.

Although the Adelphi and the Continental would have been good-sized hotels in most
U.S. cities, the erection in the 1870s of two monster hotels marked the apex of the spa's hotel
construction. A new United States Hotel was built in 1874, replacing the one destroyed by a
fire in 1865, and in 1876 extensive renovations to the Union Hotel were completed, making it
the Grand Union. Both hotels were constructed in Second Empire style, a new form imported
from Europe; it featured mansard roofs accented by central and end pavilions. The architectural firm of Vaughan and Stevens created the United States Hotel, the better designed of the
two, while John Kellum was the architect for the Grand Union.[23] The Grand Union was the
larger with 824 guest rooms, versus 768 for its rival. The United States did have additional
spaces in private cottages on its grounds. The Grand Union dining room alone seated fourteen
hundred people. A high colonnade of cast iron covered its entire front; the southern half of the
building sheltered a piazza, while on the northern half the columns extended down to the sidewalk and fronted on a row of shops. Such obviously public structures ensured that Saratoga

Springs could accommodate a diversity of visitors, boldly renewing its reputation as the most open of resorts.

However, the burning of the United States Hotel in 1865 and the Congress Hall Hotel in 1866 made many question the value of these monster hotels. Saratoga Springs realtor Philip McOmber suggested that smaller hotels like the American, Continental, and Adelphi would be more economically viable and that suburbanization, the erection of private summer homes, throughout the village would do more to increase the tax base. In 1877, after many hotels had come and gone and the village's new United States and Grand Union hotels had just been completed, McOmber condemned what he felt was the folly of its dependence on hotels. He pointed out that the loss of three hotels to fire and the consequent lack of tax revenue over the twelve years before new ones opened had left the village in dire straits. It had been a mistake, the realtor observed, to put up "costly hotels instead of attracting rich people to build cottages"; the village would then "have had strangers to pay the taxes," and the village treasury's dependence "on the accidents of the hotel seasons" would have been lessened. Plus, he added, "our cottage population would have stayed out the whole season." Without identifying it, he commented that only one of the new great hotels was financially sound.[24]

Cure Institutes

Beyond the classical hotels, at mid-century for the first time a new type of small hotel appeared. Called "cure institutes" because they specialized in hydrotherapy, they were the enterprise of physicians who prescribed the water cure. The earliest such place operated in 1855 as the Remedial Institute of Doctors Sylvester S. and Sylvester E. Strong. It was established in a four-story building, "elegant in all its appliances and appointments," with "running water and water closets on all floors."[25] The institute specialized in diseases of women and overworked professional men. It catered to the popular belief in hydrotherapy as an alternative to traditional, drug-based medicine, emphasizing the curative powers of cold baths, temperance, and a regulated diet. The Institute's Russian bath required three rooms: a steam room for sweating, a shampoo and rinsing room, and a cooling room in which to rest and reclothe. As might be expected in Saratoga Springs, the Institute's apparent spartan routine was tempered by the availability of luxuries. Meat was emphasized in a diet that went beyond vegetarian specialties, and music and entertainment were encouraged as a means of spiritual regeneration. Such attention meant that cure institutes were expensive places to stay and that the clientele had to be well-to-do.

From the 1860s, cure institutes were found especially on Franklin Square and adjoining Franklin and Washington streets. Dr. Robert Hamilton's Medical Institute on Franklin Street specialized in female lung and chronic diseases. Hamilton began his institute on Broadway in the late 1860s but soon moved it to the quieter residential precincts of Franklin Street.[26] Another establishment, the Carlsbad Hotel and Cure Institute, built in 1890 on Franklin Square, was run by Dr. Valencourt Duell, a veteran of Civil War cholera epidemics. Cure institutes advertised themselves as family-run enterprises, indicating that they were respectable and that they would give their patrons individual attention. Although the cure institutes were precursors of hydrotherapy hospitals, they were not public institutions. Municipal and state support for such projects was lacking, and it was not until 1895 that a citizens' committee completed fund raising for a small, nonspecialized public hospital.

Boarding Houses

By the 1870s, although half of the spa's visitors stayed in hotels or cure institutes, the other half stayed in boarding houses, which were more numerous than hotels. In 1850 there were only nine formal boarding houses; by 1860 this number had more than tripled to thirty-five, and in 1873 twenty-two establishments advertised that they provided rooms and, most significantly, board.[27] Compared with the hotels, boarding houses were smaller and less expensive, although in 1873 the largest, Benjamin Dyer's 120-bed facility, was the equal of most hotels. A few boarding houses also had rates as high as those of the most expensive hotels.

Homes were always potential boarding houses and small hotels that could be run by widows or married couples. The example of Number 6 Franklin Square is enlightening (Figure 38). It was built as the fashionable Harvey residence in 1870; by 1882, the now-expanded structure had become a boarding house, the Franklin Square House, run by Mrs. William

FIGURE 38. Adirondack Lodge, Franklin Square, Saratoga Springs. Built c. 1870.
Originally constructed as a home for a lumber merchant, this Second Empire structure
became a cure institute and then a boarding house.
(Photo, Theodore Corbett.)

Balch.[28] She had moved there from an expensive twenty-five-room establishment she had run on Broadway. The boarding house again changed hands and by 1890 belonged to Dr. Duell, who with his wife managed it as a cure institute. Three years later, Dr. Robert McEwen purchased the property to serve as a cure institute and added a wing on Franklin Street. When he died in 1896, his wife, Sarah, continued to run it as a boarding house; it became known as the Adirondack Lodge and was so successful it remained in business until 1917.

Most boarding houses in Saratoga Springs were found away from the Broadway business district in quieter residential areas; the hospitality business thus spread beyond Broadway. Proximity to a hotel was an advantage for boarding houses because they could catch the overflow. Albert Washington's boarding house at 41 Washington Street was well situated to take the spillover from the neighboring Grand Union Hotel.[29] Boarding establishments existed on Phila and Spring streets, on Franklin and Washington streets, and on Beekman Street, the chief street of the Irish section named Dublin. In 1873 the smallest establishment, with only eight beds, was run by G. M. Kelley on Beekman Street. Typically, boarding houses were found on streets that carried traffic between Broadway and the adjacent neighborhoods.

The growth in the number of boarding houses encouraged women to make the transition from taking in a few boarders to operating a boarding house as their chief source of income, a step they had been reluctant to take before mid-century. The 1850 federal census listed only one woman, thirty-eight-year-old Elizabeth Wilber, as managing a boarding house. It was a modest establishment run from a home that had a real estate value of only $2,000.[30] A decade later, however, she was still in business and had been joined by fourteen members of her sex, the women accounting for 43 percent of the spa's boarding-house proprietors.[31] By 1873, her Wilber House on Washington Street was a hundred-room establishment that could be considered in a league with hotels. In that year, women ran more than half the quality boarding houses advertised in guides, and ten of them were hotel proprietors.[32] The numerous boarding houses and hotels of a resort like Saratoga Springs offered women business opportunities that were not open to them in industrial communities.

Despite the appeals of people like realtor McOmber, Saratoga Springs favored hotel development, avoiding suburbanization until the 1880s. After all, the most numerous group of visitors from New York City expected hotel accommodations and reputable boarding-house living. Competition among hotels and boarding houses produced accommodations for most pocketbooks, rather than leaving the visitor at the mercy of the dominating presence of a single establishment like Ballston's Sans Souci. With their porches and pleasure grounds, Saratoga's hotels offered a choice about where one wished to see and to be seen. Investment in large hotels was risky, however, because they required extensive capital and staffing, and, given the short season, they were unused much of the year. The number of suspicious fires testifies to the risks of investment in the great hotels. Still, Saratoga Springs had its smaller hotels, its women-run boarding houses, and its doctor-run cure institutes, which could more easily than large hotels function on a year-round basis. In the last decades of the century, the spa would also have some private "cottages" on its boulevards; this development matched the trend toward such establishments in the Adirondacks and provided the more stable source of tax revenue that realtors such as McOmber had suggested. In addition, during the peak season every structure in the community, including stables, housed visitors and resort workers.

By 1880, the early Saratoga Springs crossroads had become a small city, the most urban place north of Albany. Broadway was the center for a permanent population of ten thousand, with four thousand more in the surrounding hamlets. Beyond Broadway, private development had created residential enclaves and tourist attractions that sought to compete with the main street. The West Side now extended further than the early posh residences of Franklin Square. On the East Side, the built-up area spread far beyond Circular Street, and the area between it and Broadway had been filled with inexpensive structures consisting of first-floor shops and second-floor apartments, interspersed occasionally with boarding houses. This neighborhood served as both a backdrop and an alternative to Broadway, for here the worker could obtain cheap lodgings and the middle-class visitor could find an affordable boarding house. Beyond this area, houses became increasingly expensive, even though they were built on relatively small lots. Furthermore, the East Side's most prestigious boulevard, Union Avenue, had at last begun to fill with substantial Queen Anne–style houses. And yet it was still a village, easily accessible to its country roots. After the Civil War, Jonathan Pitney gave up his position as proprietor of the Pitney House hotel to move a mile out of town and manage a farm. Ostensibly, the farm could support the hotel with fresh vegetables and milk, but in reality Pitney enjoyed farming and was pleased that the spa still offered the opportunity for rural life.

The success of Saratoga Springs did not arise simply from the provision of public spaces, hotels, boarding houses, and elegant residences. Other aspects of the community's tourism infrastructure were crucial, especially those facilities and workers that performed supporting roles behind the scenes. Alleys were a vital support space for the resorts, although they were not on most visitors' itineraries. They need to be analyzed to show the changing priorities in their use—from stables for horses to commercial development to residential enclaves. Moreover, we need to look beyond the hotel and boarding-house proprietors to those who worked in the basic resort jobs. The problems of seasonal employment and a lack of workers skilled in the hospitality business were faced by all resort communities. In the early 1800s, Low imported his staff, from architects to black waiters, for the construction of and service in the Sans Souci because he felt such workers were not to be found in the area. In Caldwell, no blacks were present, but workers were recruited from Albany to manage the family's improvements, such as the coffeehouse and eventually the Lake House hotel. The proprietor's strict landholding policies failed to encourage skilled workers to settle in the hamlet; the limited population turned over constantly and even declined from 1820 to 1850. In the coming pages, it will be apparent that Saratoga Springs was exceptional in supporting its public spaces with alleys and a diverse workforce, an achievement that ensured greater success than at Ballston Spa or Caldwell.

CHAPTER 6

Alleys as Support Spaces

Alleys and the structures that lined them were crucial public spaces in the resort infrastructure. Although a direct result of formal planning, an alley was different from a traditional public space because it took one behind the grand facades of the Broadway hotels to the back streets, to a world that might have seemed disorganized, gritty, and even dangerous. Although tourists rarely visited them, alleys housed the spa's exceptional number of horses and carriages, which were kept as a service to tourists. Nineteenth-century alleys were originally constructed as amenities, but because they were places hidden from view, they became workspaces, places where animals could be kept in barns and carriage houses and where small-scale enterprise could flourish. Alleys may be back streets, but they have subtle stories to tell. Although not as easily grasped as the stories of the main streets, they are an equally important source of information about how communities have grown. In Saratoga Springs, the alleys deserve as much attention as the hotels and great houses, as they tell how this resort functioned behind the scenes. Focusing on the back streets of Saratoga Springs, we will first examine the development of alleys, then look at the stables and carriage houses built there, and finally investigate the conversion of some alleys to residential or commercial enclaves.

Even when constructed meticulously according to plan, the alleys in Saratoga Springs were never static entities. Instead, they offered a changing array of stables, residences, and commercial enterprises. In the beginning, they were the dreams of developers; indeed, they appeared on maps before neighborhoods were settled. In design, alley structures began as vernacular, barnlike buildings, but later some were as tastefully designed and constructed as a main house. Although working people came to reside in some alleys, there were more lucrative options for the development of alley property, such as the building of commercial structures. Many well-to-do families had reasons for preventing workers from residing in their backyards. Thus, unraveling the mysteries behind the evolving alley can explain one of the most vital and yet neglected parts of resort landscape.

Certain features of these planned alleys stand out. Inspiration came from England, where London's mewses were lined with carriage houses, which several of Saratoga's developers had seen on visits to or during residence in the British capital. The London mews were laid out between two streets to serve houses fronting on both streets. Although these alleys were smaller in width than streets, they were strictly parallel to them. They were as straight as the street, despite the terrain, and required considerable land when residences were clustered around a square. Alleys contained rows of private, two-level stables situated in the absolute rear of the lot, at the utmost distance from the main house. The chief dwelling was thus kept separate from the unhealthy stable, and domestic life was protected from the alley workspace. The front of the house could remain formal and elegant, while the rear kitchen, fenced yard, and stable area progressed from housing genteel to menial activities. Houses with a mews were valuable because the upper floor of the stables provided extra lodging space for servants, and the garbage collector's night cart never had to come to the front door.[1]

This London mews pattern was modified in Saratoga Springs. Whereas the English developers constructed the residence and carriage house as part of the same project, in Saratoga Springs property owners bore the responsibility for constructing stables. Private initiative was thus necessary to make Saratoga's alleys successful public spaces. Maps make it evident that not every house with a rear alley had a stable because some owners kept no animals or made do with a shed. Therefore no rows of stables appeared. Exceptions to the strict grid pattern occurred where an alley deviated to form a dogleg in order to provide services for a third street. Some stables were entered from the yard rather than the alley, an arrangement that required access from the street through private alleys at the side of the house. As a result, some stables had entrances from both the yard and the alley. Still, the dominant pattern of Saratoga's planned alleys was a straight and narrow pathway lined with stables and sheds that backed into expansive yards; they established a buffer between the odious stable and the main house. In philosophical terms, alley structures created a barrier between nature and people.

Although the need for horse-drawn transportation remained a constant throughout the nineteenth century, the existence of the planned alley as a place for carriage houses was hardly universal. Some of the largest cities had few of them. In New York City, land values were too high to waste space on such an amenity.[2] It was common for a New York town house's service entrance to be in the front, where it provided access to basement kitchens and storage but not to the rear and a carriage house. Instead, New York's carriage houses served several patrons in a neighborhood and were placed a few blocks from these patrons' homes. Elsewhere, in southern cities such as Charleston, alleys were considered potential hiding places for slaves and free blacks and thus were rarely planned. By the middle of the nineteenth century, some New York State communities had them in certain neighborhoods, but it was rare to have alleys throughout a city. The Saratoga County community with the earliest grid supported by alleys was the village of Waterford. After a disastrous fire on July 11, 1841, much of Waterford was rebuilt in brick with elaborate stepped gables, including stables that uniquely imitated the main house (Figure 39).[3] In Waterford, the combination of early planning and determined leadership after the fire gave this canal village a model alley system. When natives of Waterford like the Doe family settled in Saratoga Springs, they supported the development and expansion of the alley system.

Among the resorts near Saratoga Springs, only Caldwell had an alley system, but it was limited. In the 1840s, William Caldwell laid out an alley to serve three blocks of Canada and Ottawa streets (see Figure 14 in Chapter 3). The rest of the village of Caldwell went without alleys. In Ballston Spa a few alleys did appear on Low's early plans as a support for Front Street, but they were not built or ultimately became streets.[4]

FIGURE 39.   Alley between Third and Second streets, Waterford, N.Y.
(Photo, Theodore Corbett.)

The Rise of Alleys

Alleys appeared as the result of four conditions in Saratoga Springs, three of which related to its role as a resort and the fourth, to its real estate market. First, as to real estate, land was abundant and therefore inexpensive in Saratoga Springs, so developers added only minimal expense to their projects by setting aside space for alleys. Because the village was not on a land-limiting body of water—a most unusual circumstance for a resort—the community could expand in every direction. Second, the village was "thought by many to be the most beautiful" in northern New York.[5] An 1844 guidebook to Niagara Falls, Canada, and the spa commented that

Saratoga Springs is "suitably laid out, a part compactly built, and many handsome dwellings and seats are observed around, some commanding fine views, and others almost hid from sight in groves of evergreens." Not just the main street, Broadway, but also the residential neighborhoods were evidently part of the village's attraction. Rare public spaces, including alleys, made the village an attractive place to visit or in which to reside. Third, the spa's leaders, such as Henry Walton, valued amenities and included alleys in their plans. Fourth, alley stables were needed to serve the resort business. The same guide asserted that "$35,000 worth of livery property is owned at the Springs, for use of strangers that to the owners produce handsome income."[6]

The fourth condition requires further elaboration. The preautomobile nineteenth century was an era of "horse culture," when that animal and facilities for its care were highly valued; most of these facilities, especially stables, were found in the alleys. The village fathers committed themselves to protecting this property in 1845, when they passed an ordinance that read, "All persons are hereby prohibited from entering any barn or livery or other stable . . . with a light of any kind, without having it well secured in a good, safe lantern." Hotels needed horses and stables to compete, and numerous businesses were devoted to transporting visitors or to renting out gigs for exercise and excursions. In Saratoga Springs it was a genteel business, for many establishments offered "horses suitable for ladies to drive."[7] Far more than the brief thoroughbred racing season, which began only in 1863, the provision of horses for visitors was a key to the resort's success. By the 1880s, the most extensive livery was Hodgman's United States Hotel Livery on Division Street next to Long Alley. Its seventy horses, twenty-five double and fifteen single vehicles, and thirty hands and drivers supplied the nearby United States Hotel exclusively and also the public. The complex of two brick and two frame buildings had been established in 1839, and it was up-to-date, well ventilated, drained, and lighted, and carefully maintained by grooms and stall men. Elegant shops devoted to outfitting for horse-drawn transportation were another aspect of the horse business. Phineas Thompson established a shop on Broadway in the late 1840s that specialized in fur robes, horse clothing, blankets, trunks, saddles, bridles, whips, fly nets, currycombs, brushes, and ladies' satchels. His first-class establishment represented the concern of Saratogians for their visitors' entertainment and comfort, a concern that was less of a priority in other U.S. communities. This commitment to the structures, employees, and goods of a horse culture was a major hallmark of a resort economy.

Unlike Waterford, Caldwell, or New York City with its 1811 street grid, nineteenth-century Saratoga Springs had no overall village plan.[8] The village government was made up of volunteers who lacked the resources to develop such a scheme, and no single property owner controlled affairs to such a degree that he could produce a comprehensive plan. The history of the spa's alleys is therefore seen in sectional or neighborhood maps representing property that developers wished to improve; thus, alleys appeared only in certain areas.

Saratoga Springs originated as a main street village, centered on a single important street —Broadway—which ran along the edge of an escarpment above the springs. Streets and alleys developed parallel to it, the neighborhood to the west of Broadway becoming the West Side, the area to the east of Broadway the East Side. Alleys appeared in support of Broadway as early as 1813 and continued to be constructed in the neighborhoods from that date until by 1850 at least eighteen existed. By the end of the Civil War, there were about forty planned alleys, and in the building boom that followed the war the number surpassed fifty. The last alleys were laid out in the 1870s, and the alley system was then complete.

The earliest alleys appear on a map dated 1813, on property owned, platted, and sold by Henry Walton.[9] From his family residence in New York City, Walton began to lay out lots on this map for his Saratoga Springs property using the street and alley pattern that would dominate much of it. His alleys, which ran along the rear of long rectangular lots at some distance from the main buildings, provided access to service structures such as barns and stables. The spa's first planned alley, Long Alley, appears in this guise on the 1813 map; it was designed as a service corridor for Broadway (see Figure 15 in Chapter 4). Confirmation of Walton's devotion to alleys is found in an 1839 map of his property.[10] To Long Alley was now added Swamp Alley and Cottage Place on the East Side and Oak Alley on the West Side. Walton did not extend his alleys throughout the village or even over his entire property, but he was the first to designate them and thereby set an example followed by many developers who purchased his land. Some entrepreneurial Saratoga families, such as the heirs of Gideon Putnam in 1825 and those of John Bryan in 1853, created plans with almost no provision for alleys.[11] Walton must therefore be regarded as the father of Saratoga's planned alleys.

Walton's Long Alley remained the most extensive in the village throughout the nineteenth century. Long Alley was the support alley for the west side of Broadway and the east side of Matilda Street, and it stretched from Division Street north to Rock Street. In 1858 at least thirteen structures lined it, making it by far the village's most built-up alley. It contained a mix of commercial and residential structures. On the East Side, Cottage Place (Chestnut Alley) must have been the earliest alley.[12] Planned by Walton in 1839 to serve Circular and Regent streets and, with its dogleg, Lake Avenue, it averaged eighteen feet across. Cottage Place boasted only one substantial building in the 1840s and 1850s, but by 1866 there were more, and by 1888 the alley was filled with structures. Its story of change over time is complex and revealing.

Walton chose not to develop all his property himself, selling portions of it to entrepreneurs such as Gideon Putnam and Dr. Samuel Freeman. Although the Putnams were generous in providing lots for a burial yard and churches, they did not show an interest in planned alleys. Freeman was different; in 1841, this Ballston Spa physician who had moved to Saratoga Springs bought an extensive tract of land on the West Side from Walton. To his credit, when Freeman developed the tract he kept Walton's alley system, and he added Railroad Alley between Church and Walton Streets in honor of the recently arrived iron horse (see Figure 21 in Chapter 4). Also on Freeman's property, parallel to Railroad Alley and north of Walton Street, was Shingle Alley, named for the product manufactured there. From the 1840s to the 1880s there were a few structures on Shingle Alley. Later Freeman became a partner of James Marvin, the developer and resident of Franklin Square. To enhance development of West Side neighborhoods, Marvin laid out an alley to the west of Franklin Street before 1850 that he named for his family, and in 1867 he created an alley to the west of Harrison Street, today's Knapp Place.[13] He therefore followed Walton's example in continuing the planned alley system. Also on the West Side, in 1838, immediately next to the Putnam property, Judiah Ellsworth, the wealthy Saratoga Springs attorney, laid out a model neighborhood that included the village's narrowest alleys (see Figure 20 in Chapter 4).[14] While Ellsworth's alley system was extensive, it did not seem to foster the building of stables; maps show that owners constructed modest sheds rather than structures of greater size (Figure 40).

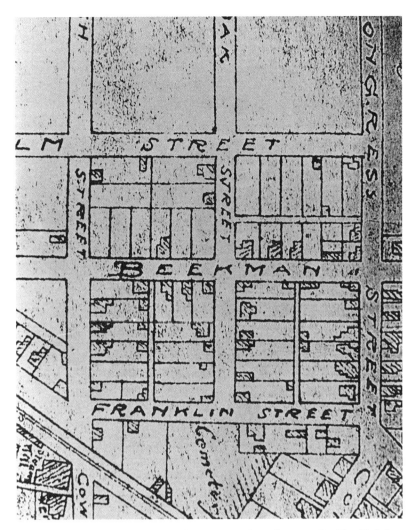

FIGURE 40. John Bevan, "Map of Saratoga Springs, Saratoga Co, New York,"
c. 1848; the structures in Ellsworth's development.
(Saratoga Room, Saratoga Springs Public Library, Saratoga Springs, N.Y.)

Between 1851 and 1854, a new area opened for development on the East Side included planned alleys. This land had once belonged to Yorkshire-born John Clarke; after the property passed to his heirs in 1846, they developed a portion south of today's Union Avenue and east of Regent Street (see Figure 19 in Chapter 4).[15] As noted, the tract designed in 1854 had alleys, but only for the largest and most fashionable lots. These alleys were laid out long before the area was settled, as housing construction here was sporadic until the early 1870s. Only in the 1880s did the alleys drawn in the 1854 plan become covered with carriage houses, which provided services to a fully populated neighborhood (Figure 41).

Alleys were still being planned on the edges of town in the 1870s; one example is Tipton Alley, which was laid out by the Wellington Brothers contracting firm between Spring Street and Phila Street. However, the need for alleys declined in the 1880s. The suburban need for

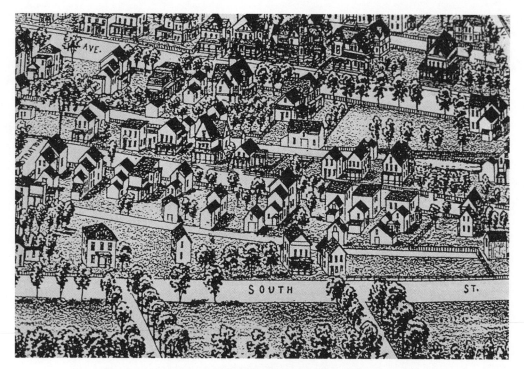

FIGURE 41. "Saratoga Springs in 1888"; the structures in North Lane,
an alley that supported Union Avenue.
(L. R. Burleigh Lithograph, Troy, N.Y.)

expansive lawns did not allow for alleys, and the prestigious new houses on North Broadway
had such extensive grounds that Long Alley was discontinued to allow the new properties to
stretch from one street to the next. By 1890 the village had reached its nineteenth-century limits; no more streets and alleys were created.

Alley Structures

Although many more structures stood along the alleys in Saratoga Springs than do today,
enough remain to show the changes in taste that modified alley streetscapes. As a rule, a
nineteenth-century stable had three functions: as a place for carriages and harness gear, horses,
and animal feed. Surveying Saratoga Springs existing historic alleys shows that three basic
stable forms provided these functions from 1840 to 1890. The three forms are associated with
three periods: pre–Civil War, post–Civil War, and the end of the century. In the pre–Civil
War period, structures were simple barns, limited in height and rectangular in form, with their
entrance on the long side facing the alley. After the Civil War the classic carriage house dominated; it was identified by its balloon frame, which increased the stable's height, and its gable
end entrance, which faced the alley. In the third era, beginning in the 1880s, the Late Victorian
Queen Anne style was most popular. It consisted of numerous planes, gables, and entrances
until the form became an expression of multiplicity. Strikingly, carriage houses now reflected
the architectural style of the main house rather than being of simple barn or stable design. By

the end of the century, both in form and in decoration, the stable was tied to the main house, and the alley had become the stylistic mirror of the street.

The three stable forms evolved over a period of six decades. In the early nineteenth century, barns similar to those built in the countryside provided residential support services. These barns were constructed with a double-door entrance on the long side, under the eaves, the building stretching along the alley and intruding minimally into the yard. The barns had a limited height of one to one and a half levels. Appearing as early as the 1820s, this form would remain common until after the Civil War. We can document such barns in the spa's alleys as early as 1828, when grocer Miles Beach's barn on Long Alley burned down.[16] Eighteen years later, Dr. Freeman reported a fire in which his "stable was enveloped in flames, in about 10 minutes, also the stables and small building of Mr. Reed directly across the alley"; however, "my horse, wagon and harness was saved."[17]

One of the earliest alley buildings, a two-level, wood-frame structure, stands on Railroad Alley (Figure 42). It has the outline of a New England saltbox, the roof outlining the transition from the high front to the rear lean-to addition, which was added fifty years after the original structure was built. The original thirty-four-by-thirteen-foot structure is sheathed with horizontal clapboards and is pierced on the alley side by two double-door openings. We can assume that carriages could enter here, but the space is extremely narrow for horses and there were no windows for ventilation. Inside, the building is divided into two bays of unequal size, both with lath-and-plaster ceilings. It is possible that one these bays served as a shop because

FIGURE 42. Two-level stable, Railroad Alley, Saratoga Springs. Built early 1850s.
(Photo, Theodore Corbett.)

there is evidence that stoves heated them. A ladder led to a covered opening in the ceiling, the entrance to the second level. From the time of the structure's construction in the mid-nineteenth century, the second floor served as a residence rather than as a hayloft. On the second level, light came from two glazed six-over-six windows in the gable ends. The second level was divided into three spaces: a hall with lath-and-plaster walls, which created rooms on either side. To the rear behind the walls of the hall was a chimney on a slate base; it conducted smoke from stovepipes that could be attached to it. Although the walls and ceiling of the second floor were unfinished, the space must have functioned as a modest residence for a family or two individuals. This structure is eighty feet from the Greek Revival house it served, and because the property is part of Dr. Freeman's development, we can assume that it dates from the 1850s. This multipurpose building illustrates the variety of uses for alley structures, but the residential space is the most unusual survival from the past.

As mid-century approached, some elements of early-nineteenth-century Federal or mid-nineteenth-century Greek Revival architecture appeared in brick and stone barns, although their form was consistent with the early barn. The commitment to brick rather than wood was in itself an event because a brick stable was far more costly to build. One such structure exists on Cottage Place. Built in the early 1840s, it has rectangular wooden lintels over the doors and windows, a wooden cornice, and a broad roof overhang (Figure 43). On the alley side, the forty-eight-foot structure has three bays, each with a double-door entrance. The second level has a

Figure 43.   Two-level brick stable, Cottage Place, Saratoga Springs. Built early 1840s.
(Photo, Theodore Corbett.)

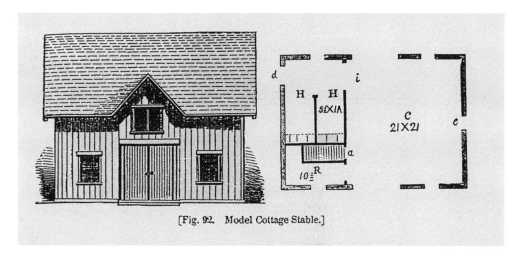

[Fig. 92. Model Cottage Stable.]

FIGURE 44. Model cottage stable.
(A. J. Downing, The Architecture of Country Houses, *New York, Dover Publications, 1969 reprint, 213–214.)*

loft door, still with its early hinges, above the right entrance. The glazed six-over-six windows at each gable end provide light for the loft. Although the stable appears from the exterior to have a third level, the loft actually extends from the second level to the roof, which is supported by post-and-beam construction. Overall this is a substantial Federal-style building, the closest structure in Saratoga Springs to the brick stables common in neighboring Waterford.

The first effort to design stables with architectural style came in the 1850s, when Andrew Jackson Downing in his *Architecture of Country Houses* devoted a chapter to "Hints for Cottage and Farm Stables," suggesting two types of cottage stable, wood-frame structures to be covered with board and batten (Figure 44). One type was identified by the dormer breaking the roofline. This dormer usually contained a door that provided access to the feed in the loft. The second is a more boxlike barn covered with a steeply pitched roof.[18] Despite the addition of Gothic-inspired vertical elements, the form of Downing's stables recalled the early barn, the height remaining one to one-and-a-half stories; his popular dormer stable required that the opening to the loft be along the alley side. His stables were compact; in fact, Downing recommended that they measure no more than eighteen by twenty feet, just enough room to keep one or two horses and a carriage. However, Downing's stables were more influential for their decoration than for their form. Covering them were vertically matched boards and batten strips at the joints, making board-and-batten siding their most distinctive feature.

A stable with Downing dimensions and such siding is found on West Harrison Street in Saratoga Springs (Figure 45). Access to it is from the twenty-foot-long street side rather than from the eighteen-foot gable ends. It is a one-and-a-half story, three-bay structure, similar in size to the barn on Railroad Alley. But here the resemblance ends. Overall, the structure is a single block, which was planned and erected at one time, rather than through a process of additions. The whole is sheathed with vertical boards and battens, which were machine made, although crudely. Based on lot-ownership records, the structure belonged with an 1850s townhouse that is three hundred feet from it.

FIGURE 45. Downing-type cottage stable, West Harrison Street, Saratoga Springs. Built 1850s.
(Photo, Theodore Corbett.)

An example of Downing's other type, the rarer center-gabled stable, can be found on Regent Street (Figure 46). Following Downing's proportions, the steeply angled roof makes up a third of the structure's height. Above the center door, in a steeply pitched dormer roof, is found the loft access door. The stable was built in the 1860s to serve the Italianate Twitchell/Hubbell House on Circular Street.

After the Civil War, barn-type structures were still built, and the side entrance continued to enjoy popularity. Before 1858, however, a Saratoga Springs businessman, Charles Burr, had introduced a wood-frame carriage house with a radically different orientation, the main entrance appearing in a gable end that faced the alley.[19] Although the new rectangular structures penetrated into the yard, reducing the distance from the house to the carriage house, by the 1870s this type of carriage house was immensely popular. These newly formal carriage houses were larger than previous barns or cottage stables. A new building technique, the balloon frame, permitted greater height and overall size; smaller and lighter studs and joists were nailed together to create a sturdy structures of two or more stories possessing individual stall windows, modest amounts of bracketed decoration, and roofs topped by a cupola. The second level of these carriage houses was a loft with an access door at the gable end rather than the side. The individual stall windows had received the blessing of architect George Woodward, whose 1865 edition of *Country Homes* claimed that "a horse needs a dry, well ventilated apartment, and enjoys fresh air, daylight, and sunlight as well as human beings."[20] This type of carriage house

FIGURE 46. Downing-type cottage stable with center gable, 113 Regent Street, Saratoga Springs.
Built 1860s.
(Photo, Theodore Corbett.)

became so desired that in the 1890s a smaller and thus more affordable version, generally without a cupola or bracketed decoration, made its appearance in Saratoga's alleys.

A post–Civil War carriage house of this new type is found on North Lane (Figure 47); it was built to serve the house at 104 Union Avenue, one of the earliest homes to be built on Union Avenue. It was constructed in 1871 by successful meat wholesaler De Voe Lohnas and is covered with board-and-batten siding, for battens were now machine-made strips of molding that came in a variety of decorative profiles. Under the eaves are Italianate brackets, which reflect a desire to modestly decorate carriage houses in the latest style.

Although in form it remained essentially the same as the gable-front carriage house, in the 1870s another type became popular. Acquiring a side shed by the gable entrance, which created an expanded roofline, this type was designated a side-shed carriage house. The side shed made the gable end as extensive as the long side so that the structure enclosed an almost square space. The motive for creating such a carriage house was often the need for interior space; constructing side-shed carriage houses was thus an artful means of expanding existing carriage houses. Although the origin of this design was practical, the sweep of the roof expressed the growing acceptance of picturesque and rustic taste. Such side-shed carriage houses came in a variety of sizes, but the largest were exceptional; one on Long Alley measures fifty-five feet at the gable end and sixty-five feet in length. Its gable end covers three levels. The stable is sheathed with the smooth horizontal clapboards that the sawmills were now producing. It is

FIGURE 47. Gable-entrance
carriage house, North Lane,
Saratoga Springs. Built 1871.
(Photo, Theodore Corbett.)

endowed with mitered, arched window heads and a pigeon roost at the high point of the gable
and is modestly decorated with stick work, which reflected contemporary architectural style
(Figure 48).

Two popular types of post–Civil War carriage houses had their roots firmly in the pre–
Civil War era. One type, a barn with side entrances, continued to be built with post-and-beam
construction, although its dimensions were greater than before. An example of this persistent
type is found on North Lane, where it was built to serve a home constructed in the 1860s. With
a length of over thirty feet and a width of twenty feet, it rivaled the main house in size. It consists of three bays, each with a double door, so it provided far more room for carriages than did

FIGURE 48. Detail of facade, side-shed carriage house, Long Alley, Saratoga Springs. Built 1870s.
(Photo, Theodore Corbett.)

early barns. There are regular entrance doors on each short side. In the front on the second level is a loft door with strap hinges, but on the left side is a decorative window, and the right side has the elegant touch of a fan light. Clearly the simple barn was now being decorated.

As previously mentioned, Downing had introduced a post-and-beam stable with a central gable. Few of these cottage stables appeared in Saratoga Springs before the Civil War, but by the 1870s a similar type, based on the balloon frame, became popular. By freeing the stable from the post-and-beam restrictions of the cottage style, the balloon type used less timber to attain greater dimensions; this type often had glazed windows, slate roofs, and decorated cornices. Such carriage houses gave the impression of being lower and wider—almost boxlike— especially when compared with the rectangular, gable-entrance carriage house. The dormer derived less from the necessity of providing a loft door and more from the wish for a decorative effect. These stables continued to follow Downing's prescription for an entrance on the long dormer side, bucking the trend for gable-end entrances. Modest bracketed decoration was added under the eaves. Although their roofs had the outline of an earlier era, such stables reflected the techniques and taste of the 1880s.

By the 1880s, a new type of multipurpose carriage house emerged. Built in the image of the main house, it was designed with living quarters and space for horses and then automobiles.

FIGURE 49.   Queen Anne carriage house, North Circular Street, Saratoga Springs. Built 1896.
(Photo, Theodore Corbett.)

The form of most of these carriage houses followed the Queen Anne style, which combined a picturesque diversity of medieval elements with innovations. Because of the eclecticism of the Queen Anne style, the Downing-inspired central dormer was easily integrated into the roof, appearing as a windowed center dormer flanked by other dormers. A Queen Anne carriage house was erected in 1896 at the rear of the home of Sydney Rickard and H. G. Ludlow at 632 North Broadway, a part of the street with lots still small enough to be served by alleys (Figure 49). The structure has a multiangled roof and several projecting gables. The upper level is shingled and the lower level is clapboard; adding yet another texture, the roof is slate. This carriage house follows the form and decoration of the main house in every way except for its lack of chimneys. A cupola also distinguished the carriage house from the main house; it provided needed ventilation to the hay loft and was doubtless a holdover from previous barnlike carriage houses. Here was a structure that brought the grandeur of the street to the alley.

Overall, the stable passed through three stages and a variety of stylistic changes, from serving a practical function as a barn to being a fashionable extension of the main house. In academic terms, the stable began as vernacular architectural history and ended as an object of architectural style.

The Functions of Alleys

Having examined the development of alleys and the structures built on them, we can now look at their use and habitation, discovering who resided or carried on business there. Back streets

FIGURE 50. Francis Guy, *Winter Scene in Brooklyn*, c. 1817–1820. The artist was a master
at showing the detail of everyday life in Brooklyn's back streets.
(Brooklyn Museum of Art, Gift of the Brooklyn Institute of Arts and Sciences)

were the centers of commercial and residential activity. We have an idea of what back streets
were like around 1820 from a view of another New York State community, rural Brooklyn (Figure 50). Francis Guy's painting of a snow scene, a rendering of a crossroads, was executed with
a concern for the detail of social life. An alley is the work's central focus, rather than a pretentious main street. Guy shows animals roaming the alley and the street. On the right the residence
of Abiel Titus is separated by the alley from his business in the barn. Titus understandably
wanted to keep his home a distance from the barn, which he operated as a slaughterhouse.[21]
Additionally, the artist portrayed the rear of a blacksmith shop and an adjacent carriage shop,
which combined a dwelling with a store. Commercial enterprise went on in the alley as an extension of the businesses that fronted on the street. At least three structures whose yards opened
onto the alley show signs of household activity, so that even residential yards were the centers
of business activity. Although the alleys in Saratoga Springs were originally built to provide access to stable lots and homes on parallel streets, as early as 1850 some alleys became residential and commercial enclaves. This trend illustrates the changing nature of alleys. By 1889, use
defined three types of alleys: carriage-house alleys, commercial alleys, and residential alleys.

    Residents began to appear in alleys in the 1820s, when accommodations were so scarce
in July and August that many visitors and workers were forced to stay in haylofts. Owners who

converted these lofts into modest rooms could demand a higher summer rent. These apartments in the alleys were at first only for seasonal use. Mid-nineteenth-century urban reformers made it clear that residence in an alley had drawbacks that should have led people to seek other housing opportunities.[22] Structures were flush to the alley, thus lacking a front or often a rear yard. Alley residents could socialize only in front of their houses or in the alley itself. Alley homes were mixed with carriage houses and sheds, opening them to the corrupting influence of animals, garbage, and waste. Nevertheless, even Saratoga's earliest alleys, Long and Cottage Place, had a few year-round residences. By the 1880s, certain Saratoga Springs alleys were one-third to almost one-half residential or commercial, although alleys dominated by stables were always the most numerous.

Two population growth spurts, from 1835 to 1860 and from 1870 to 1890, created a demand for housing and commercial establishments on alley property. During the population growth of the 1840s and 1850s alleys were inhabited, although sparsely, with barns outnumbering the residential spaces. Examples of surviving alley structures with residential spaces from that period rarely show evidence of a heating system, which should be no surprise: it was deemed unsafe to have a fire in a building where hay and feed were stored. The early residential spaces could have been used only seasonally, catching the overflow of visitors during the summer months. During the spa's population boom of the 1870s and 1880s, previously laid out lots were filled with new houses, and some lot owners put up alley housing behind the main house to enhance their investment.

These alleys were centers of laboring-class life, providing inexpensive housing for workers and for women, particularly the spa's numerous widows. Aspects of alley residential life, including occupational and social status, can be found in a sample of alleys from 1889. Although this date, the earliest for which comprehensive information exists, is late, it does provide a point from which to look back to earlier periods. Using an occupational continuum based on social status, we can describe the social mix of the spa's alleys. The continuum is divided into two status groups—"nonmanual" ("high" and "low") and "manual" ("skilled," "semiskilled," and "unskilled"). This division reflects the nineteenth-century gap between those who labored with their hands and those whose occupations required them to wield a pen.

Through an analysis of maps and street directories, the resident groups that dominated alleys have been identified. This information provides overall alley characteristics. In regard to occupational status, manual workers made up 90 percent of alley inhabitants, while nonmanual workers constituted only 10 percent, and most of these nonmanual workers were in the lower category (Table 1). The norm, then, for alley residents was laboring class, with unskilled laborers, liverymen, porters, carters, coachmen, and laundresses making up half the population. Porters, carters, liverymen, and coachmen resided close to or within the alley stables. This is not to deny the presence of many skilled workers, who constituted more than a quarter of the alley residents.

Widows and single women also added to the pool of workers in the alleys, often as household heads (Table 2). Women made up 30 percent of alley residents, and of these women 70 percent were identified as widows. In the nineteenth century, widows and single women were on their own, responsible for their livelihood; they had to be working women because they did not have the luxury of defining their status by their husband's position. Most of these

Table 1. Alley Residents' Occupational Status, 1889, by Percentage and (Number)

| ALLEY | NONMANUAL | | MANUAL | | |
	HIGH	LOW	SKILLED	SEMISKILLED	UNSKILLED
Cottage Place			75 (3)	25 (1)	
Diamond Alley		30 (3)	30 (3)	10 (1)	30 (3)
Hamilton Alley	9 (1)	18 (2)	18 (2)		55 (6)
Long Alley			36 (6)	18 (3)	46 (8)
Oak Alley			30 (3)	20 (2)	50 (5)
Pine Alley		11 (1)			89 (8)
Railroad Alley			40 (2)	40 (2)	20 (1)
Searing's Alley					100 (2)
Shingle Alley					100 (2)
White's Alley			100 (1)		
Total	1 (1)	9 (6)	28 (20)	13 (9)	50 (35)
Total Nonmanual	10 (7)				
Total Manual				90 (64)	

SOURCES: Tables 1, 2, and 3 have been created using *Kirwin's Saratoga Springs Directory* (Saratoga Springs, N.Y., 1889), and the Sanborne Insurance Map, 1889 (Saratoga Room, Saratoga Springs Public Library, Saratoga Springs, N.Y.). The classification by five groups is adapted from Clyde Griffen and Sally Griffen, *Natives and Newcomers: The Ordering of Opportunity in Mid-Nineteenth-Century Poughkeepsie* (Cambridge, Mass., 1978), 50–58. It is recognized that the use of occupational continuums has caused much controversy among historians; see especially Michael Katz, *The People of Hamilton, Canada West: Family and Class in a Mid-Nineteenth-Century City* (Cambridge, Mass., 1975). However, this study does not concern social mobility by occupation, as it seeks merely to describe the gender and occupation of those who lived in the alleys and alley neighborhoods. (The continuum used in this chapter will be used also in Chapters 8 and 9, on African Americans and the Irish.)

NOTE: This table includes only those alley residents whose occupational status can be identified; it does not include all alley residents.

women had manual-worker status, even if they made only a few dollars by occasionally taking in laundry.

Specific alleys show a populating process that was sporadic and modest and that did not lead to the formation of ethnic or racial neighborhoods. An example of a traditional carriage-house alley is North Lane, which served Union Avenue and White Street. Laid out in the early

Table 2. Women Alley Residents, 1889, by Percentage and (Number)

ALLEY	WOMEN RESIDENTS	WIDOWS, AS PERCENT OF ALL WOMEN RESIDENTS
Cottage Place	25 (2)	100 (2)
Diamond Alley	17 (2)	100 (2)
Hamilton Alley	25 (2)	50 (1)
Long Alley	35 (7)	57 (4)
Oak Alley	38 (8)	50 (4)
Pine Alley	36 (4)	100 (4)
Railroad Alley	33 (2)	50 (1)
Shingle Alley	50 (3)	100 (3)
Total	30 (30)	70 (21)

SOURCES: See Table 1.

1850s, developed with housing in the 1870s, it was still in the 1880s the ideal original alley—a series of carriage houses serving main houses some distance away. The only residence on the alley was a second-floor apartment over a stable. Then, in the 1890s, elegant Queen Anne carriage houses appeared in the alley with apartments for servants. North Lane was in an exceptionally nonmanual neighborhood because Union Avenue was a posh address. Owners in nonmanual occupations occupied all Union Avenue homes; of these almost two-thirds were professionals and proprietors (Table 3). On its south side, North Lane served White Street, where, following the original plan of the early 1850s, the properties were less substantial. Although there was a lessening of status on White Street, almost two-thirds of the residents of North Lane were nonmanual workers, an indication that White Street was still part of an upper-middle-class neighborhood.

North Lane's sister alley, South Alley, showed a similar pattern of development. In 1889 only one residence and a paint shop interrupted the series of stables. But the status of its neighborhood was not as high as that of North Lane, as confirmed by South Alley's lower number of domestic stables. The South Alley neighborhood was 82 percent manual, dominated by skilled and semiskilled workers. Despite the difference in status, the South Alley owners' respect for the 1850s plan of domestic stables was as strong. The residents of South Alley kept their fewer stables almost as readily as the professionals on Union Avenue kept their many stables.

Table 3. Neighborhood Residents' Occupational Status, 1889, by Percentage

| | NONMANUAL | | MANUAL | | |
NEIGHBORHOOD	HIGH	LOW	SKILLED	SEMISKILLED	UNSKILLED
Upper Class					
Cottage Place	27	54	14		5
Union Avenue	63	37			
North Lane	23	40	17	3	17
Working Class					
Oak Alley	14	22	35	6	24
South Alley		18	41	29	12

SOURCES: See Table 1.

Another type of alley was largely commercial. Here, although a residential and stable element was present, one-third to almost one-half of the structures were devoted to business enterprise. Such alleys developed near Broadway to support its central business district. As an example, Railroad Alley was established to provide access to the depot area. The alley served residential as well as commercial needs, for structures on Railroad Alley underwent conversion from stables to residences. The earliest stable on the alley had by 1884 been converted to a dwelling and certainly served that purpose earlier. Other Railroad Alley structures combined commercial and residential purposes. Looking out of place among the early alley barns, an elegant commercial-residential structure was erected in the 1860s or early 1870s. This two-story, brick town house raised on a high basement extends deeply into its lot toward a commercial structure on adjacent Church Street. With a heavy ornamental cornice and coursed granite lintels over the windows and doorways, the alley town house has a more impressive facade than do most of those fronting on Church Street. With its double front doors, it was a combination shop and residence. One door was for the first-floor shop, and the other was for stairs that led to the second-floor living space.

In addition to the commercial establishments, from 1882 to 1884 the eleven households on Railroad Alley made it a highly populated alley. The women residents of the alley were a widow, a seamstress, a dressmaker, an embroiderer, a stamper, two domestics, a laundress, a teacher, and one person identified simply by the title "Miss." Here was an alley with many working women; eight headed their households and three were married. They were skilled.[23] The teacher, educated, added a dimension of higher social status that was not always found in alleys, a reflection of the impoverished lot of women teachers. By 1889, however, the number of households had fallen to seven, two headed by women, five by men. The resident males were skilled and semiskilled manual workers.

More important is the fact that one alley house was vacant. The 1880s trend, then, was for a decrease in residents, particularly of women, in the face of increasing commercialization. Buildings added in the 1880s contributed to Railroad Alley's growing commercial nature. After 1885, a brick carriage house was constructed to serve the Western Hotel, and in the late 1880s the Carpenter and Miller marble works appeared. By 1889 there were only four dwellings on Railroad Alley (although some people were living in commercial buildings—over stables, for example); commercial establishments there included a carpenter shop, icehouse, oil-storage depot, wholesale liquor store, marble cutter, and several commercial stables. Here was an alley that had started mainly with stables, then became mixed residential and commercial, and then became more exclusively commercial.

A rare alley that continuously combined all three functions—domestic stable, residential, and commercial—was Cottage Place. This alley reflected social divisions within its neighborhood. Known historically as Chestnut Alley, Cottage Place appeared on Henry Walton's 1839 map, and he began leasing lots along it in 1841. The earliest structure is the early-1840s brick stable previously described, but the alley soon included at least two residences, which were built in the early 1850s.[24] One of these was a residence and possibly a shop; made of brick, it had its gable end flush to the alley (Figure 51). It was built in 1853 on the rear portion of an original Regent Street lot, which was treated as a separate property when leased the next year. The foundation is brick; the lintels are wooden. The fact that the structure's fabric contains no

FIGURE 51. Brick residence, Cottage Place, Saratoga Springs. Built 1853.
(Photo, Theodore Corbett.)

stone is a sign of the modesty of its construction, and yet it is a permanent structure. It is one of the earliest alley residences in Saratoga Springs.

Cottage Place's possibilities as a residential alley, however, were constantly challenged. By 1876 the successful insurance agent S. E. Bushnell had a rental office comprising four Cottage Place structures in a compound made up of back lots from Regent Street properties and including the 1853 house and another of the early residences. Research for 1889 indicates only four households on the alley, about the same number as in the 1850s. Although the number of residences had remained static, other alley structures had proliferated; eight carriage houses now served Circular and Regent Streets. Residents of the alley were manually employed, especially as skilled workers. Nevertheless, the alley was surrounded by a neighborhood where 81 percent of the residents were nonmanually employed. These residents of Circular Street were building or refurbishing Cottage Place's carriage houses to limit the alley's residential and commercial development.

A different story is told by Oak Alley, which was populated during and after the Civil War. This alley showed a strong tendency to be residential from the late 1860s through the 1880s. In 1889, although there were fourteen stables on the alley, there were thirteen possible dwellings, including a tenement and a dressmaker's house. All the alley residents whose occupations can be identified were manually employed, with 50 percent of them in the unskilled group. Its neighborhood, consisting of Woodlawn Avenue and State Street, was of higher status than the alley; 36 percent of the neighborhood residents had nonmanual occupations. Although more well-to-do than its alley, the neighborhood did not rise to the exalted level of the North Lane or Cottage Place neighborhoods. Oak Alley's heavy concentration of housing was a characteristic of alleys belonging to the middle class because they were willing to establish residences and shops in their backyards. A typical post–Civil War residence is found at the corner of Shingle Alley and Oak Alley (Figure 52). It dates from the late 1860s. The house was well designed for its location. It is flush to the alley, and there is no access into the house from the alley. The entrance door and rear exits are within the sheltered yard. This structure is an example of an alley residence that also served at times as a shop; it was built specifically for alley conditions. Residences like this gave Oak Alley the more prestigious characteristics of a street.

Other structures on Oak Alley continued the residential trend. A residence built in the 1880s is similar to the one on the corner of Oak and Shingle alleys with one crucial exception: it is set back thirty feet from the alley. Therefore this alley house actually had a small yard. In keeping with alley building techniques, the chief entrance to this residence faces the main house and yard, away from the alley. On the alley side is a double-door entrance to a first floor carriage space, although the bulk of the structure served as a residence. Its numerous windows as well as the fact that both floors are finished with lath and plaster confirm that its chief function was residential.

Another structure farther north on the same side of Oak Alley is similar, except that it is flush to the alley (Figure 53). It also was built in the 1880s as a residence. Evidence shows that in the 1890s the structure was converted and extended from a residence to a carriage house; about 1910 a further addition increased its capacity. Thus, alley residences had the potential to be converted in whole or in part to stables. The earlier effort to make a considerable residential enclave on Oak Alley lost impetus by 1895. The persistence of the alley stable is thus a

FIGURE 52. Wood-frame residence, corner of Shingle (Exchange) and Oak alleys, Saratoga Springs.
Built late 1860s.
(Photo, Theodore Corbett.)

FIGURE 53. Wood-frame residence, converted to side-shed carriage house, Oak Alley,
Saratoga Springs. Built 1880s, extended 1890s and ca. 1910.
(Photo, Theodore Corbett.)

phenomenon that should not be underestimated. It diminished the alley housing market and made it unsteady.

Only rarely did an alley have a substantial minority of nonmanually employed residents. In 1889 in Diamond Alley, an exceptional 30 percent of the residents were nonmanually employed. There was a simple explanation: the Diamond Alley of 1889 had been laid out originally as a street. Construction on the street in the 1870s and 1880s was limited to six homes, with no stables or commercial structures. Diamond Alley reverted to alley status with the construction of new streets around it. Its ambiguous status is indicated by the fact that over the years the title of *street* was occasionally bestowed on it. Therefore, designation as a street appears to have guaranteed a higher level of occupational and social status than designation as an alley.

By the late 1880s, owners with upper-class pretensions created a trend against the further growth of alley housing. Well-to-do Saratogians wished to retain the traditional pattern of stables as amenities as well as to limit the presence of the laboring class in their backyards. By the 1890s the appearance in some alleys of the Queen Anne–style carriage house in the image of the main house represented an effort to retain or return control of the alley to those who could afford such expensive amenities. Elegant apartments were placed above carriage and auto houses, in disregard of the earlier concern for the danger of fire. The servants and caretakers who resided in these Queen Anne carriage houses were dependents of the upper class, not heads of laboring-class households. These employees of the rich contributed to the alley mix, but only in the most posh neighborhoods and on a seasonal basis. Alleys were always the home of coachmen, hackmen, teamsters, stable hands, laborers, laundresses, and teachers, but there were never enough of them to form a distinct neighborhood. By the turn of the century the number of permanent alley residents had declined from its peak in the 1870s and early 1880s. Ultimately the middle class dominated the spa's alleys and prevented the further expansion of alley housing and the creation of ethnic or racial neighborhoods. The alleys' role as the location of stables and support facilities related directly to the resort business and outlived their role as a site for inexpensive housing or commercial development.

Resorts needed alley systems to maintain a clean and healthful environment and also to house an unusually large number of animals, especially horses. Alleys with stables removed the animals from proximity to the living quarters of both guests and residents. Moreover, during the season, when accommodations were scarce, every alley structure was pressed into use to provide accommodation for visitors or resort workers. Without alley stables, many of the social rituals of the spa, such as an excursion to Saratoga Lake, would have been impossible. In an age of horse culture, horseback riding was a popular form of recreation that attracted both sexes. The substantial alley system was a distinction of Saratoga Springs; it provided support services lacking in other resorts and cities.

PART THREE

The Resort Workforce

CHAPTER 7

The Building Trades

The teamsters, carters, widows, and laborers who resided in the alleys were the majority in Saratoga Springs. These people had no opportunity to take a vacation. They were part of that class for which leisure was deemed by authorities as a source of idleness and discontent, and, regardless, for five months of the year they were too busy entertaining or preparing for visitors to have time for leisure. Investigating them is more difficult than studying the community's developers and entrepreneurs. The majority were ordinary people, often illiterate, with limited economic or social power, and thus it requires ingenuity to find them. Moving from the lives of the workers who lived in the alleys, this chapter and the next two are devoted to uncovering the spa's laboring class: workers in the building trades, African Americans, and the Irish.

In 1860, it took employees from three distinct trades to create the resort's infrastructure (Table 4). First, the transportation workers, whom we have seen working and residing in the alleys, serviced the hotels, which could not succeed without ready access to a livery stable or railroad station. This transportation sector was divided between horse-drawn transportation, which provided connections, exercise, and entertainment within the resort, and the railroads, which brought visitors and commodities. Second, the service sector is usually thought of as young domestics in private households, but at a resort it involved a broader spectrum of women and men who were employed in the hotels, boarding houses, cure institutes, and only incidentally in private homes. Finally, the building trades were responsible for constructing and maintaining the hotels, promenades, and pleasure gardens that made the resort such a public place.

Although these three sectors also appeared in industrial communities, they took on far greater significance in Saratoga Springs, where catering to visitors was the lifeblood of the economy and where these three trades accounted for 47 percent of the village's male and female workforce. The remainder of the workforce was often indirectly involved in tourism. This 53 percent consisted of professionals, merchants, seamstresses, dressmakers, and non-construction craftsmen; the largest group of these workers was made up of laborers, and the smallest group—a fraction of 1 percent—was in industrial production (mostly machinists, not factory workers). One hallmark of industrial society, the presence of women working in their homes as shoe binders, was almost unknown in Saratoga Springs. Among women workers, there was only one shoe binder at the spa, but there were fifty-five shoemakers, a sign that the spa was perpetuating a household craft tradition. In contrast, in New England's nearby shoe industries, women shoe binders were an essential part of the outwork system—that is, the

Table 4. Workers in Resort Sectors by Gender, Ethnicity, and Race, 1860

| | GENDER | | | SERVICE, % | | SKILLED CONSTRUC- TION, % | HORSE TRANS- PORT, % | RAILROAD TRANS- PORT, % |
	MALE, %	FEMALE, %	MALE/ FEMALE RATIO	MALE	FEMALE			
Native, White	34	39	.87	5	12	71	70	86
Irish	7	11	.64	3	64	17	17	11
British	1	1	1.00	1	2	7	7	*
Canadian	1	1	1.00	*	4	1	3	*
German	1	*	1.83	*	1	3	*	*
Native, Black	1	2	.50	2	7	1	1	3
Overall			.82					

SOURCE: Eighth Census of the United States, 1860 (ms.), microfilm reels 856–857, National Archives, Washington, D.C.

*Less than 0.5 percent.

support system for the shoe factories. In New England communities engulfed by the Industrial Revolution, shoe binders were always more numerous than shoemakers.[1] However, at the resort, crafts still held sway.

For a village in the country, Saratoga Springs had surprisingly vibrant building trades. Neither the planning nor the building of hotels or public spaces could have been carried out without skilled builders, contractors, craftsmen, and architects, as well as gardeners and laborers. The components of the building trades, in order of the number of employees, were carpenters, masons and brickmakers, and painters, with fewer plumbers, stonecutters, marble dealers, paperhangers, whitewashers, and builder-contractors. In fact, after the service sector and the vague position of male laborer, the building trades constituted the largest portion of the village's economy, employing more people than transportation. Moreover, the building trades officially bridged the social gap between professional architects and builders and manual laborers. Although most members of the trades were from the laboring classes, they aspired to the middle-class ideals of domestic life, church membership, political office, and capitalistic success. As we will see, the apex of success for a tradesperson was to retire from construction and serve as the proprietor or chief of maintenance of a hotel. Overall, those in the building trades deserve credit for making Saratoga Springs a handsome, attractive community.

A Community Built of Brick and Stone

An 1875 census shows that in Saratoga County, Saratoga Springs had a preponderance of the quality building stock.[2] Because the count was taken in the midst of the post–Civil War building boom, it provides an overview of the buildings erected in the previous eras. The census shows that Saratoga Springs had 20 percent of the county's population and 19 percent of its buildings. The account reveals an emphasis on solid masonry rather than on brightly painted gingerbread trim. Saratoga Springs was predominant in the number of brick and stone buildings and in the number of expensive properties. Over half the total value of county buildings was concentrated in Saratoga Springs, and its brick and stone buildings alone accounted for almost a third of the value of the county's buildings. Although the village's brick and stone structures were greatly outnumbered by wood-frame structures, the value of the brick and stone structures surpassed the total value of the wood-frame structures. In the category of prestige housing—in 1875 housing over $10,000 in value—Saratoga Springs possessed 77 percent of the county's total. The 1820s village of tiny, wood-frame, Federal-style structures, accented by a few provincial hotels, had become a wealthy community of expensive brick buildings, which set the standard for the entire county. Before 1875, then, the building trades had given the spa an exceptional percentage of Saratoga County's most valuable real estate.

In the nineteenth century, the desire for lasting and fireproof buildings was achieved through the use of brick or stone. These materials were far more costly than the construction labor, chiefly because of the difficulty and cost of transporting of them. Because they were heavy and bulky and Saratoga Springs was not on a waterway, there was an advantage in producing them locally. The surrounding countryside to the west of the village became the chief source, as there was abundant fuel for processing and the manufacturing activity was removed from the resort.[3] In the early 1800s, brickyards in that area burned stone into slake lime. By 1831, there was another lime kiln at the edge of the village on the side of a hill near the Empire Spring. Although structures built completely of stone, such as the Bethesda Episcopal Church, the Bryan house and store, and the Augustus Bockes house on Franklin Square, were rare, every brick house needed a stone foundation and was decorated with stone dressings, especially window lintels and sills. Even wooden structures needed stone for foundations because so many homes had basement kitchens.

The stone for Bethesda Church came from quarries at Rowland's Mills and Rock City Falls, due west of the city on the extension that came to be Grand Avenue. Some also may have come from quarries in Greenfield. Masons around Rowland's Mills were already erecting stone structures, including a bridge in 1830 and the Baptist church of 1826. The small stone blocks were roughly cut on all sides with obvious imperfections; they were not the type of great blocks needed for monumental construction. However, after 1833, elegantly finished granite and brownstone dressings for sills, lintels, and hearths, which made up 10 percent of the cost of a brick house, came by railroad from quarries on the Mohawk and the Hudson rivers that used prison labor, or they came from Connecticut. Stone such as the yellow limestone of the Bockes house on Franklin Square was rare and was likely to have been shipped by the railroad because the house was conveniently located beside the tracks. In the Civil War era, slate for roofs and decoration began to be brought by railroad from Granville, on the Vermont border. Thus, much of the brick, stone, and mortar that came to characterize the spa was readily obtained in the area.

Brick was needed not only for the construction of masonry load-bearing walls but also as brick nogging to fill the cavities of Greek Revival and Regency wood-frame structures. This regional tradition of using brick nogging was perpetuated as late as 1840, when Thomas Marvin's home was constructed on Franklin Square. Although it was only a wood-frame home, the nogging was of high-quality brick, held together with mortar, reflecting the effort to make it seem as if the house were as solid as one built of stone. Bricks were constantly being fired at sites in the surrounding countryside. In the early 1800s, brick kilns were located to the north-west of the village not far from the road to Greenfield. Well-connected and politically minded Abel A. Kellogg had a brickyard on the east side of Putnam Street, an enterprise that operated seasonally because clay could not be extracted and worked in freezing winter temperatures.[4]

The Early Building Trades: A Traditional Craft System

The building trades first appear in Saratoga Springs in 1819, when the Pavilion Hotel was de-signed by Henry Walton and built by Nathan Lewis.[5] Although fashionably Georgian in de-sign, it was a wood-frame structure, built with timber cut on the spot from the pines that at that time still lined parts of Broadway. As we know, Walton was a gentleman attorney who had seen English architecture, but he was not a professional architect, and Lewis could best be de-scribed as a jack-of-all-trades. Lewis had settled in Ballston Spa as early as 1807 but had moved to Saratoga Springs when Walton did, and by 1816 he was a storekeeper. On completion of the Pavilion, he became its proprietor—a transition many builders would make. In 1812, he erected the village's first schoolhouse, its second brick building, proving his skill as a ma-son. Ultimately, in 1824, his most elaborate brick project was the United States Hotel. Still, he must have been more of an entrepreneur than a building craftsman because he depended on masters such as Jesse Morgan to do the actual work. He succeeded in becoming rich and well-connected, conveniently serving as a town assessor and a founding trustee of the First Presby-terian Church.

By the 1830s and 1840s, the building trades in Saratoga Springs had progressed to the point that a traditional craft system appeared. Skilled hands did the work, and the trade was organized around degrees of experience—that is, the rising skill levels of apprentice, journey-man, and master. The master builders were practiced men who relied on long experience and with the aid of pattern books produced buildings that followed the most popular existing style. Master and journeyman carpenters planed and dressed floor planks and clapboards and made sashes, doors, blinds, and decorations by hand, as these were not yet produced by machine.[6] Even painters, who we think of today as manual laborers, were skilled craftsmen, similar to chemists. They not only applied paint, but they produced it by mixing linseed oil from local flax presses with white lead oxide for patina and body and with powered colors that they ex-tracted from a variety of mineral and vegetable sources.

Because they labored outdoors, working hours for the building trades varied depend-ing on seasonal conditions. Like farmers, builders had a workday that extended from sunrise to sunset, and their performance was dependent on good light or a temperature that was warm enough to allow mortar to set.[7] The schedule of work was not rigid. It was interrupted by chang-ing weather, moments of leisure, holidays, and the necessity of performing household duties. Conversely, work could be intense when there were deadlines to meet. Few clocks regulated working hours; instead work time was centered on completing a task.

Work was organized around the master craftsman's household, and employment de-pended on family relationships and friendships rather than on a strict contract. Widows of master craftsmen could expect to continue the business if they had skilled sons, and thus they could keep the trade in the family. Apprenticeships were limited to the one or two that a household could support, and they went mostly to sons, relatives, or close neighbors. The master craftsman's family provided hands with instruction in skills, board within the household or nearby, and a constant supply of work, even though it did always involve the craft. Those who boarded had their daily wages reduced from $1.25 or $1.50 to $1.00. These wages were paid erratically depending on whether the master had coin, and often in-kind services or goods were substituted instead.

In 1831, a survey of the building trades gives this description of the crafts and craftsmen. Moses Trim and James Stearns were stonemasons and plasterers, master craftsmen who would practice their trade into old age. They headed households that were in practice workshops, trained their sons in masonry skills, and gradually passed on responsibility to them. By mid-century, Stearns, born in New Hampshire in 1782, and Trim, born in New York State in 1778, were aged but still practicing the masonry trade, although Trim limited himself to stone rather than brickwork. Stearns's son Calvin was now chief mason, while Trim's son Augustus played the same role, both continuing the family craft. Also in 1831, the village's boss or master carpenters were Jesse Morgan (who had made his reputation as early as 1812 building schoolhouses), Runion Martin, Elias Benedict, and the three Huling brothers, Salmon, Edmund Philip, and Beekman. Daniel T. Reed was also among them two years later, when he bought a lot from Henry Walton on Walton Street and erected a house that resembled a miniature Pavilion Hotel. Clearly, families with a monopoly of building skills dominated access to and practice in the building trades. The three Huling brothers together with their cousins formed an extended family of carpenters; the family was able to provide seven skilled craftsmen for a project, so that there was no need to hire additional hands at a wage. Not having to go outside the extended family provided a sense of security in that kinship rather than wages tied the work party together.[8]

In the late 1830s two events began to alter the building trades. The first, in 1836, was the introduction of the "city system," which favored contractual obligations at the expense of paternal ties and household production. It set a specific number of hours for the workday rather than maintaining the existing task-oriented system. The new system was introduced first to the building trades, although later it would become the norm for shoemakers, tailors, and other craftsmen. Albany carpenters introduced it when they came to Saratoga Springs to build a house; it took two or three years to be accepted. After much debate, the procedure had succeeded in Albany because it was established on the basis of a ten-hour workday. Journeymen had favored it because under the task-oriented system they could be called on to work for long hours to complete projects. In Albany the building boom that followed the completion of the Erie Canal in 1825 had fueled an effort to reduce the need for skilled craftsmen while increasing the size of the construction workforce. Master builders became contractors interested in the rapid construction of blocks of commercial and residential buildings to be sold by speculators. They looked to the cheaper and unskilled New England and Irish laborers to perform as many tasks as possible, while contracting or subcontracting with craftsmen only when their skills were absolutely needed.[9] Ultimately the system turned traditional family craftsmen into wage earners, dependent on the wage market rather than their skills. It made master craftsmen into bosses rather than "fathers," contractors who gathered men and materials for enterprises based on the lowest possible time wage rather than choosing a worker for a skill that commanded higher pay. Moreover, during the slack periods of winter, workers were let go and became unemployed. As a sign of the growing influence of wage labor, in the 1830s John Balcom opened a mechanics' boarding house on Front Street, where, for a weekly rate, one could consume salt pork and potatoes two or three times daily. Increasingly, the wage dominated the spa's building trades rather than skill, and many craftsmen were left without consistent work or the means to earn a decent living.

The second event was a nationwide depression, the Panic of 1837.[10] Unwise bank loans, excessive debt, and a dizzying rise in the price of farmland caused the U.S. economy to collapse. The depression created extensive unemployment and flour and food riots in places such as New York City. Many apprentices and journeymen found themselves without work or future prospects because the panic had ruined their masters. They were left to their own devices, and the insecurity of their future in trade caused their numbers to decline.

The tightening of the economy after 1837, specialization, and the costs involved in sophisticated production also eliminated the possibility for journeymen and apprentices to move up. Because it was becoming a highly capitalized business, brickmaking was more susceptible than carpentry to the new methods. Apprentices no longer dreamed of buying a clay pit to manufacture bricks, for by the 1840s it was a complicated enterprise that required expensive kilns and storage sheds, not to mention the costs of transportation and marketing. A brickmaking apprentice had little chance of ever owning a brick factory. By 1858, there was similar specialization in other shops that contributed to the building trades in Saratoga Springs. Two of them were F. A. Town's marble works and Dewitt Clinton Hoyt's lime manufactory.[11] Hoyt succeeded in his specialized lime business so well that by 1878, at the age of fifty-four, he retired to become the proprietor of a hotel.

Aspects of the craft system survived even after the introduction of the ten-hour day. In 1848, advertisers from the building trades included master builders Harmon S. Hoyt and Jacob P. Pitney, the builder Joseph Langdon, the mason Daniel Smith, and the house carpenters and joiners Samuel H. Wallace and Owen T. Sparks.[12] Still, it was a much altered system. The building shops at mid-century were smaller than they had been previously because they were limited to a single generation. Younger men in their thirties and even late twenties now ran the building shops, like those of Harmon Hoyt, Joseph and Alfred Langdon, Daniel Smith, and Samuel Wallace. Most builders lived with their immediate nuclear family, having only a single additional working member, usually a son trained in the trade. Exceptions included Daniel Smith, who, having no son, instead had a Scottish journeyman living in his household. In addition, there were still extended families of carpenters, but in separate households. Alexander Patterson was a twenty-three-year-old carpenter; his household consisted of a young wife and half-year-old son. He was the youngest member of an established Presbyterian Irish building family. His older brothers, Hugh and Robert, thirty-three and thirty-five years old, respectively, also lived in separate households and were the mainstays of the business. This family, at least, continued elements of the craft tradition.

The Rise of the Builder-Contractor and the Decline of the Craftsman

By mid-century, most master mechanics had put aside the craft tradition and had become builder-contractors. This trend had already enveloped New York City's building trades; there, virtually every stage of putting up a building had become open to bid and subcontracting.[13] Although some contractors were master craftsmen, many had only a smattering of carpentry knowledge; they were instead experts in cutting costs and hiring workers. The building trades did not completely ignore the craftsman, however. Contractors now divided and subdivided their work between skilled craftsmen and the unskilled, whose cheaper work was referred to as "sweating." The key to the competition for building contracts was underbidding; the contractor who substituted the most sweated labor for craft labor came in with the lowest bid and won the contract. To do so he might use sweated shops, which could produce ready-made window sashes and doorframes much more cheaply than a craftsman. New technology also played a role, as planing machines and steam-powered stone dressers cut back the need for craftsmen.

These changes were registered not only in the decline in the number of craftsmen but also in the corresponding rapid rise in the overall number of workers involved in the building trades, the bulk of whom were unskilled, often immigrants or newcomers without connections in the community. Thus, the hallmark of the trend was the mushrooming of the number of contractors and unskilled workers as the number of masters and then journeymen declined.

Of the spa's emerging master contractors in the 1850s, Hiram Owen was the most successful. Born in 1819 in Berne, Albany County, he settled in Saratoga Springs in 1838, and eleven years later he had his own carpentry business. In 1850, his traditional craft household consisted of his wife, Catherine, three young children, and, a symbol of his success, two journeyman helpers, Wealthy Carloo and Nathan Tefft. Owen's first important job was an elegant home, the Milligan House on Circular Street, built between 1853 and 1855 for a local lumber baron. The brick structure was transitional, displaying elements of the latest Italianate style and yet retaining a traditional classical outline associated with the Greek Revival. Designed as an Italianate villa, the house had an especially decorative entrance, considering the Greek Revival severity of the rest of the structure; it consisted of a portico supported by two flamboyant fluted columns, which held an entablature decorated with lead cockle shells, the classical symbol of hospitality (Figure 54). The Milligan House was a model that Owen followed in his later building designs. For twenty-four years, Owen would style himself a "master mechanic" of the carpentry business, but in 1873 he gave up construction and retired at the age of fifty-four to become the superintendent of the facilities at the Grand Union Hotel.[14] Evidently, this position was now the pinnacle of the building trades, a goal for which masters or foremen would strive. However, such a goal opened a way to leave the trade and contributed to declining numbers of master craftsmen.

From 1850 to 1860 the number of carpenters and masons in Saratoga Springs nearly doubled, while the number of painters and brickmakers tripled—but the increased numbers continued the deterioration of the craft system. Of the masons, 37 percent were foreign-born, the bulk of these being Irish, while an additional 8 percent were from New England. Although there were eight master masons—including two from Ireland—out of seventy-five members of the trade, only one was an apprentice. As for the painters, they were usually young men in their twenties and early thirties, single or recently married with young children. Almost one-quarter were of foreign birth, the greatest number from Ireland, and then England and Canada, while an additional 13 percent came from New England. Most had no kinship networks in Saratoga Springs, and many boarded in private homes or boarding houses. Only five of the sixty-nine were designated master painters, and only two teenagers were designated apprentices. Overall,

FIGURE 54. Milligan House, 102 Circular Street, Saratoga Springs. Built 1853–1855.
These leaden decorative shells are on the canopy of the front portico of a house designed
and constructed by carpenter Hiram Owen.
(Photo, Theodore Corbett.)

most members of the painting trade had no shops and no longer had the resources to train an apprentice. The Civil War buffeted the old craft system further as it drew off the few apprentices and craftsmen's sons, who exchanged the routine of the trade for the apparent glamour of military life.[15]

The building trades' growing numbers meant increased political clout. The village government intervened for the first time in 1857, when it introduced a mechanics' lien law, which provided increased security for construction mechanics and laborers.[16] Mechanics' liens guaranteed that workers would be paid even if the owner of a building they constructed went bankrupt. Filed after an owner had refused to pay for completed work or had delayed paying for it, the liens became records of the court. They were an encumbrance, comparable to a mortgage, on a new building and remained in force until the owner paid off the workers. An owner could not establish clear title to a new building until the encumbrance was cleared.

The lien law of 1857 was a sign of the difficulty that craftsmen in the building trades were having, for while the number of construction workers was expanding, the security provided by the traditional craftsmen was declining. In the 1850s and 1860s, the household workshops of the craftsmen were disintegrating as fewer sons went into the trade or went off to war, and those who were craftsmen found that the trade no longer provided them with a living. The appearance of a village clock with a timing mechanism to strike the bell, first in the First Baptist Church of 1855 and then in the Town Hall of 1871, signified that work was now measured in time, especially hours. Thus, the work environment had radically changed from the days of the task-oriented family workshop. In 1867, the New York State legislature cut the legal workday from ten to eight hours. However, because the law allowed workers to continue to work longer hours, it affected construction minimally; most builder-contractors had employees work for as long as they need them.

The decline of the craftsman's independence was mirrored in the disappearance of households as centers of production and the failure of families to pass on skills to the next generation. Like Hiram Owen and D. C. Hoyt, craftsmen were finding the proprietorship or maintenance of a hotel more attractive than construction work. By 1860, the Pitneys, a family of carpenters, were now mainly hotel proprietors; only one of them, Jacob P., continued in the carpentry business. In 1850, master carpenter Runion Martin followed Beekman Huling in giving up the carpentry trade, when he became a merchant and manager of a boarding house.

In 1871, Alexander Deal, Augustus Trim, Daniel M. Main, and Seymour Ainsworth were the leading builder-contractors in Saratoga Springs.[17] In reality, Deal was a lumber and building-materials dealer with a complex on Putnam Street near Caroline, so his construction business was an adjunct to the wholesaling of lumber. He represented the trend of builders and painters becoming wholesalers and retailers to their trade, rather than practicers of it. Trim of the firm of Trim, Latham, and Johnson was the builder of the Town Hall in 1871 and of the United States Hotel in 1874 and the renovator of the Grand Union Hotel in 1876. Main established a contracting and building firm in 1856 on Caroline Street. He was responsible for erecting the Batcheller Mansion, one of the village's most elegant wood-frame houses. Ainsworth would build several Broadway commercial structures, including the one that bears his name at the corner of Broadway and Lake Avenue, and several fashionable residences, including his own.[18] He decorated with machine-produced brackets and constructed mansard roofs in the Second Empire style. A product of the craft system, Ainsworth had been an apprentice carpenter and carriage maker at the age of fourteen. After coming to the spa in 1840, he made a fortune selling Native American goods, and with this capital he organized masons and carpenters to erect the monolithic Second Empire structures on Broadway. Although the structures he built were embellished with the most stylish machine-made decoration, the quality of his firm's basic construction techniques like framing fell short, a sign of his workers' lack of skill.

The Arrival of the Architect

Nineteenth-century architects were regarded as scientists because of their knowledge of geometry, mathematics, and sound construction techniques, as well as of the latest fashions. They had to be able to wield drawing instruments to make the most exacting designs, and they had to see to it that builders followed the designs. To establish a full-time practice, an architect also had to have business sense and be a self-promoter. The aspect of construction that emphatically did not involve the architect was working with his hands. Not everyone who claimed to be an architect at the spa met these qualifications. In 1848, young Alexander Patterson advertised that he was both a carpenter in the family building business and a professional architect.[19] We have no record of the structures he designed.

After the Civil War, the practice of architecture was on the rise, although no architect resided in the spa until 1882, when S. Gifford Slocum arrived. At first, spa architects came from nearby cities such as Fort Edward and Troy. The lack of a resident architect before 1882 reflected the fact that architects were used only for major projects, usually public buildings such as schools, churches, or hotels. However, many architects made their reputations by providing housing plans for builders' books, which were widely distributed. Thus, their designs appeared, although they were not involved in the projects. Ainsworth's favorite architect was Gilbert Croft, a Fort Edward designer, whose work he evidently copied from the 1872 edition of *Bicknell's Village Builder.* Another building book intended for owners and their builders was published in 1865. Entitled *Architecture,* it was by Marcus Cummings of Troy and Charles Crosby Miller of Toledo, Ohio. The book established Cummings's reputation, and he soon landed commissions in Glens Falls, Washington County (for its two courthouses), Vermont, and Massachusetts, as well as Troy.[20]

From 1867, Cummings would work with John Morrissey and George Dunn, Ballston contractor and mason, to erect the post–Civil War spa's most expensive structure, Morrissey's Casino. Morrissey was the leading entrepreneur in Saratoga Springs in the 1870s, the greatest developer since Walton and Clarke thirty years earlier. Morrissey was, however, scarcely like them, for he was not a resident, and most respectable people never thought of him as a gentleman (Figure 55). Born in 1831, he emigrated as a boy from Ireland, settled in Troy, and as a teenager worked in a Troy foundry and on a Hudson River steamboat.[21] Later, as a resident of New York City, he was part of the Tammany Hall political machine, became heavyweight boxing champion of the United States, lived with prostitutes, and had a criminal record. In sum, he was one of the most colorful members of New York's entertainment society. In 1861, he came to the spa and established a gambling hall in a private house on Woodlawn Street, a block behind Broadway. Rather than discreetly remaining in the background as society required, he personally participated as a dealer. His actions caused the city fathers dismay, but he bought the village off by contributing to favorite charities.

Although a large segment of the community opposed him when he started to plan the expensive casino on Congress Street in 1867, he was successful because he spared no expense in constructing this crucial amenity. It took from 1867 to 1871 to complete the $190,000 grand building, the finest gambling house in the United States. The Casino was constructed of brick in the style of an Italianate palazzo (Figure 56).[22] The projecting ledge at the top of the foundation that deflected water, the front entrance, the stoop, and the molded caps and pediments of the front windows were all of fine Connecticut brownstone. The front window caps varied in shape from arched for the first floor, to triangular for the second, to straight for the third. The brownstone was finished by being rubbed, then cemented to the wall, and was a uniform color and grain. Above the walls was a machine-made wooden cornice of carved trusses, a paneled frieze, and sawed-and-molded blocks, brackets, and drops. The sloping roof was covered with leaded roofing tin that was nailed and soldered. As planned, the materials on the sides and back of the building were inferior to those on the front. The front windows were double-thick

FIGURE 55. John Morrissey, the notorious builder of the elegant Casino at Saratoga Springs. *(*[New York] Daily Graphic, *May 3, 1878.)*

French crystal sheet glass, while those at the side and rear were ordinary American glass. Also, the window lintels and sills in the less visible areas were of modest limestone; even the foundation's rock face broken ashlar stone was pointed with colored cement only on the exterior.

The Casino resembled the homes of the wealthiest New Yorkers, and thus it exuded an aura of hospitality necessary to attract the public. The addition of 1871 was a grand parlor and dining room with great double-arched windows running the full length of the exterior walls. On the first floor, Morrissey had his own office and library, surrounded by gaming rooms. The second-floor space had both the broadest salon and numerous small rooms, a place for card games and high-stakes gambling, which could be carried out in the utmost privacy. Most ceilings were decorated with stuccoed cornices and centerpieces. To serve the structure there was a single bathroom with a tub and washstands offering hot and cold running water (hotels had only cold running water) and a single water closet, which had its own underground vault that

FIGURE 56. Morrissey's Casino, Congress Park, Saratoga Springs. Built 1867–1871. The Casino was
the most elegant and well-constructed building in Victorian Saratoga Springs.
(Photo, Theodore Corbett.)

connected with the sewer. Twenty feet from the building in the rear yard was a six-hole out-
house, the facilities for the largely male public. Most windows had blinds, those in the front being interior-pocketed with brass butts, white knobs, and silver-plated hooks, while the rest of
the exterior windows had more modest furnishings and the basement windows were merely
screened.

There were striking similarities between this structure and the Town Hall, which was
being planned by Cummings and his partner, Thomas Birt, as the Casino was completed. But
the village fathers could at best emulate the taste of the New York City gambler. The major difference between the two structures was cost: the village spent only $109,000 on its Town Hall.
Although this was more than the village could afford, it did save considerably by having the interior more modestly finished.

George Dunn, the contractor for the Casino, was born in the town of Malta and was
trained as a mason. He migrated to Ballston Spa, where by 1860 he was a leading contractor.
Dunn's skills were in marshaling materials and workers for projects rather than in the actual
construction. Contractors such as Dunn who worked with newly emerging architects were re-

sponsible for the quality of the work, the quality of the materials, and the construction of the building on time and in accordance with the architect's drawings and specifications. The contract stipulated that the architect would decide disputes over the meaning of the specifications.

In 1871, George Dunn kept track of the number of days worked and the daily wage in his leather-bound *Weekly Time-Book for Contractors, Workingmen and Others*.[23] For the six-day workweek, the wages ranged from the $5 a day he paid the foreman mason, W. A. Dunn, to $2 a day for helpers. His masonry crew ranged from twelve to nine members, and the average payroll for them was about $200 a week. Only George Dunn himself was not paid a wage. In 1871, carpentry work was subcontracted to Henry Wilson, who had a crew of fourteen to nineteen carpenters working under him. An earlier Dunn time book included a table of wages by the week, based on a ten-hour workday, with the names of the twenty-five workers on the Casino project. These workers came from throughout the region.

Dunn also gathered his building materials from the surrounding area. H. K. Cornell of Mechanicville supplied the doors, sashes, and blinds, while lime came from Jointa Lime in Glens Falls, marble mantels for each fireplace from Rutland, Vermont, and lath from Tefft and Russell Lumber Manufacturers in Fort Edward. Iron bolts and wrought iron anchors placed every 6 feet 8 inches in the brick wall came from J. B. Hodgman, a forty-four-year-old carriage smith and forger, whose shop was at the corner of Putnam and Caroline streets. The brownstone for the facade, however, was imported from Connecticut.[24]

Cummings earned his fee by producing detailed specifications for Morrissey and Dunn. The masonry specifications had headings for stone masonry, brickwork, decorative brownstone, limestone work, plastering, and vaults and drains; the carpenters' specifications covered timber, roofs, floors, furring, windows, doors, stairs, casings and base, sundries, plumbing, paint, and glazing. This document specified the gas pipes in the ceiling for lighting, the bells and speaking tubes, the bathroom and kitchen fixtures, the shelving of the dumbwaiter.[25]

The culmination of the evolution of the architecture profession in the spa came in the 1880s, when Saratoga Springs became the home of its own architects, R. Newton Brezee and S. Gifford Slocum. Although architects were certainly practicing in Saratoga Springs in 1870s, they did not reside there, and many were contractors who designed buildings as an adjunct to their chief business.[26] Slocum arrived at the resort in 1882 from Canandaigua, in western New York, while Brezee came from Garden City, Long Island, to open his architectural office two years later. Their designs in the Queen Anne and Romanesque Revival styles represented prevailing taste, but their use of the spa as their base was entirely new. Eventually, they became known for their "cottages," which were really substantial houses erected on the boulevards, but their first contracts were for public structures on Broadway. Slocum's Central Fire Station of 1884 and Brezee's Coleman Building of 1885 set the standard for their future body of work. The fire station was the second building (after the Town Hall) to represent the municipality's great commitment to civic pride and protection. It had two monumental bays for horse-drawn fire engines, each encompassed by a round stone arch in the Richardson Romanesque style. The Coleman shop and office building was more traditional in form, but the intricate decorative facade mixed Queen Anne and Romanesque styles to provide examples of three distinct levels of architectural taste. Thus although these two architects became associated with the prevailing suburban cottage ideal of the turn of the century, they were equally wed to

Broadway and expressed the community's desire for a pleasure-oriented and urbane main street. Overall, the design of buildings, which had originally appeared at the spa as a household craft, was now the preserve of trained professionals who never used their hands to construct a building.

Networks and Life Style

Outside the workplace, members of the building trades carried on a variety of religious, social, and political activities. Before the Civil War, most of the men in the building trades shared a belief in fervent Protestantism. They were usually members of the dissenting sects. The Pitneys and the Wadsworths (painters) were Baptists; the Towns, Methodists; Nathan Lewis and the Pattersons, Presbyterians; the Hulings, members of the more intellectually oriented Universalist Church. Craftsmen buffeted by market conditions and increasingly dependent on wage relationships were driven to experiment with radical Protestantism, using belief in the coming of a kingdom of God on earth as a means of explaining their increasing inability to find work.[27] Among the contractors there was a Protestant "ascendancy," which is especially evident at Greenridge Cemetery, where they occupied spacious plots on the ridge, while their Irish masons and laborers were relegated to the Catholic section on the flat land in a corner. On the incline of the ridge, for instance, is the burial monument of Seymour Ainsworth and his wife, Catherine Ham Ainsworth, who had the monument erected after her husband's death in 1890. Certainly she spared no expense in having their bronze likenesses inserted into the monument (Figure 57). However, sizeable minorities of the Irish-born masons were actually Ulster Protestants and could claim the higher ground in Greenridge. Thus, popular Protestantism was a common bond among a considerable portion of the spa's building trades, not an alien conviction that was forced on laborers by their employers to make them industrious workers.

If we could choose a book that many members of the building trades read, it would be John Foxe's *Book of Martyrs*. The middle-class novelist Marietta Holley curled up with the book on her farm in Jefferson County to prepare herself for a visit to one of most corrupt places in the United States, the nation's capital, Washington, D.C. Nineteenth-century U.S. print culture embraced this sixteenth-century tome because it was radically Protestant and anti-Catholic. In 1820, Gideon Davidson, the leading printer in Saratoga Springs, head of a publishing firm renowned for its best-selling schoolbooks and guidebooks, printed an edition of it. A modest 323 pages without illustrations, the new edition was entitled *The History of Christian Martyrdom*. Reverend John Milner edited it and added a final section on the evils of the Spanish Inquisition. More elaborate editions of Foxe with illustrations, like one published in 1836 in Hartford, Connecticut, also were sold in the area. Edited by Reverend Charles Goodrich, this edition contained material that brought the story up to contemporary times, for it covered the persecution by Catholic mobs of French Protestants in Europe from 1814 to 1820. The editor specifically warned Americans that the Pope had organized the invasion of the Catholic Church on their shores. "Already, Catholic churches are erecting; Catholic priests and emissaries are arriving by scores; publications, designed to eulogize and recommend the system, are circulating from abroad." And he recommended that "a holy vigilance should guard well the ap-

FIGURE 57. Burial monument to Seymour and Catherine Ham Ainsworth, Greenridge Cemetery,
Saratoga Springs. Erected c. 1895.
(Photo, Theodore Corbett.)

proaches of an enemy, whose triumphs here would be the ruin of the fair fabric which cost our fathers so much toil to erect. What friend of Zion does not tremble at only the possibility that papal darkness and papal thraldom may overspread even a portion of our country."[28]

That such works spread anti-Catholicism is putting it mildly. Foxe was a sixteenth-century English scholar who had grown up during the heat of the Reformation, had been forced to flee to the Continent during the reign of Catholic Queen Mary, and on his return had completed a thorough study of "martyrology."[29] Clearly, nineteenth-century editors and publishers wished to spread the same sense of urgency that had inspired Foxe and the martyrs of the Protestant Reformation. Foxe's *Book of Martyrs* appealed to the average Protestant, for it was a series of heroic stories, many of them set in times of conflict, showing how men followed their convictions and suffered indignities and even death for their faith. It was organized like a history, starting with the primitive Christian church, before the existence of a Pope, at a time when Rome was the center of Christian persecution. It traced the ingenuous efforts of the papacy to control religion by stamping out all manner of heresy, which after the Reformation was essentially Protestantism. The editor reminded American readers that their own country, the land of the Pilgrims, had been founded with these values during the religious wars. The stories gave working people examples of heroic and upright Protestant lives, leading them to "find their confidence and zeal strengthened by the examples of their forefathers."[30] In addition, when a Catholic Irishman took a job from a craftsman, it fortified a mistrust of wage labor and the contractors who fostered it.

Some journeymen and apprentices were attracted especially to Protestant revivals. These mass religious meetings were an important source of entertainment, providing as they did not only religious revival but also opportunities to drink and even to meet the opposite sex. Revivals opened the door to allowing members of the laboring class to enjoy themselves, an activity that was often frowned on by their puritanical employers. The combination of mechanics from the building trades and the drinking of alcoholic spirits was well established. Before 1830, the building trades' daily dram was as much a part of compensation as wages. When Henry Walton had his county home constructed in 1823, the records of Miles Beach's grocery show that not only did Walton pay his builders regularly but he also gave them a daily ration of rum.[31] Certainly strong drink and conviviality were a tradition in the building trades, and this tradition could be carried over to the fringes of religious revivals. After the 1830s, however, the decline of the craft system made contractors increasingly concerned about work rules, the use of time, and temperance.

Beyond religion, a few members of the building trades developed political careers, with a particular interest in law enforcement. Jesse Morgan, Runion Martin, Daniel T. Reed, Owen T. Sparks, Beekman Huling, Abel A. Kellogg, Alexander Patterson, Joseph White, Dewitt Clinton Hoyt, and Seymour Ainsworth served as village trustees from the 1830s to 1860, in the era before the Civil War, when village and town government were in their infancy.[32] Kellogg, the brickmaker, married Phila, daughter of Gideon Putnam, and used this connection to one of the village's leading families as a springboard for a political career. An original member of the Association for the Detection of Horse Thieves and Burglars, Kellogg served as village president in 1843. He clearly had aspirations as a law officer; in 1845 he became a justice of the peace, two years later justice of sessions, and in the early 1850s a police justice for Saratoga Springs. Another colleague in the Association, the brick mason Joseph White, was in 1826 one of the village's first two constables. In 1869 and 1870, respectively, Hoyt and Ainsworth would obtain the highest political prize, becoming state assembly representative for Saratoga County. The political influence of these contractors, builders, and carpenters was a result of the growth in the numbers of men who earned their living in the building trades.

Workers' organizations that emerged in Saratoga Springs remained small and served the entire working community rather than a single trade. There were no strikes, such as occurred from 1830 to 1834 with New York City's stonecutters, who violently protested the use of marble and granite cut by convicts in the state prisons. There were no construction unions in Saratoga Springs to support the bricklayers' strike in New York City in 1868, caused when they walked out for a permanent eight-hour workday.[33] The Ancient Order of United Workmen (AOUW) did appear at the resort in 1878, forming the Putnam Lodge and electing officers. Their functions included providing fellowship for workers, and funds were raised to help tide workers over during times of unemployment. The Lodge was also a member of the Workingmen's Assembly of New York State, an umbrella organization for workers throughout the state. Established because of the growth of the spa's laboring class in the 1870s, the AOUW was, however, the only organization specifically concerned with resort working conditions.

By 1875 Saratoga Springs had the most expensive and substantial real estate north of Albany, primarily because of its stock of masonry buildings. Structures at last were being built on previous housing-lot divisions, and yet Broadway remained the center of the resort's business, for construction of a hotel was still more favored than the creation of suburban developments. Masons and carpenters were needed to provide the quality decoration and details the resort demanded. At work since the early 1800s, an army of builders, carpenters, masons, and laborers, to which after the Civil War were added contractors and architects, supported the resort. The building trades went through three stages of development. At the beginning there were few craftsmen, and the jack-of-all-trades was called on to erect structures ranging from schoolhouses to hotels. From the 1820s the trades were based on a household craft system, perpetuated by extended families of master builders. The craft system underwent modification as a result of outside pressures such as the ten-hour day and the Panic of 1837, but craft organizations survived and supported the building boom of the 1840s and 1850s. From mid-century the craft system further deteriorated as master craftsmen increasingly became contractors and ultimately retailers, recruiting labor rather than practicing the skills of their trade. After the Civil War, the system of wage-oriented contractors made obsolete the traditional household craft system. Contractors and a few outside architects, hired for major building projects, dominated the expansion of the 1870s and early 1880s. Still, local recognition of the building trades' growing number of hourly wage employees appeared in 1857 with the passage of the village's mechanics' lien law.

As a group, the building trades were as anti-Catholic as any, dominated as they were by dissenting Protestants; but they were not so susceptible to the temperance advocated by captains of industry, as drink had traditionally been part of the reward for outdoor work. In addition, their leaders became politically influential, often being elected village trustees because they represented an important constituency within the village. Because the spa lacked manufacturing to support a working class, the building trades were the largest economic sector after the service business. Without them, Saratoga Springs would never have had the buildings and public spaces that were so crucial to its success as a resort.

CHAPTER 8

The African American Presence

*I*n the 1880s, the most opinionated of fictional Victorian visitors to Saratoga Springs, Marietta Holley's Samantha, commented as she walked along Broadway that "lots of black ma's had children jest as white as snow" (Figure 58). She was referring to the white children in prams being pushed by black maids. Samantha went on to affirm that she did not "believe in a mixin' of races," that she felt uneasy when she saw the black maids kissing their charges. She went even further to sympathize with the defeated South and to endorse policies of social segregation, concluding that black and white contact is "getting too loose" and that "danger is ahead" if the races become too familiar.[1] Her views can represent the racism not only of Victorian visitors but also of Saratoga area residents, for Samantha's home was in nearby Jonesville. But the separation of the races that was so widely accepted in the Victorian spa had not always been the norm. In fact, African Americans had played an important role in the making of the early spa because of the considerable degree of integration that existed.

African Americans had participated in the settling of the Saratoga region. Well before Samantha's visit, African Americans in the eighteenth century had been integrated into the white economy of the Saratoga region. Many moved from slavery to working as Samantha observed them, black females as domestics and blacks males as waiters. Yet blacks had additional skills and reasonable opportunities at the spa that made the resort the most attractive place in the area for them to make a living from 1820 to 1850. From the beginning of the nineteenth century, they filled the spa's need for workers to support the hotels, to develop the green spaces, and to entertain the visitors. While it was a living, it was not an opportunity comparable to that which white men and women had in the spa's building trades or in factory communities. Many jobs in the resort business required only domestic skills. The greatest demand was for servants, who were usually women. At the resort they could hold these jobs into middle age, whereas in industrial communities domestic work was a young woman's occupation. And the seasonal nature of work at the spa meant that even the skilled resort workers had to hold several jobs to tide them over during the off season. Trade associations failed to appear to protect and improve the lot of these workers. The spa therefore became a haven for blacks who were willing to work under less than ideal conditions.

African American bondage and work in the Saratoga area can be divided into three eras: 1720–1800, the period of slavery in the Saratoga region, well before Saratoga Springs's development; 1800–1827, the period of gradual emancipation when blacks were attracted to work at the spas; 1827–1880, the period of freedom but also of stiff competition for resort jobs, in which blacks lost out.

The first slaves held in the Saratoga region were those of Johannes Schuyler, who in the 1720s developed his lands, which were centered on a plantation at Old Saratoga, today's Schuylerville. The degree to which slave labor was present is demonstrated by the fact that when in November 1745 Native Americans and Canadians attacked the Old Saratoga settlement, the bulk of their captives were an estimated sixty black slaves.[2] These mission Indians would have adopted some captive slaves, but because black slaves were rare in Canada, it was more profitable to sell them in Montreal or have them ransomed by their owners.

Black slavery continued after both the French and Indian and Revolutionary wars, but as a source of labor it was challenged by the availability of relatively cheap New England workers. Although the Hudson Valley's slave population grew moderately until the close of the eighteenth century, it could not keep pace with the influx of New Englanders.[3] The percentage of slaves in the Hudson Valley population fell from 20 percent in the mid-eighteenth century to only 10 percent by the century's end.

Anne Grant, who resided in Albany in the 1760s, has left us information about the daily lives of black slaves. Grant observed blacks at the Schuyler family compound called the Flatts. A century before the appearance of Victorian segregationist views, she argued that the proximity of young whites and blacks, raised and educated together, fostered confidence and respect between master and slave.[4] In Albany, it was customary to give a young slave to a white child of the same sex and age, so that the two were brought up together. At least one local portrait confirms the practice; it portrays an unidentified boy watched over by a slightly older slave.[5] Although only a few Saratoga families like the Schuylers numbered their slaves in double figures, many had at least one slave and preferred black labor to other alternatives.

Northern economic conditions led to household rather than plantation slavery, and this arrangement made the growth of black families difficult. In fact, blacks were brought up with young whites to discourage early marriage and a high fertility rate.[6] Most masters had neither the acreage nor the range of duties to support more than a few slaves. Because they had greater market value, male slaves outnumbered females, creating a sex ratio that made it difficult for males to marry. The two black matrons in the household Grant described had children, but they were husbandless and could expect their children to be sold. Married black women lived in different households than their husbands, depending on frequent visits to sustain sexual relations and family development.

Even in the eighteenth century, the kitchen was the domain of female slaves; there black women developed their skills as cooks, seamstresses, and laundresses—skills that eventually would be in high demand at resorts.[7] Black men were skilled in caring for livestock, cutting wood, and serving as field hands. There was a seasonal rhythm to the work of black slaves. In the summer, the kitchen was moved from the main house, sometimes to a permanently built summer kitchen such as the one found at the Schuyler house in Old Saratoga. More often, slaves constructed a temporary wooden hut where they cooked and lived until the weather became cold. The staple of the Hudson Valley, wheat cultivation, required field hands during spring planting and summer harvesting, but slaves devoted the fall and winter to cutting timber or barrel staves and to the transport of produce to market. Saratoga's slaves thus performed

FIGURE 58. "Lots of black ma's had children jest as white as snow." The caption reveals Samantha's racism, as she was uncomfortable seeing white children being familiar with their black nannies.
(Frederick Opper, illustration for Marietta Holley, Samantha at Saratoga, *Philadelphia, 1887.)*

Lots of black ma's had childern jest as white as snov

a variety of tasks on a seasonal basis rather than following the steady routine of their southern counterparts.

The 1790 federal census provides the first identification of Saratoga area's slaveholders and where they lived.[8] The bulk of them resided along the Hudson or Mohawk Rivers. The town of Halfmoon led the list with 135 slaves, or almost 4 percent of the town's population. Ballston, Stillwater, and Saratoga—then the only towns—followed with 69, 61, and 53 slaves respectively, 318 slaves in all. However, because Ballston's population was more than twice that of Stillwater or Saratoga, these two towns had a greater density of blacks. Overall, blacks could be found throughout the Saratoga region, making them an important labor force.

Within the region, slaveholding households were divided thus: Halfmoon 55, Ballston 34, Stillwater 26, Saratoga 19. Although Halfmoon led in the number of slaves and slaveholders, only one of the five largest slaveholders resided there; thus the slaves were dispersed over the entire region. Philip Schuyler's heir in Old Saratoga, John Bradstreet Schuyler, had fourteen slaves, while Cornelius Van Vechten of Coveville, south of Old Saratoga, had ten. Dirck Swart of Stillwater followed these two masters with eight slaves, Janatie Van Vranken of Halfmoon—the only woman—and James Gordon of Ballston each had seven.[9] All were capitalists who tried to develop their property, and on occasion at least some of them or a member of their families visited the newly emerging resort at Ballston Spa. This elite group of slaveholders had supported the Revolutionary War, and as a result they monopolized postwar political offices.

More surprising than the number of slaves for the Saratoga area is the disclosure in the 1790 census that there were forty-eight free blacks. These blacks constituted 28 percent of the free blacks in the entire Albany area, while the Saratoga portion of the slave population amounted to only 8 percent. The large number of free blacks who lived in the Saratoga area foreshadowed their important role in the creation of the resort business. Their presence at Saratoga was unusual because most free blacks were found in cities. We have to assume that the conditions that Anne Grant described in the 1760s forced outmigration of free blacks from the Albany area, and they settled on small farms in the countryside. Free blacks had been slaves whom Albany patrician society considered marginal: those who were the product of a mixed racial union, those with handicaps, those beyond their prime. It was easier for slaveholders to provide such unproductive or embarrassing blacks with freedom and a small plot in the wilderness of their vast estates than to bear the cost of keeping them.

In 1799, a new era for blacks began with the passage of the State of New York's Emancipation Act. The era would conclude in the 1830s with the end of slavery. Blacks were then on their own in what became a most competitive labor market. The Emancipation Act of 1799 provided that children born to slaves after that year were to be free.[10] A second law, passed in 1817, continued the state's policy of gradual emancipation by declaring that slavery would be ended on July 4, 1827. The 1799 law did contain clauses that gave masters a measure of control over the situation because they felt they were losing property. To placate slaveholders, they were given use of a slave mother's children long after they reached adulthood; the children freed in 1799 were required to remain in bondage until they became adults: twenty-eight years old for males and twenty-five years old for females. Children born during the emancipation period could be given over as wards of the town, so that masters would not have to maintain them. Although theoretically the abandoned children were given to a new master, in practice they were given back to the original master, who received a monthly subsidy from the state to maintain the children. Thus, masters had use of the labor of freed slaves until their twenty-eighth or twenty-fifth birthdays and did not even have to pay for their subsistence.

In addition, an earlier law of 1785 obliged masters who freed adult slaves to affirm that the free blacks could support themselves and would not become community wards.[11] Able-bodied slaves who could support themselves were defined as those aged fifty years or younger, in practice those who could do productive field work. The point is that New York's emancipation laws gave slaveholders every opportunity to dispose of their slaves without any economic loss.

These laws brought a sharp decline in the number of slaves in both the Saratoga region and New York State, so that by 1830 out-of-state owners held the only remaining slaves. Historians writing in the late nineteenth century and even recently have made much of the humane spirit of those Saratoga slaveholders who freed their slaves during this period or who manumitted southern slaves who had become residents of New York.[12] The descendants of slaveholders often invented their ancestors supposed abolitionist sentiments after the Civil War because they were embarrassed; they tried to have it seem that the emancipation was based on kindness toward their family's or southern slaves. In fact, the laws of 1785, 1799, and 1817 made it inevitable that the slaves would be freed and provided masters with economic inducements that had nothing to with altruism. Slaveholders were concerned chiefly with the best means of protecting their property rights. They were relieved of the expense of maintaining children and elderly slaves, who were more costly than productive. With both the law and their business sense arguing for emancipation, most of Saratoga's slave owners were only too happy to free them.

This attitude is evident in the fact that although Saratoga County's politicians favored the abolition of slavery and emancipation, they opposed giving free black men the vote. Samuel Young, Ballston attorney, speaker of the state assembly and a leader of the Democratic Party, was usually identified with efforts to extend the franchise. In the Constitutional Convention of 1821, however, he and two other Saratoga County representatives, Salmon Child and Jeremy Rockwell, staunchly recommended that the word *white* be inserted in the measure that provided for universal male suffrage. Young's arguments were plainly racist: "The minds of blacks are not competent to vote. They are too much degraded to estimate the value, or exercise with fidelity and discretion that important right. Their vote would be at the call of the richest purchaser. Look to your jails and penitentiaries. By whom are they filled? By the very race, whom it is now proposed to clothe with the power of deciding upon political rights." Young felt that blacks could not vote until they were "raised to the level of the white man, . . . when the colours shall intermarry—when negroes shall be invited to your tables—to sit in your pew, or ride in your coach." The public was clearly not ready for such sentiments.[13]

Although Young's resolution to insert the word *white* was narrowly defeated by those of Federalist inclination, such as Stephen Van Rensselaer, and suffrage was granted to all males, it was left to the legislators to set restrictions of residence and property ownership. They burdened blacks with a three-year residency requirement and a $250 property qualification, while whites now had such requirements abolished.[14] This policy prevented most blacks from voting and relegated them to the status of second-class citizens. Although newly arrived Irish immigrants were entrusted to exercise the franchise, blacks, whose roots in the state went back to the early eighteenth century, were in practice disenfranchised. The state's electorate ratified similar laws until 1870, when the federal constitution's Fifteenth Amendment made them void. As a result of these calculated restrictions, the political status of blacks was effectively kept below that of the poorest white.

Emancipation did stimulate the development of black families. No longer attached to a master's household, emancipated slaves formed their own. In 1790 the Saratoga region had only five free black families, but by 1810 there were twenty-five, by 1830 sixty-five, and by 1840 nearly ninety.[15] Moreover, the new African American households were similar in structure to recently formed white households. A typical family comprised a young black couple with only a few children. Still, free black men, who, as a result of earlier slave conditions were more numerous than women, continued to live singly as hired hands, as they had during the slave era.

By the third era, 1830 to 1880, when blacks were emancipated, the resort business was employing black labor. Beginning in 1830 and continuing to mid-century, the black population was no longer centered on Saratoga County's rural estates and farms, but in Saratoga Springs. At the spa blacks made up about 4 percent of the population in 1830, rising to almost 6 percent in 1840, falling back to 4 percent by 1850. By 1840, the free blacks of Saratoga Springs were as numerous as the enslaved blacks had been in Halfmoon's 1790 population. Furthermore by 1850, Halfmoon, once the center of a rural slave population, had only nineteen blacks, while the nearby and growing village of Waterford, a canal town of the same size, had twenty-eight. By mid-century, free blacks had moved from the farms where they or their parents had once been slaves and were concentrated in Saratoga County's chief resort and urban center.[16]

The spa's percentage of black population in 1840 was the highest it would ever be. The doubling of the number of the spa's blacks between 1830 and 1840 rested squarely on the shoulders of black females. They constituted 58 percent of the spa's blacks in 1830 and 60 percent by the peak of 1840. Black women and girls outnumbered males in every age group except the very oldest and smallest categories of over fifty-five in 1830 and of over one hundred in 1840. The rise in the number of black females in the 1830s, from 51 to 111, can be explained only by the rise in job opportunities. The resort was already showing its need for service workers—ideal positions for black women.[17]

Blacks had acquired an important place by mid-century among the spa's 4,550 inhabitants. More than half were classified as mulattos, a definition based at the time on lightness of skin color; this classification permitted them to be competitive in the job market. Four-fifths of blacks were natives of New York State, so it is likely that many of the spa's blacks were descendants of the region's original slaves. The remainder were from free states such as Massachusetts, Pennsylvania, and New Jersey. Only three blacks were from southern slave states.[18]

The 1850 census reveals the structure of black households, and, as a result, we can discern family and work relationships. The most common type of black household, about 43 percent, was still contained within a white household, including three of the spa's hotels; there blacks were live-in servants, much as they had been in the days of slavery.[19] Most of these domestics were single black women, although there were a substantial number of men. In 1850, many black domestics were young—for example, fourteen-year-old Julia Waters and sixteen-year-old Matilda Reed and Sarah Grant. As domestics they could expect to receive $1 to $1.25 a week plus board. This domestic work not only provided a way for young girls to learn a skill but also removed a financial burden from their parents.

Some domestics were on a more professional level. Dolly Walworth, a southern slave, was freed by state law when she joined a Saratoga Springs family in 1851. Dolly was literate and skilled, and she received a salary. Her employer was the renowned judge Reuben Hyde Walworth, and his antislavery sentiments ensured that she was treated well. However, because she was free, she left the Walworths twice to work for families in Ballston Spa and New York City, returning in each case to the Walworth household. The lure of higher wages in New York City was difficult for black women to resist.[20]

At mid-century over half the village's blacks did live in their own households, a higher figure than that for the Irish immigrants who were now competing with them for jobs. Black households numbered five persons, roughly the same as white households, reflecting minimal racial distinctions in this area. The birthrate in Saratoga Springs for both blacks and whites was lower than in the countryside, but the spa households were more diverse in composition, often extended by relatives or boarders so that they were close to the size of those beyond the village's limits. Generally headed by a male, over half of black households were made up of the conjugal unit of father, mother, and children. A substantial minority of family households also had nonkin residents. Such extended households were more common among the spa's blacks than among the Irish or the blacks who lived in the countryside. The makeup of these households indicates a desire by the spa's blacks to share their home with another black family and to add to their income by taking in boarders. An example of an extended household tied to the resort business is that of Uriah Dalton, a musician from Vermont, and his wife, Margaret. The mulatto couple's household included their eight-year-old daughter and was extended by a black woman and a mulatto man who was a waiter at the Union Hall. Four whites further extended it: a male musician also from Vermont, a male waiter, and a female and a male without occupation. Evidently whites with similar occupations saw no difficulty in living with blacks, who might even be their landlord. Finally, women headed about 6 percent of the black households, a sign of the viability of black families even when a male head of household was not present.[21]

Housekeeping skills were essential to the success of the resort's hotels and range of accommodations. In practice, housekeeping positions had three levels: help, domestic service, and supervisor.[22] Help were at the bottom of the ladder; these unskilled people were hired to complete a seasonal task. Children or adolescents were usually drawn from the neighborhood to provide help and thus additional income for their family. Domestic service developed in the 1830s from this earlier tradition of help. It was based on a formal wage relationship, the result of the rise of urban and industrial society. Women who worked as domestics needed to be employed full time because they were self-supporting or at least were crucial contributors to their families' income. They were often drawn from outside the community; attracted by the job market, they were forced to settle and make their way among strangers. If they had no children, they lived in, while the presence of children required that they set up a separate household. Domestic service was not merely of way of making extra money but also a position with rules and regulations for which employers sought a certain level of skills and presence. It could be a lifelong source of income. Supervisors were at the highest level of the housekeeping sector. Their experience and skills were superior enough to warrant giving them the responsibilities of a manager. Holding the position of cook in a large household offered the best opportunity to develop supervisory experience because of the dominating role cooks played in "their" kitchens. A step above the cook, a housekeeper could go beyond managing a large household to managing a boarding house or even a hotel.

Despite the unskilled nature of the category of help, blacks tended to be least likely to be hired for these positions because whites consistently treated blacks as outsiders and reserved such casual positions for poor white neighborhood families or orphaned children. In contrast, before the influx of Irish immigrants in the 1840s, black women were predominant in the realm of domestic service. A few black women were supervisors, especially cooks in hotels and large households. Further opportunity at the highest level was shut off, however, as only whites became managers and proprietors of hotels.

Evidence indicates that black women were active in the housekeeping sector of the spa's economy. In 1850, Margaret Van Pelt worked as a domestic at the American Hotel. Fifteen years later, Mary Braxton, a Maryland native, was employed at E. A. Haggart's boarding house as a cook, as was Mary Hunter, a Brooklyn native, who shared service duties with her husband at the Saratoga Water Cure. Only a few black women had Dolly Walworth's live-in options; blacks in the servant's quarters of hotels were exploited, overworked, and underpaid by hotel proprietors, who tried to minimize wages and maximize the fact that they were giving their workers room and board.[23]

The 1850 census describes black men's occupations in detail. Black males were attracted to Saratoga Springs because they had the skills required for resort work. All had manual occupations, which we can categorize as 23 percent skilled, 70 percent semiskilled, and 7 percent unskilled. The skilled included barbers, stonecutters, a tailor, a butcher, a blacksmith, and a farmer. The semiskilled workers were waiters, musicians, teamsters, a cook, and a soda maker. The unskilled were porters and laborers. Given the limitation of the census, we can see that black men usually had a skill, particularly in resort services, and they rarely competed for un-skilled jobs. Although more black males were undoubtedly in the unskilled category than the census counts, the number of unskilled black males was still far lower the number of unskilled Irish males, who came to dominate the unskilled construction and landscape jobs.[24]

To make ends meet, free blacks held a variety of jobs for a relatively short duration. The example of Solomon Northup and his wife, Ann, is illuminating.[25] Married on Christmas Day 1828 in Fort Edward, both he and his spouse were skilled free blacks, a combination that was necessary to support the household. Born in 1808 in Minerva in the Adirondacks, Solomon was reared on farms in Washington County by his father Mintus, who saw to it that he got some education, for he read books and could sign his name. His first occupation was as a mason con-structing the Champlain Canal; then he worked as a farmer. In 1834 he moved to Saratoga Springs, where for the next seven years he held jobs as a hack driver for the Washington Hall boarding house, a railroad laborer, and a hotel staff person. During the lean winter months he supplemented his income by entertaining with his violin.

A laboring man, Solomon was no saint, especially when he worked on the rough and tumble project of building the Champlain Canal. His name appears twice, in 1834 and 1839, in court cases involving assault and battery, one of them serious enough to involve the possibil-ity of punishment by death. When contracted in 1838 to deliver goods by the Champlain Canal to Waterford, he was discharged from his job for being intoxicated. Solomon claimed damages, and, on review of witnesses, the judge found that daily drinking was common among canal workers; the judge noted that although Solomon had been drinking, it "was not so much to dis-qualify him for business," that Solomon's "general character was that he was industrious and not in the habit of being intoxicated, tho in the habit of drinking some." Although Solomon was reasonably upstanding and usually successful in finding jobs, he did feel that his happiest moments were not at the spa but rather on a farm he leased near Fort Edward. The resort, he felt, was "not calculated to preserve the simple habits of industry and economy, but on the con-trary, tending one toward shiftlessness and extravagance."[26]

Ann Hampton Northup, the mother of their three children and Solomon's helpmate, was born in 1802 in nearby Washington County and was brought up in Hudson Falls; she resided there with John Baird, proprietor of the Eagle Tavern, where she learned the cooking arts. She also lived in Salem, where she was a live-in domestic for the respectable family of Reverend Alexander Proudfit. An expert cook as a result of these early experiences, she worked at the spa's United States Hotel and in the off-season at coffeehouses in Washington County. The fact that Ann was illiterate did not stand in her way. The variety of her skills and the seasonal rhythm of her work were similar to those of her slave ancestors a century earlier, although she was now operating in a competitive labor market. At mid-century she resided in Saratoga Springs, the head of a household consisting of her eldest, nineteen-year-old daughter, Elizabeth, and an-other black family headed by a woman, the Swifts. Nearby was the Stanton family, formed when Ann's second daughter, Margaret, married Philip Stanton, teamster, and they had two children. Ann did not remain at the spa, however, moving in the early 1850s to the growing in-dustrial village of Glens Falls and in 1864 across the Hudson to Moreau, where she died six years later.[27] She continued to work as a cook, probably at the Eagle Tavern in Hudson Falls or Sherrill's Coffee House. She had a small estate of real and personal property and lived her last years in Moreau with Margaret and Philip. Although she legally remained Solomon's wife, in practice she was separated from him.

Solomon Northup is famous as an object of abolitionist sentiment, for he dictated an account of his experiences as a southern slave after he had been seized and placed in bondage. In 1841, as he was seeking work in Saratoga Springs, two strangers offered him a job in their circus accompanying their performances with his violin.[28] Northup assumed they were offering him a short-term job that would carry him to New York City and back. Instead, they abducted him, took him to the slave states, and sold him for a profit; he spent twelve years on a Louisiana plantation, until rescued by New York authorities. Such occurrences were possible in Saratoga Springs because the resort attracted a diversity of visitors during the summer season. Despite state legislation of 1840 prohibiting it, an occasional free black like Northup was kidnapped and taken south to be sold in the slave states. In 1853, New York authorities returned him to his family, who were now residing in Glens Falls.

David Wilson, a Washington County author, ghost-wrote and published Solomon's story in 1853. After publication of the bestseller, Solomon was freed and spent much of his time on the road giving testimonials that helped to promote the book and antislavery sentiment. Wilson orchestrated this endeavor. He was an antislaver, but he could not support the abolition movement, considering it an extremist attack on the rights of property. He noted in his "Editor's Preface" that it was not slavery as an institution that was responsible for Solomon's mistreatment, but its application by individuals, so that "among slave holders there are men of humanity as well as of cruelty."[29] His views were those of most in Saratoga Springs. Their moderate antislavery was appropriated and distorted by the abolitionist campaign of the 1850s, and Solomon's experience was used to promote what most northern whites regarded as a radical cause. Wilson dedicated Solomon's account to Harriet Beecher Stowe, a First Amendment abolitionist, whose *Uncle Tom's Cabin,* a landmark bestseller, had been published the year before. Doubtless, he was trying to ride on the coattails of Stowe's book, which sold ten thousand copies within a week and three hundred thousand copies by the end of 1852. Wilson's combination of individual altruism and opportunism is typical of the Saratoga area's antislavery sentiment.

Wilson's attitudes left room for racism. These prejudices dominated white opinion even as northerners advocated an end to southern slavery. In 1863, at the height of northern efforts to win the Civil War, draft riots paralyzed New York City, and blacks were the chief targets of the Irish mobs that killed 105 persons.[30] Ironically, the Irish, full citizens, led the mobs because they were subject to the draft, while blacks, disenfranchised by a web of state laws, were exempt from military service. Blacks did, however, serve in their own volunteer units, and Saratoga County had such a unit. Saratoga Springs was not directly involved in the riots, but the same tensions between the blacks and the Irish were developing at the resort, a situation that would cause a decline in the presence of blacks in the resort workforce.

After the Civil War, the spa's African American population grew moderately but not nearly enough to keep up with the flow of Irish immigrants. Blacks came from a new source. Although in 1865 most blacks were native New Yorkers, by 1875 only 65 percent were natives.[31] The newcomers were southern blacks, freed as a result of the Thirteenth Amendment.

They came to escape the grinding poverty that was the lot of a free black in the South. Also, after 1873 New York State's pioneering civil rights law, which outlawed discrimination in public accommodations, may have attracted them. Blacks could now potentially stay as guests at the very hotels in which they worked. Marietta Holley's opinionated visitor, Samantha, does not mention this development, for it probably would not have pleased her. By the 1870s, the New York City black community had a close connection with Saratoga because of the extensive number of summer visitors from that city. Often blacks first came to the spa as Samantha reported, serving a New York City family during the season. Some chose to stay or at least to spend part of their working life at the spa, although most favored life in the big city.

There is detailed information about a Saratoga Springs black resident with a New York City connection who lived in both places just after the Civil War, Emma Waite. She received a diary as a Christmas present from one of her satisfied employers.[32] It reveals her to have been a literate, skilled, and attractive person, but nonetheless a single woman, without a husband or local family connections, facing a future of spinsterhood (Figure 59). She had moved from New

FIGURE 59. Emma Waite,
c. 1870. This photograph of
Waite was purchased by the state
library along with her diary.
*(Manuscript Division, New York State
Library, Albany, N.Y.)*

York City to the spa in 1868 and resided for a time in a black teamster's household. Piecing together her employment history in 1870, we find that she supported herself in several positions that changed seasonally. She could cater parties, serve as a chief cook, do housecleaning, and mind children. Thus she was still the traditional Saratoga black domestic of pre-emancipation times, although on the highest level as a supervisor of workers. In winter, she survived by catering balls and parties, often traveling to locales as far away as Easton in Washington County. When spring came, she spent May opening houses for families who would stay through the summer. Her daily schedule of housecleaning and childcare was grueling and lasted from 5:00 A.M. to 9:00 P.M.

In June, Waite began to work at the hotels, which were adding staff. She was first employed at the Grand Union Hotel, but only for two days, as she lost her position to white help. Next the Congress Hall hired her; she was overworked and thus took a position at the new and smaller Continental Hotel. There she stayed until September 14, the end of the season. An occasional gift from a guest and the friendships she made with her fellow black workers offset the heat of summer and drudgery of work at the hotels. While she was employed at the hotels, Waite also did housework for prominent families, and this work intensified in September and October as they began to close their homes. On October 4 a telegram arrived from a New York City family that had employed her over the summer, offering her a position in the metropolis. Waite responded immediately and was in New York by 4 P.M. the next day; apparently she had no regrets about leaving the resort.[33]

The center of Waite's social life was her church, the African Methodist Episcopal Zion, and the cooperative Methodist Sabbath School. More than any other institution, the church united the black community. Evening tea meetings were popular at the church, while the school offered her an opportunity to go on an excursion to the small resort at nearby Lake Luzerne. In addition, Greenridge Cemetery was an ideal place for a Sunday afternoon promenade, away from the crowds of Congress Park and other spa pleasure grounds. A drive to Saratoga Lake for a drink was another high point in her leisure hours. Weddings, funerals, parties, shopping, and simply getting her hair cut where pleasurable activities that offered a respite from the need to make a living. These leisure-time activities were similar to those of the Irish domestics who were her competition.[34]

Waite had a reasonable amount of free time, especially during the off-season. She anticipated holidays with excitement, chiefly Christmas, Valentine's Day, Memorial Day, and July Fourth, although she was too fatigued from work to enjoy the Independence Day fireworks. Special events such as lectures and parades still had an abolitionist flavor, which was enhanced by pride in the North's victory over the South. In 1870, at a parade held in honor of the Fifteenth Amendment, articulate black abolitionist Frederick Douglass was the guest of honor; the parade was followed by a supper and ball. Another attraction was the visit of a panorama depicting the life of Lincoln. In September, the Republican State Convention was held at the spa to select a candidate for governor. As the party of Lincoln, the Republican party was favored by enfranchised blacks.[35] Waite's diary testifies to the fullness of black life at the spa.

African Americans made a substantial contribution to resort life in Saratoga Springs. The spa took advantage of a regional black labor force, which had existed from the time of the earliest settlement, when slaves had been numerous and had been regarded as the best workers by Saratoga's eighteenth-century landholders. As Saratoga Springs became the dominant resort in the 1830s, free blacks settled there because of the availability of jobs in its hotels—even if they preferred the independence of life as yeoman farmers. Free blacks could form families, claim the higher status of mulatto, establish churches, and work for most of the year if they were skilled. But a full-time job was difficult to obtain, and couples and single women needed to continually seek work to support their households.

By the mid-nineteenth century the respected place held by blacks in the resort business was being challenged. Being sold into southern slavery, a practice that abolitionists exaggerated, was not the threat. Rather blacks' second-class political and social status kept them at the bottom of society and prevented them from getting ahead. Beginning in the late 1840s, vast numbers of Catholic Irish immigrants arrived in Saratoga Springs, and, bolstered by the advantage of being white, they began competing with blacks for jobs. Increasingly, given the Irish competition, the spa's blacks sought to move to New York City for increased opportunity or to the states along the Mason-Dixon Line. At the end of the nineteenth century, blacks were less numerous in Saratoga Springs and its region than at any previous time, even though citizenship rights had been fully protected since 1870. Overall, blacks played a vital but declining role in nineteenth-century Saratoga Springs as better job opportunities appeared elsewhere.[36]

The Irish

*I*n nineteenth-century Saratoga County, foreign-born meant only one ethnic group—the Irish. Their presence is unique in that Irish immigrant women became a mainstay of the economy and remained employed in the resort business through much of their life. More than any other group the Irish were the resort's permanent laboring class. This discovery of the role of Irish women challenges the traditional emphasis on the Irish as the excavators of the canals or as urban laborers in New York City or Boston. The spa, which was not on the Champlain Canal and had no industrial jobs, had little to offer men searching for skilled employment.

Women, however, had excellent opportunities to work in the resort economy of Saratoga Springs, as is demonstrated by the facts that they were more numerous than men and that more of them were likely to have to work than were women in other parts of Saratoga County. In 1850, females constituted 53 percent of the town's population, a figure that would rise in 1860 to 55 percent and return in 1875 to 53 percent. This figure was exceptionally high by U.S. standards. For women to be more numerous was a characteristic of resorts; the population of England's Bath at the beginning of the nineteenth century was an astounding 61 percent women. The composition of the 1875 female population Saratoga Springs also set it apart from the rest of Saratoga County for two reasons: there were more widows and far more foreign-born women in all categories from single to married to widowed.[1] Most of these women were Irish immigrants. Although life was no easier for the Irish at the spa than elsewhere, they first found work as live-in servants in households or as domestics at hotels and later succeeded in contributing to the establishment of their own neighborhood, Dublin.

How Diverse the Irish Were

We must remember how diverse the Irish were in the era before 1845. The Roman Catholic peasant who came to dominate Irish emigration in the mid-nineteenth century is regarded as the typical Irish immigrant. These familiar rural Irish Catholics made up the largest portion of the population of southern and western Ireland, especially the provinces of Connaught and Munster.[2] Conservative peasants, practicing manorial subsistence farming without a viable place in the European capitalistic economy, they were firmly attached to their families and tiny plots, and therefore they did not decide to emigrate easily. They did not see emigration as an opportunity to make a new start or to earn a better living but rather as exile, a forced leaving and one not meant to be permanent. Not until the most pivotal event in nineteenth-century Irish history, the Great Hunger of 1845, did they become destitute enough to choose to migrate. Thus they were not the strong force in prefamine immigration that they became afterward. Because of their poverty, Catholic peasants usually traveled singly or in groups of siblings; they were the younger generation, which could find no future in Ireland. Unskilled in comparison with the Protestant Irish, these young women and men were the best of the peasant community, willing to work and learn a trade. So the single young Catholics who arrived in Saratoga Springs as a result of the Great Hunger came to be the largest segment of the ethnic population, but they were by no means the only Irish immigrants.

In contrast, two important groups of Irish immigrants were Protestants, and they outnumbered Catholics in the prefamine years. Especially before 1845, men and women of Protestant English and Scottish origin had emigrated from Ireland to play a part in making the spa into a flourishing resort. The most numerous were the dissenting Irish, mainly Presbyterians, who had settled in Ulster as early as the Middle Ages and were set apart from both Catholics and members of the Anglican Church.[3] Originally from Scotland, they had migrated to northern Ireland and settled, and now they were willing to try again in the United States. The Scotch-Irish, as they came to be called, had a bit of capital and could travel with their families or even in groups, often led by their Presbyterian clergy, who saw the United States as a place where they could establish a God-fearing community. They had been as oppressed as the Catholic peasants by capitalistic landlords who attempted to extract ever higher rents and dues. The industrialization of Ulster's cities, such as Londonderry and Belfast, had offered them opportunities to work in factories or in the related cottage industries, where they had performed steps in the manufacturing process. Industrialization made Ulster the most prosperous part of Ireland and gave the Scotch-Irish skills and better living conditions than those of the Catholic peasants. However, emigration was forced when the prosperity was interrupted by depression, which fostered unrest among the tenants displaced by the Industrial Revolution. The Steelboys Uprisings in the 1770s showed that the Ulster Irish were being forced off their land by speculators who bought up their unrenewed leases and drove them from their homes. To avoid further trouble, they used the United States as a safety valve, and therefore it was the Ulster Irish who dominated migration from the 1770s until the 1840s. They included in 1771 James Caldwell, who, as we have seen, would develop the resort at Lake George.

The third group of immigrants were the Irish Anglicans. In the eighteenth-century in the United States they constituted one out every five Irish emigrants, although this figure declined in the nineteenth century. The Irish Anglicans were known as "the Ascendancy," the privileged English class, who were placed above both the Catholics and the Protestant dissenters.[4] Their Anglican Church was the established church of Ireland, and until 1829 the Penal Laws gave them the exclusive privilege of holding political office. The Anglo-Irish emigrated to North America as individuals rather than in families, and they ranged from gentry to poor. The gentry blended into the Anglo-Saxon establishment more easily than the Catholic peasants or the Ulster Presbyterians. An example was William Johnson, Mohawk baronet, Indian agent, and an early user of Ballston Spa's mineral waters.

Access from Ireland to Saratoga Springs

The Irish were drawn to Saratoga Springs because of its proximity to U.S. ports of entry. The spa was on the chief routes of access to the interior. Because the passage was so much cheaper, between 1815 and 1845 most Irish immigrants landed not in New York or Boston but in Canada, near Quebec, on Grosse Island, where they were quarantined until they were deemed suitable to leave.[5] By the end of 1846, Irish immigrants escaping from the Great Hunger overwhelmed this island. From there the immigrants were barged to Montreal, where many stayed, and others were dispersed to other parts of Canada. After a few years of residence in Canada, nearly half proceeded to the United States, often by way of the Champlain Valley. The Irish did not usually become farmers but rather sought work in the largest towns and cities, and Saratoga Springs was one of the first substantial communities on this southern journey. From there the railroad offered connections to Albany and Troy or to western New York. The more well-known, but more expensive, route of Irish immigration, via Liverpool, England, to New York City and then up the Hudson River, achieved dominance over this Canadian route only after 1850.

By the 1840s, money sent from the United States paid the fares of over half the Irish passengers crossing the Atlantic from Liverpool or Belfast. The transporting of immigrants and the sending of money to Ireland had become a business. In the spa, one of the chief agents was Simon Flanigan, native of County Galway, a poor Irish county dependent on the potato, part of the western province of Connaught. Born in 1810, he emigrated to the United States in the 1840s and became a Saratoga Springs merchant with an office at the Union Hotel. His chief enterprise by 1864 was as an emigrant and ship agent, a pivotal role in Irish immigration and settlement. He could book trans-Atlantic passages or sell money drafts to send cash to the British Isles. He and his wives, Mary Hanon and then Jane Long, lived in a Greek Revival house that overlooked Dublin, the neighborhood were the Irish were most welcome; the house was a transitional station for Irish immigrants.[6] When Simon died in 1870 his burial monument in Greenridge Cemetery was the tallest obelisk in the separate Catholic section (Figure 60). His success was based on aiding his countrymen to come and settle in the spa.

Three Eras of Irish Presence

The Irish presence in Saratoga Springs can be divided into three eras. The first, before 1845, was one of diversity, in which the Protestant Irish were as numerous as the Catholics. They emigrated to the United States and then Saratoga with skills, a bit of money, and traditions not so different from those of the existing population. In the early nineteenth century, many Saratoga Springs merchants, craftsmen, Presbyterians, and Episcopalians were natives of Ireland. The second era, from 1845 to 1860, was the result of the Great Hunger of 1845, which caused a Catholic Irish exodus that single-handedly sustained the growth of Saratoga Springs. As a result, in 1850 the Irish were the largest ethnic group, vastly outnumbering English, Scottish, German, and French Canadian immigrants as well as blacks. There were 441 in the town, a figure approaching 10 percent of its population. Ten years later there were 1,180, almost three

FIGURE 60. Burial monument
of the Simon Flanigan family,
Greenridge Cemetery, Saratoga
Springs. Erected in 1874.
(Photo, Theodore Corbett.)

times as many, and because the growth of the rest of the population was dormant, they now accounted for 18 percent of the town. Additional evidence on naturalization in Saratoga County shows the effect of this post-1845 Irish emigration. Only a handful of new citizens were inducted in the county in the 1820s and 1830s, with a sharp rise after 1845 and an even sharper rise after 1852. In fact, the number of citizens naturalized in only two years, 1855 and 1856, was greater than the numbers naturalized in the 1820s, 1830s, and 1840s combined. By the third era, after 1860, Irish immigration had slowed, and the number reaching Saratoga Springs had declined. Consequently, by 1875, although the number of Irish had increased to 1,441, they constituted only a bit more than 13 percent of the population.[7] Irish growth now depended on the ability of the Irish to integrate into the spa community, to form families at the spa, and to reproduce in their new homeland—not as easy a task as it might have been in other U.S. communities. Let us look at each era in detail.

THE FIRST ERA, 1770–1844

One million Irish immigrants came to the United States in the seven decades before the Great Hunger. Two-thirds of them were from Ulster; thus a majority were Protestant, although there was a definite Catholic minority. A sizable community of Ulster Irish settled in the town of Ballston in the 1770s.[8] After the Revolution, both Americans and the British encouraged Irish emigration to the United States and Canada, which in practice was chiefly from capitalistic Ulster. In 1810, Judge William Cooper's *Guide to the Wilderness* was published in Ireland. It emphasized the generous landownership terms offered to the Irish who settled in upstate New York. Crop failures that had occurred in Ireland in 1800, 1807, 1816, 1822, and 1839 created conditions favorable for emigration long before the Great Hunger.[9] The end of the War of 1812 marked the opening of the sea lanes between the British Isles and North America, and after 1815, British legislation encouraged emigration from Ireland to Canada because the authorities wished to see Canada populated. These developments made that passage the fastest and most inexpensive available.

In Saratoga Springs, this was an era when families arrived from Ireland rather than single women; hence the Irish were not yet the mainstay of the resort labor force. Protestant Irish such as John Patterson and his three sons, Hugh, Robert, and Alexander, came and settled. This family probably arrived at the spa in the early 1830s; Robert's eldest son, John, was born here in 1835. All three sons married Americans and followed their father's trade as carpenters. Alexander, the youngest brother, born in Ireland in 1827, would become not only a carpenter but also a self-styled architect and a civic leader. His Protestant background helped him to become a village trustee (1862 to 1865), to be elected a member of the school board (1869 to 1876), and to serve as a trustee of the First Presbyterian Church.[10] Nonconformist Irish like the Pattersons could rapidly play a significant role in community affairs.

Irish Catholic families did arrive in the spa before the Great Hunger. Some of the earliest Catholic families to settle in Saratoga were those of Owen and John Dinnen, who came around 1835. These brothers were born in Ireland in 1813, grew up in County Longford, and probably were twins. They were skilled, Owen a tailor and John a teamster. At mid-century Owen's household consisted of his wife, Ann, and their five U.S.-born children. John's household consisted of his wife, Mary, an Irish native of the same age, and their children, at least three of whom were born in the United States. Three more Dinnen families followed Owen and John to the spa by the beginning of the Great Hunger. They were headed by Hugh, James, and Michael, who came from the same Longford-Cavan counties and purchased plots adjacent to each other in Greenridge Cemetery.[11] Here is an example of the strong family ties of the first Irish settlers at the spa, who encouraged their relatives to migrate to the same place.

THE SECOND ERA, 1845–1860

The second era of Irish immigration involved those who came to the United States between 1845 and 1860 as a result the Great Hunger of 1845 to 1849. By 1845, young, single Catholic immigrants had come to dominate the exodus. Efforts were made to aid the Irish in reaching Albany, where 8 percent were of Irish birth in 1830; the Albany Irish population rose by 1855 to a peak of 40 percent, when they composed 60 percent of the paupers in the Albany Alms

House. Bishop McCloskey of Albany raised funds for victims of the Great Hunger, coordinating immigration with travel agents and government authorities to facilitate their arrival and settlement in the Albany area. The entire Albany area, including Saratoga Springs, became a magnet for the Irish. Even today, there are more residents of Irish descent than any other ethnic group in Saratoga Springs.[12] Thus by the late 1840s the spa's largest ethnic group had shifted from being Protestant Irish to being Catholic Irish.

The other notable characteristic of the Irish population in Saratoga Springs was the predominance of females; in 1850, there were 263 women, who made up 61 percent of the Irish population. If only adults were counted, that figure was even higher, pointing to a substantial surplus of women over men. This surplus was unusual. In other New York State communities, such as nearby Cohoes, males predominated or were at least equal in number to females.[13] Irish women were attracted to the spa at mid-century in exceptional numbers because they filled the resort's need for workers in domestic service, food preparation, and entertainment.

At the time of the Great Hunger, women immigrants probably outnumbered men 53 percent to 47 percent, although after the crisis their numbers evened out.[14] Still, the Irish were the only European immigrant group that was ever weighted in favor of women. Single Irish women or groups of them — often made up of sisters — arrived in North America with no relatives to depend on and the need to go immediately to work. Without skills they could not easily work in factories, but they could become domestics and laundresses, and it was this employment that brought them to Saratoga Springs.

We get an indication that the Irish women of Saratoga Springs were largely domestics when we look at their places of residence and their ages. Most of the single Irish women are found residing in middle-class households, hotels, or boarding houses, where it is likely they performed domestic duties. If we look at the ages of these live-in, single women, we see an unusual pattern for domestic workers. In the youngest category (and this included children) 60 percent worked, while in the twenties group, the percentage fell only slightly to 58 percent. Because two out of every five Irish women were in their twenties, this group provided the greatest number of resort workers. The youngest group ranked next in providing workers. In the two older categories, only 20 to 25 percent worked; this percentage was still much higher, however, than in other New York cities like Buffalo, where Irish women rarely worked beyond the age of twenty-one.[15] What is most striking about the resort, therefore, is that almost a quarter of older Saratoga women were still drawn from their homes to join their younger sisters as servants, washerwomen, and cooks. The resort business of Saratoga Springs could offer women employment not just in their youth but for much of their adult lives.

Typical of these single live-in women was Catherine McCarty, twenty-five years old at mid-century and residing in the American Hotel. She had emigrated from Ireland with her parents. Her extended family, headed by her father, Florence McCarty, recent immigrant and shoemaker, consisted of nine members, but only her parents and their one-and-a-half-year-old child, Angel, resided together; the rest boarded throughout the spa. The tradition of starting domestic service at a young age was strong among the spa's Irish community. In 1850, well-to-do families of such leaders as Rockwell Putnam or Reuben Hyde Walworth had teenage Irish servants. With marriage prospects in the Irish community dim, finding a good position in service must have been the best opportunity for a single Irish woman, and many chose to keep these positions into middle age. Thus Irish households were often small, with their families extended to reside and work throughout the village.

A decade later, the 1860 census showed continued growth in the Irish population, which outpaced the town's modest population increase in the 1850s. But the pattern of the Irish presence was not affected by the growth. Females still made up 61 percent of the native Irish population. A new category in the census revealed that a high percentage of Irish women were illiterate. Here also is the first indication of where women worked. Although 57 percent of Irish women listed no occupation, of those who did, 83 percent were servants. Washerwomen, cooks, and seamstresses were the remaining occupations, all of which were related to the resort economy. Irish women constituted 55 percent of the spa's servants and 64 percent of its washerwomen. U.S.-born servants were next in number at 28 percent, while blacks were a distant third at 7 percent. For an upstate New York community, this was an unusually high percentage for Irish servants and an unusually low number of blacks. In New York City in 1880, Irish servants constituted only 44 percent of domestics; the resort was thus exceptionally dependent on this ethnic group.[16]

On arrival in Saratoga Springs, Irish women and men were on the same social level as blacks, competing with them for jobs and often living in the same neighborhoods. White observers commented on the need of both ethnic groups for benevolent guidance: "The negro is something like the Irishman in his blundering good nature, his impulsiveness and improvidence, and he is like a child in having always had someone to think and act for him." Irish women did not accept such benevolence, and although they were at the bottom of the white social structure, they were able to take jobs from free blacks because blacks were completely outside the social structure. As early as 1830 in New York City, Irish domestics had come to outnumber black servants by more than three to one.[17]

This trend was even more pronounced in Saratoga Springs, where the number of black domestics declined throughout the nineteenth century. As a result of the competition between blacks and the Irish, only a few households brought them together. The exceptions were mostly live-in situations. In 1850, Dolley Corey, a fifty-six-year-old mulatto, headed a household that included Bridget Holton, a thirty-five-year-old Irish companion or domestic. Thomas Marvin's household had a thirty-year-old mulatto cook, Clarissa Evens, and four younger Irish domestics, Harriet, Mary Ann, Bridget, and Margaret Frazer, probably sisters. Ten years later, James Marvin's household had one black female and two Irish servants plus one black and one white laborer, both natives of New York.[18]

Residence in hotels brought the greatest numbers of Irish and blacks together. At mid-century the Congress Hall, the American Hotel, Union Hall, and the United States Hotel were the permanent residences of fifty Irish, forty-two women and eight men, and eighteen blacks, thirteen men and five women. Although at this time the hotel staffs evidently consisted chiefly of Irish women and black men, by 1860 blacks no longer boarded at hotels in such numbers, the buildings having become the almost exclusive home of Irish women and a few Irish men. The American Hotel now had ten Irish female boarders, all between the ages of seventeen and twenty-four except for one forty-year-old, and one Irish male of twenty-eight. There were no blacks at all. Increasingly, blacks lived in their own households and were a secondary factor in the servant market. The forty-six black women who claimed to be servants or washerwomen constituted only 7 percent of domestics, while more than half were Irish. Thus, as the number of blacks residing in hotels or working as servants declined, the number of Irish women rose to meet the demand.[19]

In contrast with Irish women in New York's industrial and commercial cities, Irish women in Saratoga Springs had a unique life cycle. The majority of Irish women in Saratoga remained single immigrants who lacked the support of a family structure at the spa, which explains why they continued to work as they grew older. Marriage did not draw young women off in Saratoga Springs to set up their own households as it did in Cohoes and Buffalo; only a minority of the spa's Irish women married. Because these single women regarded themselves as exiled and were still strongly tied to their families in Ireland, their chief aim was to earn quick cash that would pay for the passage of a sister or brother from Ireland rather than to save for a dowry that would attract a husband.[20] And employment as a domestic in Saratoga Springs had its advantages in this regard. There was always a market for white, English-speaking servants, so Irish girls could move around in the Saratoga labor market. During the season, Saratoga's hotel owners were forced to pay high wages to prevent domestics from moving from one establishment to another. The resort market for domestics, beyond the traditional live-in household work, meant that there was a greater demand for domestics in Saratoga Springs than in any other area community.

From their upbringing in the old country, Irish women regarded domestic service as a suitable position, for a lifetime if necessary. In the United States, however, the prevalent view was that domestic service was a demeaning and therefore only a temporary situation. In 1842, Catherine Beecher attributed the poor quality of U.S. domestic service to this situation and urged that efforts be made to make the field more honorable and professional, as in the British Isles.[21] Large Irish households and hotels in Ireland required chambermaids for bedrooms, housemaids for public rooms, nursery maids to mind children, and scullions or undercooks for the kitchen. Those Irish girls with experience in domestic service in their homeland were well trained, but they were the exception. Most girls came from the poor Irish countryside, without training in household duties.

Although domestics were needed to sustain the resort industry, bigotry against immigrants and Catholics remained widespread in the United States. Mistresses of private households constantly complained about the skills of Irish domestics. The personal relationship between mistress and servant always seemed to be betrayed, as Irish girls moved from one opportunity to the next.[22] Moreover, the Irish domestics were often described as dirty because they were brought up in dirt-floored farmhouses. Domestic work was also backbreaking and often health-threatening, and women usually sought an easier workload or avoided such burdens as they grew older. Furthermore, employers feared that Roman Catholic superstitions would infect their children, and mistresses fruitlessly attempted to convert their domestics to Protestantism.

A minority of Irish women came to the United States and the spa as married ladies with their husbands and children; these women had the advantages of being part of a family unit and being able to depend on their husbands. It must be remembered, however, that their marriages had been arranged, and the Irish dowry system caused them to be treated like closely guarded property. Irish women were reared to be docile and submissive, and after their children were raised and their older husband died, they experienced a frustrating widowhood.[23] This pattern continued even with their new life in the United States. As an example, Mary Dinnen was in her late twenties, twenty-one years her husband Hugh's junior, when they married in Cavan County. In 1843, she bore him a son, John. The family immigrated to the United States around 1846, with a daughter, Catherine, born that year. Eight-year-old John died at the spa in 1851. Hugh died five years later. He was clearly an exceptional Irish immigrant, a capitalistic merchant who owned land, supported an extended family, and was devoted to his church. Mary Dinnen was left a widow with the responsibility of providing for her family until her death almost thirty years later in 1884.

Julia Clair Flanigan also was a mother who outlived her entire family. She migrated with her husband, Thomas, to the United States in 1848 or 1849. By mid-century they had set up a household in Saratoga Springs. Born in Queens County, Leinster, between 1823 and 1826, she married Thomas a year before coming to the United States. Julia's husband was a blacksmith; with a partner he established a successful business at the spa and eventually became a community leader. Her principal roles were as a housekeeper and a mother. The family monument in Greenridge Cemetery is a record of tragedy. Although her first-born, John, lived to be an adult, dying at twenty-four, few of her children survived their early years. Eight other children were born between 1851 and 1866. Although all survived at least seven months, five of them died on or before their third birthdays. Of the three remaining, Ellen died in 1861, a bit beyond her tenth birthday; Margaret survived the longest to the age of thirty-four; and William, the last born, lived to be twenty-five. None of Julia's nine children outlived her, and only two of them outlived their father. Julia was widowed in 1882 and survived in this lonely state for another six years.

More easily than Irish women, Irish men in Saratoga Springs obtained nonresort jobs and became married heads of households. Irish families traditionally gave their sons every advantage over their daughters, and thus at the spa Irish males lived like their counterparts in cities. In Cohoes and Buffalo, for example, Irish males led lives not so different from those of the natives; their life cycle was almost identical, the chief differences being a matter of degree, for the Irishman held less property, rarely opened his household to boarders, and had a less secure job. Moreover, the spa's single Irish men made little attempt to marry the extensive pool of Irish women, instead marrying women of other backgrounds. By 1850, eighteen Irish men had married outside the Irish community, while only four of the numerous Irish women had been able to. The small number of single Irish men—a marriage pool of only forty-four—were usually boarders or helpers, living in the households of craftsmen, without the wherewithal to marry. Also, Irish-born male children outnumbered their female counterparts thirty-two to twenty-two, implying a favoring of males in emigration to the United States. Households of Irish immigrant families at the spa at mid-century usually consisted of parents and an eldest son born in Ireland, a continued sign of the exalted state of males in Irish family life.[24]

Both the 1850 and 1860 Saratoga censuses provide information about Irish male occupations and thus give an idea of the economic and social status of the households they headed, especially compared with those headed by women. In 1850 and 1860 more Irishmen claimed to be laborers than any other occupation, and there were probably more laborers than the 40 and 65 percent of men recorded respectively in those years. At mid-century, for instance, Jacob Pitney, the Baptist builder and hotel proprietor, had a household extended by three Irish males and a female between the ages of twenty-two and thirty.[25] Although no occupations were given for the males, it is likely they were laborers working for Pitney in his carpentry business, and the woman was doubtless the domestic for the hotel. As previously seen, there was work for unskilled laborers at the spa in the building trades or in the improvement of Congress Park or in the maintenance of hotel pleasure grounds.

Comparing Irish to African American men, the Irish participated in a greater variety of occupations, especially the more lucrative and prestigious, and they were less important in the resort business. Of the Irish in 1850, 48 percent were skilled craftsmen, 12 percent were semiskilled, and 20 percent were unskilled. The remaining 20 percent were in a category not open to blacks—namely, entrepreneurs, merchants, and grocers.[26] Although the Irish were thought of as being at the bottom of the social ladder, in fact, in Saratoga Springs they were found at all levels of society—a reflection of Ireland's varied religious, economic, and social conditions. Irish males were more skilled than blacks; many were tinsmiths, watchmakers, basket weavers, machinists, tailors, masons, carpenters, brickmakers, painters, wagon makers, butchers, and shoemakers. They competed with blacks for jobs as laborers, but they did not follow blacks into the semiskilled jobs in the hotel business. In contrast to black males, no Irish men were musicians, waiters, cooks, or barbers. The 1860 census mentions only one Irish servant and one Irish porter. Among the Irish, retailing and craft production were most important, with considerable participation in the building trades and a concentration in the resort's transportation business as teamsters, carters, blacksmiths, and railroad workers. In contrast to Irish women, Irish men played a minor role in the resort labor pool, few of them being employed in domestic service or entertainment.

Saratoga's Irish immigrant males had an additional advantage over Irish women: they were able to obtain the benefits of citizenship. By mid-century, Irish males were being integrated into the spa's political system and social organization. Of immigrants who became citizens in Saratoga County from 1820 to 1856, nearly all were males, and of the males 99 percent were from Great Britain and Ireland, the remainder being Germans.[27] Although separating Irish from English or Scottish immigrants is impossible, we can assume that the Irish were in the majority. Moreover, their citizenship made them active members of the Democratic Party, which was pro-immigrant; before the Civil War it accepted slavery as inevitable, thereby protecting the jobs of immigrants at the expense of slaves and free blacks. Participation in Democratic Party activities became an important vehicle for the Americanization for Irish males. Thus, Irish males had advantages over their sisters from the old country; they were able to marry into the native population, obtain citizenship and political clout, and gain better-paying employment that was not dependent on the seasonal resort business.

The institution that brought most Irish men and women together was the Catholic Church. Baptism, marriage, and the last rites were sacraments only the Church could administer, so its influence pervaded everyday life. A visiting priest, John Kelly, held the first Catholic mass in Saratoga Springs in 1834. By the late 1850s the Irish had a formal Catholic church,

St. Peter's, which provided the full educational and social services they had been familiar with in Ireland. In 1870, when Simon Flanigan, the wealthy ship agent, made his will, he gave sums not only St. Peter's, but to its priests and to the Sisters of St. Joseph's schools, with the remainder of his estate to be distributed among the poor of St. Peter's.[28] The church was now a formidable institution, ministering to Irish women and men and encouraging the growth of Catholic families.

THE THIRD ERA, 1861–1880

After 1860, the memories of the Great Hunger were distant, and the third era of Irish presence was one of consolidation: families were formed at the spa, and the Irish were increasingly integrated into the community. By 1875 the decline in the number of immigrants slowed Irish growth, so that they were a maturing portion of the community; late marriage and a high birthrate were now the competing factors in growth. On account of the attraction of resort work for Irish females, the Saratoga Springs Irish were three times as numerous as the Irish in nearby Ballston Spa, where they made up only 9 percent of the population.[29] As a result, the overall population in Saratoga Springs showed an unusual surplus of women and widows in contrast to industrial Ballston Spa. The Irish influx was the chief force in creating the surplus; the pattern of long-term domestic employment set resort communities apart.

In the 1860s, enough Irish families resided in a section of Saratoga Springs to form a neighborhood named for the capital of the old country, Dublin. With at least a quarter of the village's Irish families concentrated there, they became the leading if not the only ethnic group in the neighborhood.[30] Laid out by Judiah Ellsworth adjacent to the Putnam Burial Yard in 1838, the Dublin area consisted of inexpensive properties that came to be the site of compact Greek Revival houses. By 1850 the chief public building in the neighborhood was the Pitney House Hotel, which served as the pub and social center of the community. Here residents gathered in 1890 to form the spa's chapter of the Ancient Order of Hibernians.[31] Next to it was the home of Simon Flanigan, the village's unrivaled friend of and agent for Irish immigrants.

The Irish had a reputation for cherishing a house and land, in contrast to other immigrant groups. In another upstate New York community, Poughkeepsie, almost half the Irish owned a house in 1860.[32] Dublin's inexpensive lots and the modest houses on them attracted immigrants. Before houses were built, many an Irish family temporarily lived in a shanty. Typically they were small, one-room wooden huts seven feet high with a sloped roof. They could be identified among other outbuildings by their chimneys, which were needed for heat and cooking. (One of these houses survives in a backyard in Dublin at the corner of Franklin and Ash Streets.) One Dublin family was that of Jeremiah McCarty on Oak Street near the corner of Beekman. Born in Groom, County Limerick, Munster, in 1817, he had come to Saratoga Springs after mid-century, in the era of the Great Hunger. He practiced the trade of tailor and had another Dublin resident, Florence McCarty, shoemaker, for a relative. Florence, thirteen years Jeremiah's senior, had arrived in the spa with his wife, Bridget, a few years before Jeremiah and lived three houses away. Homeownership gave the Irish a stake in Saratoga, allowing them to marry and increase the size of their families. By the late 1880s, the Irish presence in Dublin was on the wane, as Italian families began to occupy their homes in the old neighborhood.[33] This trend would continue—a sign of the full integration of the Irish into the broader community.

Acceptance

The key element in the assimilation of the Irish within the community in the 1860s and 1870s was the well-to-do Catholic Irish. Their condition was different from that of the majority of the Irish found in Saratoga Springs. They were skilled, migrated as families, which were often extended by a common interest in a particular craft, and had a bit of capital. Overall, they were from the wealthy north and east of Ireland, not the subsistence potato plots of the western and southern provinces. Once settled at the spa, they prospered, and they served as the transitional element in the community, smoothing the way for less-fortunate Irish Catholics. They gained a place in Saratoga Springs and became community leaders.[34] In the Dinnen clan, John, with his skills as a teamster, was foreman of the Second Exempt Steamer Fire Company in 1877. Dinnen also had another interest, becoming a member in 1869 of the board of managers of the newly formed Saratoga Musical Association. Other Irish males had roles to play in the village's political, educational, and firefighting leadership. Thomas Flanigan, the blacksmith, was appointed in 1867 to the first Board of Education of the Saratoga Springs Union Free School District. Ten years later, Flanigan was president of the William B. White Volunteer Fire Company. Firefighting companies attracted Irish men, who made them their secret societies.

An indication of Irish strength is found in a sample of thirty native Irish men and women buried in the Catholic section of Greenridge Rural Cemetery between 1851 and 1890. Census information confirms that most came to the spa in the 1840s and 1850s, so their migration was a product of the Great Hunger. The fact that they were buried in Greenridge shows that they were integrated into the community's social hierarchy, willing to purchase a lot in the village's most prestigious and most Protestant burial place. Even then, the Catholic section of Greenridge was the least desirable spot, a stretch of level land divided into a monotonous grid of tiny plots, a great contrast to the picturesque nature of the rest of the cemetery. But, regardless of the bleakness of the section, Irish merchants and craftsmen were buried there in lots dominated by costly monuments. Simon Flanigan set aside $1,500 in his will to erect the section's tallest obelisk (Figure 60).[35] He and others who came from Ireland with their families had only minimal difficulty in becoming citizens. Except for their Catholicism, they were not typical Irish immigrants.

In the Civil War era, the family of Reuben Hyde Walworth came to exemplify the ultimate acceptance of Irish Catholicism. The chancellor of the Equity Court, Walworth was a Presbyterian and a temperance man; an Irish visitor in 1864 said that "he sticks as fast and as tight to Protestantism as Prometheus did to the mountain."[36] But his family, from his wife, Sarah Hardin, to his three children, including his son Mansfield, and even his black servant, Dolly, were Catholic converts. Their conversion was the result of the influence of his eldest son, Clarence, who converted from Episcopalianism to Catholicism in 1845 and four years later was ordained a priest. He went on to become a missionary and a founder of the Paulist Fathers Catholic order. With the exception of Reuben, the family's Catholicism endured; all the converts from Sarah to Clarence are buried in the Catholic section of Greenridge Cemetery. So accepted had Catholicism become by the 1860s that the Irish visitor could hint at the possibility that someday even the chancellor might become a Catholic.

Irish emigrants in the pre-1845 era came to the spa chiefly from Protestant Ulster and the Ascendancy Pale around Dublin rather than from the impoverished rural south and west. Peasants from the south and west became the most numerous Irish immigrants after 1845; they were able to take domestic positions from the native-born and black labor force and became a mainstay of the resort economy. Although most were the illiterate and unskilled Catholic daughters of peasant families, they worked diligently as live-ins or at hotels to earn the money necessary to bring additional family members to the United States. Saratoga Springs could not have managed its hotels without single Irish women, who remained in domestic service even into middle age. Because of the excess of single, young Irish women, there were not enough Irish men to court them, and therefore family development among the Irish community was delayed or did not happen. In the third era, after 1860, immigration slowed, and the growth of the Irish population depended on their ability to create homes. Irishmen were now accepted as businessmen, in volunteer organizations, and in village government. Homeownership in the Dublin neighborhood contributed to the Americanization of the resort's Irish. The transition was smoothed by the presence of well-to-do Catholic Irish from Ulster and the Pale, who helped immigrants get a start and find mates within Irish Catholic families. Yet their role was limited; the longevity of Irish women in domestic service was this ethnic group's chief contribution to the resort. From being a town mostly of Protestants, the spa grew to have a substantial Catholic Irish minority, which constituted its largest ethnic group. By 1880 the Catholic Irish would be fully integrated into the community.

If we look back on the rise of the spa's emerging service industry, it is evident that those who catered to visitors could not come together or move toward a working-class consciousness. Anti-Catholicism dominated the building trades, separating Protestant craftsmen and contractors from the largely wage-earning Irish. Blacks rivaled the Irish for the same resort positions. Social Darwinism—the application of the great naturalist's studies on birds and plants to human societies to justify the survival and progress of the "fittest" races—nurtured white racial superiority. Racial hostility distanced the Irish maid from the black teamster or the Indian basket maker. Alike, the Catholic Irish, African Americans, and, as we will see in the next chapter, Native Americans suffered from class prejudice and the religious bigotry of visitors and Saratogians. However, abolitionist literature gave blacks dignity, while other authors liberally applied the concept of the noble savage to Indians. The Irish, however, were on their own; few came forward to advocate their cause.

PART FOUR

Catering
to a
Diverse
Clientele

C H A P T E R   1 0

Native American Encampments as Tourist Attractions

ative Americans had exploited the Saratoga area for resources such as sturgeon and deer long before whites appeared. In the mid-eighteenth century, they also peacefully coexisted with whites, annually visiting the Saratoga area not only for game but to camp quietly near Hudson Valley settlements and sell wooden and deerskin crafts to the farming households. With the end of the War of 1812, they had ceased to be a military or political force in the Champlain-Hudson valleys, and gradually they faded into the background. By the middle of the nineteenth century, they were unknown to most whites in the eastern United States because they had been driven to the West or had been restricted to reservations or had retreated to isolated patches of land where they lived in poverty. At Saratoga Springs, however, Native Americans appeared annually in encampments, which provided Victorians with a rare opportunity to view a people who they felt were both respectfully exotic and innately savage.

The Need for a Native American Past

Although most U.S. communities ignored Indian land claims and perpetuated a myth that they were established on virgin territory, Saratoga Springs sought to have an Indian past. The springs appeared in novels set in the colonial period, such as *The Last of the Mohicans,* as the forested place where the chief characters first make their appearance; a spot where the "cooler vapors of the springs and fountains rose above their leafy heads" is a definite reference to Saratoga Springs.[1] Native Americans were needed to give credence to the medicinal value of the springs; the inference was that they had been using the springs since before whites came—that is, they had been taking the cure from time immemorial. To perpetuate the myth, when workers retubed High Rock Spring in 1866, promoters attributed the remains of platforms and tubing apparatus not to whites but to ancient Indians. In spring excavation, when definite evidence of Indian occupation failed to be uncovered by the workers, this lack of a Native American past was explained away by claiming that springs were a secret place, reserved only for Indians.[2] Thus the spa needed a Native American past in order to substantiate its claim that the springs had always had medicinal powers.

Confirmation of an Indian presence at the springs came from the pen of historian William Stone Jr. An admirer of eighteenth-century Mohawks, he had completed his father's biography of Sir William Johnson in 1865, which for the times treated Indians honorably, almost as though they were whites. Stone's knowledge of the Indians and of Johnson came from his father, William Stone Sr., who first introduced the possibility that Johnson had used Saratoga's mineral springs. This event would mark the beginning of the spa in most histories and was significant as a tale of cooperation between whites and Indians. According to the younger Stone, this process began in 1767, when the Mohawk's special affection for the ill Sir William Johnson "led them to communicate to him" about the Saratoga springs. He was carried to the springs in a litter by his fellow Mohawks. Johnson, "amid a wild and strange chant raised by the Indians to their Deity," entered a rude bark lodge by the springs; in "this primitive hotel reclined the first white man that had ever visited this Spring." After only four days of treatment at the spring, he was able to give up his litter and travel some of the way on foot to Schenectady.[3] Here we have a dash of early promotion mixed with a romantic concern to show Indians sharing their secrets with certain whites.

This often-repeated story of Johnson's visiting Saratoga's or more likely Ballston's springs is used to suggest that the Mohawks wished to control the springs as private property, reserving them for whom they chose. In fact, the Mohawks did not believe in the sanctity of property or hoard resources or place particular medicinal value on these springs. The person who believed in them was Stone's subject, Johnson himself, who was a European by birth and familiar with English spas such as Bath. The Mohawks valued the fish and game of the Saratoga area far more than the springs and also hoped that Johnson's presence would help them maintain their claim to the Saratoga region. For nineteenth-century Saratogians and promoters, however, the Johnson story became an ideal starting point for a history of the miraculous powers of the springs.

Thus, the existence of Indian camps at the spa was meant to confirm for Victorian visitors an Indian presence before whites arrived and found the springs. Promoters and authors established the Saratoga region as a center of Indian lore because of the continuous presence of Indians in the area. To the Indians, the encampments perpetuated their fading eighteenth-century ways and allowed them to ignore the problems they were having in coming to grips with Victorian society.

Visitors' Views of Native Americans

Most spa visitors, however, brought a different image of the Native American past. They had been indoctrinated with the idea of Indians as bloodthirsty devils whose barbarism stood in the way of the republic's manifest destiny. They remembered that the Indians in the Saratoga region had supported the British during the American Revolution. During the colonial wars and the Revolution, Indian raids and ambushes and their irregular style of warfare helped the British push back borders and take captives, successes that made whites both respect and fear them. This past was not forgotten in nineteenth-century histories and guidebooks, which reminded Victorian visitors of eighteenth-century Indian depredations against whites. Going against the trend of seeing the Mohawks as bloodthirsty was difficult and rare. One such effort was the 1838 biography of Joseph Brant by William Stone Sr., in which he took pains to dispel the negative reputation of the Mohawk chief. He treated Indians as human beings rather than portraying them as "cold, cruel, morose and revengeful." He defended their culture better than anyone in the nineteenth century, even to admiring the scalp lock as "an emblem of chivalry."[4]

But Stone's and his son's romantic views were in a minority, contending with a sea of hostility toward Indians.

One of the first attractions in the Saratoga area portrayed Native Americans in the destructive role of irrational savages. At nearby Fort Edward, a popular shrine that was developed around the personage of Jane McCrea featured only the barbarism of the Native American past. She was a heroine of the Saratoga Revolutionary frontier who had stayed to join her fiancé, a loyalist serving with Burgoyne's invading army. Her fiancé's own Indian auxiliaries, the very men who should have offered her safe passage to her fiancé, had cut her down. Historic sites, paintings, and finally a historical account magnified this incident for visitors out of all proportion to the event's actual importance.

By 1828, guidebooks began to popularize the sites associated with Jane McCrea; her grave was the object of intense romantic devotion.[5] A pine tree marked the earliest site; at a convenient nearby spring, the culprits reputedly covered her remains with brush and bushes. Her name was inscribed on the pine tree with the date 1777 and the words "no traveler passes this spot without spending a plaintive moment in contemplating the untimely fate of youth and loveliness." In fact, by eighteenth-century standards, Jane McCrea was a flawed heroine, a spinster without remarkable looks; but again poetic license prevailed over reality. The trip to the tree became a favorite excursion from Saratoga Springs, as it was only fifteen miles away. The message conveyed at the pine tree was that Indians were irrational, impossible to trust, and the source of fear among whites, especially helpless young women.

This impression is found in one of the earliest portrayals of the Jane McCrea story, a painting completed in France in 1804 by John Vanderlyn, a Kingston painter whom Henry Walton had patronized.[6] Entitled *The Death of Jane McCrea,* the painting depicts a helpless white woman, the personification of innocence, held and threatened by two fierce Indians. Although the Indian figures are as muscular and frozen as neoclassical statues, they are not so much heroic as brutish. In 1816, the painting was brought to New York City and exhibited at the American Academy of Fine Arts as the creation of an American artist portraying a supposedly heroic American subject. It was an immediate favorite and was much copied, which spread interest in seeing where the event took place (Figure 61). The emphasis on this incident in some of the nation's early artistic efforts perpetuated the idea that the "savage" was too irrational and bloodthirsty to coexist with whites.

In 1853, David Wilson, the Hudson Falls literary promoter of Solomon Northup, wrote and published *The Life of Jane McCrea* to serve as a guide to sites associated with her. Wilson's book summed up the tradition, offering nineteenth-century historical scholarship without divesting "the story of all the romantic interest which actually belongs to it."[7] He implies that Jane McCrea's fate was in the hands of savages, that neither Burgoyne nor her fiancé could control the Indians' innate savagery. Wilson uses the story to explain the misguided Burgoyne campaign. He describes a grand council of more than four hundred Mohawks, Algonquins, Caughnawagas, and Ottawas that Burgoyne convened on Lake Champlain for the expedition. There the British commander prepared them for the expedition, unaware of the force that he was unleashing. Burgoyne's fault, Wilson contends, was that he thought he could "restrain the ferocious spirit of the savage, within the limit of civilized humanity." Wilson plays to popular Protestant prejudices when he inserts that the Indian chiefs were "headed by a priest of Rome,"

FIGURE 61. Unidentified artist, after John Vanderlyn, *The Murder of Jane McCrea,* c. 1839. This picture was so popular that it was reproduced in numerous lithographs. Note that the term *Murder* had now replaced the more moderate *Death.* *(New York State Historical Association, Cooperstown, N.Y.)*

a reference to the mission Catholicism of many of Burgoyne's Indians. He offers a white view of the Indians' war dance as "imitating the act of scalping, of lying in ambush, the sudden attack, the struggle, the carnage and the victory." Although the chiefs promised Burgoyne to obey the laws of civilized war, including respect for civilians, in fact, "their ferocity was aroused as soon as their nostrils snuffed the first scent of blood." Burgoyne's early victories would be marred by "their butcheries"; and in the hour of his sorest need "they deserted him like cowards." Ultimately the rebels triumphed over Burgoyne, and Jane became "a sacrifice to the drooping spirit of Liberty."[8] In this way, Jane McCrea entered the lexicon of American heroines.

Another perspective treated Native Americans more sympathetically. The spa visitor Washington Irving contrasted their eighteenth-century independence with their deterioration in his own time. Irving's essays on "Traits of Indian Character" and "Philip of Pokanoket" were not nearly as popular with readers as folklore pieces like "Rip Van Winkle," but he was able to defend Native Americans' actions. He explained that Indians were not cowardly in war, that "the bravest warrior thinks it no disgrace to lurk in the silence" and triumph through his "superior craft and sagacity by which he has been enabled to surprise and destroy an enemy." As to Native American barbarity toward prisoners, Irving contended that captives were adopted into Indian families in the place of the slain and were treated as if they were relatives and friends; when adopted whites were offered the possibility of returning to their original homes, "they will often prefer to remain with their adopted brethren."[9]

Irving found Indians to be noble savages and portrayed them as a separate nation with simple virtues, corrupted by the spread of American civilization. After their dominating presence in the eighteenth-century Saratoga area, the status of Indians underwent considerable change. Irving felt that the closer Indians came to participating in American society, the more degraded they became. Irving admitted that the remains of the Indian nations could no longer hunt nonexistent game and that Native Americans were relegated to a life of starvation, poverty, and drunkenness. He noted, "The miserable hordes which infest the frontiers, and hung on the outskirts of settlements . . . are composed of degenerate beings," corrupted and enfeebled by the vices of white society, "without being benefitted by its civilization."[10] Irving concluded that Native Americans had suffered from exposure to American society, in which they now were socially at the bottom, along with blacks and poor whites.

From 1826, when Cooper published *The Last of the Mohicans,* he introduced readers and visitors to the idea of contrasting the noble and the bloodthirsty aspects of Indian life. As a boy in Cooperstown, Cooper had met the few Oneidas who camped in the surrounding woods and made baskets and brooms to sell in his village.[11] Like Irving, he found them to be dirty and degraded, not the kind of material he wanted for his novels. Later Cooper traveled to the western United States and saw the Pawnee and Sioux, whose warriors seemed to him to still have heroic qualities such as loftiness of bearing, gravity, courtesy, and boldness. These qualities were given to Chingachgook and Uncas in this novel; as the last of their tribe, they are noble and redeeming figures, even though they represented a cultural world different from Cooper's own. Still, he also needed villains to counter their nobility, and thus the bloodthirsty savage appeared. Played against Uncas is, Magua, the Huron, the savage with sinister motives who makes a sport of cruelty. Cooper explains Magua's motivations as based on the fact that the English had taken advantage of him by getting him drunk, while the rival French promised him a share of booty and captives. As a result, Magua turns on his abusive ally and seeks revenge by capturing an English woman, Cora, daughter of the commandant of Fort William Henry. In Cooper's work certain Indians, particularly the Hurons like Magua, with their ties to fanatical French Catholic missionaries, were more prone to be irrational savages than Mohicans like Uncas. Both aspects of Indian character continued to appear in the nineteenth-century literature that brought visitors to the area, and Irving's and Cooper's views of Native Americans were the most influential ones at the spa.

The Tradition of the Encampments

In contrast to the message of the Jane McCrea stories, where Native American were portrayed as feared warriors, the spa took a different direction by encouraging Indian encampments. One of the rare opportunities for easterners to see Native Americans firsthand was at Saratoga Springs or Caldwell, where each summer they arrived and established a camp. In both communities, the Indian encampments became an important feature of the tourist economy. The encamped Native Americans were an exotic relic of their early past, an object of pity because they had lost their land and power and an object of curiosity because they did not accept the industrialization that was sweeping the nation. Fashionable racism became a means of explaining both the failure of Native Americans to stem westward expansion in the nineteenth century and their stubborn resistance to Victorian values.

The practice of sending Native American hunting and fishing parties to camp in the Saratoga area predated white occupation. It was part of an annual cycle in which villages migrated there to gather the fish and game that would sustain them elsewhere over the long winter. Thus, from the Indian standpoint, the later Victorian encampments were a logical extension of their seventeenth- and eighteenth-century visits, a seasonal link in their life cycle. There was no need for Saratogians to ask the encampment Indians to move on in the fall, for of all the parties at the spa they understood the seasonal nature of the place, and they were prepared to leave before the winter set in, as they had been doing for centuries.

In the mid-eighteenth century, visits of River or Schaghticoke Indians to the white settlements around Albany had offered both Native Americans and whites opportunities for peaceful interaction in close proximity to each other. Anne Grant, a keen observer of the Native Americans at Schuyler Flatts, north of Albany, gives us a glimpse of a part of their life cycle.[12] In the summer, Indians erected their wigwams along the orchard in the Schuyler family compound at the Flatts. Contact was carried on between the women of the Schuyler family and their Indian counterparts. The Indian women and children made objects needed by white households. These included wooden baking trays, dishes, ladles, spoons, shovels and rakes, birch-bark brooms and containers, colorful baskets, ornamented deer-skin leggings, moccasins, belts, and garters. For these goods, white families bartered the milk, bread, and foodstuffs that sustained the Indian families through the summer. Meanwhile the braves went back and forth from the camp, catching the sturgeon and eels that abounded in the Hudson and smoking the meat to preserve it for the winter. The role of the Indian as a fisherman is expected, but as craftspeople Indian women had a business role; they provided the type of goods that would later be popular at the spa.

Native Americans in the Saratoga area were honored when they were still a political and military force to be cultivated. In eighteenth-century England, that bedrock of civilization from which Victorianism sprang, Native Americans were treated with generosity and esteem, welcomed into the best houses, and honored as noble savages and allies. In 1766 a concerned group of Stockbridge Indians sought the crown's protection for their lands from Massachusetts speculators by making a voyage to England.[13] They stayed in suburban London, where their every public movement became a social occasion, and the newspapers supplied the demand for information about them by publishing their social calendar. They enjoyed visiting English pleasure gardens such as Marybone Gardens and their favorite, Vauxhall Gardens, a privately owned park with landscaping, goldfish ponds, statues, promenades, gazebos, music pavilions, and boxes for listening to the concerts and for elegant dining. At the pleasure gardens, the Stockbridge Indians entertained the public by singing their warlike songs, and in turn they were honored with fireworks and given the choice of what entertainment was presented. Unofficially, the Indians became a featured attraction, drawing large crowds of people eager to see and learn about this exotic, primitive, and yet noble people. Thus it was in most civilized England that Native Americans had the earliest hint that they could be an attraction at a pleasure ground.

By the mid-nineteenth century, the motivation to display Indian culture was the dire poverty in which they lived on their reservations. Those who ran the schools at St. Regis blamed the poverty on truancy and hence on the lack of education Mohawk children received. They recognized that Indians had no time for school. "Nearly one-half of them are now absent from the reservation, some of them spending their time in the cities and villages of the United States and Canada, vending their trinkets, while others go far into the western and northern forests, in pursuit of game for manufacturing blankets and trinkets. Were it not for this roaming disposition, much more might be done in forwarding the education and moral interest of this unfortunate tribe."[14] Indians did not take easily to the ways of the white men, and the encampments offered them a better means of earning a living than did the schools.

In Saratoga Springs between 1840 and 1900, Native Americans erected wigwams and makeshift housing in order to spend the summer season on or near Broadway, selling their crafts and entertaining visitors by demonstrating their way of life (Figure 62). In 1856, a sedate visitor from Philadelphia commented that the Indian encampment, along with Congress Water and Saratoga Lake, were the highlights of a five-day sojourn.[15] Traditional handmade crafts, such as a three-cup sewing basket made from birch bark and incised with Indian motifs, were purchased by Victorian visitors (Figure 63). Newspaper engravings show that the Indian encampments fostered native traditions and thereby perpetuated elements of Native American

FIGURE 62. *Old Indian Encampment,* c. 1870. The encampments were an attraction that gave tourists a glimpse of Native American life, and they also provided a way for the Indians to obtain income by selling crafts and entertaining visitors.
Postcard Collection, Saratoga Room, Saratoga Springs Public Library, Saratoga Springs, N.Y.

Figure 63. Three-cup sewing basket, birch bark, Saratoga Springs, c. 1880.
Such Native American crafts were popular souvenirs.
(Author's collection.)

culture. Soon Indian families were as crucial to the tourist economy as Irish domestics or black musicians.

The encampments were similar to large outdoor markets. Instead of building and maintaining a shop for Indian goods, such as was done at the Indian Emporium on Goat Island, Niagara Falls, Saratoga left Native Americans to create their own booths and sell goods without a middleman.[16] The encampments required no buildings, the workers needed neither a wage nor housing, and thus the attractions were inexpensive to produce. They were an entity of their own, separate from Congress Park and the spa's other pleasure grounds, and their sites could be changed frequently. The earliest encampment, in the 1840s, was located on the west side of Broadway, just before the entrance to Congress Park. Later encampments were moved north to the pine grove on the west side of Broadway, near Chancellor Walworth's home. In the 1880s, according to Samantha, two encampments were operating at the same time. By the 1880s, besides the Native American craft shops, the encampments included fortune tellers, museums of curiosities, games of chance and skill, croquet grounds, photographic galleries, swings, and all manner of other diversions.[17] A decade later, another encampment developed at the southwest corner of Circular and Spring Streets; it consisted of a line of wooden booths, which housed a glass blower and a bowling alley.

The Composition of the Encampments

Historian William Stone Jr. described Saratoga's Indian encampments in the 1870s as being run by "so-called Indians," a diverse group that he noted was no longer limited to the descendants of eighteenth-century Mohawks. To his displeasure, he found three Indian groups in the

Saratoga encampments: "half and quarter breeds," with both white and black blood; French-Canadian Indians, who were in reality Caughnawagas; and true Mohawks. He felt that the true Mohawks were descended from Johnson's and Brant's Mohawks, who had migrated to Canada during the Revolution.[18] Although enlightened in his portrayal of Indians, Stone showed little grasp of the diverse cultural, religious, and racial conditions of the encampments. In fact, each of the three groups he identified, including his idealized Mohawks, was multicultural.

By the mid-nineteenth century, the Kayaderosseras was no longer the hunting ground of the "pure blooded" Mohawks whom Stone idealized. During the Revolutionary War, the Mohawks had sided with the British, serving with Burgoyne, and therefore were gradually expelled by the rebels from their homeland.[19] At the end of the war in 1783, the Mohawks had migrated to lands at the eastern end of Lake Ontario near Kingston or to the Grand River at the western end of the lake, or they had joined their Caughnawaga brothers at St. Regis.

It is doubtful that more than a handful of nineteenth-century Mohawks were in any sense pure-blooded. In the eighteenth century, the Mohawks had been amenable to the adoption of new tribal members. From the mid-century seventeenth century on, the tribe had suffered a drastic population decline, not only from the post-Revolution exodus to Canada but also as a result of contracting European diseases.[20] To replenish their population, the Mohawks encouraged the adoption of white, black, and Indian captives. Women and children were the favorite captives because they could be taken easily; and because they commanded less ransom, they were less likely to be exchanged. As Irving noted, the Indians systematically acculturated white captives to the point that they lost the desire to return to European civilization. By the end of the eighteenth century, the Mohawk adoption of captives had created a diverse Native American society.

The second and probably most numerous group of Indians discerned by Stone was the group he called the "French Canadians." In fact, they were Caughnawagas. By the nineteenth century, they came to the spa chiefly from the St. Regis Reservation. Although they were the kin of the Mohawks, their development was separate from that of the Native Americans in Mohawk Valley villages. The Caughnawagas were originally Mohawks and Oneidas whom the Jesuits and Canadian government had coaxed from the Mohawk Valley in 1667 and 1668 to live at missions around Montreal.[21] This Caughnawaga mission grew in the 1670s and 1680s by attracting Mohawks, including Kateri Tekakwitha, a Mohawk maiden of ecstatic piety, who after her death in 1680 would be recognized by the Catholic Church for her saintliness. Frustrating as it was to Protestant New Yorkers, the Caughnawaga Mohawks of the mission were genuinely devout Catholics.

To offset French influence over the Caughnawagas and to prevent the drain on the Mohawk population caused by the Canadian mission, New York's colonial governors had encouraged the Caughnawagas to return by offering them a Saratoga homeland.[22] This land in the Saratoga-Stillwater area was part of the traditional Mohawk hunting and fishing grounds, and the Mohawks had allowed the Caughnawagas to use it. However, despite the efforts of the British governors, the Caughnawagas could not be permanently attracted away from their Canadian mission.

The Caughnawagas came to play the role of intermediaries between Montreal and Albany. From 1699 until the French and Indian War, they were the middlemen in a lucrative trade in which Montreal received cheap and good-quality trade goods from Albany, while offering in exchange the furs that no longer appeared in the Hudson River city.[23] This trade was carried on despite growing hostility between England and France and the continual hostility of New Englanders toward French Canadians. The Caughnawagas therefore maintained ties with the Mohawks and the Saratoga area, but they remained securely in the French camp.

Although the Caughnawaga mission near Montreal still exists, a branch mission was established that became the St. Regis reservation, the chief source of Indians for the Saratoga encampments. St. Regis had been an Indian village as early as 1754, when the remaining Schaghticokes had migrated there from the Hoosic Valley. When the British conquered Montreal in 1760, Jesuit father Anthony Gordan led some Caughnawagas away from the original mission, which he felt was too close to the corrupting influence of the Protestant British and the alcoholic spirits available at Montreal.[24] They formed a new community at St. Regis, which was on what would become, in 1783, the New York–Canadian border. With their presence at St. Regis assured, the Caughnawagas were party to the Jay Treaty of 1794, which guaranteed Indians the right to cross the U.S.–Canadian border at will because the Native American tribes were sovereign nations. Two years later, the Caughnawagas sold all their land claims in New York State, including the Saratoga area, to the new state government. Thus, St. Regis Mohawks were mostly mission Caughnawagas with a strong Catholic faith and a French Canadian culture.

By the mid-nineteenth century, the St. Regis Reservation still covered land on both sides of the U.S.–Canadian border, and it was an important reservation for Caughnawagas and, to a lesser extent, Mohawks. Because of the influence of both Canada and the United States, during the War of 1812, inhabitants of the eleven-by-three-mile reservation split their loyalty between the Americans and the British.[25] St. Regis Mohawk Eleazer Williams, a descendant of a white captive from the Deerfield Raid of 1704, had grown up a Caughnawaga, was educated in New England, and supported the Americans. In the war, he served as a U.S. agent, commander of the U.S.-funded Corps of Observation. His influence and the rations he distributed helped to keep some St. Regis Indians on the U.S. side, although a majority favored the British. The Americans also failed at efforts to bribe Caughnawaga chiefs to keep their main mission near Montreal neutral. Warriors joined both sides, arousing suspicions about their loyalty. The Indians suffered most from Anglo-American restriction on their travel because they could not carry on their seasonal hunting and foraging expeditions.

By 1860 the St. Regis Indians numbered about one thousand, the greatest number of whom lived on the Canadian side. The Native Americans were increasing in numbers, but as a white reporter noted, they might have been even more populous had they not suffered "from filthy habits" of sanitation, which left them open to epidemics, such as the cholera outbreak of 1832. Because whites did not understand the Indian method of farming, their cultivation was regarded as "extremely slovenly and improvident." In addition, although there were two state-supported schools on the reservation, this reporter felt that they were "thinly attended" and "of little benefit."[26] He failed to see that the Indians did not have time for sustained education or intense cultivation because of a seasonal life cycle that included visits to the spa.

Stone identified the third Indian group within the Saratoga encampments as half-breeds, a term he used negatively, for he felt they represented the debasement of the Indian character. He overlooked the mixing of the races that began in the seventeenth century, which allowed many Native Americans to acquire both black and white blood. Interracial marriage between

Native Americans and African Americans was commonplace in mid-eighteenth century Albany County and in the Saratoga area. The Schuyler family had black slaves on their Old Saratoga estate; from the 1720s trade with Montreal led to miscegenation between Native Americans and the Schuylers' black slaves. Those of mixed race included the famed warrior Louis Cook, the son of an Abenaki mother and a black slave father.[27] Where black slavery was concentrated —in Old Saratoga, the Hoosic Valley, and Halfmoon—there were opportunities for black and Indian unions. Because Saratoga's type of slavery made it difficult for black couples to live in the same household and limited the supply of mates for black men, the seasonal visits of Native American families provided opportunities for black men to find wives. By the end of the century, many black-Indian families had been created by choice, invitation, and love—without racist commentary from eighteenth-century whites, who viewed such mingling as acceptable for the lower classes.

Early-nineteenth-century racism made Cooper hesitant to portray the mixing of races in *The Last of the Mohicans.* Although Hawkeye, a rare sensitive frontiersman, can be a "brother" to Indians who are the last of the Mohicans, Cora, Colonel Munro's daughter, has her options limited. A white with traces of black blood from her birth during her father's assignment in the West Indies, she rejects Magua and is attracted to Uncas's manly charms. Still, she conveniently dies along with Uncas to avoid the possibility of an amorous affair.[28] In deference to nineteenth-century sensibilities, Cooper's admiration for his Mohicans stopped short of his portraying interracial marriage. These inconsistencies neither affected the popularity of the novel nor reduced spa visitors' expectations of seeing in the encampments noble characters like Uncas or Chingachgook or even the contrasting Magua.

Such a mixture of blood was viewed as ideal for only one occupation: the fabled Adirondack guide, who from the mid-nineteenth century took visitors from the spa to these northern mountains, unquestionably the wildest part of the region. Most of these guides were from the St. Regis reservation and were trying to make a few extra dollars during the summer season; the going rate in the 1850s was a dollar a day per person. Indian families served visitors not only as guides but also as cooks and as camp organizers. City-bred whites assumed that because the guides were Indians who would deal with whites and who had an understanding of some of their ways, they must have the blood of both races.[29] The city folks proved this to their satisfaction by simply observing Indian facial features and skin color and then concluding that these Native American guides were half-breeds. Overall, the guide relationship was positive for both races: white men bragged about their wilderness experience when they returned to the city because they felt it was so authentic, and Native Americans used their traditional skills to earn badly needed cash.

Half-breeds residing in the spa area were not viewed so favorably. Saratogian Daniel Shepherd displayed conflicting attitudes toward Indians in a novel set at the springs in 1787; it was published in 1856 as *Saratoga: An Indian Tale of Frontier Life.*[30] He tried to present a noble view of Native Americans and yet found them to be alien and unpredictable, and he explained the contrast by stereotyping them as half-breeds. Shepherd's main Indian character, Indian Joe, is a half-breed, loyal and yet equally sinister. His features are those of an Indian, but he dresses like a white person and likes to associate with them. He is knowledgeable about medicine and is a crack shot with his rifle. Whites see Indian Joe as a lurking menace to the civilized folk attempting to settle the region. They accuse him of talking insolently like a "colored man," of being an "infernal sneak," and of letting his passions dominate his character. Yet if a white person were "on the right side of him, . . . he'll go through fire and water for you."[31] Here is the white stereotype of Native Americans: not totally savage, but alienated from the mainstream of white society, fit to live only with blacks or white misfits. Shepherd's message is similar to that of Stone: if the Indian's blood had only remained pure, noble values would dominate his character, and white society would have respected him. Shepherd and Stone viewed halfbreeds, personified by Indian Joe, as a debasement of the true Indian, when in fact the mixing of races was a vital part of the richness of Native American society. Stimulated by popular social Darwinism, white racism continued, and it would hinder the understanding of Native Americans for generations to come.

Native Americans Residing at the Spa

Shepherd's novel shows the Saratoga region's Native American community before the encampments existed. He aimed to portray "local peculiarities, arising in part from the various races of the settlers, partly from the different relations in which they stood to the Aborigines and partly from the character of the country itself." The novel describes the small number of Indians who remained in the Saratoga area after the Revolution. Most are shown as living an isolated or solitary life in a few wigwams next to their corn patches. Indian males are portrayed as "grouped together in lazy clusters, either dozing upon the ground, or sitting in sluggish silence, leading just the life of unoccupied animals." Doubtless, this characterization reflects their inability to hunt, fish, and make war as they had done in the past. Most of the Native Americans portrayed in the novel are individual males without family connections who are more active than those described above. Although they do not figure as characters, Indian women are viewed as more redeeming; they are recognized for their skill in "making or staining baskets, cooking their rude meals, hanging out strips of meat to dry, or working upon gayly-fringed moccasins."[32] Such skills would prove useful in attracting tourists when the encampments were established.

As the nineteenth century evolved, some Indians or mixed bloods accepted enough white culture to be able to live permanently in the Saratoga area, where they were often involved in the resort business. The cook Ann Hampton, whom the free black Solomon Northup married in 1829, was described by her husband as having "the blood of the three races in her veins." This had "given her a singular but pleasing expression, . . . resembling a quadroon," a term used for a mixture of mostly white and some Indian and black blood.[33] Unlike Stone or Shepherd, Northup reflected an African American attitude of pleasure regarding her mixed lineage. At the spa, Ann Hampton overcame prejudice by being industrious and talented; she succeeded in gaining employment with many white persons by showing traits not associated with Indians.

Another resort business figure, Peter Francis, a St. Regis half-breed who resided on the southwest shore of Saratoga Lake, became a renowned local guide.[34] Although illiterate, he was a frank and social person and a wonderful teller of tall tales. As a youngster, Andrew Berger had seen Francis's talent and employed him at the Sans Souci Hotel in Ballston Spa, where he was an expert in cooking fish in the French style. Francis made a living by serving as host, cook, and waiter to Saratoga Lake fishing parties consisting of the rich and famous. He died in 1874.

He had been content to live from the tourist trade, but he failed to become completely accul-turated to middle-class ways, for he kept his cash in his house rather than in a bank account.

What many Victorians experienced in their dealings with Indians was a matter more of culture than of blood. Some whites participated in the resort business by adopting a Native American life style, even if they failed to become members of a Native American village. These whites were considered oddities by the white community because they acted like Indians. Angeline Tubbs was one such white; she lived a solitary life outside of Saratoga Springs in an Indian-style wigwam.[35] She followed the Native American manner of making a living through a variety of trades, such as fortune teller, trapper, mendicant, and even occasionally thief. She plied her trades not only in the encampments but whenever she came to town. Tubbs claimed she was fifteen in 1777 when Burgoyne surrendered and had been a camp follower of the Brit-ish army. Once beautiful, by the 1820s she was regarded as a dark-haired sorceress, with sharp, sallow, wrinkled features, and a hooked nose. The butt of practical jokes, she was dressed in bloomers and paraded on Broadway by village fathers hostile to the radical women's move-ment that advocated wearing pants as a symbol of independence. Yet influential women such as Mrs. Rockwell Putnam and Madame Jumel sought her spiritual powers, and she became a

FIGURE 64. "He wuz one of the last left of his tribe"; an off-duty Native American at the encampments dressed like any white laborer.
(Frederick Opper, illustration for Marietta Holley, Samantha at Saratoga, *Philadelphia, 1887.)*

respected figure at revivalist camp meetings because of these supposed powers. She died in 1865, presumably at the age of 103. She represents those who lived the ways of their Native American sisters even though they apparently had no Indian blood.

White racist views kept Native Americans separate, players whose cultural distance made them at best an adjunct to white society. Angeline Tubbs shows us that Victorians regarded Native Americans as outsiders, losers, at the lower end of the social spectrum. When Samantha visited the spa she ran across an "Injun" away from the encampment, out of his eighteenth-century regalia, dressed in the shirt, pants, suspenders, and straw hat of a white laborer, no longer the type of exotic cultural icon that Victorians admired (Figure 64).[36] To Samantha, the country's manifest destiny made it inevitable that the values of Native Americans, part of the lowest strata of society, would be replaced by her middle-class values. At the spa Native Americans had come to have experiences similar to those of others of their class like widows, blacks, and the Irish.

Saratoga's entrepreneurs wanted an Indian encampment so that those who had read Cooper or knew of Jane McCrea or admired the noble character of Brant or Johnson would not be disappointed. Although Saratogians saw them as seasonal visitors, the Native Americans who participated in the Victorian encampments had occupied the area since before the time of contact with whites. In the eighteenth century, Native Americans had hunted, fished, and sold crafts to Saratoga's white families and participated in the wars in which they primarily sought captives. The Mohawks and Caughnawagas claimed the Saratoga area, but it was lost to them after the Revolution, when they were forced to sell their claim to the State of New York. In the nineteenth century, Native Americans coexisted in a few isolated places in the Saratoga area with outcast whites and blacks, at the bottom of the social ladder, or they resided among their own at the St. Regis Reservation. Yet, without their presence, the resort life at the spa would have been much diminished. Moreover, the encampments offered them a chance to practice their traditions and their crafts, activities that might have disappeared altogether under the onslaught of white civilization. Here was one the few moments in the nineteenth century when whites and Native Americans made peaceful and mutually rewarding contact, which could happen only at resorts like Saratoga Springs.

CHAPTER 11

Wickedness versus Pleasure
The Religious Solution

*I*n the late nineteenth century, Saratoga Springs had the reputation of being one of the country's most wicked cities, where the fabled mineral waters served as a mere chaser for champagne. The popular historian of Saratoga Springs, George Waller, makes much of this wickedness as the special ingredient in the spa's success. Still, sin had not been the only road to the spa's prosperity; in fact, religious conviction played an equal role in the growth of the spa. We need to be reminded that medieval European tourism was based on the religious pilgrimage, in which roads, signposts, hostels, and shrines were built to cater to those who felt that religious renewal was the chief aim of travel. From such a perspective it is possible to portray the spa as a "heavenly city"—the destination and home of God-fearing pilgrims.

The nature of nineteenth-century wickedness is revealed in a print, popular in the 1840s, which was found in a nineteenth-century Granville, Washington County, farmhouse. Entitled *The Tree of Life*, it symbolizes the state of religious belief in the Saratoga region by presenting two contrasting worlds: an earthly one of sin and possible redemption through gospel ministers and a heavenly "New Jerusalem" of bright order and assured redemption (Figure 65). The first world is shown to be the place of corrupt human nature. On the left of the print are the barren wastes of the devil, seen residing in a bottomless pit, flanked by loose women. Well-dressed men and women labeled "quacks," "usury," and "extortion" parade along "The Broadway," the main street of business activity, and, incidentally, the main street of Saratoga Springs. To the right, a couple drives a fine team of horses labeled "pride of life." Below them appear carousing dandies and their women, draped around a table laden with alcoholic spirits. Above there is a warning: "the end of these things is death"—a sentiment often echoed by temperance visitors to Saratoga Springs. The top section of the print portrays a much more serene heavenly city. It is readily accessible through a gate labeled "knock and it shall be opened." It represents a utopian community planned and executed by the hand of God, who has imposed urban order without diminishing the natural beauty of the countryside.[1] The print offered Saratogians planning and developing their community a choice between spiritual death or a heavenly utopia.

FIGURE 65. *The Tree of Life,* c. 1840,
E. B. & E. C. Keliogg, New York
and Hartford, Conn. This popular
conception of religious faith and the
pitfalls of maintaining it was found
in Washington County.
(Author's collection.)

Dissenters versus Episcopalians

This fundamental division between two worlds—one of earthly sin, the other of heavenly
order—appeared in New York's post-Revolutionary era as a division between evangelism and
the traditional, established churches.[2] These churches were associated with the gentry and
their way of life, which included permissive child rearing, open-house hospitality, the natural
acceptance of strong drink, a casual respect for the Sabbath, and a belief in the prerogatives of

a natural aristocracy. In New York State, the gentry could include only gentlemen who attended the Episcopal Church and in the post-Revolutionary era those who favored Federalist political principles. In contrast, there were the guilt-ridden and God-possessed dissenters, who in England had been Methodists but in the New York frontier were more likely to be Baptists. Their austere religion eschewed the refinements of the gentry in favor of solemn, silent fellowship. Their faith allowed them an escape from the realities of disease, debt, overindulgence, violence, and fear, which were common to ordinary people. Their religious practice involved a sharing of emotion that was distasteful to the gentry. To the Baptists, conversion was a decisive communal experience based on a deep feeling of fellowship. The idea of fellowship emphasized equality, rather than rank and precedence. These republican principles attracted the poor, the unlearned, and even blacks. Religious convictions thus produced divergent life styles and contrasting ideas of what it was to be sinful.

From the late eighteenth century, Presbyterians, Baptists, and Methodists on the Saratoga frontier were hostile to the established Anglican and new Episcopal churches, as well as to the Congregational Church in New England. They were regarded as established churches, for the colonial and the new republic's legislatures had recognized them as state-supported churches, and hence they received government funds. The dissenters were critical of liturgy and organization that had even the remotest association with the Roman Catholic Church, aspects that they disdainfully called "Popery." In post-Revolution New York, their particular object of scorn was the Episcopal Church, whose leaders had often been loyalists. They ignored the fact that Anglicans such as George Washington and Alexander Hamilton had supported the establishment of an independent American Episcopal Church, severed from the English monarchy. To dissenters, the elaborate Episcopal liturgy smacked of papal influence, urban sophistication, and aristocratic dominance, a combination that fostered luxury and sin rather than morality.

After the Revolution, the dissenting opposition kept the Episcopal Church on the defensive. Still, New York City's Trinity Episcopal Church, where Washington and Hamilton attended among more than one thousand communicants, remained wealthy and powerful and was determined to spread Episcopal churches on the New York frontier.[3] It was also the church of Hamilton's and Washington's political party, the Federalist, and thus their politics supported this church.

Among the members of Trinity Church, Henry Walton moved to Ballston in 1790. Two years later the lay preacher Ammi Rogers, Walton, and others erected Christ Episcopal Church a few miles from the Saratoga County courthouse, the first church to be built in the area.[4] Rogers was a Yale graduate who became a priest in 1794, after having been ordained a deacon of Trinity Church. Funding for Christ Church and for Rogers came directly from Trinity Church, an indication at this early date of the influence of New York City. After the Federalist defeat in the election of 1800, the party gave even more support to the establishment of traditional churches as a means of maintaining their political influence. They chose to support Presbyterian, Congregational, and especially Episcopal churches rather than those associated with the French Revolution's republican principles, like the Baptist church.

By 1800, the Ballston Episcopal church was coming into conflict with dissenting churches that were not about to relinquish the frontier to Papists. The new minister of the

Ballston Spa Baptist church, Elias Lee, challenged Ammi Rogers to a debate in the county courthouse on the merits of their theologies. Lee was schooled in the rights of man and the compatibility of reason with evangelical religion. He claimed to have found support for his arguments in a borrowed 1769 edition of Thomas De Laune's *A Plea for the Nonconformists,* which had mysteriously disappeared from the courtroom where he was using it, a circumstance that he blamed on Rogers. This book had been first published in England in 1683 as an attack on the Anglican Church by Baptist martyr Thomas De Laune, who had died in prison while writing it. The book had been republished often, including the 1769 New York edition, which aimed at preventing the establishment of an Anglican bishopric in that city and the surrounding counties. Lee had come to the Ballston Spa church from Connecticut in 1800; he would remain there as pastor for thirty years. His first action was to reprint De Laune, for which he raised a subscription from dissenters throughout the Saratoga region.[5] A determined preacher, Lee wanted to organize an opposition among dissenters to counteract Rogers's work and thus demonstrate the strength of dissent.

Rogers's reaction to Lee's threat to reprint De Laune's works was to write an article in the newspaper against it, claiming that the seventeenth-century Baptist was "lying malicious" and asserting that English dissenters had foolishly preserved copies of the book and sent it to their American compatriots. Rogers reasoned that the seventeenth-century English conditions of persecution for dissenters had subsided and that "parents' faults should not be forced upon their children."[6] He also condemned the Ballston printer William Child, a known Baptist sympathizer, who was turning out the new edition.

Regardless, Lee published an 1800 edition of De Laune's *Plea for the Nonconformists.* Printed at Child's office north of the courthouse, it was only the second book published in Saratoga County, a sign of the significance of the controversy. Lee's preface summed up the hostility of dissenters toward the expanding Episcopal Church. He argued that Episcopalians were inevitable monarchists, while Baptists were republicans or "friends of liberty." The monarchical and aristocratic portions of a mixed constitution, favored by the Episcopalians, tended "to overbalance the rights and liberties of the people." The head of the American Episcopal Church, Lee reasoned, was in reality the English monarch, who had the trappings of the Pope, a situation alien to American republican aspirations. The Episcopal clergy were, in fact, the monarch's allies, for they claimed to derive their powers through a type of divine right, the uninterrupted succession from St. Paul, also a Catholic saint. He asserted that Anglicans and American Episcopalians denied "the people under Christ to be the source of ecclesiastical authority," and therefore they must support "the divine right of kings and popish successions." Lee believed Episcopalians had a political agenda that threatened the young republic, but a dissenting minister like himself was the "servant of the people" because his congregations paid his wages and regulated the church.[7]

The French Revolution's religious free-thinking impressed Lee, who defended it against the Episcopal charge that it was caused by "infidelity and atheism." Instead he argued that it was inspired by religious millenarians, for "God has promised in his word . . . that the time was coming when the tyrannies of the earth shall be dissolved, and a system of politics should spread through the world in harmony with true religion and the rights of mankind." His vision was that of a political Second Coming, when dissenters with republican rights would overwhelm a corrupting monarchy and aristocracy, including by its very nature the Episcopal Church.[8] To the traditional sins shown in the Granville print, the Baptist had added a lack of republican virtue.

Lee was not totally moved by religious convictions, for 1800 was a year of political upheaval in which the Democratic-Republican Party drove the Federalist Party from office on both the state and the national level. In the election, the Federalist Party of Washington, Hamilton, and the current President John Adams was defeated by Jefferson. The Federalists were in trouble because they had initiated the Alien and Sedition Acts, which sought to muzzle criticism of the government in an attempt to protect the country from an impending war against Revolutionary France.[9] More important, the Federalists were seen as natural aristocrats who believed that government should be handled by men of property and gentility, who were often members of the Episcopal Church. The Republican party of Jefferson and Aaron Burr appealed to the more democratic and leveling instincts of the French Revolution, even though its founders admitted that the Revolution had gone too far. It was common for evangelical preachers to campaign for the Republicans by following an itinerant path, much as Baptist or Methodist ministers did in order to establish their churches. The Baptist and Methodist message appealed to less sophisticated farmers, so it was only logical that the message be mixed with the more democratic ideals of the Republicans. Because farmers largely settled the Saratoga region, Lee sought their support for his religious and political cause.

To support the reprint and to counteract Rogers's pastoral and Federalist convictions, Lee created a dissenting Republican organization. In this effort he gained the financial support of more than a thousand subscribers from throughout the region — as far north as the Adirondacks, as far east as Vermont, as far south and west as Schenectady.[10] This 1800 list of subscribers offers an indication of the strength of dissent in the towns of Saratoga Springs and Saratoga. It included leaders of the local Baptist, Presbyterian, and Dutch Reformed Churches. Andrew Sprague and Nathaniel and Gesham Saxton were trustees of the Saratoga Baptist Church in the 1790s. From 1796, Nathaniel's home had served as the meeting place for Baptists. Ziba Taylor would help to organize the First Presbyterian Church of Saratoga Springs in 1816. In 1794, he had settled above High Rock Spring, opening a store and dealing in lumber. Later he became a landowner and operator of mills on Loughberry Creek, which made him the Upper Village's leading businessman. By 1813 he was a judge of the county Court of Common Pleas. Reverend Samuel Smith was the pastor of the Dutch Reformed Church at Schuylerville from 1790 to 1800 and thus an influential dissenter. Also counted was John Cady, who had established a farm in 1780 at Cady Hill, to the southwest of Saratoga Springs, and Daniel Bull and Cyrel Carpenter, physicians. The most notable Saratoga Springs subscriber was tavern and boardinghouse owner Gideon Putnam, who threw his support to the dissenters and their Republican politics. Many subscribers, like Taylor, went on to become political leaders, to serve as militia officers, town clerks, justices of the peace, sheriffs, and tax collectors. These dissenting Republicans were a force to be reckoned with.

In 1817, the Ballston Episcopal church was moved to Ballston Spa. Three years later the rival Baptists also moved their church building from Ballston to Ballston Spa.[11] The Episcopal Church continued to develop with a sister church in nearby Burnt Hills. Like other Episcopal churches on the New York frontier, it was forced to modify its practices to meet the complaints of dissenters. In essence, the Episcopal church survived the Revolutionary War backlash by becoming more like a dissenting church.

Three decades after the De Laune controversy, an effort was finally made to establish an Episcopal church in Saratoga Springs. Such a church would seem to have been essential for attracting wealthy New Yorkers of that denomination; instead, however, there was delay. Walton encouraged the building of churches by offering free lots in prime locations near Broadway. To Walton's chagrin, the first churches erected were not Episcopal, but rather Presbyterian in 1816-1820 and Universalist in 1825. Not until October 1830 did a small Episcopalian chapel near Congress Spring become the center of the parish of Bethesda, its name evoking Christ's healing activities at the well in Biblical Bethesda.[12] But this early church could not afford a rector and had to depend on clergy from Burnt Hills and Ballston. Brought up in the Church of England, John Clarke joined Walton and worked for more than a decade to move the spa's Episcopalian church out of its missionary stage, giving the young church its first furnishings. By then the controversy between dissenters and Episcopalians had mellowed, and the emerging Roman Catholic Church became a far more obvious target of hostility. Still, the spa's Episcopal Church remained a fledgling institution, and the construction of its own building was delayed until the 1840s. The early split between Episcopalians and Baptists faded in the nineteenth century as more important issues, like temperance, revival, and the construction of great churches, brought the Protestant denominations together. Yet it remained latent and would have an effect on how spa society developed.

The Temperance Debate

In the nineteenth century, the consumption of alcoholic beverages was much higher than it is today.[13] It had risen rapidly after the American Revolution and reached a peak in the 1830s, paralleling the rise of Saratoga Springs to its position as the country's most prominent spa. Men consumed much less wine and about the same amount of beer as now, although the alcoholic content of beer in the nineteenth century was almost three times higher than it is today. The major difference lay in the consumption of spirits, which was four times what it is today. The result was an intake of absolute alcohol that was almost three times the current level. The effect is clearly seen in those nineteenth-century genre paintings that portrayed a wife with her child in the tavern urging her working-class husband to come home before he became drunk and spent all his pay. Conversely, those who partook claimed it did not impair their ability to work; in fact, they claimed that the conviviality it fostered among workingmen enhanced their ability to achieve.

The concept of drinking as sinful as opposed to being a pleasant complement to a meal is age-old, and the movement cut across social divisions, attracting many traditionalists as well as evangelicals. Some Federalist gentlemen like Stephen Van Rensselaer viewed temperance as a way to reform the lower classes and to reinforce the political power Federalists had lost at the ballot box through moral control; to set a good example gentlemen had to practice it themselves. Because temperance leaders were often manufacturers, their interest in the cause has been called "a capitalist plot" to maintain order and morality among their workers.[14] The broader temperance movement rapidly became diverse, as temperance leaders formed associations of voters to pass temperance laws that would turn communities like Saratoga Springs into godly cities. It seemed like a cause ideally suited for a community famous for its mineral springs. Ultimately, however, the issue of temperance would split rather than unify Saratoga Springs.

Temperance appeared in the Saratoga area in 1808, when a gathering was held in Moreau, ten miles north of Saratoga Springs, with the purpose of cleansing the body and soul through the adoption of temperance. Twenty men met at Captain Peter Mawney's licensed tavern to form the Union Temperance Society of Moreau and Northumberland, which was aimed at a membership that would "wholly abstain from all spiritual liquors."[15] A week later they had completed bylaws that prohibited members from taking drinks of rum, gin, brandy, whisky, or distilled spirits, except on the advice of a physician. Financial penalties enforced the policy and raised revenues for the cause. The bylaws did allow the consumption of the small amounts of alcohol in wine, beer, and cider. This was the young nation's earliest temperance society.

The elected officers were Sidney Berry, president; Ichabod Hawley, vice president; Billy J. Clark, secretary; and Thomas Thompson, treasurer. Both Berry and Hawley had signed the De Laune subscription eight years before, an indication of the connection between dissent and the temperance movement. Sidney Berry typified the respectable leaders of the local temperance movement. He was a wealthy slaveholder and Revolutionary War veteran from New Jersey who had settled in Northumberland after the war. He also became a county judge and then it's the county's first surrogate judge, and in 1791 he was elected to the State Assembly.[16] In 1811, his daughter married a twenty-five-year-old attorney, Esek Cowen, who would become a judge and leading citizen of Saratoga Springs. A year later Cowen joined the Temperance Society and became a conduit between the spa and the original temperance movement.

Less than a year after the formation of the Moreau temperance society, a second temperance society was established in Greenfield, northwest of Saratoga Springs. Its constitution prohibited the use of ardent spirits on all occasions, without medicinal or holiday exceptions, making the organization the first "thorough" total-abstinence society in the United States. Ultimately, in 1829, the members would take the radical position of total abstinence from anything that could intoxicate, thus eliminating even cider. The organization grew rapidly to a membership of 1,791, and in 1814 the society was the first in New York State to have a total-abstinence tract published. It aimed at eliminating drinking on holidays and public occasions, even though popular opinion felt it was acceptable at these times. To this end it held its meetings on the Fourth of July and George Washington's birthday to celebrate these anniversaries in a quiet manner.[17] Clearly, this organization was serious, not afraid to carry temperance principles to their logical conclusion. Temperance societies viewed the consumption of alcohol as a social ill that could be cured through community reform. While welcoming the support of churches, temperance followers were nondenominational, and the earliest meetings were actually held in taverns like Mawney's to show the secular nature of their effort. Ultimately it was neither the church nor the tavern that they sought to dominate; rather they advocated a political solution, rallying public opinion at the ballot box in support of laws that would abolish the sale of spirits.

Temperance leaders noted that New York State's licensing of taverns, including granting the right to sell spirits, had originally been relatively harmless. Soon, however, the meals and occasional sling or toddy gave way to harder spirits, which became the dominant sector of the business. From the taverns, drinking spread to the corner grocery stores. The impetus came during the War of 1812, when army contractors and sutlers supplied the troops defending Lake Champlain with cheap but potent spirits. When the war was over, the trade did not abate, and the state and local governments nurtured it by viewing it as matter of excise—a major source of tax revenue, ironically for the maintenance of poorhouses and penitentiaries, the very places for which the worst offenders were destined.[18] The prospect of tax revenues led to the liberal granting of licenses, which did, however, contain restrictions on behavior within the establishment.

Beginning in the 1820s and culminating in 1838, Saratoga Springs was a crucial battleground for temperance. The opposition to the temperance agenda was formidable, especially on Broadway. Businessmen, the leading retailers of liquor, were advocates of expansive licensing. These men were not manufacturers interested in maintaining order among their workers. To placate them, the village incorporators of 1826 were most liberal in issuing licenses for the sale of liquor. They immediately issued nine tavern licenses and legalized the sale of gallon jugs and liquor by the glass at twelve groceries. In the 1830s, at least seven grocery stores, one candy store, and one cigar store sold liquor.[19] These included the very reputable Broadway grocery of Miles Beach, constructed in 1814 and expanded to become the Post Office. Beach was not only the village's second postmaster but also a founder of the Presbyterian Church, a village trustee, a leading spa booster, and a friend of temperance leaders.

In 1829, the spa was described as the resort for men of pleasure, where "every other store, almost, was a dram-shop and intemperance was universal."[20] In practice, many retailers operated without even obtaining a village license. By the 1850s, in defiance of licensing laws, whiskey dens were dug in at the street corners and under village stores. Thus the sites of the trade were not just hotels, taverns, and restaurants but also a substantial portion of the retail stores and potentially any nook where an enterprising seller could set up shop. Dealers were united in the informal but powerful Liquor Sellers' Association, which claimed to have the good of the community at heart. It opposed prohibition and temperance by simply lobbying to leave village laws on the sale of spirits unchanged.

The inherent connection between the hotel and grocery trade and the sale of alcoholic spirits would prevent most of the spa's business leaders from supporting temperance. Licenses were issued annually in April and May by the village's Board of Trustees; the trustees were often hotel owners or retailers who regarded the sale of such beverages as a key to their success. The United States, Union Hall, Congress Hall, and Pavilion hotels purchased licenses in the 1840s.[21] Smaller establishments like B. J. Goldsmith's on Broadway specialized in fine groceries, wines, liquors, and cigars to supply "all the principal hotels in the town."[22] Goldsmith imported spirits directly from European houses, including famous champagnes, claret from J. Calvert & Co., and brandy from Hennessey & Co. With Goldsmith's and similar establishments supporting the tourist trade, the spa's leadership paid only passing attention to temperance. On leaving his post at the Presbyterian Church in 1829, Reverend Samuel Wipley lamented, "I labored hard in Saratoga Springs for nearly three years, but with very little success" in spreading temperance.[23]

True, a segment of the spa's business community found temperance to be compatible with profit. In the 1850s water-cure establishments recommended complete abstinence from spirits, advocating instead consumption of the village's famed mineral waters. Temperance hotels and boarding houses existed, although none of the largest establishments remained in this category for long. The Congress Hall Hotel was conducted as a temperance house by Joshua Collins for a limited time from 1846 to about 1850.[24] In temperance hotels, daily blessings, prayer meetings, sermons, and psalm singing were standard entertainment.

To overcome the Liquor Sellers' Association, the temperance movement had leaders among the clergy and prominent citizens. They included Reuben Hyde Walworth and Edward Cornelius Delavan, a seasonal resident of Ballston.[25] Walworth was a member of the First Presbyterian Church in Saratoga Springs when he became a total abstinence man. He was the first president of the New York State Temperance Society; later he would be president of the American Temperance Society. Delavan had made a fortune in the wine trade and in Albany land speculation, yet by the 1820s he was a temperance man and a founding member of the state society. At his estate near Ballston Center, he created a temperance community, where his tenants neither distilled grain for spirits nor turned apple juice into hard cider. These leaders believed that people were not innately corrupt, that large numbers of sinners could be converted and communities perfected. To achieve these goals they became evangelicals who supported temperance and religious revivals as a way of providing society with a measure of order and control. In 1835, Delavan and Walworth arranged to hold the National Temperance Convention in Saratoga Springs. During the convention, the spa briefly appeared to be a heavenly city on earth.

The third important temperance leader, Esek Cowen, led the battle for temperance after the 1835 convention. Three years later, he drafted a petition in favor of temperance and presented it to the village trustees. Sidney Berry's son-in-law was now a prominent village attorney of robust physique, standing something over six feet tall. Cowen claimed that his adherence to temperance from an early age had given him the robust health to grow so tall.[26] In the petition, the temperance community asked for repeal of the village's authority to grant licenses for the selling and drinking of spirits on the premises of a grocery store, although the document wisely stopped short of asking the same for hotels. The petition opposed these licenses on several accounts. To begin, already existing village statutes limited such sales to places that accommodated travelers. In addition, the sales created idleness, dissipation, and pressure on family budgets; increased the number of paupers and the taxes needed to support them; prevented a spirit of capitalistic enterprise that made the village an attractive place to settle; caused wives and children to suffer; and caused crime and had a demoralizing influence on youths. Finally, the majority of the spa's citizens opposed the sales and were willing to make up by private subscription any resulting loss in village revenue. This petition was the most serious effort to make Saratoga Springs into a heavenly city.

The village trustees who presumably read the petition were Thomas Marvin, president, Seth Covel, Runion Martin, Robert Gardner, and Washington Putnam.[27] The trustees met in Judge Marvin's office; as a partner in the United States Hotel, he had clear interests, and he had an ally in Washington Putnam, who had a similar connection to the Union Hall. Marvin and Putnam dominated trustees like Covel, a tinsmith, and Martin, a master carpenter. We do not know the trustees' personal opinions, but it can be surmised that Covel and Martin as craftsmen supported the use of spirits to cement working and social relationships. Cowen's petition failed to address the effect of temperance on tourism, although it did promise that crime would be reduced and that respectable individuals would be encouraged to settle in the spa. The attitude of the trustees on temperance must have been similar to that expressed in a local newspaper, which explained why Saratoga Springs could not accept temperance; it argued:

> This is a fashionable watering place. The crowds of strangers who come to Saratoga are from all quarters of the world. They know nothing of the laws and customs and regulations of the state. They have been in the habit of visiting other places where gaming and its kindred vices were tolerated and licensed by law. If when they arrive in the village they are told that all things are strictly prohibited — that they must attend church and live as quietly and temperantly as many of the New England villages, where strangers seldom or never go, . . . and if they are to be restricted by law in the enjoyment of their pastimes and pleasures, then they will be likely to bid us "good-bye," and go where there is less restraint upon their habits and manner of life.[28]

Essentially, the spa was not suited to such political reform because it had to be open to diverse pleasures and provide all forms of entertainment to retain its visitors.

The five village trustees set Cowen's petition aside and failed to act on it; as an alternative they encouraged a religious solution, offering the opportunity for temperance advocates to preach against drink. As a result, Lyman Beecher, the founder of the American Temperance Society in 1826, attracted crowds from the spa's pulpits; the community took this obligation seriously, for in the 1840s and 1850s it would erect monumental churches worthy of such preachers.[29] This, of course, was not the political solution desired by temperance leaders. Cowen's failure to convince the village trustees to limit licenses left the community as divided as ever.

Although the resort had excellent temperance chiefs, there were few Indians. The bulk of the resort workers were women of Irish dissent, who were unaffected by the movement. Walworth and Cowen were men of the bar; only Delavan actually employed numbers of workers. In 1842, there were finally enough followers in the village to form a division of the Sons of Temperance — a full seven years after the statewide convention. By 1850, temperance leaders had converted Oscar Granger, owner of the Saratoga area's largest glass-making factory, whose enterprises were staffed only by workers who took a temperance pledge. Judge William Hay added his pen to the temperance cause after moving to Saratoga Springs in 1840. He became the conscience of the movement by using his literary skills to praise Saratoga County's temperance effort in a history published in 1855.[30]

This was a crucial year because during it the New York State legislature passed a temperance law banning the sale of spirits throughout the state. However, this legislation was not the watershed it seemed; the law was repealed in less than two years, having been found unenforceable. Temperance leaders in Saratoga Springs blamed its failure and the failure of their earlier efforts on the village's leaders; they called these men "self-styled patriots and rich re-spectables" who were in reality rum sellers, lacking any respect for moral public opinion.[31] In fact, temperance began to fade as a political issue because of the rise of other concerns, such as the abolition of slavery. For the rest of the century, Saratoga Springs remained tolerant, avoiding a political solution to the temperance issue. In the 1890s, when Diamond Jim Brady came to town, he chose fresh-squeezed orange juice to accompany his epicurean meals, while for his friends there was a display of beer, wine, and spirits.[32] At the spa, the tastes of both Brady and his friends would be honored.

The Revival Sects

Attracting supporters of temperance were the newly established free-thinking sects, an alternative to the dissenting and Episcopal traditions. Taking advantage of the hostility between the dissenting and Episcopal churches, these sects attracted members because of the looseness of their doctrine and organization. Church buildings were not necessary for the free thinkers: assembly halls, temple groves, cemeteries, and natural beauty spots were acceptable sites for their worship services—which were, in fact, religious revivals. Dissenting churches had used these spiritual meetings as a way to enhance religious devotion, often where a church was failing or sinfulness was especially blatant. In the nineteenth century, however, revivals lost their denominational association, as they became open meetings for all, often reaching entire communities and reviving the spirit in every church in an area. In practice, revivals were detrimental to many established Presbyterian, Congregational, Methodist, and Baptist churches because they inspired congregations to change their denominational affiliation or even to associate with free-thinking religious groups.

The formula for a revival meeting was relatively simple.[33] Sometimes denominational authorities were asked by the local church to send a not necessarily ordained preacher to visit a community in order to conduct services that would renew religious conviction. Sometimes the revivalist came on his own, moved simply by the spirit to preach. Regular pastors stepped aside or shared their pulpits with the revivalist, who was willing to speak to several denominations. The itinerant revivalist held frequent and protracted services, well beyond the Sabbath. For best effect, he preferred an outdoor tent meeting, where the largest crowds could be gathered. To hold the crowd, eloquent speaking, singing, and other music were necessary. Speedy admission to the communion and the sacraments encouraged the commitment of as many onlookers as possible, even the young and uninstructed. If handled properly, a revival could reinforce the spiritual commitment of a church or community, but it could also reach a point of emotional excess, bringing a community to a standstill.

The earliest revival in the Saratoga Springs area dates from 1819–1820, when Reverend Asahel Nettleton, a thirty-five-year-old native of Connecticut and an ordained Presbyterian minister, held a series of meetings.[34] The Albany Presbytery had contracted with Nettleton to hold the revivals to help the pastors around Saratoga Springs. He posed no threat to existing ministers because of this contract. Nettleton was described as a subdued preacher of "old fashioned New England orthodoxy," a man of practical piety who may have lacked eloquence and manners but who offset these deficits by being a man of strong convictions. He began his mission in Saratoga Springs quietly because he was also seeking to improve his failing health. Nettleton found the village to be spiritually dead, especially during the tourist season, when he observed its social life to be a contrasting mixture of "coldness and gaiety." The newly formed and erected Presbyterian Church, the village's largest, had only twenty-two members, not much beyond those present when the church was organized in 1816. Nettleton chose to avoid preaching in the village's largest church; instead he picked a schoolhouse where in limited space he held a series of crowded services. He eventually produced eighty converts, a good beginning, he thought, to bolster the resort's Presbyterian Church and surrounding dissenting churches. Like the leaders of the temperance movement, however, Nettleton found his message was better received in the countryside than in Saratoga Springs. He was among the earliest revivalists to note Saratoga Springs's lack of religious ferment in contrast to the communities around it.[35] This condition would prevent Saratoga Springs from becoming a heavenly city.

The popularity of free-thinking threatened the dominance of both the dissenter and the Episcopal churches. The Granville print (Figure 65) of the heavenly and earthly cities offers help in understanding the popularity of the new sects. Here in visual form is their essence, a simple and direct relationship with Christ. In the earthly city two preachers are attracting crowds, but out in the open rather than in a church. The black-robed and collared clerics' message is clear; when one is asked, "What shall I do to be saved?" he responds, "Believe on the Lord Jesus Christ." This is the limit of the pastor's role; neither preacher leads a following to the heavenly gates. The role of the pastor as mediator between God and humans was reduced to that of helpmate; individuals could then follow their own conscience.

In Saratoga Springs an example of a free-thinking sect was the Universalists. They disagreed with the Calvinist concept of salvation only for God's elect, which dominated the Presbyterian and Congregational churches.[36] Universalist support came from those who were frustrated and confused by Calvinist doctrines such as predestination. They argued that the love of God was so inclusive that no person could avoid salvation, despite his or her willful sins. Theological concepts such as the trinity of Father, Son, and Holy Spirit were abandoned in favor of rational precepts. The Bible was the basis of their teaching, but it was to be interpreted by each individual, aided by unordained preachers who were often laymen or laywomen. The Universalist message was simple, democratic, and initially appealing to both rich and poor, free-thinking and evangelical. It was also anticlerical and antidogmatic, an alternative to both the dissenting and the Episcopal churches.

The Universalist Church was established at Saratoga Springs in 1824. The Universalists' intellectual approach drew booksellers like Beekman Huling and his son, Edmund, a newspaper publisher. As a free thinker, Edmund reflected the hostility of Universalists toward the emotional religious fervor of camp meetings. In his diary he called those attracted by the meetings "fanatics" and gleefully noted that a revivalist meeting had been broken up because liquor was being sold on the edge of it.[37] Yet the Universalists were also hostile to the formal beliefs of the established churches. The church appealed chiefly to working-class men and to intellectuals who reflected their social concerns. From Walton, the Universalists obtained a choice lot across from the Presbyterian Church near Broadway. Subscriptions covered the cost of the structure's brick walls, but the congregation had to borrow funds to complete the project. The carpenter tradesmen of the Huling family were the leaders of the effort, and they did much of

FIGURE 66. Universalist Church (popularly known as "the Brick Church"), Church Street,
Saratoga Springs. Completed in 1825. Membership in this free-thinking church, meant to embrace
a diversity of doctrines, waxed and then waned in Saratoga Springs between 1824 and 1858.
(Photo, Theodore Corbett.)

the carpentry work at their own expense. It was the community's first brick church, a permanent structure that stood in striking contrast to the impermanence of the revivalist tents.

Completed in 1825, the new church was a two-story, masonry Georgian structure, raised
on a stone foundation (Figure 66). It put the wood-frame churches in the spa area to shame. In
the countryside, where religion was stronger than in the village, it served as a model; a similarly designed stone Baptist church would be built a year later near Beekman Huling's farm in
Milton. Fenestration was the chief decoration of both buildings; in the spa church there were
windows along the front and rear, and eight windows along its west side. The three-bay facade
had two entrances, one for men and one for women. Inside the family unit was separated as
men occupied pews on one side while women sat on the other; there was a gallery on the second
floor for children. This arrangement prevented rich families from purchasing pews in prominent locations, so they could not overawe the congregation by their presence in front seats.
The roof was covered with wooden shakes, but there was no steeple such as that on the neighboring Presbyterian Church. The church was so commodious that in the 1830s and 1840s it
was used as a courtroom, when the crush of people on Chancellor Walworth's piazza became

too great. Among those attorneys who practiced law at the church were none other than Daniel Webster and William Kent.

Despite its commodious building, the Universalist congregation did not flourish. In the 1830s and 1840s, the congregation dwindled and the Huling family paid the mounting debts.[38] In addition, Beekman Huling found it difficult to keep a pastor for more than six months, although he offered candidates free room and board at his own house. By 1858, needed repairs and mounting debt forced the board of trustees to vote in favor of selling the building, and it was purchased for commercial purposes. During the thirty-four years in which it existed, the Universalist Church represented an alternative to traditional dissent, but its loose doctrines and equal attraction for both traditionalists and evangelicals made its survival precarious.

At the opposite theological extreme from Universalism was another popular spiritual movement, millenarianism. It contended that the second coming of Christ was imminent, a time when he would reign over a heavenly city on earth similar to the one portrayed in the Granville print. In the Saratoga area, Elias Lee had first endorsed a millenarianism inspired by the events of the French Revolution. The doctrine also had the support of one of the leading intellectuals and theologians of the region, Union College's president, Eliphalet Nott.[39] He preached at the spa and also served as a mentor for its college-educated. Nott was convinced that the world had to be readied for the millennial jubilee, the triumphant second coming of Christ. He supported the abolition of slavery, temperance, and educational reform in order to make the world fit for the reign of Christ on earth. Nott's intellectual millenarianism appealed principally to the well-educated, while economic catastrophes like the Panic of 1837 spurred a more popular millenarianism.

The Saratoga region's leading purveyor of these views, William Miller, technically only a Baptist lay preacher, began to preach in Washington County in the early 1830s.[40] He found the Bible's words to be the only source of salvation in a corrupt world, which included its prominent religious institutions. To him, it was unquestionable that sinful man was the creator of his plight and stood in need of redemption. Through his reading of the Bible, he concluded that salvation lay in the second coming of Christ. He attacked free-thinking denominations like the Universalists, who reacted by criticizing his calculations and his personal life, claiming that his theology was built on "sandy foundations." Caught up in revivals, he advocated temperance, condemned rum sellers, and claimed to have converted their shops into places of worship.

In 1832, Miller began speaking extensively and preaching the Second Advent.[41] He did not seek to create a separate church but rather to convey his views to other Christians and to lead them in revivals and prayer meetings. His book *Evidence from Scripture and History of the Second Coming of Christ* was published in 1836; in it he predicted that the second coming of Christ would occur around 1843. From 1832 to 1844, Miller lectured thirty-two hundred times throughout the Northeast, Saratoga Springs included. At the spa he developed a following, and these followers gathered in the Gideon Putnam Burial Ground in 1843 to await the second coming. When the event failed to materialize, Miller revised his Biblical calculations and predicted the second coming the following year, but his supporters again waited in vain. As a result Miller and his followers were expelled from the Baptist Church; Miller died in 1849, discredited because his predictions had failed to come true. A year before his death, Miller's

FIGURE 67. William Miller Chapel, Town of Hampton, Washington County, New York. Built 1848. Built a year before Miller's death on his farm, it commemorated the spot where his family had awaited the second coming. *(Photo, Philip Haggerty.)*

family built a small Greek Revival chapel on their Hampton farm, near the stone outcropping where they had awaited the second coming (Figure 67). Enough faithful followers remained to spread his word and eventually to create the Adventist Church. In sum, Miller's thought combined several popular spiritual causes: support of temperance, hostility to capitalistic practices, ambivalence toward the ordained clergy of the traditional churches, belief in the second coming. No one would accuse him of being a traditionalist; he stretched his Baptist background and carried its evangelical tenets to a logical conclusion.

The Building of Monumental Churches

The Baptists who expelled Miller were not above adopting ideas from free thinkers like him, of moving a degree of the emotion found under the revival tent into their sanctuaries. Dissenting and Episcopal churches in Saratoga Springs came together and began in the 1840s to create elegant houses of worship capable of holding crowds; the construction of these buildings made it unnecessary to rent lecture halls or hold outdoor tent meetings. These structures offered comforts not found under a tent, such as stoves to ward off the cold and cushioned seats. Elaborate Greek Revival or Gothic decorative elements helped demonstrate a denominational theology and drew an extensive membership that translated into financial security and power. When staffed by a series of distinguished preachers who visited the spa for the summer, the new churches became tourist attractions. The need to build substantial churches gave Saratoga Springs at last a skyline of steeples, the appearance of a heavenly city—even if firm religious convictions may have been lacking. These churches of varying styles would provide the spa with moral fiber, taking this burden from local government.

    The Saratoga region's earliest churches had been small and without benefit of a pastor. In the late eighteenth and early nineteenth centuries, churches were no more than crude log structures built by a public subscription of members or the patronage of a wealthy citizen.[42] When completed, most churches were without a pastor, the congregations often waiting several years before a preacher could be assigned. Part of the problem was support; although a few churches had glebes—land grants from the British crown that provided the income of a church —most depended on an annual subscription to cover the building's maintenance and a minister's salary. Therefore, a pastor's employment contracts were for short duration, and ministers were often directly dependent on their congregations for their livelihood. As a result, only young, untried, or retiring ministers could be permanently lured to places like early Saratoga Springs or Caldwell. Churches could only afford to share a minister cooperatively, and most congregations were conservative, unwilling to tolerate innovative theology. Thus, there was a rapid turnover of ministers, who looked forward to moving to better positions in the cities.

In the early years, religion did not appear to be a priority in Ballston Spa and Caldwell, and they lacked churches and preachers for visitors and citizens alike. Low had no interest in churches, and the Boston visitor Abby May complained in 1800 that there were no church bells on Sunday in Ballston Spa because no congregation had a building for services. In Caldwell, the only church was supported entirely by the landlord, who did not make its support a priority. James Caldwell established a Presbyterian congregation, but there was no permanent pastor until after his death in 1830, when William was able to secure Edwin Ball. His tenure was short, for in the mid-1830s the church held regular services only during the summer season. In the 1840s a schoolhouse-like church held a maximum of sixty for services. The summer preaching was evaluated by a Boston visitor as quite respectable; it followed the Episcopalian style, although the Caldwells were Presbyterians.[43] In practice, like other early churches, the Caldwells' church was nondenominational, the proprietors seeking merely to attract a decent pastor for the summer. Finally in 1855, after the death of William Caldwell, a substantial Greek Revival Presbyterian church was erected, a sign that the community was maturing from the days when it was dependent on its proprietary landlord.

It took a while for the chief dissenters in Saratoga Springs, the Baptists, to reach the point where they could support a major church. They had organized their earliest church in 1793, and three years later a log building was erected four miles south of the spa.[44] Another church followed in 1809 closer to the spa, but not until 1822 did the Reverend Francis Wayland erect a church on a Washington Street lot obtained from the heirs of Gideon Putnam, who had designated it for a church in 1813. These early churches were constructed of logs or wood frame; they were tiny and flimsy and scarcely reflected the growing power of the Baptist church. Finally, in 1855 the Baptists built an extensive church on the Washington Street site, which was now conveniently located between the United States and the Union Hall hotels, and the preaching offered there became a major spa attraction.[45] From that year on, Washington Street would take on the aspect of a miniature heavenly city in which visitors and citizens could partake of religion in respectable surroundings.

When completed, the First Baptist Church was the largest interior assembly space and brick structure in the village, rivaled only by the American Hotel. It was an example of the Greek Revival style, a republican classical design that was by then old-fashioned. The church's front recalled a Greek temple, as its facade was decorated with six pilasters that supported an entablature and pediment (Figure 68). The spaces between the pilasters were slightly recessed in the severe Greek Revival manner. In the front, window lintels and sills were of brownstone and the foundation was covered with the same material, while side windows had granite heads

FIGURE 68. First Baptist Church, 45 Washington Street, Saratoga Springs. Built 1855.
This monumental brick structure had seats for six hundred; the bell tower was so lofty
that the village trustees made it the official community timepiece.
(Photo, Philip Haggerty.)

and sills. A few decorative details showed the exuberance of the emerging Italianate style, especially the extended cornice and pediment supported by dentils and that style's hallmark, rudimentary brackets. An octagonal drum surmounted the whole on which rested the bell tower. In the tower, the highest in Saratoga Springs, the village trustees were allowed to place a clock mechanism so that the bell struck hourly. Thus the bell was at the service of the entire community, a circumstance that gave this church the greatest claim to being the community's meeting house.

One entered the Baptist Church through a lengthy vestibule, which contained three entrances to offices and Sunday School facilities, with stairways at either end. The sanctuary was actually on the second floor to symbolize the upper room in which Christ met his disciples for the Last Supper. Facing the sanctuary was a vestibule, and above it was a choir loft supported by a single cast-iron post. A brick load-bearing wall and eight massive vertical beams ensured support of the tower. The rear choir loft had a few plaster moldings decorated with acanthus leaves and rosettes; Gothic ribbed vaulting decorated the choir ceiling. The expansive sanctuary contained pews for six hundred people, making additional galleries unnecessary. The easily viewed altar was centered on the baptismal fount, whose decoration was limited to single Corinthian columns that supported a dentated entablature. The walls opened with six vertical windows on each side, an exceptionally large expanse of clear glass. Where the plaster-over-lath wall met the ceiling there were three sets of plaster moldings. Above the plain ceiling, hidden from the public, was a roofing system of suspending timbers that supported the tin roof, which covered the entire sanctuary. In the sanctuary, the emphasis was on the lines of free pews from which the faithful could easily view the altar, follow the service, and see and meet their brethren.

The other great dissenting-church building that appeared on Washington Street at mid-century was Methodist. At first the church was slow to gain converts at the spa, but in the 1850s it became the fastest expanding denomination. In the 1830s, the Methodists used a system of circuit preachers; they would appear for a Sunday service and after it was finished move on to another church, so that each small congregation could have the use of the preacher.[46] Moreover, Methodists were not above holding revivals, although of a more dignified nature than those of the free-thinking sects. Saratoga Springs was a stop in their Stillwater Circuit, but in 1829 the Methodist meeting was so weak that only two members turned out to meet the circuit preacher. Over the next decades, women would be attracted to the congregation in greater numbers than men, as the membership rose from fewer than 100 in 1841, to 320 by 1861, 420 by 1870, and 662 by 1878, making it the largest Protestant denomination.

Why were Saratogians so attracted to the Methodist Church in the 1850s and beyond? Unlike the Presbyterians and Congregationalists, the Methodists had done away with Calvin's doctrine of predestination, replacing it with the idea that people were not inherently sinful but instead had personal autonomy to attain salvation. Moreover, they ran their services like indoor revival meetings, numerous converts being made based on no more than their personal confession of faith. Furthermore, the symbolic communion of bread and grape juice was not restricted but was widely distributed to all believers. Women were especially drawn because they had a role to play at the church. Methodist marriages were a spiritualized union between two partners, without the constraints of old-fashioned patriarchal authority, and wives were given the responsibility of teaching their husbands and children to pray and to be Christian gentlemen and ladies.[47] Methodist women managed their households and ordered their domestic life with a concern for the piety they learned in church and were a major source of support for the Methodists' charitable activities. Such a church was appealing to Saratoga's growing middle class, who were not interested in denominational constraints but who were concerned to do good works within the community.

In 1841 the Methodists purchased a site on Washington Street from John Clarke for $1,000 and built their first substantial sanctuary, an effort that put them in dire financial straits; it took them twenty-four years to pay off the debt. However, the great popularity of the Methodist message eventually cleared their debt, and in 1871 they built a new church on the site, creating a structure to rival and even surpass the nearby Baptist sanctuary. It was dedicated in 1872; the total value of $125,000 put the church in a rarified league with the Town Hall and the Casino. The Methodists followed the Baptists in erecting a boxlike structure meant to hold as many of the faithful as possible in order to bring the feeling of the camp meeting and outdoor revival into the sanctuary. However, unlike the austere Baptist sanctuary, the Methodist Church was designed in the latest and most fashionable Gothic Victorian style; a rare style for the area, it had little in common with traditional Gothic or Greek Revival designs.[48] Various hues and textures of marble, granite, and limestone highlighted columns, capitals, and Gothic arches and gave the facade a polychrome effect (Figure 69). The bell tower surpassed even that of the Baptists in height and was of Germanic inspiration. The numerous pointed gothic openings in the facade were filled with stained glass to create an effect of splintered light. The sanctuary was the largest meeting space in the city, seating up to one thousand. In addition to the pews on the floor, the feature that gave the structure so much capacity was the extensive public balcony, which covered three sides of the building. The Methodists thus showed themselves to be open to all brethren in the most up-to-date fashion. In front, the altar was easily accessible, as Methodist theology demanded, while the pulpit and choir receded behind it. Breaking the surface of the plain walls, Gothic windows surrounded by wooden ribbing contained stained glass. Inspiration for the vast space derived from popular stick-style housing rather than from the soaring English Gothic style.

The First Baptist Church and the Methodist Church would dwarf a third church built across the street, Bethesda Episcopal. The concentration of the churches on Washington Street showed that Protestants had reached a degree of toleration, if not respect. As mentioned, Episcopal services had commenced at the spa in 1830, but no meeting place existed beyond a rustic chapel. The key figure in the establishment of a permanent church was Rockwell Putnam, who put aside his father's support of religious dissent. When in May 1841 the parish decided to plan for the erection of a permanent church, Henry Walton, John Clarke, and Rockwell Putnam each offered a choice lot as its site.[49] Walton's lot was in the grove on the east side of Broadway near his elegant Pavilion Hotel; Clarke presented a grove close to his Circular Street house; Putnam offered a site on Washington Street, where he lived, among the lots his family had already provided for the Baptist and Methodist churches. Ultimately opinion favored Putnam's Washington Street lot. The cost of $3,500 put the church in debt, but the vestry favored this location. Putnam actually had to move his house to a Broadway site to make way for the new building.

Bethesda Episcopal Church followed plans drawn by Richard Upjohn, a famous New York City architect and romantic, who dreamed of restoring medieval spiritual values.[50] An English cabinetmaker and craftsman who had come to United Stares in 1829, Upjohn had

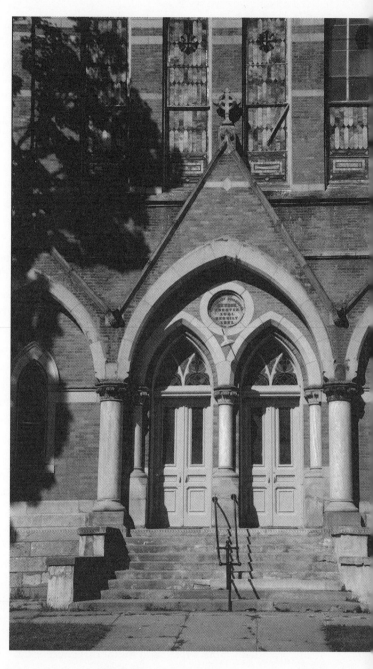

FIGURE 69. Main entrance,
Methodist Church, Washington
Street, Saratoga Springs.
Completed in 1872.
(Photo, Theodore Corbett.)

designed New York's Trinity Church in the traditional style of an English Gothic cathedral. Upjohn sandwiched in plans for Bethesda while working on Trinity, and thus the two structures are similar. Bethesda was built in Gothic style from 1842 to 1844, when the Baptists and Methodists had yet to build their grand churches (Figure 70). Bethesda's Roman Catholic and Anglican precedents created a sanctuary different from those of the nearby Baptist and Metho-

FIGURE 70. Bethesda Episcopal Church, Washington Street, Saratoga Springs. Built 1842–1844.
The church was erected according to a Gothic design of Richard Upjohn; the parish struggled
to pay for it, and it was not consecrated until 1866.
(Photo, Theodore Corbett.)

dist churches. Inside, an elaborate English-style hammer-beamed ceiling was its focal point, encouraging visitors to look upward toward a pointed ceiling that beckoned the heavens. In contrast, the altar, in English fashion, was distantly obscured from the faithful by the elaborate rail and transept arms and the deep choir. The aristocratic nature of the Episcopal Church was evident in the decision to keep the altar and the realm of the priesthood separate from the congregation.

From 1858 to 1861, in reaction to the size of the neighboring Baptist and Methodist churches, Bethesda was expanded to increase its modest seating capacity.[51] The walls of the nave between the tower and the transept arms were moved out and lined up with the outer wall of the transepts. However, the Episcopal hierarchy did not consecrate the church until October 1866, when it was finally free of debt. Clearly, financial and organizational concerns were paramount in the minds of the Episcopal hierarchy, in contrast to the spiritual fervor that had led to the erection of other Protestant churches.

The building of Bethesda Episcopal, the Methodist, and the First Baptist churches in close proximity did not bring an end to spiritual rivalry. Each church had a different architectural style to fit its theological, evangelical, and social mission. The fundamental division between the Episcopalians and the Baptists that had existed after the Revolution remained in a diluted form. It is seen in the writing of the Chancellor's son, spa native and novelist Mansfield Walworth. His *Lulu: A Tale of the National Hotel Poisoning*, published in New York City in

1863, portrays a community, "Tattletown," that resembles his hometown. It is divided between two sets, the Reds and the Blues, each representing contrasting religious and social values.[52] The Reds, of whom Mansfield is one, are for fine linen, brocade, silks, diamonds, turkey and oysters, dancing, whist, fun-loving activities, and, most notably, champagne and mint juleps. The Blues are for calico, plain black silks, cameo breastpins, veal pot pies and hasty pudding, the game of fox and geese, spiritual prayers, and most definitely tea parties and lemonade. Further divergence reveals the Reds providing charity for all the poor, while the Blues offer it only to the worthy poor, much as if it were an investment. The Blues are dissenters, hating the Pope, calling the Episcopal church "the nursery of popery," and referred to its priests as "jesuits." The Reds go to church but are tolerant of all faiths, even Catholicism. The Reds promenade in the evening; the Blues hide behind their window shutters. The Reds mind their own business, while the Blues mind everyone else's business. Overall there is a hint that the Reds are the descendants of New Yorkers, while Blues have their roots among New England puritans. The contrast is overdrawn, but it shows how the spa's Episcopalians and Baptists, with the Methodists falling somewhere in between, could still divide, as late as the Civil War era. Yet, both the Blues and Reds were part of the spa's social fabric, each group appealing to a segment of visitors — a division that made the spa's attractions as diverse as possible.

Did the building of the great churches benefit the development of the spa? The answer is unquestionably yes. The churches helped the spa by providing entertainment and relieved the village government of responsibility for setting moral standards. The early resorts lacked churches as amenities and suffered because they could not observe the Sabbath with proper services. The revival movement caused a temporary setback for the mainline churches, but they were able to combat it by building grand church structures that incorporated features that had been developed under the revival tent. Many visitors to the spa oriented their daily schedules around religious services and visits to these grand churches. For the middle class, religious uplift was a natural complement to the healthful uplift of the springs. Saratogians of both Red and Blue persuasions were willing to invest their limited resources in the building of churches and the placement of eloquent preachers in order to attract visitors and maintain moral standards. If there was a problem with drink, it would not be solved through village legislation. Forceful messages from the village's pulpits would curb the consumption of strong drink and would restrain the potential for the pauperism, crime, and disorder associated with strong drink. Thus the churches were encouraged to take on the role of moral arbiters, even to solving secular problems. On Washington Street, at least, the towers of a heavenly city were a reality by 1871.

Nineteenth-century sin took many forms, of which those seen in the Granville print were merely the most prominent. The consumption of alcohol was an obvious sin, but imposing the political solution of the temperance advocates was impossible for an open resort. Business interests and village trustees were unwilling to restrict licenses and instead established strong churches to provide the spa with moral fiber. Dealing with capitalistic greed, however, was better left to secular authorities, especially as churches sought to gain business support for their capital campaigns. Local government was better at restraining capitalism, as witnessed by the mechanics' lien law of 1857.

True, outsiders like Morrissey could sweep away the opposition to gambling by establishing a clubhouse more costly than the most monumental church. His Casino, however, catered to a narrow crowd, high-rolling gentlemen visitors, and it was off limits to the community's Reds and to the Blues. Ultimately, the community was religious, despite the loose division between traditionalists and evangelicals, and both these groups agreed on the need to provide religion for visitors. The resort did not embrace the wickedness that the press found everywhere. The spa partook of both heavenly and earthly cities, balancing the needs of the flesh with the desires of the spirit.

CHAPTER 12

Setting the Standards for Resort Society

N ineteenth-century social life at the resorts was a matter of tension between a high level of civility and an abundant amount of rudeness. Society lacked a set of rules to guide it and to smooth over the inevitable diversity of viewpoints. Morrissey had codified rules for the patrons of his Casino, but those rules were a matter of business and highly restrictive, not the kind of informal essence that would bring society together. A lesson could be learned from the example of England's Bath, where Beau Nash had provided crucial leadership to establish a degree of social unity. So effective was he, it was claimed when he retired from the position of master of ceremonies that society splintered, and Bath declined as a resort. To bring society together, resorts needed to be led by someone as powerful as Nash. White Sulphur Springs followed the English ideal of appointing a master of ceremonies, of whom Colonel William Pope of Alabama was the most renowned.[1] He established the Billing, Wooing, and Cooing Society, with its own constitution and membership list, which included seventeen hundred eligible young men. The constitution set down the rules for how respectable gentlemen should pursue ladies, and to be omitted from the list meant that one was unknown to southern society. The younger generation of males was thus regulated. The task at the Virginia spa, however, was easier than at Saratoga because the limited number of visitors in Virginia created a society that was intimate and closed to outsiders.

Leadership by a master of ceremonies failed to happen at Saratoga Springs. There society was diverse, and its public nature prevented anyone from controlling the agenda of social life. The spa's best potential master of ceremonies was Reuben Hyde Walworth. He had come to Saratoga Springs in 1823 as judge of the area circuit court, having already served in Washington as a congressman. In 1826, he bought Henry Walton's Pine Grove, a wood-frame Federal-style structure with four porches, an extensive garden, and a well-stocked woodhouse. It was the finest house on Broadway, a conducive place for summer entertainment. Walworth added lots to the property from 1827 to 1845, surrounding the house with orchards and woods. He drew the New York City literati to this expansive home. He became the Chancellor of New York's equity court in 1828.[2] After working in Albany from 1828 to 1833, he was able to move the court to Saratoga Springs, running it from his home or the nearby Universalist Church. His hospitality was renowned, and he was a great conversationalist, gamesman, and athlete, who would challenge his guests to jumping contests. He was the only local who was regarded as the social equal of Manhattan's old-money aristocrats.

Still, the Chancellor had limitations as a host, for he was unable to please all the guests who frequented his porches. Although in his early years he had stocked his house with wine and cider, as we have seen he later became a leading temperance man, taking a pledge to drink only cold water.[3] He made the Saratoga water famous by having it freshly scooped up for his guests, but many visitors found it impossible to be festive without spirits. He was also a firm Presbyterian who found it difficult to accept the popular religious enthusiasm that was sweeping neighboring communities or his own family's sudden conversion to Catholicism. Among his own peers, the attorneys and politicians of the courts and government, his legal methods at the Chancery Court were regarded as arbitrary and autocratic. Many of his colleagues were pleased to see his court abolished by the Constitution of 1848. Finally, Chancellor Walworth was aristocratic by nature and made no effort to organize community events or to entertain ordinary visitors. These negatives ensured that the Chancellor would not be Saratoga's Beau Nash.

For resorts to succeed socially, the ideal was to get reluctant guests to participate in social gatherings and to meet people from outside the social circles they enjoyed at home. This was not an easy task. Evidence shows that the number of attractive women visitors was limited, that among men backwoods hunting and fishing were favored over the grandest party, that the diversity of visitors caused confusion as to status, and that boredom was a pressing social problem. Although the middle class was soon the most numerous, they did not set social values at the resorts but rather emulated the values of their "betters," waiting to see how the fashionables would act. To remedy the situation, hotelkeepers, prominent New York City matrons, and an occasional physician sought to unify the visitors by providing them with a consensus on standards for manners, relationships, and entertainment. In this effort women played a most crucial role because they had the greatest stake in social rituals.

The Hotel Porch and Doctors as Social Arbiters

Hotelkeepers already exercised a degree of control over public access and decorum because they controlled the required hotel porch. A visitor in the late 1820s observed, "Saratoga is laid out in one long street, which has a most cheerful appearance; having columns and verandas, overgrown with woodbine, clematis, . . . the whole town is pleasing and gay."[4] These columns and verandas were a form of porch, a roofed space outside the main walls of a building. At its smallest, the porch was no more than a portico covering only the entrance to a building. In the Federal style of the early nineteenth century the porch seemed an afterthought. These porches were only one story in height, but they were landscaped along the front with lines of evergreens and ornamental trees, which were fenced to guide the visitor to the stairs. When the Greek Revival style followed toward the mid-nineteenth century, the porch cover was raised above the entire facade to create a temple front. A porch front comprising a triangular pediment supported by heavy freestanding columns was a main feature of Greek Revival architecture. However, the temple front did not provide an ideal sitting space because there was no room for chairs between the columns; thus the Greek Revival portico served mainly as a large formal entrance.

By mid-century, the porches of the spa's hotels had become more open and substantial, serving as important social space. They were called piazzas and were long, covered galleries with widely spaced columns supporting the roof, completely open for walking and social activities. Andrew Jackson Downing, who promoted the Italian word *piazza,* claimed that the piazza's quality of being partially closed and open related it to the natural environment. Piazzas extended not only across a building's front and sides but also along open courtyards in the center or rear. A veranda, such as the 1820s' visitor mentioned, was a continuous piazza, one covering more than two sides of a structure, designed for outdoor living in hot weather. Sitters were protected from the sun during the day and caught cool breezes at night. At the spa, hotels had to have a piazza or veranda to be socially successful. The ultimate porch had many levels; it rose from below the street and was carried to a second or even third story, thus covering the structure's facade (Figure 71).[5] In the rear, multilevel porches provided access to rooms. These porches appeared to be light and airy because they used decorative and slender cast-iron piers to support the overall wooden porch structure.

In contrast to the porches and terraces of English hotels, which were on the second floor and thus removed from public access, most spa porches were immediately accessible from the street. The fact that most porches were above the street level, however, created a partial barrier because a person had to navigate steep wooden stairs to reach them. Porches were ideal places for entertaining casual acquaintances because they did not require the formality necessary in

FIGURE 71. Broadway porch, Saratoga Springs. Built c. 1870. The earliest remaining two-tiered porch on Broadway, it was recently removed to meet building codes.
(Photo, Philip Haggerty)

parlors. They were perfect for gathering after meals and for making friends and alliances. Those sitting on the piazza were both in touch with and yet protected from the disorganized life of the sidewalk and street, a necessary balance when practicing the art of seeing and being seen. Porches also linked various parts of hotels, making it unnecessary to take a route through the hotel's interior. Overall, porches served both as a transition from the street to the hotel interior and as a barrier, beckoning those who belonged, but discouraging those who did not.

To get guests to navigate their porches and to meet people, hotelkeepers sponsored and regulated social events. They were eager to provide social events that would constantly fill the hotel's extensive public rooms. Efforts were made to cooperate with other hotels so that clients would meet new company, even if they preferred the restricted company of their own hotel. In 1823, the ladies at one Saratoga Springs hotel, the Pavilion, held a brilliant affair for "the ladies of Congress Hall." Five years later, a visitor commented, "The proprietors of these hotels take it by turns to give nightly balls; . . . and they enforce such excellent regulations, by turning any person out of the three houses [hotels], who misconducts himself in either, that although the company consists of all classes, very few quarrels take place."[6] In practice, hotel managers encouraged prominent ladies to volunteer to create fashionable and charitable events. These ranged from intimate affairs to amateur theatricals, which if held at the Town Hall might draw twelve hundred spectators. As the century progressed, such activities helped to create a semblance of social unity for the visitors at the various hotels.

Beyond hotelkeepers, doctors of every age and experience set rules at the spa. The rules chiefly involved health, but they overlapped with the requirements of social decorum. By the 1840s, male physicians such as R. L. Allen were intervening, warning women that an ambitious schedule of drinking the waters could be beneficial to only a few "Amazon belles." Instead, "judicious" drinking and bathing and limited exercise were recommended for a sex that supposedly was not accustomed to rising early, was not used to strenuous walking, possessed weak stomachs, and was regarded as having health that the doctor described as "feeble."[7] Allen felt that women's participation in the cure should also be limited because of their retiring personalities. Men, in contrast, could drink the waters in greater quantities. Such advice would have surprised many women fifty years earlier. In taking the waters, Victorian women faced new restrictions from advising physicians, who also ventured into offering opinions on manners, a field in which they had no expertise.

The Role of New York City Women

Despite the best efforts of hotelkeepers and doctors, as a whole male visitors, even though they were more numerous at the spa, had little interest in social relations or fashionable activities. Men deferred to women in matters of social decorum because they did not have to follow the rules as closely as did women. As the observer of New York society and novelist Edith Wharton put it, "Social tolerance was not dealt in the same measure to men and women." Men could go astray and be forgiven, while "the young women of their class . . . simply bowed to the ineluctable." Men wanted balls and dances, yet they did nothing to organize them. Men thought spas were boring; as early as 1806, Irving complained when Ballston Spa was dull, calling it "the slaughterhouse of time," yet men did nothing to remedy this situation.[8] To prevent the

spas from becoming boring, women had the duty of stimulating social activities. In allowing them to organize these functions, men were willing to spare no expense because women
planned occasions where the quality of dress was high, etiquette prevailed, and the fare was on
the exalted level of champagne, ice cream, and blancmange. Thus women were most influential in setting the spa's social standards.

The matrons of New York City were a dominant force in these social activities. In the
1840s, the old-money families of New York separated themselves from the newly rich or the
socially radical, keeping within a narrow circle of acquaintances that was maintained by subtle
distinctions.[9] Women were more concerned with the fine points of decorum because they were
the arbiters of them, especially exclusivity. Their outward gentility and patrician elegance often concealed a scheming, sneaky, meddlesome, and snobbish effort to elevate their own importance. They defined style. In the matter of dress, clothes were to be somber although of rich
material. Entertainment was at home rather than in public places, and alliances were made only
between old families, who abhorred the new rich or the intellectual crowd. These informal but
obsessively adhered to standards of conduct created a New York society where malicious gossip determined social rank and boredom was an expected burden.

New York's social life boiled down to a monotonous round of private dinners and balls,
nights at the now acceptable opera, and visits to each others' house. Even young men were
restricted, forbidden, according to Wharton, from "horse-racing, and running down south to
those d—d Springs, and gambling at New Orleans." Going out, especially for women, was
restricted. The paterfamiliases still did the shopping in these leading families, women fearing
to promenade or even window-shop without a male escort. This remained the norm until
the 1890s, when the establishment of elegant shopping districts such as "Ladies Mile," along
Broadway from Fourteenth Street to Twenty-third Street, at last allowed women to walk on
their own.[10]

Admission to New York society was not specifically codified, and yet the women who already shared the distinction firmly controlled it. The chief requirement was to possess "old
money," wealth that had been in the family for a generation.[11] Admission to society resembled
the model set by European aristocracy in that it was hereditary. The process of admission included sending sons to the right boarding schools, giving daughters the most advantageous
marriage, and summering at a place that had the most social distinction. Newcomers had to
go through a time-consuming ordeal meant to make certain that a family's fortune was intact
because the volatile economy caused fortunes to be unmade as quickly as made. Along the way,
established matrons tested the candidates and kept them on their toes. Effective and venom-
ous techniques included the public cut, social exile, and the rigors of betrothal and marriage.
These rituals at the spa were carried on with a vengeance because society from the rest of the
country was present to watch.

New Yorkers made up the majority of spa visitors. They are often portrayed as artists
and entertainers, the creators of a flamboyant summer social life, but clearly this was not the
society that old-money matrons frequented. In reality, Manhattan was divided into several social groups. There were the literary and theater types such as Catharine Maria Sedgwick, the
newly rich entrepreneurs like Madame Jumel, and members of the old-money families like
Catherine Clinton. Saratoga Springs was not the type of resort where the closed society of the

old New Yorkers could flourish. At this spa everyone was on display, social democracy was rampant, and the newly rich continued to be drawn, making up for the defection of some old-money families to Newport.

De Witt Clinton's widow, Catherine Jones, remained a social leader and continued to come to Saratoga Springs after his death. Her position in New York society depended on Clinton, twice mayor of New York City, candidate for the presidency of the United States in 1812, and governor of New York until his premature death in 1828. At the spa, she practiced the "cut," establishing it as an instrument of the social scene. She was a woman of some education, talent, and breeding; her family of physicians included a grandfather who had been a surgeon to George Washington during the Revolutionary War and a father who was one of New York City's leading doctors.[12] She continued to be antagonistic toward her husband's political rivals, especially President Martin Van Buren. This hostile attitude carried over to Saratoga Springs, where in 1839, according to Philip Hone, she cut the president at a reception in the United States Hotel ballroom by scornfully turning her back on him. Hone described Mrs. Clinton as a woman of "a great many airs," whose insult was "a piece of rudeness, . . . not . . . justified by any person whom I have heard speak of it."[13] The incident got to the New York press and was portrayed in a cartoon (Figure 72).

Families with newly made fortunes were also victims of the distinctions that women like Mrs. Clinton maintained. Despite their wealth and breeding, some New Yorkers who visited the spas were never accepted by her or her society. One such lady was Eliza Bowen, Madame Jumel. She was an exceptionally wealthy New York visitor, but her scandalous past and her extravagance prevented her from being a member of high society. Visiting the spa annually from the 1820s to the 1850s, she was among the first summer residents to take an interest in the spa's real estate, and she was the first to build a summer cottage on her land, which was a small estate. In 1832, she purchased twenty acres from innkeeper Jose Villalase of Saratoga Springs in a prime location on the newly laid out Circular Street.[14] Seven years later, she acquired adjacent land, including the Circular Street house of John Hodgman, using Nelson Chase as her agent. Her Greek Revival farmhouse was constructed in the early 1830s and was a smaller version of the home of Circular Street developer John Clarke (Figure 73). It became her cottage and was maintained year-round by black servants, who prepared it for her annual visit. In 1832, Madame Jumel's first visit to her completed home not only was for pleasure but also was an escape from the cholera epidemic that was sweeping New York City and the rest of the state. Her adopted niece, Mary Marilla Chase, and her two children were frequent visitors at the cottage. Yet, Madame Jumel never spent her entire time at the cottage; in New York fashion, she often took her meals on Broadway at the United States Hotel.

In New York City, Madame Jumel controlled a real estate empire, yet she preferred to reside at the city's finest hotel, the Astor House. She attended church and at her death left substantial sums to charities, including the Association for the Relief of Respectable Aged Indigent Females.[15] But she was never acceptable in polite society because of her disreputable background. After failing as a housemaid, young Eliza, like her mother, had drifted toward prostitution. Becoming the mistress of a Providence sea captain saved her from her mother's fate, for he took her to New York City, where he set her up in style. Her marriages to Jumel and to Aaron Burr—the once vice president of the United States, but by consensus a most unsavory

FIGURE 72. "The Direct Cut." This cartoon of Catherine Jones Clinton snubbing Martin Van Buren,
president of the United States, illustrates a use of social prerogative at Saratoga Springs.
(Found in George Waller, Saratoga, Saga of an Imperious Era, New York, 1966, 106.)

fellow—did not enhance her reputation. Despite her wealth, she could make no better match
for her niece than Chase, a Cherry Valley law student. Her religious devoutness and good
business sense were not enough to endear her to the women who dominated New York's old-
money society, and they cruelly ostracized her. To them she dressed too extravagantly, spent
money too freely, and resided too often in hotels rather than her own home. Saratogians aped
the elite New Yorkers, accepting their judgment of her conduct. When Madame Jumel rode to
the United States Hotel in the finest equipage, they made mimicked her, rather than respect-
ing her wealth. This ridicule and her inability to travel reduced her desire to return to the spa,
and she was there less frequently in the 1850s.

Other influential New York women ignored the practice of rigid social distinctions except to criticize their cruel excesses, especially in courting techniques. Catharine Maria Sedgwick, a novelist, had been introduced to Saratoga Springs by her eldest brother, Theodore

FIGURE 73. Madame Jumel Cottage, 129 Circular Street, Saratoga Springs. Built 1832. The Greek
Revival house stood at the edge of the village when it was constructed as the spa's first summer home.
This extravagance set the lady apart from the rest of New York City society.
(Photo, Theodore Corbett.)

Sedgwick Jr., an Albany attorney, who had been the first of his family to frequent the spa because of his ill health and forced retirement (Figure 74). Visits to Saratoga Springs helped to
advance the sales of her books, and in July 1827, at the age of thirty-eight, she was feted at the
spa because her novel *Hope Leslie* was rivaling Cooper's books in sales and attention. She and
her brothers became annual visitors to the spa and brought friends such as James Kirke Paulding. She was a native of the Berkshire Mountains in Massachusetts and kept a home in Lenox,
near Stockbridge, but she also spent much of her time with her brothers in Albany and New
York City.[16] At an early age, she had decided not to marry, a position in life that she rigorously
defended in print as allowing for happiness. Sedgwick enjoyed the social whirl at the spa with
the support of her four brothers, all attorneys, who saw the spa as a place to advance her literary career and their own interests in writing and publishing. Charles was a modest Berkshire
attorney, while Robert and Henry were in the thick of New York City's affairs, combining their
literary interests with Unitarian religious convictions. Robert and Henry introduced their sister to New York's literary circles, pushed to have her first novels published, and encouraged
her to promote the books by travels that in 1839 took her to England.

The upper crust of New York society regarded Sedgwick as an oddity. Her position was
an extreme one, for spinsterhood was not the acceptable norm that marriage was. Sedgwick

FIGURE 74. Auguste Edouart, *Miss Catharine Maria Sedgwick of Stockbridge (Saratoga Springs 16th August. 1842)*. Sedgwick was the leading female novelist of the age; she chose to remain a spinster and yet was a respected member of literary society in New York City and Saratoga Springs. *(From* Auguste Edouart's Silhouettes of Eminent Americans, 1839–1844, *ed. Andrew Oliver, Charlottesville, Va., 1977, 141.)*

was a free-thinking bluestocking who followed her brothers enthusiastically into the enlightened Unitarian Society of New York. She was at pains to separate herself from Puritans because their "bigotry, their superstition, and above all, their intolerance, were too apparent on the page of history to be forgotten. . . . They were still in the thraldom of Judaic superstition, and adhered steadfastly, as unhappily a majority of their descendants do, to Calvin's gloomy interpretation of the Scripture, even now popular dogmas in our enlightened country." In 1848, she delineated the contrast between the Puritanism of her native Massachusetts and the openness of New York City. "My Sundays are not days of rest [in New York City]. I wish you would recommend to those enlightened Bostonians who are on the ultra pinnacle, and wish to abrogate the restrictive institution of the Sabbath, to take a walk along Anthony and Orange Streets . . . in New York, and see it virtually annulled, all the shops open, and apparently no recollection of this old abuse of man's precious liberty."[17] Thus her attitudes firmly aligned her with the Saratoga Springs Reds, although she was not especially fond of the spa's excessive emphasis on fashion, considering it to be a major obstacle to human happiness.

Easing Women's Conduct: The Rise of Confidence

To an extent, resorts, especially in their early years, eased the rigid social decorum that Mrs. Clinton personified. Parental control over children was less strict at the spas than at home. A father usually could not stay at the resort for the season, the demands of business allowing for only periodic appearances. Although mothers regarded it as mandatory to pack their daughters off to Saratoga for the entire season, they themselves were often unable to reside at the spa for that span of time. The rules of chaperoning were less rigorous at the spas than at home. At Ballston Spa from May to August 1800, a twenty-four-year-old resident of Boston, Abigail May, kept a diary featuring her social experiences. She was at first well-chaperoned, but as her stay wore on she was increasingly left on her own. She had arrived with her mother and younger brother and a gentleman friend of the family. The gentleman soon returned to Boston; her mother sent her brother to Schenectady to recuperate from a smallpox vaccination, and her mother chose to join him. Eventually both her mother and brother returned to Boston, leaving Abby to fend for herself. At first she felt helpless without her mother, but she made up for it by adopting matrons from the guests as her "mothers," accepting their advice on keeping late hours and social decorum. Thus, young and single women who were alone at the spa could survive by adopting older women as their chaperones.[18]

Abby May gradually developed her own rules for taking the cure. At that time, there was nothing like the competition to sample the springs that there would be in later years. At first she would walk only to the springs across from the hotel; then she began to drink the water early in the morning before breakfast; and finally she would go for a bath at 5 or 6 A.M., but always took a container of laudanum in case she fainted. She gained an appreciation of the waters and was able eventually to distinguish the taste of the iron, salt, and sulfur mix; by the middle of her stay, she had a routine and had entered completely into the spirit of taking the waters.[19]

The "fairer" sex had the duty of setting the degrees of propriety in the relationship between the sexes. When her mother first left Abby alone, a group of forty lawyers appeared at the hotel. This onslaught of men left her so insecure that she sulked about it, commenting that "among so many men a female does not feel pleasantly."[20] Later, she did join a mixed group of beaus and belles on an excursion to Lake George, during which they camped under a tent fashioned from a sail; for propriety the shared tent had only a makeshift curtain divider. Although the excursion might have been judged scandalous had she been at home, the entire experience delighted her because it was a needed social activity that prevented boredom at the spa.

Sixty years later the situation of women like Abby May had not appreciably changed, and yet a journalist, the artist-correspondent Winslow Homer, did find women at the spa to be a bit more independent. In his late twenties he had covered the Civil War, drawing battle and camp scenes for *Harper's Weekly*.[21] After the war, he came into his own as the artist of the American vacation and especially of women at leisure. He favored the scenery of the coast of Maine, the Bahamas, the Adirondacks, and Saratoga Springs. Homer did not copy exactly from nature; rather he sought to convey the myths that defined the United States in the late nineteenth century. His picnic, bathing, sporting, and camping scenes included visions of a new woman; sometimes she was confidently playing croquet, the summer lawn game that put her on the same footing as men. Only months after the Civil War ended, he was assigned to the summer season at Saratoga Springs and thus had an opportunity to watch society, including its rituals at the recently inaugurated racetrack.

Homer's work at Saratoga portrayed the post–Civil War woman visitor, who now came to the spa in parties of her own sex rather than being the helpless young woman that Sedgwick portrayed. Although a minority, after 1865 younger women were more emancipated than they had been previously from traditional domesticity and from the influence of overbearing matrons. On their vacations, younger women experimented with new situations, from mountain hiking to attending horse races—activities that men had previously regarded as too strenuous and socially compromising for them. Dressing fashionably—although it still restricted them physically—gave younger women a degree of confidence and independence of spirit. Homer rendered women at leisure as if they were Greek statues, making them look like heroic figures. This symbolism was evident in a grandstand view of the younger generation of women watching the Saratoga race meet (Figure 75).[22] Although different from Abby May's milieu, the race-

FIGURE 75. Winslow Homer, *Our Watering Places—Horse Racing at Saratoga;* the affluent, stylish, and unmarried women who dominated the flimsy grandstand at the racetrack.
(Print from Harper's Weekly: A Journal of Civilization, *August 26, 1865.)*

track had a spirit of emancipation that was meant for women only at events like the meet and that was limited to the younger generation of women of the most acceptable families.

The New York Literati and the National Press

The spa attracted writers, journalists, historians, and artists, a media group that bestowed on the resort some of its most infamous social institutions. Wharton made much of the forbidden fruit of New York's intellectual and cultural community because as a young woman she was so attracted to it. Her plots portrayed matrons pining for the creative artist whom they might have married if he "could have supported a wife, or if he had consented to give up painting and Rome for New York, and the law."[23] New Yorkers who left the city and went to Europe to learn about and to practice the fine arts were free spirits, disdainful of social distinctions. Saratoga Springs served as an alternative to Europe and was an enduring summer home for New York's intellectual and cultural community. There they met their fellow artists, admired the history and scenery of the region as a romantic backdrop, and found the society at the spa to be conducive to the critical observation of human nature.

Because few writers wanted to spend their time at the spa secluded in a boarding house, they needed a meeting place. But outside hotels their choices were limited. In the 1830s and 1840s, the village's only salon was at Walworth's home on Broadway. He reviewed the hotel registers daily and invited visiting literati, artists, and politicians. Washington Irving, who spent his early years at Ballston Spa, was a fixture of Walworth's salon. He came to Saratoga Springs in 1832 after an extended residence in Europe. His companion was his sister-in-law's brother, the writer James Kirke Paulding. Irving knew Walworth through his son, the budding novelist Mansfield Tracy Walworth, for whom he served as best man at his Saratoga Springs wedding in 1852.[24] Attendees at Walworth's soirees also included Cooper, Sedgwick, and the historian William Leete Stone, Sr.

Cooper stayed in Saratoga Springs in 1824 and 1825, using it as a base for his research for *The Last of the Mohicans.* His novel had described the chief character, Hawkeye, drinking at a spring that bore striking similarities to Saratoga's High Rock, an incident that helped spread the reputation of its waters. Two years after its publication in 1826, Cooper was lionized at the United States Hotel, just before he left for Europe. Saratoga's temperance judge, Esek Cowen, held the reception in his honor, but Cooper responded with anti-American sentiments, toasting "England! with all thy faults I love thee still. Thou art my country."[25] Many guests were crestfallen when the man who had done so much for American literature and the spa's region made such an Anglophile statement.

In 1832, Sedgwick and Paulding contributed to *Tales of Glauber Spa,* a book about life at a fictitious resort. The book's editor was Robert Sands, a youthful bachelor and Columbia University graduate who had given up the law for a literary career. His claim to fame was a versified tale about King Philip's War, which initiated a wave of writings and plays on the noble savage as a stoic figure. He edited several short-lived literary reviews and died at the age of only thirty-three, the same year the book of tales was published.[26]

Sands's introduction claimed that the book manuscript was found at Glauber Spa in Sheep Neck near New York City, a fictional resort that had gone bankrupt. Although Sands's ideas about spas came from stays at Saratoga Springs, it was definitely not the resort portrayed in these tales. Sands shows Glauber "spaw" to have been created by a farmer's wife and daughter who convinced the farmer that his well water had healing powers and that their home could become a fashionable hotel. The chief villain is the local doctor, who certifies the springs' health-giving powers and sets up his office at the farm. The farmer mortgages his property to turn it into a spa, and at first it is a success. However, one of the farmer's black servants dies during a cholera epidemic, and no one wishes to stay at the spa; as a result they are ruined.[27] Although a cholera epidemic did strike New York in 1832, the rest is fiction, meant to discredit the growing number of spas by showing that their popularity and credibility were built on pure promotion and fickle crowds. The New York City literati had a tradition of being cynical about claims of the spas' healing powers, especially when developers had an opportunity to make a financial killing. This disdain for the proliferation of spas was popular in the first half of the century, but it disappeared as visits to places like Saratoga Springs became permanent fixtures on the New York social schedule.

Novelists occasionally attracted readers to the spas, but newspaper reporters provided news about the spas to a far wider audience. After the Civil War, Saratoga Springs became a mecca in July and August for the society reporters of every urban newspaper in the country. Reporters sought the plum assignment of going to Saratoga in order to enhance their careers and personal welfare by detailing the trivia and gossip that sold newspapers. One such reporter for New York City's *Mail and Express* was Arthur Aldridge, a young man who in 1887 wrote revealing letters about the spa to his sweetheart Georgina Warhurst, a secretary in his employer's office. He confided that he disliked the expense of staying at the resort and the heartless flirting that went on there, but he enjoyed being the center of attention because all the fine young ladies "want me to give them nice notices." One belle bought "20 copies of the paper and sent them to her friends." His daily articles were on mundane topics: "cutlery, neckties, trunks, chain bracelets, medallions, floral jewelry," and of course "Saratoga gossip." He soon found his articles were in demand by other newspapers, and he made extra money by selling them to three other papers.[28] Thus an inexperienced reporter became a center of attention at the spa, and his work perpetuated the spa's reputation as the center of the country's summer social life. Reporters like Arthur Aldridge put to rest the carping of the early novelists by promoting and giving a degree of reality to the spa's cultural and social life.

The Myth of the Marriage Market

The most famous literary creations of the 1820s and 1830s involved courtship and marriage rituals, the crucial question being whether to wed for love or for money. Rather than containing any information on accommodations or attractions, Paulding's 1828 edition of *The New Mirror for Travelers and Guide to the Springs* featured permissible decorum for ladies and gentlemen, tongue-in-cheek advice designed to enhance their marriage opportunities. Although Paulding's critique was exaggerated, other visitors confirmed his view that the spa's courting rituals stimulated both social coarseness and genteel manners. Paulding believed that the fashionables had created the Ballston and Saratoga resorts, and he was the first to describe their favorite pastime, the management of the supposed marriage market in Saratoga Springs. His book was not meant to provide serious advice for spa visitors but was intended as a satire on the pretensions and extravagance of young and married ladies. He claimed that young ladies at the spa acted ill-bred because they were encouraged to drink and dance too much or to push for seats at the dinner table. He ignored the possibility for affection in relationships between the sexes, asserting that the number one attraction in a beau at Saratoga was his income. He also suggested how married ladies and gentlemen could participate in the social whirl by using subterfuge to appear as if they were single and youthful—especially if they had neither of these attributes. Thus the springs were "a great place for scandal" where a lady might "gain her health and lose her reputation."[29]

Another piece of fiction perpetuated by Paulding that appeared four years later was the notion that Saratoga Springs society fostered a marriage market. He contributed a short story about the spa's courting rituals, which was included in Sands's *Tales of Glauber Spa*.[30] Set in the summer of 1828, the tale is entitled "Childe Roeliff's Pilgrimage." It focuses on Roeliff, a successful New York tinsmith, who takes his family, including his daughter Minerva, to Saratoga Springs. Much is made of how Minerva, a delicate, shy, and blushing girl, is encouraged by experienced socialites to be noisy, flirtatious, and fashionable. Minerva is put to several tests, including singing in front of an "intimate" gathering of three hundred, dancing with perfect strangers, and accepting the advances of a charming gentleman whom she correctly suspects of being a fraud. A fortune hunter pursues her to Lake George, but she has the good sense to turn down his advances. Luckily, the suitor becomes more interested in having an affair with an older married woman, so she is saved from him. She does find romance with Reuben, a young man rejected by the socialites because of the old-fashioned cut of his coat. They fall in love and are eventually married in Montreal. Paulding faulted men and women equally for this state of affairs, making special villains of male fortune hunters and of the fathers who ignored their daughters' feelings in favor of rich alliances. Still, his fiction made the notion of the marriage market a standard feature of the spa's social life.

In truth, in courting the emphasis at the spas was on chivalry, the display of manners, rather than on the serious business of marriage, let alone sexual relationships. Women of varying social convictions believed that the presence of the opposite sex was necessary for pastimes such as dancing, listening to music, and even walking. Socializing between the sexes was termed the mixing of beaus and belles—friends who enjoyed each others' company but who were not interested in the prospect of marriage. In 1800, while staying at Aldridge's hotel, Abby May observed as the Ballston season progressed that "we have plenty of beaus now and some very good of the kind tho' some are rather shy—there are but very few ladies here at present." The main attribute of a beau was that he was a smart young man who would pay attention to and flatter a lady: "ladies must be flattered—tis the part of gentlemen to administer the soothing essence." However, Abby did feel there was an excess of this essence. She enjoyed the company of men who did not overuse it and treated her as an intellectual equal by discussing books, politics, and agriculture. Likewise, she admired women who were accomplished enough to converse on many subjects with fluency and propriety, not on their future marriage prospects.[31]

It was deemed offensive for women to walk, ride, and converse with a man too frequently or to lead a man to offering himself in marriage, especially if her parents were not present. Although Abby May had a variety of social experiences at Ballston Spa, marriage was a concern that appeared only once, and it was regarded as a scandalous situation. A girl visiting Ballston Spa raised the possibility of her marriage; but once the man was identified as an adventurer, the girl's "mother was sent for and she was urged to return to her New York home." Abby could not decide who was most at fault, the girl—who may not have been so innocent—or the mother, who sent her there alone.[32] Because it was assumed that there were adventurers at a spa, it was not an ideal place to look for suitors. In fact, the highest success a beau could expect was to gain an introduction to a belle so that he might call upon her when she returned home.

Although courtship was possible at spas, betrothals, engagements, or marriages were unlikely. To parents, the object of a young lady's spending a season at the spa was to obtain experience and breeding so that she might handle serious courtship at home. The spa was an ideal place to contemplate a future courtship because of the presence of a variety of attractive visitors from throughout the country. Parents could arrange to have their daughter meet likely prospects in the spa's casual atmosphere. Nevertheless, if their daughter took no interest in a suitor, parents were powerless to move the relationship along because romantic writers like Sedgwick advised that affection between a couple was a prime requirement of a successful marriage.

More to the point, women themselves believed in long-drawn-out courtships.[33] Many feared marriage because it meant leaving the security of their father's household. They were also not eager to set up their own households, an undertaking that required attention to management and domestic affairs. Finally, they viewed sex as something a new husband would force on them, not necessarily a pleasurable experience. The short time spent at a spa was far too brief to iron out any of these concerns, especially while parents were forcing a daughter to make new friends. True courtship took place over an extensive period at home, not at the hectic social affairs of a spa.

Overall, social life at the spas was a loose arrangement, depending on the force of a few restrictive groups to sustain it. From the beginning men claimed to defer to women on social matters, so women had the burden of preventing the boredom that could plague even the gayest resort. Because women made the rules, men took them less seriously, seeing them as binding on women only. The arbiters of social conduct ranged from Manhattan matrons to hotel proprietors to some opinionated doctors to news reporters. None of them was especially successful because social power depended on a consensus about conduct that remained elusive. We have only to contrast the social views of Catherine Jones Clinton, Madame Jumel, and Catharine Maria Sedgwick to see how opinion varied. Although all were from New York City, they represented the diverging social views of that metropolis, and regardless of wealth, breeding, or talent, they shunned each other's company.

Saratoga Springs and Ballston Spa would not have a master of ceremonies to set rules of conduct as Nash did at Bath or Pope did at White Sulphur Springs. Instead the press would provide each spa with social myths, such as the marriage market that Paulding created. And the press had its redeeming moments, especially when Winslow Homer recognized that the post–Civil War woman was a new type of visitor, confident that she could perform the social rituals on her own, without the presence of her parents or brother. Conduct at the Saratoga spas was based on public display and diverse audiences, in contrast to conduct at resorts that appealed to exclusiveness and intimacy. The tourism infrastructure at Saratoga Springs drew a wide spectrum of society, including the middle class, so that any social rules would always have their detractors and never be acceptable to all.

C H A P T E R   1 3

The Nature of Visitors

Visitors were the lifeblood of resorts; their presence drove the resort economy, spreading a resort's reputation and attracting the ideal audience. Saratoga Springs chose to be open to both an aristocratic clientele and the growing middle class. It was the first resort to be publicized as a place where the middle class could rub shoulders with the rich and famous. In Marietta Holley's 1887 novel *Samantha at Saratoga,* Samantha personified the spa visitor of the centennial era; she exemplified the change that had taken place over the nineteenth century, during which the early majority of visitors, the wealthy and the prominent, came to be out-numbered by the middle-class throng.[1] These later visitors were not fashionable; rather their taste was homespun and positively austere. Samantha's dressmaker in Jonesville, a farming village near the spa, had warned her about the need to be fashionable at the spa by displaying her neck and arms. Samantha responded indignantly and chose to wear a "black straw bonnet, green veil, umbrella, black alpacy, that good moral dress."[2] Needless to say, the dress had long sleeves and the highest collar. At the spa, she and her husband, Josiah, like Holley herself, chose not to stay at a hotel, residing instead at a respectable "boardin house." No servants, friends, or children accompanied Samantha; her party consisted of herself and her spouse, the middle-class norm for the season.

Holley was born in 1836, the youngest of seven children, on a woodland farm in New York State's Jefferson County along the Canadian border. She had a simple, hard-working, Christian upbringing.[3] Her father was a Universalist, while her mother was drawn to revivals and chose to be a Baptist. After her father died and her brothers left home, she and her mother were left to eke out a hardscabble existence. She earned some income from teaching music and publishing poems, an occupation that led to a writing career. The character of Samantha first appeared in 1873 in *My Opinions and Betsey Bobberts's.* Samantha would appear in at least twenty-two more novels, many of them featuring her travels to the centennial at Philadelphia, the World's Fair at Chicago, Europe, the St. Louis Exposition, Coney Island, and, most notably, Saratoga Springs. An upstate recluse, who spoke with a slight lisp, Holley left the farm only when she went to see her publisher in New York City. Finally in 1881 she took the plunge, not only visiting her publisher but on her return stopping at Saratoga Springs. Five years later Holley spent the entire summer at the spa, writing the novel in which her stock middle-class character, Samantha, was introduced to the spa. This on-the-spot writing was new to her for she had usually used guidebooks in the past. In her boarding-house room high above the street to avoid noise, she made drafts every morning; she was interrupted only for her spring water, which was left outside the door. With the publication of *Samantha at Saratoga,* the details of visiting the spas were open to a broad reading public; such knowledge had once been the preserve of a limited elite.

Early Resort Visitors

In 1800 travelers in the United States had limited resort destinations, a scant number in comparison with their English counterparts, because few places existed in the United States for the conspicuous consumption of leisure. The cliffs of Newport and the beaches of Cape May did not become destinations until amenities appeared after the Civil War. Ease of transportation played a minimal role in the development of destinations; most resorts were located in rugged natural surroundings, far from the turnpikes and population centers. The earliest destinations were obscure villages or plantations built around modest facilities; often these facilities did not even include a hotel.[4] Virginia's White Sulphur Springs was developed around a mere tavern, with guests staying in private rows of cottages. Eventually, the erection of a hotel and the arrival of the railroad would allow it to become a resort of consequence, but until then it depended on its good company to attract a restricted number of visitors.

The basic piece of resort infrastructure was the hotel. Stafford Springs, Connecticut, and later Clarendon Springs, Vermont, were centered on single hotels. Stafford Springs was an early spa; in 1771 John Adams enjoyed its sulfur- and iron-impregnated waters. By 1810, Stafford Springs had a four-story hotel and bathhouses managed as an early cure institute. At Clarendon Springs, Thomas McLaughlin erected a three-story brick hotel in 1835. He had expanded the springs from what had been a small hotel in 1798 to a fashionable village around his new hotel and a green. By 1850, the chief characteristic of both spa hotels was multistoried porches that encouraged visitors to sit outdoors but protected them from the often-inclement northeastern weather.

The resort with the country's largest hotel in 1804 was Ballston Spa. Its delights and those of the region around it were described by early visitors as being especially attractive. Although the number of visitors was still small, Ballston's region was already recognized as a destination because of its historical romance and natural beauty. Early visitors traveled in parties of two or three and usually had their destinations to themselves. In the snowy December of 1780, the Marquis de Chastellux, a cultivated officer of Rochambeau's army at Newport, Rhode Island, was among the first tourists at the Saratoga battlefield. His guide was none other than Philip Schuyler, the former commander in the Saratoga campaign and an early advocate of protection for Saratoga's valuable springs. Four years later, the Venezuelan revolutionary Francisco de Miranda took time between visits with Thomas Paine and Alexander Hamilton to travel north of Albany. He commented, "The grasses of the fields exuded such an aromatic odor, the forests presented a sight so fertile, the grain and other crops appeared so beautiful and luxuriant, and the land was so rich that I thought I was in Puerto Rico, Cuba, or part of our [Latin] American continent."[5] His goal was also a tour of the Saratoga battlefield, and this time the guide was Samuel Bemis, a local farmer who owned part of the site and would make a reputation showing visitors the remains of the conflict.

In these early years, men traveled on excursions to the area to get away from the cares of politics and responsibilities. In May 1791, Secretary of State Thomas Jefferson sought to cure the migraine headaches he was suffering from in New York City by coaxing his friend James Madison to join him on a tour up the Hudson River to Albany, Lake George, and Lake Champlain. New York's Federalist leaders were suspicious that this apparent holiday was a trip aimed at undermining their political hold on the region, but it was soon evident that Jefferson and Madison wished to do no more than collect botanical specimens and visit historical sites. Ever the gentlemanly host, Philip Schuyler had his son John Bradstreet Schuyler offer them the hospitality of his Saratoga farm and accompany them on a tour of the Saratoga battlefield. What Jefferson saw on the journey impressed him; he commented to his daughter that Lake George was "unquestionably the most beautiful water I ever saw: formed by a contour of mountains into a basin thirty-five miles long, . . . finely interspersed with islands, its water limpid as crystal."[6] Such an evaluation, from an authority who had traveled widely and had a great depth of learning, confirms that at this early date the region had become a favorite tourist destination.

Women visitors were fewer and were expected to have more limited interests. In July 1792, when John Bradstreet Schuyler was asked to entertain a party of gentlemen and ladies at the Saratoga farm, only the men wished to see the battlefield. Women discovered the attractions of the Saratoga area by chance, although after the initial visit they returned faithfully year after year. Julia Stockton Rush, wife of Philadelphia's most famous doctor and enlightened reformer, Benjamin Rush, discovered Ballston Spa in 1809 during a journey to visit her two married daughters in Montreal. Like her husband an advocate of hydrotherapy, she became a devotee of taking the waters and a social leader at Ballston Spa and later Saratoga Springs.[7] Her social standing attracted a select circle of friends to stay at the hotel of her choosing. She even convinced the proprietor of the Congress Hall Hotel to hire a Philadelphia band of black musicians, led by Frank Johnson, to play for several seasons. At this early date, visitors came to experience the healthy benefits, social life, and beauty of the region.

The Company They Kept

The appearance of crowds at resorts by 1800 requires a closer look into their composition than is demanded by the small parties of early visitors. The keenest observer of these early visitors was the budding novelist Washington Irving. In 1806, less than a year after his first visit to Bath, England, the youthful and debonair observer of human nature chose to spend the summer at Ballston Spa. He commented on the stages of village growth, noting that at first it had attracted only health seekers; as it became more popular, it was dedicated to simple country pleasures such as a gathering for a hop; and by the time of his visit it had matured to become a center of style, where pleasure and amenities were the primary attractions.[8] Significantly, Ballston Spa had in only a dozen years passed through all three stages—from cure center to site of rustic pleasure to a fashion center; by 1806 it was the nation's premier resort. Its spectacular rise was known even to foreigners; in 1834 an English visitor commented, "On account of the preference and patronage given to 'Ballston' by the capricious goddess Fashion, . . . many are found who certainly have heard of the name of Ballston, but know nothing of the place itself."[9]

Irving established a continuum of visitors. Resorts began by catering to an exclusive clientele, not because of purposeful planning but because their facilities were limited. Hotel-keepers sought to establish a clientele that would return annually and that felt the resort offered "agreeable company"—that is, visitors just like them. As resorts became more popular, this clientele was increasingly described as "fashionables," visitors who had a certain claim to wealth and sophistication. As resorts expanded, however, the ability to entertain more than one class of visitor was crucial in order to fill expansive accommodations. Eventually, so broad a company was entertained that social relations were in flux.[10]

Figures for visitation at Saratoga Springs are impressionistic, depending on the estimator's perspective. Francis Johnson Dallam of Baltimore visited the spa in 1827 and commented that "the company is large about 700 but not such as are agreeable to me, all strangers and many of them foreigners."[11] Dallam's figure is too modest and may include visitors at only one or several hotels. One authority claims twelve thousand visitors in 1823, while another numbered the crowd in 1832 at three thousand; the year after it was estimated at thirty-five hundred.[12] These figures contrast with those for White Sulphur Springs, the favorite of people such as Dallam, which until 1858 had no hotel and could fit no more than 150—the obvious source of its exclusivity. The aristocracy was always concerned that tourists were overrunning a resort that had once been the preserve of a few.

By mid-century, visitors who came to Saratoga Springs emphasized the diversity of the crowd. The throng at Congress Spring in 1851 consisted of "the drooping invalid, the hale and hearty man, the gay Lothario, the dashing belle, the pretty maiden, the happy child, the young, the middle aged and old, the rich and poor, the learned and unlearned, the wise and unwise."[13] Here was a diversity of class and age. While the aristocracy came mostly for the amenities, the promise of health and spiritual revival drew the middle class. Families of this sort were willing to make financial sacrifices to send a family member to be cured.

In fact, resort visitors became compartmentalized depending on their origin, their hotel, and their idea of pleasure. Aristocrats, especially from Baltimore, Philadelphia, and Boston, who lacked the recognition they had at home and had nothing but their apparent gentility to separate them from the throng, were never comfortable with Saratoga's diverse and growing crowds. In 1824, a New Yorker observed at a Saratoga hop that visitors from the three rival cities "formed in the same manner. And group seemed sneering at group, with looks indicating conscious superiority, and each appeared to be scrutinizing and criticizing the sayings and doings of his neighbor. . . . We found an unusual share of reserve and local jealousies and distinctions prevailing."[14] Similarly, Irving observed a sectional rivalry among representatives of the eastern, middle, and southern states, as evidenced by the distinctive exhibition of ladies' riding equipages and wardrobes and gentlemen's abilities with horses.[15] The crush of visitors from every corner of the nation meant that the crucial social distinctions of one's home turf were lacking; this lack led to the formation of cliques of visitors from the same city.

Because of the diversity of the crowd, class distinctions were also based on the choice of accommodations. It was the hotel that led to the compartmentalization of Saratoga's society. Each group of visitors had its own standards of conduct, its own expectations of the price of accommodations, and its favorite place to stay. One visitor explained in 1844 that "people while at Saratoga fall into a particular class; not one formed by any arbitrary rule, but as they are pleased to rank themselves with each other at the different hotels." Thus, there were separate hotel clienteles: "the great and would be great" politicians, women who were "belles of the highest pretensions," country squires who were "gentlemen of the turf," rich tradesmen and farmers, "sober and retiring—yet affable and genteel" clergymen with their families, and those of religious persuasions from Presbyterian to Episcopalian, from "romanist" to Universalist.[16] This observer recognized each group's choice of a different hotel and observed that this segmentation prevented society from having a single set of rules, as was the ideal in Bath.

Others found simple pleasures more to their liking than the established social calendar. In 1842, when nineteen-year-old Francis Parkman, the future historian and Boston Brahman, visited Lake George, he traveled with his backpack, camped on its islands, and washed his soiled clothes in the limpid waters. He found the tavern at Caldwell to be "full of fashionable New Yorkers"; he was out of place, looking "like Old Nick," and "evidently looked upon in a manner corresponding."[17] Parkman had no love for New Yorkers and after a night in these surroundings, he went on to the rustic pleasures of the islands. His experience shows that resorts drew college students as well as fashionables. The ability to entertain more than a small elite became crucial if resorts were to survive. Saratoga Springs took the early lead among the resorts in being open to visitors by providing the greatest range of facilities, and it maintained its lead throughout the nineteenth century.

The major change in visitation was the arrival of the middle class at resorts, a movement that began in the 1830s and reached its peak after the Civil War. Their appearance was a development that Irving had not contemplated. This change was a matter not only of numbers but of culture, as middle-class values were now those held by a majority of visitors. Such values, which included domesticity, the abolition of slavery, strict Sabbath observance, self-improvement, and total abstinence from alcoholic drinks, gave the middle class of the 1830s and 1840s their own consciousness.[18] The spread of these values redefined the way many people used their leisure, as it affected the activities they expected and enjoyed at resorts. Those resorts that were able to cater to this new audience survived and flourished. Those resorts that attempted to survive by continuing to depend on the gentleman's ideal of English spas, found themselves restricted to a smaller, more competitive market, which became very tight after the Civil War. This was the case with Clarendon Springs, a rival of Saratoga Springs in the 1830s and 1840s, which lost its aristocratic clientele and closed after the Civil War.

The number of middle-class visitors at resorts grew as a result of their devotion to the water cure, the secular equivalent of the religious conversion that entranced the bulk of Victorians. In 1846, Harriet Beecher Stowe, the future author of *Uncle Tom's Cabin,* began a short stay at the Brattleboro (Vermont) Water Cure that expanded into two years—despite the protests of her husband. Sickly on account of the primitive methods used by her previous doctors, Stowe emerged fully recovered and a devotee of the practices of hydrotherapists, whom she regarded as secular saviors. Her experience was not an isolated one. The water cure had been a medicinal possibility in the late eighteenth century, but it became popular only in the 1840s.[19] It was appealing to the middle class because it was a do-it-yourself type of cure that made a physician's constant attention unnecessary—unless of course one was willing to pay for it. It also satisfied a growing middle-class concern for physical fitness, for which walking to, drinking at, and bathing in cold spring water was ideal. The sick came after more widespread treatments had failed, but even healthy visitors were interested in drinking the waters as a preventive measure. The loosening of restrictions on physicians' licenses allowed numerous cure institutes run by doctors to appear from the 1840s on. Although a cure institute could be established anywhere that "pure" water was available, in practice Saratoga's mineral waters remained the most reputable and therefore its cure institutes were the most respected.

In the 1870s new conditions contributed to the further expansion of the spa's middle-class markets and made it the most popular resort of its time. The opening of two mammoth hotels in 1874 gave the middle class dominance and ended much of the compartmentalization that had identified the earlier Saratoga experience. The Grand Union Hotel and the United States Hotel had places for three thousand guests between them, the maximum accommodation of the entire village only a decade before.[20] Lesser hotels like the Congress Hall had room for eleven hundred guests. When we remember that in 1803 Ballston Spa's Sans Souci, with space for two hundred guests, had been the county's largest hotel, the contrast is striking. Filling these new rooms required that old barriers fall and that anyone who could afford a hotel room be allowed to stay. This openness was not totally the result of market conditions. In 1873, the New York State Civil Rights Law for the first time forbade discrimination against blacks, preventing innkeepers from turning away anyone whom they deemed unacceptable. Additionally, the centennial celebration of the American Revolution, which locally focused on the Battle of Saratoga, stimulated hotel development to provide access to the historic sites and festivities. This was a celebration not just for the upper class but for the American public as a whole, of which many elements were for the first time part of the vacation market. All visitors did not welcome this expansion; as expected, long-standing visitors were upset by the diverse crowds the centennial and the mammoth hotels attracted. Although some continued to frequent Saratoga's more intimate hotels, such as the newly opened Adelphi, others left the spa and retired to the seclusion of a villa in Newport. To attract the mass market created by the middle class, certain segments of the quality market had to be lost.

Country folk like Marietta Holley's Allens were now going to Saratoga Springs. Samantha ridiculed old-money New Yorkers with their "diamond ear-rings, cuff-bottoms, Saratoga trunks and big accounts at the banks."[21] There had always been ordinary people at the spa who looked on the social endeavors of the rich with fascination and disdain, but the public criticism of the rituals of the old society found in the account of Samantha's visit made the old families uneasy about the Saratoga crowd. The early tradition of the spas as the exclusive preserve of the rich and infirm had given way to the point that a visit had now become the expectation of the many.

Only one class was excluded from centennial Saratoga Springs, and this exclusion was the result of circumstances outside the community's control. Members of the laboring class could not come because in the nineteenth century they had no formal vacations, paid or unpaid. At best they had Sunday holidays, which were restricted because they were at least partially devoted to the Sabbath. Sunday excursions for the working class, which Thomas Cook had developed in England, were much more limited in the United States because distances were greater and most excursions were to places in immediate proximity to the largest cities.

Even urban public parks were restricted, the most notable being New York City's Central Park, where officials did allow the laboring class to attend band concerts.[22] Catskill vacations for the working class were in the future; nineteenth-century employers felt their workers did not need vacations.

Male Dominance

Throughout the nineteenth century, gender was a factor in the makeup of resort visitation. Traveling and spending time on a vacation was regarded as a male preserve. Commenting on the Ballston Spa of the 1790s and early 1800s, Washington Irving noted that before "style" appeared, it had been a male enclave for simple pleasures like fishing and hunting; a man could enjoy the lack of formality and ceremony and be free from the disconcerting presence of his wife. The ideal of a male enclave was modified as the century progressed; by the 1840s, the trustees of the Village of Saratoga Springs definitely prohibited "disorderly houses and houses of ill fame," a reference that certainly implies that they had existed.[23] However, the dominating presence of males at resorts remained constant, even if their ideas of entertainment changed.

The first vacations were battlefield excursions or hunting and fishing parties, which were regarded as too strenuous for the fairer sex. The War of 1812 had been fought in two of the most scenic parts of New York State: along the Niagara frontier and on the northern section of Lake Champlain near the Adirondacks. After 1815, soldiers who served at these locations, such as Solomon Van Rensselaer of Albany, wished to relive their past exploits and incidentally to view natural wonders like the falls at Niagara.[24] Solomon did take his wife, Arriet, along to familiarize her with his exploits, but she came primarily improve her poor health; it was much more common for a man to go with a party of comrades-in-arms. The simple pleasures at resorts drew men away from their work and home, giving them a chance to renew themselves through contact with nature and refreshing them so that they could handle work when they returned.

The tradition of hunting as a relaxing sport was a well-established male pastime. The ideal was expressed in the 1850s and 1860s in the paintings of the English artist Arthur Fitzwilliam Tait, which were distributed as popular Currier and Ives prints.[25] Tait depicted men in their prime with firearms and dogs, stalking abundant prey in the Adirondacks or the Catskills. The genre was far from new. More revealing of hunting as the perfect male recreation in relation to the family are the idealized, uncomplicated portrayals of middle-class family life also found in Currier and Ives prints.[26] A set of prints designed by Fanny Palmer in 1855 celebrates the domestic pleasures of country life. Among these is *October Afternoon,* in which the man of the house returns with a friend from a hunting expedition (Figure 76). His wife and children greet him at the gate, and he displays his kill of rabbits and birds. His young son grasps his father's rifle on his shoulder, and the dogs leap up as if to laud his exploits. Another Palmer print of 1857, *Home from the Brook,* shows a husband and friend with their catch returning to his wife, son, and daughter (Figure 77). The proud fisherman displays his largest fish and the children transfer the basketful of catch to a platter, while his wife remains passively seated, reading a book. The wife's detachment hints that not all wives welcomed the cleaning and preparing of their husband's game and fish. Men hunted and fished exclusively with their own sex; women

FIGURE 76. F. F. Palmer, del., *American Country Life. October Afternoon,* 1855; a man returning
from an outing to be honored by the family he has left at home.
(Lithograph of N. Currier.)

FIGURE 77. *Home from the Brook. The Lucky Fishermen,* 1857. Women generally had passive roles
in male outings, even though they would be required to gut and clean the fish for dinner.
(Lithograph of Currier and Ives, New York.)

remained at home with the children, properly occupied with domestic duties. Male outings, the basis of nineteenth-century vacations, offered no opportunity for women's participation.

Male visitors came to the Ballston Spa – Saratoga area in the early 1800s because they still regarded it as a wilderness and thus found it unnecessary to journey to the remote and inaccessible Adirondacks. In the 1820s and 1830s, Saratoga Springs had its own version of a fishing camp only two miles to the east of town. This camp belonged to German-born Jacobus Barhyte and included a trout pond and tavern. Barhyte provided instruction in catching trout and cooked elegant meals with the same skill as did later Adirondack guides. He did not think of himself as an innkeeper; however, he would prepare trout and provide cider or peach brandy, "quite indifferent about whether or what you pay him," as one guest commented.[27] Barhyte's guests included the most renowned sportsmen and politicians of the day: Joseph Bonaparte, Prince Jerome Napoleon, De Witt Clinton, Martin Van Buren, and Henry Walton. Although women did catch an occasional trout at his pond, Barhyte's clientele was overwhelmingly male.

As the spa succeeded in attracting larger crowds, another activity was introduced that fortified the resort as a male bastion: nineteenth-century electioneering. This was a male preserve because women were not enfranchised. In the season, politicians were drawn to Saratoga Springs because they could address a considerable and geographically diverse crowd of male voters. After the railroad arrived in 1832, the spa became a crucial whistle stop for presidential and gubernatorial campaigns. The great Saratoga Springs jurist and socializer Reuben Hyde Walworth held open house at his Broadway home, Pine Knot, for politicians of diverging convictions. His guests included three presidents—Martin Van Buren, Millard Fillmore, and James Buchanan—and also-rans such as De Witt Clinton, Silas Wright, William Marcy, Daniel Tompkins, Churchill Cambreleng, Francis Granger, William Seward, Steven Douglas, Albert Tracy, and Enos Throop.[28] Beyond Walworth's threshold, other politicians making stops at the spa were John Quincy Adams, Daniel Webster, Henry Clay, and, after the Civil War, U. S. Grant. These figures did more than draw crowds; they helped the community obtain political favors. Cambreleng, a New York congressman and U.S. ambassador, made Saratoga Springs and Ballston Spa accessible to the outside world by sponsoring the legislation that enabled the first railroad to be built between Schenectady and the spas; he also became the railroad's first president. A spa celebration in 1840 honored the great Whig politician Daniel Webster. Webster addressed a crowd of ten thousand at Temple Grove near Congress Park, of which three-quarters were men.[29] A Broadway parade followed in which the centerpiece was a float with a log cabin, covered with Whig banners; it seated fifty of the village's most handsome beaux and belles and was drawn by sixteen gray horses. Thus by 1840 women were attending political speeches and riding on parade floats, although they could not vote.

Males were given the choice facilities at the spa. Gambling was entirely off-limits to women if only because of their own distaste for it. Samantha was approached at the track by a chap who asked her to "buy a French pool"; she replied that she could not see how a duck pond would benefit her. Then she realized that he wanted her to bet on a horse, and she retorted, "No, I shall not gamble, neither on foot, nor on horseback."[30] The Casino, the village's most expensive and elegant building, excluded all respectable women by limiting the gaming to high-rolling gentlemen visitors. Morrissey acted as the Casino's master of ceremonies. To honor the Blues he did not permit gambling on Sunday. To maintain the established barriers, no women were allowed in the gaming rooms, although they could accompany gentlemen in

FIGURE 78. "At Saratoga,—Morrissey's Gambling House." Gambling in the public gaming room
of the Casino was an activity restricted to male visitors.
(Every Saturday, *September 9, 1871.*)

the salon. However, in 1871, Morrissey forbade even these visits to discourage any impression
that women had the possibility of gambling. No locals were allowed in the gaming rooms, the
implication being that Morrissey's gambling was too serious for them, especially as credit was
not extended.[31] Although Morrissey eventually relaxed some of his rules, their effect is seen in
a view of the grand parlor where not a single woman is in sight; the Casino was decidedly a male
bastion (Figure 78).

     The epitome of a male visitor was Ulysses S. Grant, victorious Union general and presi-
dent of the United States from 1869 to 1877. He had come to Saratoga Springs for the July 4,
1865, celebration as a victorious general; the crowd gave him an ovation at the Leland Opera
House and wherever he went. Twenty years later, he returned to the Saratoga area to spend
his last days before he died of cancer of the throat. After his notoriously corrupt presidency,
Grant had adopted New York City as his home and came to Saratoga Springs with the New
York crowd. An outdoorsman, he used the spa as a base to fish and hunt at Lake George and
other parts of the Adirondacks. By 1884 Grant was bankrupt, but he could still come to Sara-
toga because his New York friends supported him. They included Joseph W. Drexel, of the high-
society banking family, who offered the dying Grant and his family a modest cottage at Mount
McGregor, five miles to the north of Saratoga Springs. The press followed Grant's family to
Mount McGregor, providing coverage that enhanced the reputation of the Saratoga area as a

vacation spot. Grant upheld the male ideal of spending a vacation in rustic surroundings, although the presence of his devoted family showed that middle-class values had modified ideas about how to take a vacation. After Grant's death, his Mount McGregor cottage became a favorite excursion from the spa, rivaling Lake George and Saratoga Lake. Intrepid tourists such as Samantha and Josiah Allen had to see the spot where "the Hero met his last foe and fell victorious."[32]

Although Grant's family was present to sustain the dying hero, most men came to the spa without their families. Spa hotel registers throughout the nineteenth century show that three out of every five registered parties consisted of a single male.[33] How did these male visitors handle the social situation of being alone in a place that demanded public display? Charles West Thomson of Philadelphia came to the spa alone, and his 1824 journal gives an indication of how he overcame the difficulty of making friends. He stayed at the Union Hall, which he described as a "sober house where there are no balls," where the company was reserved, and which thus provided no help in meeting people. He had planned to meet friends, but they had left by the time he arrived, so he was on his own. Everyone was a stranger until he spied a familiar face from Philadelphia, who "reconciled me to my situation." Later Thompson made a few acquaintances among males like himself. He found that mingling to take the waters was the great icebreaker because in that ritual there was a lack of distinction by age or class.[34] For a single male like himself to make his way among a crush of strangers at the springs was regarded as normal and proper. This was not the case, however, for women, who were denied the same freedom of movement.

Women's Place

Women did come to play a growing role in the development of the spas even if they were excluded from male-dominated recreation and politics. In the early nineteenth century, women did not expect to use their leisure time to stay at a resort. Albany patrician women such as Maria Van Rensselaer, the aged and widowed matriarch of that influential family, traveled extensively in her twilight years, but among her extended family's homes, not to a resort.[35] She crisscrossed the Albany area on prolonged visits to her relatives' and friends' country houses and invited them to her country home, but, like most women of the upper class, she would not patronize country inns or public places. Moreover, patrician families saw these country homes as investments. There the wife labored more intensively than she did in the city, overseeing the planting and harvesting of crops, producing cheese and preserves, or seeing to the management of the sawmill and gristmill. For most women, time spent at a country house was scarcely a vacation.

Among other acts of visiting, young women of well-to-do families were also encouraged to stay in cities as part of their finishing; these visits prepared them for marriage and taking a place in society. In 1800, urban centers such as Boston, Philadelphia, and especially New York City were the favorite places for such experiences. Normally, the young women stayed with relatives or friends for a winter or spring season, during which she was prepared for the world.[36] By the 1820s, however, the finishing of young ladies by a season in a city had declined. Ironically, as cities grew, they came to be seen as centers of corruption rather than as places of education. The summer season at the spas offered an alternative; there a young lady might gain the same finishing and avoid the effects of the Industrial Revolution.

The transition from visiting relatives and friends to spending a season at a resort was slow because in this age of domesticity women were encouraged to retreat into the refuge of the home and devote themselves to domestic duty.[37] Middle-class women were taught that their sphere was the home and that they would be honored for achievements in the management of their household and in the moral education of their children. In contrast, public achievements outside the home were a male preserve, although women were granted a limited role in religious and charitable activities. Women who traveled and spent time at the spas were leaving their home, their natural sphere, thereby failing to fulfill their domestic duty.

Although women had to avoid too much activity in the public arena, some did leave home to take the waters at a spa. Initially they came for reasons of health, a result of the growing respectability of the cure among elements of the medical profession. Uniquely at spas, they could exercise some freedom over their public life. Women became important participants in such spa activities as the ritual of taking the waters and the business of socializing and establishing relationships between the sexes, and they even added to the spa's intellectual life. Also, when summer homes appeared at the resorts, women were given the domestic duty of establishing a temporary home away from home. It was their job to leave for the resort before and return home after their husbands, so as to open and close the summer cottage. In managing a summer house or a country house, they were perpetuating the tradition of the spheres rather than taking the risk of joining the public at a hotel. In contrast, men, while a majority, increasingly played a more passive role at the spas, hiding out in smoke-filled rooms or hunting and fishing retreats and avoiding social life—except for occasional required displays of gallantry toward women.

Women come to the spas for their health as early as men. When Abigail May visited Ballston Spa from May to August 1800, she was a twenty-four-year-old woman, almost beyond the conventional marrying age, faced with the prospect of spinsterhood. She was ill and would not live long, dying within a year of her stay. We do not know the exact nature of her ailment, but she came to Ballston to have her hand treated with the mineral waters. Despite her malady, she traveled by stagecoach from Boston to Ballston Spa and back and followed a strenuous schedule at the spa. Yet her poor health blunted her spirit, as we find her writing that she had lived "long enough to see the insufficiency of earthly things; to have my fairest prospects blasted; to experience old age in all its helplessness; to find myself a useless being in society."[38] Her views were typical of women who came to the spa in a desperate attempt to set right a life plagued by illness.

Washington Irving's 1807 observations about women visitors at Ballston Spa indicate a growing role for them. By then, the male bastion of Ballston was changing because of the invasion of women. He complained they came not so much for health and good company but rather to exhibit themselves and their finery, to excite admiration and envy. To strike the proper appearance, Irving noted, "a sober citizen's wife will break half-a-dozen milliners' shops, and sometimes starve her family a whole season, to enable herself to make the Springs campaign in style."[39] Irving's observations show that women had introduced the style of urban centers to the resorts; in doing so, they disrupted masculine pursuits and led a life that was far from the recommended one of domestic seclusion. Unintentionally, he foretold that visiting women would set the standards for the social activities that would become one of the spas' chief attractions.

To exert this social influence, women had to overcome the fact that their numbers were not great. Our knowledge that they were a minority comes from hotel registers at Ballston Spa and Saratoga Springs covering 1824 to 1883. Analysis of the parties registered at Ballston's elegant Sans Souci Hotel in 1823 and 1825 show that females were a decided minority.[40] Only about a third of the parties contained females; most of the guests, more than 60 percent, were single males traveling alone. Of the females, over half came as wives, registering with their husbands. About 30 percent were in parties made up exclusively of women, whether titled "Mrs." or "Miss." The remaining 17 percent consisted of females whom a male accompanied, usually a father or brother. Men thus outnumbered women more than two to one, and unmarried women were even more of a rarity. Irving's comment about men escaping their wives may have a ring of truth.

Twenty-seven years later, the Union Hall Hotel was the leading Saratoga Springs establishment. In 1852, single males still made up most of the hotel visitors, 57 percent. Only 41 percent of the parties contained females, the vast majority, 81 percent, being wives, most often accompanied by their husbands, although children and servants were also part of their parties. All-female parties made up 14 percent of the women, those with the title of "Miss" slightly outnumbering those with the title of "Mrs." The misses registered in groups of two to four women, while those with the title "Mrs." were usually with their children and servants but without their menfolk. Finally, only 5 percent of the female visitors were accompanied by a male, usually a father or a brother.[41]

After the Civil War, male dominance of parties staying at fashionable hotels was still pervasive. The 1869 register of the Union Hotel—an expanded version of the Union Hall and still the spa's leading hotel—shows little change in composition of parties from the 1820s. Bolstered by numerous veterans of the Civil War, single males made up 63 percent of the parties, and parties exclusively of several males made that figure 3 percent higher. Thus, only one-third of the parties contained women and this one-third was divided among wives at 52 percent, parties exclusively of women at 37 percent, and females accompanied by a male at 11 percent.[42] The sole indication of change from the 1852 Union Hall register is the rise in the number of parties made up exclusively of women, with the corresponding decline in the number of wives. Although the percentage of women accompanied by a male was up slightly from 1852, it would never again reach the heights it had at the Sans Souci in the 1820s. Clearly, more women were staying at the hotels without a male escort, and the majority were now identified as unmarried. Therefore, groups of unmarried and unescorted women were staying at the mid-century Union Hall and Union Hotel in greater numbers than at the Sans Souci in the 1820s. Still women were a decided minority at the spas' hotels—even after the Civil War.

A fourth hotel register, from the Continental Hotel, takes us closer to the end of the era, namely 1883. It was a smaller and less elegant hotel than the previous three, although it was as respectable—many clergymen stayed there. At this late date, 62 percent of the Continental's registrants were still single males. Among the female visitors, for the first time all-female parties of unrelated married ladies or widows narrowly outnumbered wives, 50 percent to 48 percent. As before, the number of parties with a female accompanied by a male declined, now to only

2 percent.[43] In the sixty years between the Sans Souci and the Continental, three trends stand out: the continued dominance of single males at all the hotels; the decline as the century progressed in the number of females accompanied by a close male relative; and the emphasis on wives as the chief female occupants at hotels and yet after the Civil War the increasing number of all-female parties. Although the percentage of females in hotels scarcely changed, after the Civil War the rise in the number of parties made up exclusively of women and the decline in male chaperones gave women more freedom in staying at a spa hotel.

The figures do not tell the whole story of women's increasing independence at resorts. When, in 1860, Susan B. Anthony, the women's rights organizer, breakfasted at the Fort William Henry Hotel in Caldwell, she insisted on placing her own order for "coffee, cornbread and beefsteak," while the formally trained black waiter ignored her. He turned to the only male in the party and asked him to exercise his prerogative and order for all. Anthony was not about to have a "middleman" decide what she would eat, and after an embarrassing moment the waiter was forced to acquiesce.[44]

More telling than this incident, the earliest gatherings of women's rights advocates coordinated by Anthony were held in Saratoga Springs. The first three conventions she organized took place at the spa in the summers of 1854, 1855, and 1856. Her supporters, including William Hay, the temperance historian of Saratoga Springs, felt the spa to be an ideal place to expose the "curious fashionables" to the cause of women's rights. A superb organizer of meetings, if a reluctant speaker in her early career, Anthony held the 1854 convention at the same time as the Temperance and Anti-Nebraska Convention, at which her brother, Daniel, spoke on preventing slavery in the western territories. She was able to draft Matilda Joslyn Gage, who was already at the spa to support the temperance and antislavery meeting, to address her convention. The 1855 convention was a "who's who" of the women's rights movement, with powerful leaders like Lucy Stone, Martha Wright, and Mary L. Booth contributing to its success. However, 1856 was a presidential-election year, and women's rights were regarded as an eccentricity; the speakers failed to show at the convention, and Anthony was left to deliver the speeches on her own. Despite this setback, in the summer of 1869 she returned to organize the Woman's Suffrage Convention at the Congress Hall Hotel, where the "on-lookers" included ex-president Millard Fillmore. In 1870 the convention was back, organized by Gage, and Anthony received the princely sum of $100 as a paid speaker, a vindication of her earlier efforts at the spa.[45] Surely the women at these conventions debated the social and political issues of the day and each summer found the spa a conducive place to gather—a far cry from the times when women did not go to resorts.

An Urban Crowd

City dwellers were the most likely to visit spas. They came not only from New York City, Philadelphia, New England's Boston and Salem, and nearby Albany and Troy, but also from Charleston, South Carolina, and New Orleans. Given their wealth and sophistication, urban dwellers could afford to travel great distances to be properly cared for and entertained. Additionally, even the most northerly cities suffered from summer heat, making the seasonal visit to the northern uplands a necessity. Epidemics in cities such as New York helped Saratoga Springs, which in 1832 boasted it was immune from the cholera epidemic that struck other northeastern communities. In the South, summer was the fever season, so visiting a healthy, cooler northern climate became a necessity.

Patricians of nearby Albany and Schenectady, who sought the springs for reasons of health, were influential at Ballston Spa during its early years as a resort. In 1798, Sarah Maria Nott, wife of Eliphalet Nott, the future president of Schenectady's Union College, sought Ballston's waters because she had failed to recover from the rigors of childbirth. Six years later, she again sought relief at the springs but died after a four-day stay, leaving her husband with four small children. In July 1803, Ann Van Cortlandt Van Rensselaer, wife of the mayor of Albany, Philip Van Rensselaer, was present at Ballston Spa. As noted, ailing Stephen Van Rensselaer often stayed at its Sans Souci Hotel in the summer and then would winter in Charleston, South Carolina. There Van Rensselaer developed a circle of friends who would join him annually in a summer pilgrimage to Ballston Spa.[46]

Much as with entrepreneurial activity, the role of New York City in spa development cannot be underestimated. In 1852, the register of the Union Hall shows that New York City with 34 percent, New England with 30 percent, and the Albany area with 14 percent were the guests' most frequent homes. Seventeen years later at the same hotel, a single group was now dominant, residents of Manhattan and Brooklyn, who made up 56 percent; New Englanders fell to a distant second with 15 percent. Visitors from the rest of the country, and from Cuba and Paris, France, were a minority.[47] Such exceptional domination of the visitor market by one city shows how crucial social and economic ties were between Saratoga Springs and New York City.

The accessibility of Ballston Spa and Saratoga Springs to New York City was fundamental to their success. New York had become the nation's greatest metropolis because its port attracted coastal and international Atlantic trade. It was possible for travelers from Charleston or New Orleans to take a sailing packet to New York City and then follow New Yorkers to the spas. At first sloops made the trip up the Hudson River to Albany, but after the introduction of the steamboat in 1807, New York's port became a center for this form of transportation. By 1825, twelve steamboats plied the Hudson daily from New York to Albany or Troy. This accessibility led Henry McCall Jr. to write home to Philadelphia in August 1848 that Saratoga was not for him but "for the New Yorkers, . . . of all sorts and sizes from Van Buren down."[48]

An aristocratic New York City visitor to Saratoga Springs, Philip Hone, was enamored with the quality of his accommodations and the company. He came to Saratoga Springs annually and could afford to bring his extensive family with him. Mayor of New York City in 1825, Hone had made a fortune in the import and auction business.[49] After 1824, he often stayed at a private cottage on the grounds of the United States Hotel. Hone enjoyed meeting political leaders and writers at the spa, asserting that the quality of the company made a vacation successful. Although a supporter of Henry Clay in 1839, at the spa Hone was not above fraternizing with Martin Van Buren, a Democrat. Hone had been favored with the most elegant accommodations in the United States Hotel, while, in contrast, President Van Buren could obtain only a closetlike room. Thus, it gratified the former mayor of New York that he was better lodged than the president of the United States.

Boston, Salem, Providence, Hartford, and New England's towns provided the second largest number of visitors. New Englanders had requirements that set them apart, especially strict observance of the Sabbath. An English visitor reported that at Lake George's Lake House, the proprietor wisely ceased all activities on Saturday evening so that the hotel would be ready for "a state of Sunday quietness."[50] This restriction was required by the hotel's New England visitors, even though there was no preacher in Caldwell village to officiate at a Sunday service.

Philadelphia, the rival urban center to New York City, was also represented at Saratoga Springs. Philadelphians had a choice of resorts, many of them more accessible, such as the bathing beaches of Cape May, New Jersey, or the cool hills of White Sulphur Springs. They were critical of Saratoga Springs, Ballston Spa, and Caldwell, most often for the lack of well-bred company—that is, visitors who belonged to their aristocratic social set. Henry McCall Jr. carped about Saratoga Springs, noting its crowds as "such a collection of swells and rowdies [as] it has rarely been my chance to lay my eyes upon." He went on, "All exclaim against the dullness of the season and yet we are crowded to death."[51] Still, Philadelphians appreciated the medicinal value of the waters, and the city's newspapers, especially the *Herald,* were not above sending reporters to cover Saratoga's social season.

Southerners were an important constituency in the first half of the nineteenth century. Gideon Davidson's earliest guidebook to Saratoga Springs and Ballston Spa began by giving the mileage from Charleston to Philadelphia and eventually to the spas. He encouraged south-erners to get away from the oppressive heat and illness of the summer, to enjoy the North's bet-ter roads and accommodations, and to witness the sublime beauties of New York's mountains and splendid cities. In 1822, James and Mary Chestnut of Mulberry Plantation, South Caro-lina, visited Saratoga Springs on a journey that included a voyage from Charleston, South Carolina, to New York, an excursion to Newport, and another voyage to England. For twenty-two-year-old Mary, the spa was a welcome change from the isolated work routine of a south-ern plantation, which she felt had caused her to be ill. Later she would be a social fixture at White Sulphur Springs, but her initial spa experience was at Saratoga, and she remembered it fondly. Until it burned in 1821, the spa's elegant Pavilion Hotel was the southerners' favor-ite residence. Five years later, a dozen Charleston families stayed at Saratoga's United States Hotel. Southern students in northern schools also made Saratoga Springs a stop on their grand tours. The majority of southern visitors were men who traveled with numbers of black slaves. More than any other group, southerners had a reputation for coming to "display themselves" and participate in the spa's gay and diverse social life.[52]

Visitors from the South were numerous until northerners' sympathy for the abolition of slavery sorrowed this relationship. The *New York Times* of August 5, 1856, reported that "the number of Southern visitors at the Springs has never been so large"; this was an impressionis-tic observation, however, meant to smooth over political differences and increase visitation. Only thirteen miles to the east of Saratoga Springs in Union Village, militant abolitionists led by Dr. Hiram Corliss had been active in promoting the underground railroad. Additionally, the Fugitive Slave Act of 1850 aroused such hostility in northern abolitionists that southern-ers did not feel welcome at northern spas. Rumors spread of the insults abolitionists heaped on the southern women who visited the spas. The disappearance of southerners in the 1850s doomed Clarendon Springs, and in 1866 the original developer was forced to sell the prop-erty at a loss. Saratoga Springs experienced the same defection of southerners because of its political climate.[53]

There was a modest revival of southern visitation to Saratoga after the Civil War because of the interest of southerners in the newly established thoroughbred racetrack. Instead of visiting Saratoga Springs, however, many southerners frequented Quebec's lake district, the Eastern Townships, which looked like the Adirondacks. Here the descendants of Loyalists were the hosts, people who had sympathized with the South during the Civil War and deserved southern patronage. Thus, southern visitation at the spa never returned to what it had been from 1820 to 1850.

Foreigners were also present at the spas. Europeans, especially the English, made Saratoga Springs a stop on their grand tours; however, they did not repeat these visits in succeeding years as the English tended to choose another part of the globe to explore. More consistent visitors from 1815 to the end of the century were Cubans, West Indians, and Central Americans. Cubans had trading connections with the New York City, providing wholesalers there with sugar, cigars, and coffee, commodities that were then distributed throughout the county. They also had an interest in horse racing, and they followed the Manhattan crowd to the spas. In 1882, they had a favorite establishment in Saratoga Springs for their sojourn, the Everett House.[54] The proprietor, P. M. Suarez, was a native of Spain who had come to New York City in 1854, where he became a hotelkeeper. At the spa, his fully equipped ninety-five-room hotel had space for two hundred guests, many of them from Latin America. Thus, foreigners were welcome at Saratoga and added to the cosmopolitan atmosphere.

The Defection to Newport and the Rise of Suburban Ideal

Before the Civil War, Saratoga Springs was the dominant resort for the fashionable and rich, even if some claimed not to enjoy it. In the post–Civil War era, a gradual shift took place in where the upper strata of spa society spent their summer vacations. Residents of Manhattan did not easily give up their devotion to Saratoga's hotels to partake of the rugged Atlantic coast or the Adirondack wilderness. But southerners and upstate New Yorkers were drawn to the sea at Newport, although few of them swam in the ocean. The example of Erastus Corning's family vacation is illustrative. Beginning as a clerk in an Albany hardware store, Corning became mayor of Albany and one the richest men in the state capital, having profited as a merchant, land speculator, railroad developer, and president of the Albany City Bank. In the early years of his marriage, his wife, Harriet, took her children for a change of air to a farm in Canaan, New York, while Erastus, consumed by business affairs, visited only when he could get away.[55] This pattern followed the tradition of patrician families such as the Van Rensselaers of Cherry Hill, who had country houses within a reasonable distance of Albany. By the 1840s, however, the Cornings had acquired a summer house at Sachem's Head, Connecticut, recognition of the pleasures of the seaside. Nevertheless, after Erastus's greatest financial successes in the 1850s, the entire family also went to Saratoga Springs, which they could now afford. In the 1860s, Erastus Corning retired, and he and Harriet chose to join the summer colony of mainly southerners at Newport, Rhode Island. Still, his family did not entirely abandon the spa for the seashore; his two sons and their families continued to spend their summers at Saratoga. A generation gap appeared, as some continued to favor the spa, while others went to Newport.

In the 1880s, in their search for exclusivity, some old-money New Yorkers established themselves at Newport, the ideal place to continue their studied aloofness. The shift was gradual and hardly universal. Commodore Cornelius Vanderbilt, who built a fortune creating the New York Central Railroad, always summered in Saratoga.[56] After the Commodore's death, his son, William (Billy) continued the tradition of summering at the spa. The next generation of Vanderbilts, however, had other ideas. Billy's two sons, Cornelius II and William Kissam (Willie), purchased or built "cottages" in Newport in the mid-1880s. The shift to Newport by some New Yorkers reflected a change in social values from taking a vacation that was publicly oriented to one that was completely private. Among the rich, to see and to be seen in public was no longer the fashion, so they avoided hotels in favor of summer homes, where they could entertain their exclusive circle of friends with a staff and amenities comparable to those of a hotel. The rich who joined the summer colony at Newport built their homes beyond the town in a suburban oceanside enclave, with extensive grounds to give them the ultimate in privacy. These grand homes emulate the country houses of and were to attract the European aristocracy, especially titled Englishmen.[57]

The concern to create an English country house fit the suburban revolution sweeping the country and influenced the development of resorts. The Victorian ideal of family and home had become a standard for the elements of the aristocracy that summered at Newport and also for the emulating middle class. It emphasized the home as a healthy refugee for nurturing the family; there the mother dominated, while the father spent most of his time away from business affairs. The ideal housing was suburban — that is, beyond the city center, although not too distant from its attractions.[58] A family could retreat to the suburbs from the crowding caused by immigrant populations and from the unhealthy conditions and perceived dangers of the urban core. Privacy was the watchword in the suburbs as homes were built in the latest architectural styles in the midst of expansive lawns, which provided healthful recreation and a barrier to the public street. The middle class could emulate their betters in suburban housing because of the wide variety of new products that the Industrial Revolution made available. The latest styles of architecture were inexpensively obtainable, for example, because sawmills mass-produced Victorian gingerbread trim.

The suburban home and the summer vacation cottage drew on each other. At first, only the most wealthy, with their own carriages, or retirees could partake of the suburban ideal because the suburbs were too distant for the middle class to commute to work. However, in the 1880s a transportation revolution remedied this problem. New broad boulevards leading to the city center, with houses lining them, created a parklike residential atmosphere and allowed for more direct access to the downtown. The addition of streetcar lines along the boulevards by the turn of the century provided easy and inexpensive access to the downtown and thus made the distant suburban areas accessible to the middle class.

The best example of suburban development in the region we are considering here, similar to that at Newport, was at Lake George, just north of Caldwell. There the rich soon became tired of Caldwell's few crowded hotels and even the most elaborate camping. Although hotels were the place to stay in the 1850s and cottages remained private structures on their grounds, after the Civil War the New York City crowd became more adventurous and wanted their own place on the lake. With land now available, the west and east sides of the south end of Lake George came to be dotted with summer cottages and camps. The earliest cottages on the west side were Colonel Walter Price's summer houses, both completed by 1872, closely followed in 1876 by Dr. I. H. Tuttle's Rockledge estate near Tea Island.[59] Colonel Price was an English immigrant who had made a fortune brewing beer in Manhattan and had purchased all his land in 1869 from locals. In contrast, the Reverend Doctor Tuttle, the rector of St. Luke's Episcopal Church in New York City, had more limited resources but made up for it with his impeccable connections to many of the city's best families. From 1856, he purchased at least sixteen parcels along the lake in preparation for building his summer house. In these transactions, Tuttle dealt directly with the Caldwell proprietary heirs. It took him twenty years to decide to build his cottage, proof of the novelty of having one's own place on the lake. These new owners from New York City continued the process of opening the lake to a wider spectrum of society. The new cottages, in the Second Empire style, looked out of place along the mountainside because of their mansard roofs, a feature more appropriate to an urban setting. Eventually, cottages would be more compatible with the environment, constructed of natural materials such as the logs and stone found in the Adirondacks, but the early cottages represented a suburban ideal.

In contrast to development in Newport and Lake George, suburban development in Saratoga Springs was nuanced. True, in 1832 Madame Jumel built her own cottage. Still, because New York society was prepared to recognize only her sins, none dared to follow her lead, and the idea of summering in one's own cottage languished. Even in the 1880s, suburbanization was only moderately successful in Saratoga Springs, where life centered on Broadway and society revolved around numerous hotels. The building of elaborate summer cottages in Saratoga Springs was tied to the development of boulevards in the 1870s and 1880s: Grand Avenue, North Broadway, Union Avenue, Lake Avenue. Some of the earliest summer homes built in the 1870s were on Grand Avenue, including one by New York City stockbroker Edward T. Noble. Georgia lumberman Joseph Gilson's home on Lake Avenue followed it in 1885, and two years later a cottage was built on North Broadway by New York banker Isaac Phelps.[60] As noted, however, the lots were not usually expansive, and the crowding of large homes along the boulevards made them appear distinctly urban. Only at the far reaches of North Broadway would Saratoga Springs have lots of the size needed to create the parklike aspect advocated by suburban developers. Despite the need for suburban development expressed by realtors, Saratoga Springs was slow to adopt the summer home, concentrating instead on its hotels, boarding houses, pleasure grounds, and outdoor public spaces. Downtown Broadway continued to resemble the highly urban milieu that was popular with the middle class and held the suburban ideal at arm's length.

In the century from 1780 to 1880, the number of Americans who traveled to a destination for health, education, or pleasure increased significantly. In the last years of the eighteenth century, visitors had vacation places mostly to themselves. Concern for health was the earliest motive for the visit, followed by the enjoyment of simple country pleasures; ultimately style drove people to visit resorts. By the early 1800s, the fashionables of the cities were addicted to vacations, and the search for gentility and entertainment brought crowds to even the most isolated places. In the Civil War era, political convictions and the rise of new resorts caused defections of visitors from one place to another. Southerners abandoned Saratoga Springs and northern resorts in the 1850s as hostility to slavery became open, and they did not return in considerable numbers, even after the Civil War.

The makeup of the spa's clientele varied over time. As to class, visitors until the 1830s were aristocratic, refined, and limited in number, but after then the middle class appeared in increasing numbers, emulating their betters, diluting the exclusiveness of the resort experience wherever they congregated. At resorts, there was a gender gap in favor of men. Social precepts limited women's ability to travel to, stay at, and enjoy a resort. Men turned traditional hunting and fishing excursions into full-fledged vacations that reinforced the notion that women were not able to participate in such activities. After the Civil War, for the first time, women did appear at resorts in parties made up exclusively of their sex, confident that they did not need a male escort. In origin, visitors were usually city dwellers who fled from the urban conditions of heat, disease, crowding, and the presence of the lower classes—especially in the summer. Visitors annually made a trip to Saratoga Springs from cities as distant as Charleston, New Orleans, and Havana, Cuba. The shift by some of the rich to Newport was the result of their need for exclusivity, which could be found in a suburban setting, most often on the edges of the ocean or lakes. Saratoga Springs, however, resisted this shift by capitalizing on its urbanity and openness, developing social rituals that brought the aristocracy and the middle class together.

Epilogue
Why Do Resorts Succeed?

As we review the nineteenth century and glimpse beyond it, we see how accepted it had become to believe that resort life could provide a dynamic economic basis for a community. By the end of the century, spas and resorts were sprouting throughout the nation. On November 13, 1886, western New York's *Buffalo Express* reported that Breesport, a hamlet near Elmira, New York, had become a center of great attention. The reporter enthused, "It is the last place in the world anyone would ever expect anything of, but within a few weeks the quiet little village has sprung prominently forward and bids fair to bloom and blossom like a rose." The reason for the hubbub was the discovery of a mineral spring, which proved on analysis to have the proper content for good health. Development by local worthies was in full swing, and a former sheriff from Buffalo had leased the local hotel and was having it enlarged and renovated for the expected summer guests. The article concluded, "Breesport evidently means to make hay while the sun shines."[1] Thus discovering mineral springs was like finding a gold mine; it could turn a community around, bringing an economic boom.

Over the years, most of these new spas, which were completely dependent on the shifting sands of the visitor market, would disappear, victims of the weakness of their tourism infrastructure and lack of a service workforce. Ballston Spa and Caldwell, not Saratoga Springs, represent the norm for communities that became resorts. They failed to reach the nineteenth-century "urban threshold" of Saratoga Springs and other New York communities because their tourism was too slender a base on which to build an economy. They faltered and went no further than a limited tourism or saved themselves by switching to an industrial base.

It was difficult for Ballston Spa and Caldwell to build a tourism infrastructure when only a single person was in control of the resort. True, the landlords of Ballston Spa and Caldwell were willing to expend resources on embellishments and experiments. Ballston Spa had the county's first great resort hotel and was the first center of fashion, a place where the presence of agreeable company sustained a resort economy. Caldwell was as well planned as Saratoga Springs; centered on its courthouse, it had a broad and straight main street, flanked on one side by alleys. Nestled below Prospect Mountain on the shore of a peerlessly scenic lake, Caldwell's white Greek Revival structures were regarded by visitors as exceptionally picturesque. After William Caldwell died in 1848 and Low left Ballston Spa in 1823, however, each community was on its own and had to shift its economic base to survive. Ballston Spa abruptly turned its back on tourism and went in the direction of Utica and Rochester, becoming a manufacturing center and home to middle-class values. Caldwell embraced tourism as never before, welcoming the construction of several hotels and eventually summer cottages. Yet tourism in Caldwell remained highly seasonal, never being enough to support the local economy year-round. It is instructive that a local businessman placed his gang sawmill among the grand lakeshore cottages; it marred the beauty of the lake by belching steam and consuming the forest, all for the sake of year-round employment. In Caldwell, tourism provided only a partial basis on which to build an economy.

As we look to the twentieth century, at the heart of the success of resort communities are five concerns: resort infrastructure, the public nature of amenities, the quality of entrepreneurial leadership, puritanism versus the pursuit of pleasure, and exclusivity versus openness in attracting visitors.

The first key to the success of Saratoga Springs as a community and resort was its ability to build an infrastructure of accommodations, amenities, and services; such an infrastructure is recognized by today's tourism managers as the hallmark of a vacation destination. To investigate this infrastructure has required the integration of planning and architectural history with social and economic history. The motives of the planner-developers have been scrutinized to trace the erection of buildings and then to show how the streets, alleys, hotels, boarding houses, and public amenities were populated with citizens ready to serve visitors. The tourism industry in Saratoga Springs was similar to twentieth-century service economies and was thus able to deal with the new century.

The Saratoga Springs model was distinct because most resorts in the twentieth century would adopt extensive suburban development, with its emphasis on summer cottages. At Lake George, the suburban ideal was paramount from the 1870s into the twentieth century as the so-called cottages spread up its west side and along the lower east side until the road veered away from the lake. Residents of New York City were prominent in this activity; even their religious institutions sought the serenity of the lake. The influx included the Paulist Fathers, a New York City–based Catholic order that Clarence Walworth, son of the Chancellor, helped to found. They built a monastery on a tranquil bay, at the termination of the east-side road. Grand as the cottages and establishments were, however, they were only seasonal, not conducive to the creation of a permanent community. The dispersion of activities throughout the lake to other hamlets, like Bolton Landing, prevented Caldwell village from increasing its year-round population much above what it had been when it was part of the proprietors' estate. At a time when nearby Glens Falls was growing by leaps and bounds as a result of lime and the wood-products industry, Caldwell remained a sleepy hamlet.

A sign of a strong resort infrastructure was the expansion of the building trades. The architectural distinction of Saratoga Springs was the dignified red-brick buildings of its masons, rather than wood-frame "painted ladies." Moreover, the most substantial and expensive real estate north of Albany was not the result of the efforts of professional architects. They were hired only after the Civil War to design public buildings, and Saratoga Springs had no resident, full-time architects until the 1880s. Instead, the spa progressed through three stages of building-trades development. In the early years, jacks-of-all-trades such as Gideon Putnam and Nathan Lewis found construction to be one means of making a living. From 1830 to 1860, extended families of craftsmen, especially masons, carpenters, and painters, controlled the trade by passing their skills on to a few apprentices, who were relatives or friends. In the last stage, from the 1850s to the 1880s, contractors came to dominate through their ability to collect materials and offer day wages to workers, who were not usually skilled. Most building tradesmen were Protestants of a fiercely anti-Catholic mentality who tried to support their families as an increasingly competitive labor market made conditions more difficult. A few of the craftsmen and contractors held local government office, but they never organized their fellow working-men for collective action.

After the U.S. centennial, the spa's infrastructure continued to grow. In the twilight of the nineteenth century, an effort was made to renew European roots through the addition of an amenity to Congress Park. At the spa, Richard Canfield, a legendary New Yorker who combined a passion for gambling with patronage of the arts, introduced projects promoting European taste. He acquired the Casino and the property around it in 1893 and 1902, acquisitions that allowed him to expand pleasure grounds to the east and north. Here, he had Italian gardens laid out in rectangular shapes of the classical style around a pool that contained several pieces of sculpture.[2] Two marble columns, copies of the work of Giacomo da Vignola, an architect for St. Peter's in Rome, marked the entrance. A marble sundial was based on one existing in Lugano, Switzerland. The figures included Hermes, the messenger of the gods, and in the pool, two sea tritons who were nicknamed by the residents "Spit" and "Spat" for the streams that flowed from their shell trumpets (Figure 79). Neither Jane McCrea nor noble Indians but rather

FIGURE 79. Sea Triton, Congress Park, Saratoga Springs. Placed in the park by Canfield in 1902. This baroque sculpture helped to put Saratoga Springs in a class with European spas.
(Photo, Theodore Corbett.)

Canfield's two imported Baroque tritons became the spa's mascots just after the turn of the century. Thus, Canfield followed a long line of entrepreneurs who were willing to extravagantly invest in the resort's infrastructure; he also represented the continuing fascination of New Yorkers for the spa and their need to embellish it with European art.

In their fascination with European embellishments, the entrepreneurs of Saratoga Springs turned their back on the region's history and showed no practical restraint in the expense devoted to building monuments. Resorts and spas had first appeared in the Old World, and it was these resorts that this spa sought to emulate. English spas, in particular, were models, for the founding fathers of Saratoga Springs, Henry Walton and John Clarke, knew them well. Their ability to introduce expensive buildings, landscaped pleasure grounds, street paving, plantings and lighting, support alleys, and a water-supply system would carry Saratoga Springs into the twentieth century. Morrissey and Canfield continued what Walton and Clark started, sharing a concern to produce a community with pleasures and monuments to match the those in the Old World. This European connection in the arts would place Saratoga Springs a step above the resorts and communities around it.

Uniquely, Saratoga Springs depended on a service economy; its leaders had early experience in managing a nonindustrial workforce. Native American families found a summer home here and at a very few other resorts, such as Caldwell and Niagara Falls, where their encampments provided a rare opportunity for them to coexist with Victorian society. Also, African Americans and the Irish provided labor and services for the resort communities. Until the 1850s, there was a greater proportion of blacks in Saratoga Springs than in most upstate New York cities because they could make a living in the resort business. By then, however, the Irish were present in even greater numbers, and in the next decades they took resort jobs from blacks. The Irish settled throughout upstate New York, but Saratoga Springs had more single Irish women in domestic service; they worked not just in their youth but permanently into their forties, devoting much of their life to the resort trade. Thus, the interrelationship between domestic service and tourism was established in the early 1800s and was perfected throughout the century. These forgotten Americans provided an important skilled labor force for a service economy and made work at a nineteenth-century resort a multicultural experience.

Women played a crucial but neglected role in the resort workforce, as they do now. Their presence was greater in the service business than is realized, for they were ideal resort workers, and their skills in housewifery allowed them to dominate all levels of the domestic service industry. They ran boarding houses or hotels, or they managed the kitchen on which a hotel's reputation depended, or they joined the growing number of domestics necessary to keep the community looking elegant and pristine. At the top of the resort trade, women could do better than their counterparts in other communities because they had opportunities to become respectable boarding-house proprietors. Yet there was tragedy in their lives; poor women and widows did not always succeed financially or in marrying into the community, as witnessed by the number forced to live in inexpensive alley housing. The service-based economy of today has its origin in the backbreaking labor and suffering of these nineteenth-century women.

Resort life was public in every aspect, and consequently the hotel drove the community's economic and social engine. Broadway, where the greatest number of hotels existed, was from the beginning the center of attraction. Its concentration of commercial structures created an urban aspect only a few blocks from the contrasting open fields and wilderness; as a result it could offer both experiences to visitors. The public aspect of Saratoga Springs forced the development of amenities to entertain visitors rather than to solve the village's social problems. Private investors gave the spa some of the nation's earliest and most sophisticated pleasure grounds, parks, Native American encampments, theaters, a casino, and a rural cemetery. These became the setting for the round of parties and events that were necessary to set social standards. Even churches were eventually built for the spa's public life; their monumental auditoriums with comfortable seats served as an inspiration for preachers whose eloquence captivated audiences.

To create these public spaces, resorts needed a unique type of investor to orchestrate development. Spa leaders had to be willing to designate space—commercial promoters would say waste—for squares, pleasure grounds, alleys, and expansive hotels in order to enhance the community's attractiveness and quality of life. This was not the type of investment for a commercial promoter because it brought no quick return. The need for public spaces drove investors and contractors to organize the building trades for the construction of the nineteenth-century buildings and amenities that are still the Victorian backdrop present-day visitors enjoy in Saratoga Springs. Thus, the early development of a tourism infrastructure was the product of an enlightened leadership. Saratoga Springs and ultimately Caldwell also prospered from a leadership that shared development responsibility and did not dictate a single direction for enterprise. Henry Walton's willingness to sell land rather than rent it out has been documented. The sale of extensive portions of his estate made possible the enterprises of Gideon Putnam, John Clarke, the Marvin brothers, and Judiah Ellsworth.

In Caldwell, responsibility for development also came to be dispersed. Caldwell was more affected by the penetration of the automobile than Saratoga Springs. In the mid-twentieth century interstate access to the village and its location as a gateway to the Adirondacks made it immensely popular, so much so that it has been accused of becoming an Adirondack Coney Island. A decision to appeal to the vast middle-class family market made Caldwell discard any pretensions to exclusivity that remained from its past. The very name of the founding family was now viewed detrimental to the village and town, which sought a means of making tourists believe that it was the only community on Lake George. As a result of its concern for mass marketing, in 1962 the town fathers jettisoned the Caldwell name in favor of Lake George Village and Town, ensuring that most traces of the Caldwell family legacy would disappear. By the 1990s, the commercialization of Caldwell by overzealous development had split the community: on the one side were the cottage owners, who wanted to save the famous lake from the polluting effects of overuse by boaters; on the other side were the motel and shop operators, who stood for "progress, mass tourism, and fun."[3] Lake George Village and resorts like it attract both types of citizens, the public-spirited conservationist and the free-wheeling commercial developer, and both share a claim to the resort's stewardship.

Another split occurred between puritanism and the pursuit of pleasure. Puritanism in the nineteenth century was powerful enough to delay the development of resorts and leisure activities. In Saratoga Springs the Blues and Reds were divided on the religious and moral issue of how much pleasure was proper at a resort. Waller was correct in calling attention to the conflict between the restrained and the epicurean as a dominant force in the building of a resort. But he saw only the fun lovers as succeeding and enhancing a resort when, in reality, both Blues and Reds had religious and moral convictions. Tolerance for both the Blues and the Reds and for diverging nineteenth-century viewpoints on religion, drink, and social custom allowed Saratoga Springs to flourish as a resort. Religious revival and temperance made resort leaders uneasy, but such movements were allowed, although they never had as extensive a role as in other places. Public consumption of alcoholic spirits was more crucial to a resort's restaurant and entertainment trade than it was in manufacturing communities, where drinking was private or limited to the laboring class. Saratoga Springs never become a heavenly city on earth or fell to religious zealots; instead it made compromises and entertained both spiritual and secular visitors.

In the twentieth century, the debate over religion and morality continued, with resorts often finding themselves the victims of efforts to legislate morality. The temperance movement continued, spawning in 1919 a national prohibition of spirits, the Twenty-third Amendment. Like early efforts, it failed to stop drinking in the 1920s, merely forcing it underground, where it became the domain of organized crime. Although the amendment was repealed only fourteen years later, temperance was accompanied by a groundswell of antigambling sentiment in New York State.[4] Morrissey's Casino was an early victim of this sentiment; its new owner, Richard Canfield, was forced to close the Casino first in 1904 and finally three years later, and the structure was sold to the City of Saratoga Springs in 1911. Municipal intervention thus saved a public space that might have been lost, as the Casino was turned into today's lavish social center and historical museum. In contrast to Morrissey's time, today anyone with an invitation to the numerous parties held at the Casino can enjoy a glass of champagne. Gambling no longer takes place, and efforts to revive it have been opposed by most elements of the community because it would hurt the wagering that already exists at its tracks. This late twentieth-century compromise dispensed with both Morrissey's rules and gambling.

Nineteenth-century Saratoga Springs at its most open also fostered social distinctions, for leisure was a product of aristocratic, not democratic, ideals. Regarding the spa of the 1830s, the words of an English visitor are perceptive: "Here, more than elsewhere, may be discovered the distinction that really prevails among persons of the different classes in America. Certain it is, that exorbitant prices, combined with ridiculous extravagance in dress," have caused one Saratoga hotel "to be frequented by the first company in the Union."[5] The audience for nineteenth-century resorts remained limited. From 1780 to 1880, more Americans were excluded from resorts than visited them. There were those who took no vacations; in 1780 they were the vast majority, and even by 1880 the entire laboring class was still in that category. There were also those, especially among middle-class families, who chose not to bear the cost of an expensive resort like Saratoga Springs. Finally, there were those who could not enjoy a resort because of social convention, this group consisting largely of women. Although they had abundant leisure and often the financial means, women remained a minority at resorts, restricted from enjoying the spa by the requirements of their supposed duties at home. Even those who came could not enter the men's preserves, such as the Casino's gaming rooms. Thus only males from the upper and middle classes, usually traveling as individuals, had complete freedom to use the spa. Leisure and pleasure remained commodities that Americans and foreigners associated with an aristocracy that could afford them. Although Saratoga Springs was more open than Newport or White Sulphur Springs, it was certainly not open to all.

Today the typical visitor is far from fitting the profile of our 1880s older couple, Samantha and Josiah. Surveys of American travelers for the summer of 1996 show that almost half of us (43 percent) vacation as families. Families even account for 40 percent of the Club Med crowd; when Club Med was founded in the 1950s, it was the exclusive preserve of swinging singles. Only a small minority in the nineteenth century considered the possibility of a family vacation. Today, couples (not necessarily married) make up 27 percent of vacationers, while threesomes or more add an additional 4 percent. At 26 percent, the smallest remaining group is singles, the nineteenth-century's dominant group. In contrast to the past, current singles face considerable obstacles in traveling. The travel industry is set up for double occupancy, and to break that norm requires financial supplements that can double the cost of a room. In addition, there is the trauma of eating alone, of being assigned the middle seat on an airplane, and of women dealing with foreign, male-oriented cultures. The odd-person-out predicament of the single traveler would have surprised the nineteenth-century traveler, who enjoyed being independent of his family, the ideal state for a gentleman. Interestingly, one of today's few types of resort that does attract singles are spas, now expensive and elegant establishments, not unlike the cure institute. The argument for singles in this market niche is the same as in the nineteenth-century spas, that "feeling well . . . is an individual matter," that health needs vary so much by the individual that they cannot be met in a family group.[6]

Resorts can choose to be open or exclusive in attracting visitors. Clearly, resorts such as White Sulphur Springs and Newport or at times Ballston Spa and Caldwell succeeded with exclusivity, and White Sulphur Springs and Newport have retained that tradition today. The ideal of an exclusivity that fosters intimacy, quiet relaxation, and solitude remains popular. Current glitzy vacation advertisements show a couple on an empty beach, languidly sunning themselves, an image that supposedly appeals to the high-powered but exhausted businessperson in search of nothing more than rest and relaxation. This kind of experience is not what Saratoga Springs offered because it violated the cardinal rule of public participation in the enjoyment of attractions and activities. Such intimacy could be found only in one of its secluded cure institutes.

A reality of both the past and present is the transitory nature of resort audiences—the defections of groups from one resort to another, and especially the appearance of different social classes at resorts. The arrival of the middle class at resorts was certainly much earlier than the post–Civil War era. Saratoga Springs was serving ever-widening audiences in the 1830s, including them because of its open tradition. Most of its amenities were free, and even the Casino was open to all visitors—although locals were excluded. From the 1850s, the number of people taking vacations increased, and the spa's mammoth hotels could survive only by filling their hundreds of rooms with such visitors. They easily filled the vacuum left by the disappearance of southerners to their own resorts and the aristocratic elements drawn to Newport. The popular press found people-watching to be best at Saratoga Springs; reporters fearlessly offered innuendo and gossip to feed their growing middle-class readership. By the 1880s, homespun Marietta Holley had brought her values to the spa to compete with those established by the earlier generation of Mrs. Clinton, Madame Jumel, and Catharine Maria Sedgwick. These new middle-class values were not so vulgar as the rich thought; after all, during Samantha's visit, she expressed a sympathetic appreciation of the condition of Native Americans and a strong concern for the rights of women.

Women visitors were less numerous than men in the nineteenth century because society decreed that they could not travel or enjoy a vacation on their own. However, as the nineteenth century progressed, their confidence increased, and more hotel groups consisted exclusively of women traveling together, without their husbands or brothers. The women organized social events that set the standards of conduct for guests who were the cream of society from every part of the Union. This social role remains their preserve today, and they now are an equal presence at all resorts, even in those that cater to singles.

The road to today's mass-marketed tourism would twist and turn for Saratoga Springs, Caldwell, and Ballston Spa. From the medieval pilgrimage to the taking of the waters at Bath to the porch gatherings at Victorian spas to the current historic-house tours, the hospitality industry has come a long way. By the turn of the nineteenth century, the success of resorts was already a matter of a tourism infrastructure, of sophisticated architecture and necessary public spaces, of a service workforce, of a degree of spiritual uplift, and of investors' planning to meet these needs. The rise of tourism created resort communities that debated and chose the best way of entertaining the visitors. By the end of the nineteenth century, success as a resort meant that visitors had to be entertained in a sophisticated infrastructure, where compromise and public spirit prevailed, so that a wide spectrum of Americans could enjoy a vacation.

Notes

❦ ❧

These notes are not meant to serve as a bibliography or as a record of all sources consulted. For example, one of my most productive research experiences was at the American Antiquarian Society Library in Worcester, Massachusetts. That institution is not cited here because the works consulted were all published and could be found — although never as comprehensively — at other libraries.

ABBREVIATIONS

BM   Brookside Museum, Saratoga County Historical Society, Ballston Spa, N.Y.

HCHP   Historic Cherry Hill Papers, Special Collections, New York State Library, Albany, N.Y.

HS   Historical Society of Saratoga Springs, Saratoga Springs, N.Y.

HSP   Historical Society of Pennsylvania, Philadelphia.

JAM   Journal of Abigail May, Library, New York State Historical Association, Cooperstown, N.Y.

MCP   Miscellaneous Caldwell Papers, McKinney Library, Albany Institute of History and Art, Albany, N.Y.

MD   Manuscript Division, New York State Library, Albany, N.Y.

NLP   Nicholas Low Papers, Collections of the Manuscript Division, Library of Congress, Washington, D.C.

NYHS   Library, New-York Historical Society, New York, N.Y.

SCC   Saratoga County Clerk, Ballston Spa, N.Y.

SCCO   Saratoga County Clerk's Office, Ballston Spa, N.Y.

SSCH   Saratoga Springs City Historian, Saratoga Springs, N.Y.

SR   Saratoga Room, Saratoga Springs Public Library, Saratoga Springs, N.Y.

WCCO   Warren County Clerk's Office, Lake George, N.Y.

WCEP   William Caldwell Estate Papers, Special Collections, New York State Library, Albany, N.Y.

WCHO   Warren County Historian's Office, Lake George, N.Y.

WRSI   Warren County Records Storage and Information Center, Lake George, N.Y.

INTRODUCTION: *The Creation of Resorts*

1. George Waller, *Saratoga, Saga of an Imperious Era* (New York, 1966), 63–69, 75–79.

2. Harley McGee, *Recording Historic Buildings* (Washington, D.C., 1970); National Museum of American Art and National Institute for the Conservation of Cultural Property, *Handbook, Save Outdoor Sculpture!* (Washington, D.C., 1992); Brandywine Conservancy, *Protecting Historic Properties: A Guide to Research and Preservation* (Caddice Ford, Pa., 1984). On the superiority of visual over written sources, see Thomas Schlereth, ed., *Material Culture Studies in America* (Nashville, Tenn., 1982), 79–102, 106–113, 124–140, 143–152, 174–191, 195–258, 289–305, 316–324.

3. J. H. French, *Gazetteer of the State of New York* (Syracuse, N.Y., 1860), 455, 492.

4. Ibid., 457, 494.

5. Dona Brown, *Inventing New England, Regional Tourism in the Nineteenth Century* (Washington, D.C., 1995), 8–16, 43–67.

6. John Sears, *Sacred Places* (New York, 1989), 2–30, 209–216.

7. David Maldwyn Ellis, *Landlords and Farmers in the Hudson-Mohawk Region 1790–1850* (New York, 1967), 16–71, 288–302.

8. Waller, *Saratoga*, 81–86, 122–126, 228–235.

9. Ellen Weiss, *City in the Woods: The Life and Design of an American Camp Meeting on Martha's Vineyard* (New York, 1987), 19–32, 64–73.

10. Neil Harris, "On Vacation," in *Resorts of the Catskills*, ed. Neil Harris (New York, 1979), 2–7.

11. The tour was outlined in print in Gideon M. Davison, *The Fashionable Tour: or, A Trip to the Springs, Niagara, Quebeck, and Boston in the Summer of 1821* (Saratoga Springs, N.Y., 1822); Louise Roomet, "Vermont as a Resort Area in the Nineteenth Century," *Vermont History* 44 (winter 1976): 1–5.

12. Robert Conte, *The History of the Greenbrier, America's Resort* (Charleston, W. Va., 1989), 6–31, 64–73.

13. John Hope Franklin, *A Southern Odyssey, Travelers in the Antebellum North* (Baton Rouge, La., 1976), 81–166; Phoebe Ann Lewis, *The Equinox, Historic Home of Hospitality* (Manchester, Vt., 1993), 8–11; Robert Albion, *The Rise of New York Port (1815–1860)* (Devon, U.K., 1970), 95–121.

14. Betsy Blackmar, "Going to the Mountains: A Social History," in Harris, *Resorts of the Catskills*, 64–79.

CHAPTER 1: *The Tradition of the English Spa*

1. Michael Kraus, *The Atlantic Civilization—18th Century Origins* (Ithaca, N.Y., 1949), 1–22; Bayard Still, *Mirror for Gotham: New York as Seen by Contemporaries from Dutch Days to the Present* (New York, 1956), 46.

2. P. J. Corfield, *The Impact of English Towns 1700–1800* (Oxford, U.K., 1982), 51–65; Phyllis Hembly, *The English Spa 1560–1815: A Social History* (Cranbury, N.J., 1990); J. H. Plumb, *The Commercialization of Leisure in Eighteenth-Century England* (Reading, U.K., 1973).

3. E. P. Thompson, "Time, Work-Discipline and Industrial Capitalism," in *Customs in Common* (Harmondsworth, U.K., 1993), 352–403.

4. Quoted in Edward Wagenknecht, *Washington Irving, Moderation Displayed* (New York, 1962), 101.

5. Don Gerlach, *Philip Schuyler and the American Revolution in New York, 1733–1777* (Lincoln, Neb., 1964), 32–35; NYHS, Nicholas Low Papers (1784–1825), William Wallace to Nicholas Low, October 9, 1801.

6. NYHS, "Genealogical Chart showing the descent and alliances from the Colonial Period of the issue of Cruger son of Henry Walton" (New York). On Peter Van Schaack's time in England, see Henry Cruger Van Schaack, *The Life of Peter Van Schaack, LL.D., Embracing Selections from His Correspondence and Other Writings* (New York, 1842), 132–135, quote on 132; William Benton, "Peter Van Schaack: The Conscience of a Loyalist," in *The Loyalist Americans: A Focus on Greater New York*, ed. Robert East and Jacob Judd (Tarrytown, N.Y., 1975), 44–55; Carl Lotus Becker, *The History of Political Parties in the Province of New York, 1760–1776* (Madison, Wis., 1960), 10, 19, 60, 75, 107, 177, 264.

7. On the Cruger family, see Lewis Einstein, *Divided Loyalties, Americans in England during the War of Independence* (London, 1933), 245–266; Catherine Crary, *The Price of Loyalty, Tory Writings from the Revolutionary Era* (New York, 1973), 9, 179, 274–275, 346. On the Walton family, see William L. Stone, *Reminiscences of Saratoga and Ballston* (New York, 1875), 287–292.

8. Bryan Homer, *Charles Dickens and Leamington Spa: Fact, Fiction and Fancy* (Coventry, U.K., 1991); Anne-Marie Edwards, *In the Steps of Jane Austin* (Southampton, U.K., 1985), 75–99.

9. J. H. Plumb, *Men and Centuries* (Boston, 1963), 104–106; Hembly, *The English Spa 1560–1815,* 115–117, 136–138, 234–235.

10. Barry Cunliffe, *The City of Bath* (New Haven, Conn., and London, 1986), 118–127; Christopher Woodward, *The Building of Bath* (Bath, U.K., 1994), 10–15.

11. Steven Blake, *The Pittville Pump Room* (Cheltenham, U.K., 1980), n.p.

12. Cunliffe, *The City of Bath,* 125–134; Woodward, *The Building of Bath,* 28–29.

13. National Trust, *Bath Assembly Rooms* (London, 1985), 17–27; Corfield, *The Impact of English Towns,* 56–61.

14. George Rowe, *Illustrated Cheltenham Guide* (Cheltenham, U.K., 1845), 65–66.

15. Theodore Corbett, *Our Sense of Place* (Elmira, N.Y., 1995), 3–4, 8–17.

16. David Burt, *Elizabeth's England* (London, 1981), 143–147.

17. Rowe, *Illustrated Cheltenham Guide,* 1–2.

18. R. Grundy Heape, *Buxton under the Dukes of Devonshire* (London, 1948), 24–28.

19. Martin Smith, *The Story of Stamford* (Stamford, U.K., 1994), 81–96.

20. Rowe, *Illustrated Cheltenham Guide,* 1–2, 4–5, 15, 22, 31, 57, 72, 86–87.

21. Ibid., xxxiii.

22. Nicholas Pevsner, *The Buildings of England—Derbyshire* (Harmondsworth, U.K., 1986), 12–14; Mike Langham and Colin Wells, *Buxton: A Pictorial History* (Chichester, U.K., 1993), n.p.

23. J. Jean Hecht, *The Domestic Servant Class in Eighteenth-Century England* (London, 1956).

24. Lyndon Cave, *Royal Leamington Spa, Its History and Development* (Chichester, U.K., 1988), 63–65, 105.

25. Ibid., 105.

26. Edward P. Thompson, *The Making of the English Working Class* (New York, 1966), 234–237.

27. Cheltenham Borough Council, *Cheltenham* (Cambridge, 1990), 55.

28. Ibid., 17; Langham and Wells, *Buxton.*

29. Thompson, *Working Class,* 264–265.

30. Rowe, *Illustrated Cheltenham Guide,* 2, 4, 67, 72, 87, 91, 94.

31. Ibid., 32, 40–41, 71, 73, 79–80, 88, 92–93, 94–96.

32. Cheltenham Borough Council, *Cheltenham,* 15–16.

33. Ibid., 55.

CHAPTER 2: *The Rise and Fall of Ballston Spa as a Resort*

1. Franklin Ellis, *History of Columbia County, New York* (Philadelphia, 1878), 305; among the visitors to Lebanon Springs in 1780 were Ethan Allen, the Vermont hero, and Ezra Stiles, president of Yale, who shared the springs despite their diverging religious views, 78–82. See also John Pell, *Ethan Allen* (Boston and New York, 1929), 258.

2. Don Gerlach, *Philip Schuyler's Saratoga* (Schuylerville, N.Y., n.d.), n.p.; G. Turner, "Account of the Chalybeate Springs near Saratoga," *Columbian Magazine or Monthly Miscellany,* March 1787, 306–307.

3. Gerlach, *Philip Schuyler and the American Revolution in New York,* 32–35.

4. For a mid-nineteenth-century overview of Stephen Van Rensselaer, see Benson Lossing, *Eminent Americans* (New York, 1890), 2:260–261.

5. Douglas Sinclair, *Three Villages, One City* (Rensselaer, N.Y., 1992), 17–23; F. W. Beers, *County Atlas of Rensselaer, New York* (New York, 1876), 14–16.

6. BM, Sans Souci Hotel Register, 1823–1825; HSP, Philip Schuyler to Stephen Van Rensselaer, Saratoga, August 14, 1783.

7. Robert Sands et al., *Tales of Glauber Spa* (New York, 1832), 15–17.

8. Elizabeth Blackmar, *Manhattan for Rent, 1785–1850* (Ithaca, N.Y., 1989), 9, 28–42, 177–178, 210–211.

9. Sung Bok Kim, *Landlord and Tenant in Colonial New York, Manorial Society, 1664–1775* (Chapel Hill, N.C., 1978), 176, 194–195, 213.

10. NLP, Returns of Mr. Nicholas Low: Surveys in the Patent of Kayaderosseras, December 6, 1790; Nathaniel Bartlett Sylvester, *History of Saratoga County* (Philadelphia, 1878), 229.

11. Field Horne, *The First Respectable House* (Ballston Spa, N.Y., 1985), 14–18.

12. NLP, Map according to Mr. Baldwin's plans as a map of the Town of Bath or of lots near Ballston Salt Springs, June 18, 1803; NLP, A Map of Lot #2, December 7, 1790, Seth Baldwin; NLP, Beriah Palmer to Nicholas Low, May 17, 1796.

13. NLP, George White to Nicholas Low, December 10, 1803.

14. Davison, *The Fashionable Tour,* 34; Sylvester, *History of Saratoga County,* 240.

15. SCCO, A Copy of a Map and Survey of Subdivision of Lots no. 1 and no. 2 of the subdivision of lot 13, October 28, 1814, and August 31, 1819, H. Goodrich. The history of the wash house and what it became has a detailed study: John Cromie, "Doubleday Slept Here," *Local History* 2 (January 1992): 1–6.

16. Sylvester, *History of Saratoga County,* 240.

17. Ibid., 232–233.

18. NLP, Ballston Spa Company Report by Benjamin Peck, July 1, 1814; NLP, Samuel Hicks to Nicholas Low, April 22, 1820; NLP, Factory Hamilton Street 50 feet wide.

19. NLP, Map according to Mr. Baldwin's plans as a map of the Town of Bath or of lots near Ballston Salt Springs, June 18, 1803.

20. SCCO, A Copy of a Map and Survey of Subdivision of Lots no. 1 and no. 2 of the subdivision of lot 13, October 28, 1814, and August 31, 1819, H. Goodrich.

21. NLP, Map of Seth Baldwin & James Scott, November 15, 1815.

22. NLP, John DeWitt to Nicholas Low, November 21, 1796; NLP, Ballston Spa Company to Nicholas Low, March 8, 1814.

23. NLP, Peter Williams, Archy Kidd, Joel Lee, Samuel Pittman, Faugher McBain, Andy Fesson, R. Gwens, John Warren, James O'Connor, Eli Barnum, Harvey Loomis, Amos Altcott, Thomas Palmer to Nicholas Low, October 30, 1810.

24. Saratoga County Historical Society, *In a Pleasant Situation* (Ballston Spa, N.Y., 1986), 12; Horne, *The First Respectable House,* 25.

25. Ballston Spa's population history from 1790 to 1830—the most crucial period for developing a profile of the village as a resort community—is difficult to trace. Detailed information does not exist before the U.S. Census of 1850, and by that time Ballston Spa had ceased to be a resort. In addition, the village's population can only be approximated because of the available town censuses. Ballston Spa was located in the towns of both Milton and Ballston, although the greater portion of the village was in Milton, and thus an exact count from the town censuses is difficult to determine. In contrast, Saratoga Springs was created as a single township, and the boundaries of the city came to encompass the town, making a population study far more credible.

26. NLP, Peter Williams, Archy Kidd, Joel Lee, Samuel Pittman, Faugher McBain, Andy Fesson, R. Gwens, John Warren, James O'Connor, Eli Barnum, Harvey Loomis, Amos Altcott, Thomas Palmer to Nicholas Low, October 30, 1810.

27. Sylvester, *History of Saratoga County,* 231, 236, 240, 243–254.

28. NLP, Nicholas Low, Bromeling's bill, July 28, 1804, to September 12, 1804; NLP, Andre Berger to Nicholas Low, bill for May 7 to June 14 and bill for August 13 to September 27, 1811; NLP, Andre Berger to Nicholas Low, bill for October 1812; NYHS, Low Papers, Henrietta Low to Nicholas Low, May 15, 1816.

29. NLP, Martin Bromeling to Nicholas Low, January 24, 1805; Sylvester, *History of Saratoga County,* 240.

30. NLP, Peter Williams, Archy Kidd, Joel Lee, Samuel Pittman, Faugher McBain, Andy Fesson, R. Gwens, John Warren, James O'Connor, Eli Barnum, Harvey Loomis, Amos Altcott, Thomas Palmer to Nicholas Low, October 30, 1810.

31. Stone, *Reminiscences,* 287–292.

32. Sylvester, *History of Saratoga County,* 235–237.

33. Manuscripts Division, New York Public Library, New York, N.Y., Nicholas Low, Land Book II, 186; NLP, Estate at Ballston Springs, April 27, 1793–December 31, 1806; D. R. Preston, *The Wonders of Creation; Natural and Artificial* (Boston, 1807), 158–159; Benhard Puckhaber, "The Washington Spring of Ballston Spa," *The Grist Mill* 1 (winter 1968): 2–3; Sylvester, *History of Saratoga County,* 240–242; Stone, *Reminiscences,* 405–411.

34. NLP, Beriah Palmer to Nicholas Low, January 11, 1787.

35. Sylvester, *History of Saratoga County,* 240–242; Edward Grose, *Centennial History of the Village at Ballston Spa* (Ballston Spa, 1907), 60–62.

36. NYHS, Henry Walton to John Taylor, Saratoga Springs, February 17, 1831; David Nestle, "Ballston Spa—An Important Railroad Center," *The Grist Mill* 1 (fall 1967): 1; Taylor Crest, *Charlton Worthy, John W. Taylor* (Ballston Spa, N.Y., 1984).

37. On Hiro Jones's cotton mill, see MD, Hiro Jones Mill Book; Sylvester, *History of Saratoga County,* 233, 236–238, 248. On the bank, see Ruth Roerig, *History of Ballston Spa National Bank* (Ballston Spa, N.Y., 1988).

CHAPTER 3: *The Reluctant Resort*

1. Abigail May left an 1800 account of an excursion to Lake George in her Journal, JAM, n.p.; see also Theodore Corbett, "Women at the Spas, 1790–1850," *Local History* 1 (September 1991): 2–5; for an overall view of the development of tourism in the Adirondacks, see Craig Gilborn and Alice Gilborn, *Museum of the Adirondacks* (Utica, N.Y., 1984), 32–51.

2. An important source of information for the entire Caldwell family is MCP, Letter from Augusta Sewell Dwinford, daughter of Jane Caldwell Sewell to Catherine Beck Van Cortlandt, daughter of Harriet Caldwell Swell, 1885, Folder 25. See also Joel Munsell, *The Annals of Albany* (Albany, N.Y., 1850–1859), 5:26; Loretta Bates, "The Caldwells of Lake George" (paper for Adirondack Community College Course 272, December 1994).

3. Quoted in Munsell, *The Annals of Albany,* 3:405, 8:187; quote on 3:435.

4. Alice Kenney defined these patricians in *The Gansevoorts of Albany* (Syracuse, N.Y., 1969). On the material culture of the Caldwell family, see Joseph Butler, *Sleepy Hollow Restorations: A Cross-Section of the Collection* (Tarrytown, N.Y., 1983), 65, 97; *The Family Collections at Van Cortlandt Manor* (Tarrytown, N.Y., 1967), 24–25, 50–51, 63, 66–67, 74; MCP, "James Dobb's certificate that he did not see James Caldwell in N.York in 1782," Folder 2.

5. Isabel Thompson Kelsay, *Joseph Brant, 1743–1807* (Syracuse, N.Y., 1984), 645; Theodore Bolton and Irwin Cortelyou, *Ezra Ames of Albany, 1768–1836* (New York, 1955), 44, 210.

6. On the Gansevoorts' Snook Kill development, see Kenney, *The Gansevoorts of Albany,* 121–123, 145–149, 171, 174, 208, 217, 246–248, 294. On the creation of Schuylerville (Old Saratoga), see Gerlach, *Philip Schuyler's Saratoga.*

7. SCCO, C, 518, September 10, 1796, William Stillwell and wife to James Caldwell.

8. On James Caldwell's Warren County landholdings, see H. P. Smith, ed., *History of Warren County* (Syracuse, N.Y., 1885), 212, 219, 561, 565; WCCO, Deed Book A, 434, Trustees of Columbia College to James E. Caldwell, April 29, 1818; WCHO, Caldwell Estate Records, Udney Hay to James Caldwell, January 13, 1787.

9. WCHO, James Caldwell to John Beebee, August 14, 1810; William Brown, ed., *History of Warren County New York* (Glens Falls, N.Y., 1963), 209.

10. WCEP, James Caldwell to William Baird, July 1, 1823; Lake George Historical Association, *The Lake George Institute of History, Art and Science* (Lake George, N.Y., 1969), n.p.; Stone, *Reminiscences*, 393.

11. S. R. Stoddard, *Lake George: A Book of To-Day* (Glens Falls, N.Y., 1881), 59–64.

12. James Stuart, *Three Years in North America* (Edinburgh, Scotland, 1833), 1:179; WRSI, Map showing survey of Lots nos. 15 & 16 Kennedy Patent with its relation to the village of Caldwell, September 20, 1887.

13. On Walton's land policies, see Chapter 4; WCHO, James Caldwell to John Beebee, August 14, 1810; MCP, Village Lots of Caldwell, Folder 11.

14. Bolton and Cortelyou, *Ezra Ames of Albany*, 67–69.

15. On James Fenimore Cooper, see *The Letters and Journals of James Fenimore Cooper*, ed. James Franklin Beard (Cambridge, Mass., 1960), 1:128; Henry Walcott Boynton, *James Fenimore Cooper* (New York, 1931), 132–134; W. B. Shubrick Cymer, *James Fenimore Cooper* (New York, 1968), 43.

16. On Thomas Cole, see Henry T. Tuckerman, *Book of the Artists* (New York, 1966), 223–232; Louis Legrand Noble, *The Life and Works of Thomas Cole* (Cambridge, Mass., 1964), 176–190. On Cole's trip to Lake George in 1826, see Elwood Perry III, *The Art of Thomas Cole: Ambition and Imagination* (Newark, N.J., 1988), 47–67.

17. Smith, *History of Warren County*, 571; WRSI, House Bill from John Simpson, Sept. 1808.

18. Walter Harding, ed., "The Diary of Margaret Miller Davidson," *Journal of the Rutgers University Library* (December 1949): 7; WCHO, William Caldwell's Will, December 29, 1841; MCP, Daniel McConnelly to William Caldwell, November 4, 1813, Folder 3.

19. Munsell, *The Annals of Albany,* 10:217.

20. WCHO, William Caldwell bill for Union Hall, June 27, 1835, and Repair on Mansion House, June 3, 1846; WCEP, William Caldwell to William Sherrill, 1840; Betty Buckell, *Old Lake George Hotels* (Lake George, N.Y., 1986), 25; Mason Wade, ed., *The Journals of Francis Parkman* (New York, 1969), 45–47; WCCO, Deed Book I, 237, Hiram Hawley to William Caldwell, October 10, 1837.

21. WRSI, Map showing survey of Lots nos. 15 & 16 Kennedy Patent with its relation to the village of Caldwell, September 20, 1887.

22. Smith, *History of Warren County,* 567.

23. Ibid., 567–573, 649, 667.

24. Brown, *History of Warren County New York,* 284–285. Bolton and Cortelyou, *Ezra Ames of Albany,* 100–102.

25. L. H. Clark, ed., *Report of the Debates and Proceedings of the Convention* (New York, 1821), 121–122; Edward P. Cheyney, "The Antirent Movement and the Constitution of 1846," in *The History of New York,* ed. A. C. Flick (New York, 1933–1937), 6:283–321.

26. Trip Sinnott, *Tea Island: A Perfect Little Gem* (Topsham, Maine, 1983), 39–40.

27. Wade, *The Journals of Francis Parkman,* 59.

28. George William Curtis, *Lotus-Eating: A Summer Book* (New York, 1852), 128–129.

29. WCHO, William Caldwell's Will, December 29, 1841, and Settlement of Caldwell Heirs in the Supreme Court of the State of New York, September 2, 1852.

30. WCCO, William Caldwell by executor to John H. Smith, Deed Book P, 448, November 13, 1848; WCCO, William Caldwell by executor to Frederick B. Hubbell, Deed Book S, 429, October 18, 1851; Smith, *History of Warren County,* 252, 321, 536, 602, 660, 668–669, 673, 687, 695; WCHO, Ledger Caldwell Lake George, 1814–1856, 17, 44. On Hubbell, see Cynthia Corbett, "Frederick B. Hubbell: Caldwell Lumber Baron," *Caldwell Quarterly* 1 (summer 1978): 1–3.

31. Stoddard, *Lake George,* 33–41; Buckell, *Old Lake George Hotels,* 8, 17–21.

32. WCHO, William Caldwell's executors to Thomas Thomas, January 18, 1855; WCCO, Thomas Thomas to Daniel Gale, Deed Book 13, 328, November 22, 1865.

33. Quoted in Smith, *History of Warren County,* 573; F. W. Beers, *County Atlas of Warren County, New York* (New York, 1876), 72.

34. Beers, *County Atlas of Warren County,* 72; Stoddard, *Lake George,* 46.

35. Kenneth Maddox, *In Search of the Picturesque* (Rhinebeck, N.Y., 1983); Kathryn O'Brien, *The Great and the Gracious on Millionaire's Row* (Sylvan Beach, N.Y., 1978), 29–33, 73–82.

36. Society of Colonial Wars, *Report of the Secretary* (New York, 1898); *Laws of the State of New York, Passed at the One Hundred and Twentieth Session of the Legislature* (Albany and New York, 1897), 147, and *Laws of the State of New York, Passed at the One Hundred and Twenty-Third Session of the Legislature* (Albany, 1900), 924–925; Society of Colonial Wars, *Program Commemorating Battle of Lake George* (New York, September 8, 1903); "At the Dedication of the Lake George Battle Monument at Lake George, September 8, 1903," in *Public Papers of Governor Odell* (Albany, 1903), 235.

CHAPTER 4: *The Development of Public Spaces*

1. *New York State Legislative Manual,* 1820, 1825, 1830, 1835, 1840, 1845, 1850, 1855, 1860, 1865, 1870, 1875, 1880; the basic guide to sources for the history of Saratoga Springs is Beatrice Sweeney and Marion Taub, *Bibliography of Research Materials on Saratoga Springs* (Saratoga Springs, N.Y., 1977).

2. SSCH, Village of Saratoga Springs, Board of Trustees Minutes, March 26, 1844, 34–40, and March 30, 1857, 376–377; Daniel D. Benedict, Diary, July 17, 1835–November 18, 1866, published as "The Late Daniel D. Benedict's Diary," *Supplement to the Saratoga Sentinel,* no. 16, Saratoga Springs, N.Y., April 28, 1881, n.p.; R. L. Allen, *A Historical, Chemical and Therapeutical Analysis of the Principal Mineral Fountains at Saratoga Springs* (Saratoga Springs, N.Y., 1848), 24–25; Edward Fuller, "Our Thoroughfare, Past and Present Reminiscences, 1819–1918," series in *Saratoga Sun,* April-July 1918, n.p.; Sylvester, *History of Saratoga County,* 191; Cornelius Durkee, *Reminiscences of Saratoga* (Saratoga Springs, N.Y., 1929), 150; MD, Waterbury Family Papers, Association for the Detection of Horse Thieves and Burglars of Every Description, minutes, October 4, 1823.

3. The leaders cited here are not the ones found in popular local histories. Evelyn Barrett Britten states in her *Chronicles of Saratoga* (Saratoga Springs, N.Y., 1959),, "To Gideon Putnam more than any other person, Saratoga Springs is indebted for the first foundation of our Spa." She cites as her source Dr. R. L. Allen, who had talked to many of Putnam's friends and relatives and published his *Analysis* in 1848, thirty-six years after Putnam died. In contrast, "Judge Henry Walton" is scarcely mentioned in her book. For the legal profession in the area, see E. R. Mann, *The Bench and Bar of Saratoga County* (Ballston, N.Y., 1876).

4. SCC, 1825, "Map of a number of Building Lots & Buildings . . . near the Congress Spring, . . . being the property of the Heirs of Gideon Putnam, deceased, April 1810, copied by Theodore C. Hails, 1922"; Edmund Huling, "Saratoga in 1831," *Huling's Saratoga Springs, Ballston Spa and Schuylerville Directory for 1882–83* (Saratoga Springs, N.Y., 1883), 19; SCC, Map of Lands Belonging to Henry Walton at the Village of Saratoga Springs, in December 1813, January 1, 1814, copied by Theodore C. Hails, 1923.

5. SCCO, 1807, "Henry Walton and wife to Gideon Putnam, Deed Book CD, 150, March 20, 1804, receiving an annual rent of $1862. This is a Release of all rents and dower rights received in the foregoing deed." SCC, 1825, "Map of a number of Building Lots & Buildings . . . near the Congress Spring, . . . being the property of the Heirs of Gideon Putnam, deceased, April 1810, copied by Theodore C. Hails, 1922."

6. Stone, *Reminiscences,* 287–292; Durkee, *Reminiscences of Saratoga,* 5, 50, 68–69, 80–81, 117–118, 124, 141, 152–153, 257, 291.

7. Stone, *Reminiscences,* 292–297; on Clarke's water system, see Huling, "Saratoga in 1831," 32–33.

8. SCC, H. Scoffed, Map of Lands Lately Owned by J. Clarke, 1854, copied by Theodore Hails, 1922.

9. SCC, H. Scoffed, Map of Lots owned by A. S. Maxwell, Saratoga Springs, N.Y., 1854, copied by Theodore C. Hails, 1922.

10. SCC, Map of Village Lots Surveyed for J. Ellsworth, Esq., June 3, 1838.

11. SCC, S. R. Ostrander, Map of Property at Saratoga Springs Owned by Dr. S. Freeman, 1841, copied by Theodore C. Hails, 1923; "Death of Dr. Samuel Freeman," *The Daily Saratogian,* December 19, 1870, 2.

12. SCC, Plan of Part of the Village of Saratoga Springs Showing Property Owned by J. M. Marvin and Others, 1867. Stone, *Reminiscences,* 69–71; SCC, Peckham H. Green and W. Henry Vibbard, Map of the Property of John A. Bryan at Saratoga Springs, 1853, copied by Theodore C. Hails.

13. Theodore Corbett, "Saratoga's Franklin Square," *Classic America* 3 (1988): 14–17; Sylvester, *History of Saratoga County,* 192–193, 196–197. For the railroad station, see *Endicotts Picture of Saratoga for 1843 Containing Thirteen Accurate Views from Original Drawings of the Principal Buildings and Places of the Village, with Brief Descriptions of Each* (New York, 1843), no. 7; Benedict, Diary.

14. SSCH, Union Avenue Association, 1865–1870, 1–4; quote on 1. For architectural descriptions of existing structures in Saratoga Springs, the indispensable volume is James Kettlewell's *Saratoga Springs: An Architectural History, 1790–1990* (Saratoga Springs, N.Y., 1991), 59–60, 81–87.

15. Britten, *Chronicles of Saratoga,* 117, 131, 417, 527.

16. For Tabor Reynolds, see Sylvester, *History of Saratoga County,* 31, 87–88, 99, 149, 188, 202, 504.

17. Marietta Holley, *Samantha at Saratoga or Flirting with Fashion* (Philadelphia, 1887), 145–149.

18. Blackmar, *Manhattan,* 72–107.

19. Dorothy Stroud, *Capability Brown* (London, 1984), 47–53; Dudley Dodd, "The Stourhead Pleasure Grounds in Wiltshire," *The Magazine Antiques* 127 (June 1985): 1324–1332; Brian Allen, "The Landscape," in *Vauxhall Gardens,* by T. J. Edelstein (New Haven, Conn., 1983), 17–23.

20. Charles Lockwood, *Bricks and Brownstones: The New York Row House, 1783–1929* (New York, 1972), 38, 65, 69, 112, 139; Laura Wood Roper, *FLO: A Biography of Frederick Law Olmstead* (Baltimore, 1973), 66–76; Roy Rosenzweig and Elizabeth Blackmar, *The Park and the People* (Ithaca, N.Y., 1992), 1–36, 104–105, 110–111, 117, 130–131. Rosenzweig and Blackmar are at pains to distinguish between New York's pleasure gardens and Central Park. They emphasize two distinctions: Central Park was a natural space, while pleasure gardens were eclectic spaces with a variety of contrasting novelties; and pleasure gardens were open to and enjoyed by the working class, while Central Park was regulated to discourage the presence of working-class people. These authors seem to miss the fact that the English landscape tradition included the picturesque; English architects designed landscapes that were not only natural but also included focal points such as classical temples and Chinese pagodas. Pleasure gardens in this tradition were designed and constructed in early-nineteenth-century Saratoga Springs. After mid-century, a modest number of novelties were added to Congress Park in the tradition of a New York pleasure ground, ensuring that the park would remain open to as wide an audience as possible.

21. SCCO, Map of Lands Belonging to Henry Walton, 1813; SCCO, Joseph E. Westcot, Map of Building lots on the Land of Henry Walton at Saratoga Springs, Compiled on the Half Scale of the original from Walton's Map of January 1839, Showing the Lots as then Sub-divided, Marked and Numbered, copied by Theodore C. Hails, 1923.

22. Durkee, *Reminiscences of Saratoga,* 9–10, 13, 120–121.

23. "Rear View, United States Hotel," *Endicotts,* no. 7.

24. Arthur Merrill, *Confessions of Congress Park* (Saratoga Springs, N.Y., 1955), n.p.

25. Britten, *Chronicles of Saratoga,* 58–59, 68–71.

26. Holley, *Samantha at Saratoga,* 171–176.

27. *Endicotts,* no. 4.

28. Sylvester, *History of Saratoga County,* 161.

29. David Schuyler, *The New Urban Landscape* (Baltimore, 1986), 37–56; Thomas Bender, "The Rural Cemetery Movement: Urban Travail and the Appeal of Nature," *New England Quarterly* 47 (1974): 196–211.

30. Schuyler, *The New Urban Landscape,* 45–46, 49, 53.

31. Stone, *Reminiscences,* 198–199.

32. "Gateway Given by Mrs. Sackett Dedicated Sunday," *Saratogian,* May 21, 1927.

33. Durkee, *Reminiscences of Saratoga,* 12–13.

34. Ibid., 16; Fuller, "Our Thoroughfare."

35. Durkee, *Reminiscences of Saratoga,* 23; Kettlewell, *Saratoga Springs,* 43.

36. Gerald Carson, *A Good Day at Saratoga* (Chicago, 1978), 3–24, 42–46.

CHAPTER 5: *Accommodations*

1. J. Milbert, *Picturesque Itinerary of the Hudson River and the Peripheral Parts of North America,* trans. Constance Sherman (Ridgewood, N.J., 1959), 49. On the suburban ideal, see Clifford Clark Jr., *The American Family Home, 1800–1960* (Chapel Hill, N.C., 1986), 72–102; Huling, "Saratoga in 1831," 34.

2. Blackmar, *Manhattan,* 60, 63, 88, 134–135; Eighth Census of the United States, 1860 (ms.), microfilm reels 856–857, National Archives, Washington, D.C. (hereinafter, 1860 U.S. Census).

3. Stone, *Reminiscences,* 409; Huling, "Saratoga in 1831," 28–29. In the 1830s, Methodist preacher John Morrill ran Harmony Hall on Broadway, while, under the proprietorship of Deacon Isaac Taylor, the Washington on North Broadway was a destination for Presbyterian ministers.

4. *The Empire State: Its Industries and Wealth* (New York, 1889), 193; *Saratoga Springs Directory,* 1885–1890; Kettlewell, *Saratoga Springs,* 92.

5. Noah Webster, *An American Dictionary of the English Language* (Springfield, Mass., 1859), 563.

6. Conte, *The History of the Greenbrier,* 8–57; HSP, Dreer Collection, Yarnall Letters, R. S. Mercer to Peter McCall, White Sulphur Springs, Green Brier County, September 4, 1848.

7. Basil Hall, *Travels in North America in the Years 1827, 1828* (London, 1829), 2:23–25, 27–28.

8. John Honeywood Steel, *An Analysis of the Mineral Waters* (New York, 1831), 39. *Endicotts,* nos. 2 and 3; Harding, "The Diary of Margaret Miller Davidson," 8–9; Stuart, *Three Years in North America,* 1:192–200; Hall, *Travels in North America,* 2:23–25, 27–28; the quote from Strong is found in Hans Huth, *Nature and the American: Three Centuries of Changing Attitudes* (Berkeley, Calif., 1957), 107.

9. Sylvester, *History of Saratoga County,* 154.

10. Benedict, Diary.

11. Stone, *Reminiscences,* 292; Sylvester, *History of Saratoga County,* 167.

12. Benedict, Diary.

13. Sydney Ernest Hammersley, *The History of Waterford, New York* (Waterford, N.Y., 1957), 266–277.

14. *Endicotts,* no. 1; Benedict, Diary; Sylvester, *History of Saratoga County,* 166–167.

15. A. T. Goodrich, publisher, *The Northern Traveller* (New York, 1825), 147–151; Caroline Gilman, *Poetry of Traveling in the United States* (New York, 1838), 84–85.

16. Alexander Mackay, *The Western World; or, Travels in the United States in 1846–47 . . .* (Philadelphia, 1849), 2:213–216; *The Diary of Philip Hone, 1828–1851,* ed. Allan Nevins, (New York, 1969), 405–406.

17. Sylvester, *History of Saratoga County,* 168; Durkee, *Reminiscences of Saratoga,* 9–10; Benedict, Diary; Seventh Census of the United States, 1850 (ms.) microfilm reels 522–523, National Archives, Washington, D.C. (hereinafter, 1850 U.S. Census); Kettlewell, *Saratoga Springs,* 16.

18. Sylvester, *History of Saratoga County,* 169; SR, John Bevan, "Map of Saratoga Springs, Saratoga County, New York," c. 1848; F. W. Beers, *County Atlas of Saratoga, New York* (New York, 1876), 30; Saratoga Springs Preservation Foundation, Saratoga Springs, N.Y., Paula Dennis, "Historic Structures Report of the Pitney House Hotel," February 1999.

19. SCCO, 54, 314–315, 317–318, November 14, 1845, and October 31, 1844, Washington Putnam and Amos Stafford to Jonathan Pitney; SCCO, ZZ, 218, November 6, 1847, Abraham Best to Jacob Pitney Junior; *Boyd's Saratoga Springs Directory for 1868–9* (Saratoga Springs, 1868), 4; "The Pitney Family" and exhibition materials for "Reclaiming African-American and Irish-American Heritage," at the Saratoga Springs Urban Heritage Center, Saratoga Springs, N.Y., October 1999.

20. *Boyd's Saratoga Springs Directory for 1868–9,* n.p.

21. Sylvester, *History of Saratoga County,* 168; Beers, *County Atlas of Saratoga,* 29.

22. Sylvester, *History of Saratoga County,* 165–167; Kettlewell, *Saratoga Springs,* 56–58.

23. Beatrice Sweeney, *The Grand Union Hotel* (Saratoga Springs, N.Y., 1973).

24. "Costly Experiment of Mammoth Summer Hotels—Cottages Are More Profitable," *The Daily Graphic,* September 7, 1877.

25. Durkee, *Reminiscences of Saratoga,* 22.

26. SR, "Dr. Robert Hamilton's Institute," *The Saratoga Union,* December 25, 1889, 3.

27. 1850 U.S. Census and 1860 U.S. Census; *Guide to Saratoga Springs* (New York, 1873), 45–46; Suzanne Lebsock, *The Free Women of Petersburg: Status and Culture in a Southern Town, 1784–1860* (New York, 1984), 178.

28. Durkee, *Reminiscences of Saratoga,* 22; *Saratoga Springs Directory,* 1870–1876; Kettlewell, *Saratoga Springs,* 58.

29. *Boyd's Saratoga Springs Directory for 1872–1873* (Saratoga Springs, N.Y., 1872).

30. 1850 U.S. Census.

31. *Guide to Saratoga Springs,* 45–46.

32. Ibid.

CHAPTER 6: *Alleys as Support Spaces*

1. On the English mewses, see Mark Girouard, *Cities and People* (New Haven, Conn., and London, 1985), 225–226. The barn and stable in U.S. cities have not been studied; still, there are helpful works on rural barns in the Northeast: on the spacing of the residence with attached farm buildings in northern New England, see Thomas Hubka, *Big House, Little House, Back House, Barn* (Hanover, N.H., 1984); on survey techniques for barns, consult Henry Glassie, "The Variation of Concepts within Tradition: Barn Building in Otsego County, New York," in *Man and Cultural Heritage,* ed. H. J. Walker and W. G. Haag (Baton Rouge, La., 1976).

2. Lockwood, *Bricks and Brownstones,* 26, 45, 82, 182, 184, 203; Blackmar, *Manhattan,* 94–99, 104–106, 164–166; John Stilgoe, *Common Landscape of America, 1580–1845* (New Haven, Conn., 1982), 68–72.

3. Hammersley, *The History of Waterford,* 132–178. In 1831 Waterford investors tried to convince Saratogians to develop a railroad connection by way of their town rather than Schenectady. Four years later a railroad line to Waterford and Troy was completed. From 1802 Waterford was also a center for step-gabled architecture, identified by distinct brick extensions formed in the pattern of a step. Several step-gabled structures were constructed on Broadway in Saratoga Springs; the most notable was built in 1841 for Judge Nicholas Doe (see Figure 33 in Chapter 5). He was a previous resident of Waterford, where he grew up in a similar step-gabled town house. On Waterford gables, see Hammersley, *The History of Waterford,* 266–277.

4. Beers, *County Atlas of Warren County,* 72; NLP, George White to Nicholas Low, March 25, 1804. See Chapters 2 and 3.

5. *The Traveler's Guide to Montreal, Quebec and Saratoga Springs* (Montreal, 1859), 26.

6. S. DeVeaux, *The Traveller's Own Book to Saratoga Springs, Niagara Falls and Canada* (Buffalo, 1844), 87–88, 90.

7. SSCH, Village of Saratoga Springs, Board of Trustees Minutes, April 22, 1845, between 52 and 53; *The Empire State,* 187, 194.

8. Edward Spann, "The Greatest Grid: The New York Plan of 1811," in *Two Centuries of American Planning,* ed. Daniel Schaffer (Baltimore, 1988), 11–39.

9. SCC, Map of Lands Belonging to Henry Walton at the Village of Saratoga Springs, in December 1813, January 1, 1814, copied by Theodore C. Hails, 1923.

10. SCC, Joseph E. Westcot, Map of Building Lots on the Land of Henry Walton at Saratoga Springs, Compiled on the Half Scale of the Original from Walton's Map of January 1839, Showing the Lots as then Sub-divided, Marked and Numbered, copied by Theodore C. Hails, 1923.

11. SCC, Peckham H. Green and W. Henry Vibbard, Map of the Property of John A. Bryan at Saratoga Springs, 1853, copied by Theodore C. Hails.

12. SCC, Joseph E. Westcot, Map of Building Lots on the Land of Henry Walton at Saratoga Springs, Compiled on the Half Scale of the Original from Walton's Map of January 1839, Showing the Lots as then Sub-divided, Marked and Numbered, copied by Theodore C. Hails, 1923.

13. SCC, S. R. Ostrander, Map of Property at Saratoga Springs Owned by Dr. S. Freeman, 1841, copied by Theodore C. Hails, 1923, and Plan of Part of the Village of Saratoga Springs Showing Property Owned by J. M. Marvin and Others, 1867.

14. SCC, Map of Village Lots Surveyed for J. Ellsworth, Esq., June 3, 1838.

15. SCC, H. Scoffed, Map of Lots Owned by A. S. Maxwell, Saratoga Springs, N.Y. 1854, copied by Theodore C. Hails, 1922.

16. Durkee, *Reminiscences of Saratoga,* 7.

17. SR, Dr. Samuel Freeman Papers, 1797–1862, letters, 1840s.

18. A. J. Downing, *The Architecture of Country Houses* (1850; reprint, New York, 1969), 213–214.

19. Saratoga Springs Preservation Foundation, Saratoga Springs, N.Y., Richard Clark, "Map of the village of Saratoga Springs," 1858.

20. George E. Woodward, *Woodward's Country Homes* (New York, 1865), 87.

21. On the personages and structures within the Guy painting, see Gabriel Furman, *Notes Geographical and Historical Relating to the Town of Brooklyn in Kings County on Long Island* (1824; reprint, Brooklyn, N.Y., 1968).

22. Schuyler, *The New Urban Landscape,* 24–36, 59–66. Despite limitations, housing on alleys was attractive to the nineteenth-century working class because it was inexpensive; this attraction is demonstrated by the alleys of one U.S. city: James Borchert, *Alley Life in Washington: Family, Community, Religion and Folklife in the City, 1850–1970* (Urbana, Ill., 1980).

23. Figures come from analysis of the *Saratoga Springs Directory for 1881–2* (Saratoga Springs, N.Y., 1882); *Saratoga Springs Directory 1882–83* (Saratoga Springs, N.Y., 1882); Huling, *Huling's Saratoga Springs, Ballston Spa and Schuylerville Directory for 1882–83; Huling's Saratoga Springs and Ballston Spa Directory for 1883–84* (Saratoga Springs, N.Y., 1884); *Kirwin's Saratoga Springs Directory* (Saratoga Springs, N.Y., 1889).

24. Analysis of Cottage Place residents and alley structures is based on: SCC, Lot 254, Book 63, p. 417, April 1, 1841, Henry and Margaret Walton to Maro Eaton, Watch Maker, lease for $1 and $21 yearly rent; Lot 257, Book RR, p. 339, April 12, 1841, Henry and Margaret Walton to Henry Benedict, carpenter, lease for $21 yearly rent; Lots 259 and 260, Book NY, p. 23, September 23, 1841, Henry and Margaret Walton to Brainard Spencer of Middletown in Connecticut, Merchant, lease for $49 yearly rent.

CHAPTER 7: *The Building Trades*

1. 1860 U.S. Census; Mary Blewett, *Men, Women, and Work, Class, Gender, and Protest in the New England Shoe Industry, 1780–1910* (Urbana, Ill., 1988), 14–19.

2. Conveniently found in Sylvester, *History of Saratoga County,* 135.

3. Durkee, *Reminiscences of Saratoga,* 10; Jan Johnstone, *Saratoga County Communities: An Historic Perspective* (Clifton Park, N.Y., 1980), 50–51, 74–75.

4. Durkee, *Reminiscences of Saratoga,* 150.

5. Ibid., 10.

6. On the nature of the crafts, see Edward Hazen, *Encyclopedia of E. A. Trades: The Panorama or Professions and Trades* (Philadelphia, 1837), 198–218; Harley McKee, *Introduction to Early American Masonry, Stone, Brick, Mortar and Plaster* (Washington, D.C., 1973).

7. Huling, *Some Reminiscences,* n.p., SR. Carpenters in rural New York State followed this pattern much longer than carpenters did in major building centers like Saratoga Springs. The life of an Otsego County carpenter in 1869 is described by Wayne Franklin in *A Rural Carpenter's World: The Craft in a Nineteenth-Century New York Township* (Iowa City, 1990), 9–36.

8. Durkee, *Reminiscences of Saratoga,* 161–163; Esther Littlefield Woodworth-Barnes, *Huling Genealogy* (Clemson, S.C., 1984), 194–195, 205–208, 211.

9. Huling, *Some Reminiscences,* n.p., SR. On Albany's building trades after the completion of the Erie Canal, see David Hackett, *The Rude Hand of Innovation, Religion and Social Order in Albany, New York 1652–1836* (New York, 1991), 102–103.

10. W. J. Rorabaugh, *The Craft Apprentice from Franklin to the Age of the Machine* (New York, 1986), 60–61, 102–103.

11. Saratoga Preservation Foundation, Saratoga Springs, N.Y., Richard Clark, "Map of the village of Saratoga Springs," 1858.

12. SR, John Bevan, "Map of Saratoga Springs, Saratoga County, New York," c. 1848.

13. Sean Wilentz, *Chants Democratic New York City & the Rise of the American Working Class, 1788–1850* (New York, 1984), 30–32, 45–46, 132–134; Sylvester, *History of Saratoga County,* 191.

14. Marvin Swartz, *American Interiors: The Brooklyn Museum* (Brooklyn, N.Y., 1968), 89–95; Kettlewell, *Saratoga Springs,* 39.

15. 1850 U.S. Census and 1860 U.S. Census; Sylvester, *History of Saratoga County,* 170, 225; *Saratoga County Directory,* 1870.

16. Sylvester, *History of Saratoga County,* 222–227; SSCH, Village of Saratoga Springs, Board of Trustees Minutes, October 6, 1857, 396. On the effects of similar legislation in New York City, see Blackmar, *Manhattan,* 190–191.

17. Sylvester, *History of Saratoga County,* 81, 154–158, 165, 181, 188, 191, 218, 504; *Saratoga County Directory,* 1870.

18. Durkee, *Reminiscences of Saratoga,* 14, 140.

19. SR, John Bevan, "Map of Saratoga Springs, Saratoga County, New York," c. 1848.

20. *Bicknell's Village Builder* (N.p., 1872). On Croft's career in Glens Falls, N.Y., see Theodore Corbett, *The Community by the Falls* (Lake George, N.Y., 1978), 22, 26; Diana Waite, "Introduction," in *Victorian Architectural Details, Two Pattern Books by Marcus Fayette Cummings and Charles Crosby Miller* (Watkins Glen, N.Y., 1980), n.p.

21. Britten, *Chronicles of Saratoga,* 62–84.

22. Saratoga County History Center, Ballston Spa, N.Y., George Dunn Papers, 1860–1874, "Masons' Specification for a Three Story Brick Building, to be erected in the Village of Saratoga Springs, N.Y. for John Morrissey"; Kettlewell, *Saratoga Springs,* 41–43.

23. HS, Library, George Dunn, *Weekly Time-Book for Contractors, Workingmen and Others* (1869, 1871). See also Saratoga County History Center, Ballston Spa, N.Y., George Dunn Papers; HS, Library, George Dunn, *Time Book* (1873).

24. BM, "J. B. Hodgman to Mr. Morrissey for bolts and anchors"; "r'ceipt Dec. 3, 1870 C. Rap received from Dunn for brownstone on Morrissey's Building"; "bid on Mr. Morris[s]ey's, Oct. 25, 1870 for marble mantels from Rutland, Vt."; "T. S. Coolidge to George Dunn, April 18, 1874 order for carload of lime from Jointa Lime Company, Glens Falls, N.Y."

25. Saratoga County History Center, Ballston Spa, N.Y., George Dunn Papers, 1868, "Carpenters' Specifications for a Three Story Brick Building, to be erected in the Village of Saratoga Springs, N.Y. for John Morrissey."

26. Catherine Burns, "R. Newton Brezee in Saratoga Springs" (master's thesis, American University, 1980); Kettlewell, *Saratoga Springs,* 77–81, 93.

27. There were a growing number of self-professed messiahs like Robert Matthews, alias the Prophet Matthias. A carpenter from Coila, thirty miles from the spa in Washington County, this prophet promoted the patriarchal-centered traditions of the Old Testament, emphasizing patriarchal authority in the family and workplace at the expense of women, a reflection of his own difficulties in establishing a viable household and workshop. See Paul E. Johnson and Sean Wilentz, *The Kingdom of Matthias* (New York, 1994).

28. John Foxe, *The History of Christian Martyrdom: Being an Authentic Account of the Lives, Sufferings, and Triumphant Deaths of Many of the Primitive, as well as Protestant Martyrs, in Different Parts of the World* (1563 reprint of *The Book of Martyrs;* Saratoga Springs, N.Y., 1820); John Foxe, *The Book of Martyrs; or, A History of the Lives, Sufferings, and Triumphant Deaths, of the Primitive as well as Protestant Martyrs: From the Commencement of Christianity, to the Latest Periods of Pagan and Popish Persecution* (1563; reprint, Hartford, Conn., 1836), iv, xxi–xxiii, 571–592, quotes on xxii. For Holley's reading it, see Kate Winter, *Life with "Josiah Allen's Wife"* (Syracuse, N.Y., 1984), 91.

29. "The Life of the Rev. John Foxe," in Foxe, *Book of Martyrs,* v–x.

30. Foxe, *Book of Martyrs,* iii.

31. NYHS, Miles Beach, Day Book, 1816–1818, September 18, 19, and 30, 1816; Howard Rock, *Artisans of the New Republic: The Tradesmen of New York City in the Age of Jefferson* (New York, 1979), 295–300; Paul Gilje and Howard Rock, eds., *Keepers of the Revolution: New Yorkers at Work in the Early Republic* (Ithaca, N.Y., 1992), 101–105.

32. Sylvester, *History of Saratoga County,* 154–156, 218–219; MD, Waterbury Family Papers, Association for the Detection of Horse Thieves and Burglars of Every Description, minutes, October 4, 1823.

33. Irwin Yellowitz, "Eight Hours and the Bricklayers' Strike of 1868 in New York City," in *Essays in the History of New York City,* ed. Irwin Yellowitz (Port Washington, N.Y., 1978), 78–100; Sylvester, *History of Saratoga County,* 187.

CHAPTER 8: The African American Presence

1. Holley, *Samantha at Saratoga,* 162–163. This chapter is an expansion of Theodore Corbett, "Saratoga County Blacks, 1720–1870," *Quarterly Journal of the Saratoga County Historical Society* 20 (1986): 1–6.

2. On the Saratoga attack as slave trading, see New York Public Library, *Journal de la Campagne de Sarastaugue* (1745), n.p.; Marcel Trudel, *L'esclavage au Canada* (Quebec, 1960), 141, 276, 337, 353, 357, 360–363; Edmund O'Callaghan and B. Fernow, eds., *Documents Relative to the Colonial History of the State of New York* (Albany, N.Y., 1848–1851), 6:240.

3. Kim, *Landlord and Tenant,* 7, 23, 114, 125, 289; Robert Wells, *The Population of the British Colonies in America before 1776* (Princeton, N.J., 1975), 111–116; O'Callaghan and Fernow, *Documents*

Relative to the Colonial History of the State of New York, 6:245; Corbett, "Saratoga County Blacks," 1–2.

4. Anne Grant, *Memoirs of an American Lady* (New York, 1901), 1:86–87, 92–95.

5. The painting, owned by Mr. and Mrs. Rodman C. Rockefeller, is reproduced in Roderic Blackburn and Ruth Privonka, *Remembrance of Patria Dutch Arts and Culture in Colonial America, 1609–1776* (Albany, 1988), 196, 231.

6. Ira Berlin, "Time, Space and the Evolution of Afro-American Society on British Mainland North America," *American Historical Review* 80 (1980): 47–78; Ira Berlin, *Many Thousands Gone: The First Two Centuries of Slavery in North America* (Cambridge, Mass., 1998), 177–194, 228–255.

7. Grant, *Memoirs of an American Lady,* 2:264–270.

8. Bureau of the Census, Department of Commerce and Labor, *Heads of Families at the First Census of the United States Taken in the Year 1790, New York* (Washington, D.C., 1908), 14–18, 27–30, 39–41.

9. Ibid., 17, 28, 39.

10. Edgar McManus, *A History of Negro Slavery in New York* (Syracuse, N.Y., 1970), 161–196.

11. Carl Nordstrom, "The New York Slave Code," *Afro-Americans in New York Life and History* (January 1980): 7–26; Carl Nordstrom, "Blacks in the Hudson Valley," Cherry Hill Forum Paper on the Ethnic Heritage of the Upper Hudson (October 1981), 34–52.

12. Britten, *Chronicles of Saratoga,* 335–342.

13. Clark, *Report on the Debates and Proceedings of the Convention,* 100–101, 104, 137, 140, 168, 186; quotes on 101.

14. Nordstrom, "Blacks in the Hudson Valley," 37–38.

15. Bureau of the Census, *Heads of Families,* 12–55; *New York Legislative Manual,* 1810, 1830, 1840.

16. 1850 U.S. Census. A hand-drawn map of 1890 by Jno. M. Davidson Jr. in the Saratoga Room, Saratoga Springs Public Library, supposedly shows blacks residing in Saratoga Springs on "Johnny Cake Road" (near present-day Congress Street) c. 1820. On the movement of blacks from the farm to the town, see Stephen Thernstrom and Peter Knights, "Men in Motion: Some Data and Speculations about Urban Population Mobility in Nineteenth-Century America," in *Anonymous Americans: Explorations in Nineteenth-Century Social History,* ed. Tamara Hareven (Englewood Cliffs, N.J., 1971), 20, 25–33.

17. *New York State Legislative Manual,* 1830, 1840.

18. Ibid.

19. 1850 U.S. Census.

20. Britten, *Chronicles of Saratoga,* 201, 229–233.

21. 1850 U.S. Census.

22. Faye Dudden, *Serving Women, Household Service in Nineteenth-Century America* (Middletown, Conn., 1983), 12–48.

23. Britten, *Chronicles of Saratoga,* 230–233; Herman Bloch, *The Circle of Discrimination: An Economic and Social Study of the Black Man in New York* (New York, 1964), 19–31.

24. 1850 U.S. Census.

25. Solomon Northup, *Twelve Years a Slave,* ed. Sue Eakin and Joseph Logsdon (Baton Rouge, La., 1968), 3–11.

26. SCCO, Contract between Solomon Northup and Washington Allen, Box A33, June 8, 1838. SCCO, *Index of Convictions,* February 1834, Solomon Northup, Assault and Battery, Special Sessions; May 1, 1839, Solomon Northup, Assault and Battery, Special Sessions. SCCO, "The Saratoga," 1st quarter, 1994, 2:28; Census Office, New York, *The 1885 New York State Census of Population, Queensbury, Warren County, New York.*

27. 1850 U.S. Census and 1860 U.S. Census.

28. Northup, *Twelve Years a Slave,* 12–50.

29. Sue Eakin and Joseph Logsdon, "Introduction," in Northup, *Twelve Years a Slave,* xiii–xiv, xxi–xxii, quote on xxxvii; Joan Hedrick, *Harriet Beecher Stowe, a Life* (New York, 1994), 102–137.

30. Iver Bernstein, *The New York City Draft Riots* (New York, 1990), 17–72.

31. Census Office, New York, *The 1865 New York State Census of Population, Saratoga County, New York* and *The 1875 New York State Census of Population, Saratoga County, New York.*

32. MD, Diary of a black woman Emma Waite (1870), "Happy New Year from M. E. Hunter," January 6; HS, *Patterns: Saratoga's Nineteenth-Century Women* (Saratoga Springs, N.Y., 1989), 3.

33. MD, Emma Waite diary, February 28, May 5, May 14, June 2, June 14, July 12, August 12, September 14, October 4–5.

34. Ibid., March 26, April 1, April 16, April 27, June 1, June 9, August 5; Sylvester, *History of Saratoga County,* 178.

35. MD, Emma Waite diary, February 14, March 19, April 21, September 7.

36. On blacks in Saratoga Springs after 1880, see Myra Young Armstead, *"Lord, Please Don't Take Me in August": African Americans in Newport and Saratoga Springs, 1870–1930* (Urbana, Ill., 1999).

CHAPTER 9: *The Irish*

1. Census Office, New York, *The 1875 New York State Census of Population, Saratoga County, New York.*

2. Kerby Miller, *Emigrants and Exiles, Ireland and the Irish Exodus to North America* (Oxford, 1985), 137–149.

3. Ibid., 151–168.

4. Ibid., 149–151.

5. Cecil Woodham-Smith, *The Great Hunger: Ireland 1845–1849* (London, 1962), 208–238; Miller, *Emigrants and Exiles,* 292, 296; Bureau of the Census, *1990 Census of Population, Social and Economic Characteristics, New York* (Washington, D.C., 1993).

6. 1850 U.S. Census and 1860 U.S. Census; F. W. Beers, *Combination Atlas of Saratoga and Ballston* (New York, 1876), 18–33; Jeremiah O'Donovan, *A Brief Account of the Author's Interview with His Countrymen* (Pittsburgh, 1864), 300–306.

7. 1850 U.S. Census; 1860 U.S. Census; SCC, Naturalization Records, 1820–1856.

8. Stone, *Reminiscences,* 399–405, 416–422.

9. Alan Taylor, *William Cooper's Town, Power and Persuasion on the Frontier of the Early American Republic* (New York, 1995), 317–318; Woodham-Smith, *The Great Hunger,* 207–217.

10. Sylvester, *History of Saratoga County,* 155, 171, 181.

11. 1850 U.S. Census; analysis of burials and stones in Greenridge Cemetery.

12. William Rowley, "Albany: A Tale of Two Cities, 1820–1880" (Ph.D. diss., Harvard University, 1967), 168–175; New York State Department of Commerce, *1980 Census of Population, Characteristics of People and Housing,* New York State Data Center, Summary Tape File 3.

13. 1850 U.S. Census; Daniel Walkowitz, *Worker City, Company Town* (Urbana, Ill., 1978), 52–54; Mary Ryan, *Cradle of the Middle Class: The Family in Oneida County, New York, 1790–1865* (New York, 1983), 148–149; Edward Spann, *The New Metropolis, New York City, 1840–1857* (New York, 1981), 26; Rowley, "Albany," 168–175.

14. Halsa Diner, *Erin's Daughters in America* (Baltimore, 1983), 30–33.

15. 1850 U.S. Census.

16. 1860 U.S. Census.

17. Quoted in Noel Ignatiev, *How the Irish Became White* (New York, 1995), 92–121, quote on 99; Dudden, *Serving Women,* 64–65.

18. 1850 U.S. Census; 1860 U.S. Census.

19. Ibid.

20. Dudden, *Serving Women,* 219–221, 59–71.

21. Catherine Beecher, *Letters to Persons Who Are Engaged in Domestic Service* (New York, 1842), 87–89.

22. Miller, *Emigrants and Exiles,* 406–407.

23. Ibid., 176, 237, 275.

24. 1850 U.S. Census.

25. Ibid.; 1860 U.S. Census.

26. 1850 U.S. Census.

27. SCC, Naturalization Records, 1820–1856.

28. Sylvester, *History of Saratoga County,* 175; Record of Wills, Surrogate's Court, Saratoga County, Box 82, no. 40, Will of Simon Flanigan, July 22, 1872.

29. Census Office, New York, *The 1875 New York State Census of Population, Saratoga County, New York.*

30. Beers, *Combination Atlas of Saratoga and Ballston,* 37.

31. Hibernian records are in the collection of William J. Burke & Sons Funeral Home, Saratoga Springs, N.Y.

32. Clyde Griffen and Sally Griffen, *Natives and Newcomers: The Ordering of Opportunity in Mid-Nineteenth-Century Poughkeepsie* (Cambridge, Mass., 1978), 78–79.

33. Mary Jane Ellis, "The Rise and Fall of the Irish and Italians" (term seminar paper for Saratoga County History course, Adirondack Community College, fall 1995).

34. Sylvester, *History of Saratoga County,* 155, 180, 188–189.

35. Analysis of burials and stones in Greenridge Cemetery; Record of Wills, Surrogate's Court, Saratoga County, Box 82, no. 40, Will of Simon Flanigan, July 22, 1872.

36. O'Donovan, *A Brief Account of the Author's Interview with His Countrymen,* 300–306; quote on 300.

CHAPTER 10: *Native American Encampments as Tourist Attractions*

1. James Fenimore Cooper, *The Last of the Mohicans* (1826; reprint, New York, 1962), 27.

2. Britten, *Chronicles of Saratoga,* 142–143.

3. Stone, *Reminiscences,* 6–10.

4. William Stone (Sr.), *Life of Joseph Brant-Thayendanegea including the American Revolution* (New York, 1838), 1:xiii–xxi.

5. John Barber and Henry Howe, *Historical Collections of the State of New York* (New York, 1841), 570; Milbert, *Picturesque Itinerary of the Hudson River,* vi–viii, 48–49; Eugene O'Connor, "The Love That Changed History," in *Saratoga County Heritage,* ed. Violet Dunn (Ballston Spa, N.Y., 1974), 447–454; June Namias, *White Captives* (Chapel Hill, N.C., 1995), 117–144.

6. Kenneth Lindsay, *The Works of John Vanderlyn* (Binghamton, N.Y., 1970), 86–87, 141–142.

7. David Wilson, *The Life of Jane McCrea with an Account of Burgoyne's Expedition in 1777* (New York, 1853), 38.

8. Ibid., 117.

9. Washington Irving, *The Sketch-Book of Geoffrey Crayon, Gent.* (1820; reprint, New York, 1897), 313.

10. Ibid., 308.

11. Robert Spiller, "Afterward," in James Fenimore Cooper, *The Pioneers* (1823; reprint, New York, 1964), 440–443.

12. Grant, *Memoirs of an American Lady,* 1:131–133, 1:156–157, 1:204–205, 1:233–234. On the River Indians' contact with white communities, see Patrick Frazier, *The Mohicans of Stockbridge* (Lincoln, Neb., 1992), 75–78, 148–149, 164–165, 204–205; William Cronon, *Changes in the Land: Indians, Colonists, and the Ecology of New England* (New York, 1983), 58–67; Daniel Richter, *The Ordeal of the Longhouse: The Peoples of the Iroquois in the Era of European Colonization* (Chapel Hill, N.C., 1992), 32–35, 60–62, 65–66.

13. Frazier, *The Mohicans of Stockbridge,* 161–163; John Garrant, *The Four Kings* (Ottawa, 1985); Kelsay, *Joseph Brant,* 168–169, 388–389.

14. Quoted in Laurence Hauptman, *The Iroquois in the Civil War: From Battlefield to Reservation* (Syracuse, N.Y., 1993), 140.

15. Stone, *Reminiscences,* 105.

16. Gilbert Vincent, "An Iroquois Sampling at Fenimore House Museum," *Heritage* 10 (summer 1994): 9; Todd DeGarmo, "Indian Camps and Upstate Tourism," *New York Folklore Newsletter* (summer 1993): 4–5, 10.

17. Britten, *Chronicles of Saratoga,* 66, 347, 354; Stone, *Reminiscences,* 97–113; Durkee, *Reminiscences of Saratoga,* 64–65; Holley, *Samantha at Saratoga,* 321–340.

18. Stone, *Reminiscences,* 121–128.

19. Kelsay, *Joseph Brant,* 161–348, 546–552.

20. Gunther Michelson, "Iroquois Population Statistics," *Man in the Northeast* 14 (fall 1977): 4; William Starna, "Mohawk Iroquois Populations: A Revision," *Ethnohistory* 27 (fall 1980): 371–382; Theodore Corbett, "The Clash of Cultures in the Champlain-Hudson Valley," manuscript to be published by Purple Mountain Press.

21. Claude Chauchetiere, *Narrative of the Mission of Sault St. Louis 1667–1685* (Kahnawake, Canada, 1981), 35–39, 51–67, 103–105; Richter, *The Ordeal of the Longhouse,* 126–127; James Axtell, *The Invasion Within* (New York, 1985), 65–66, 118–119, 125.

22. Lawrence Leader, *Robert Livingston* (Chapel Hill, N.C., 1961), 47–48; O'Callaghan and Fernow, *Documents Relative to the Colonial History of the State of New York,* 6:973. On the persistence of Caughnawaga interest in the Albany area, see D. Peter MacLeod, *The Canadian Iroquois and the Seven Years' War* (Toronto, 1996), 1–36.

23. Peter Wraxall, *An Abridgement of Indian Affairs,* ed. Charles Howard McIlwain (New York, 1968), 244; O'Callaghan and Fernow, *Documents Relative to the Colonial History of the State of New York,* 6:851, 7:576–577, 7:672, 8:92, 10:317. On the gradual divergence of Iroquois and Caughnawaga interests, see Richter, *The Ordeal of the Longhouse,* 166–180; Thomas Elliot Norton, *The Fur Trade in Colonial New York 1688–1776* (Madison, Wis., 1974), 138–139.

24. Francis Parkman, *Montcalm and Wolf* (Boston, 1912), 1:65–71, 2:369.

25. Quoted in French, *Gazetteer of the State of New York,* 308.

26. Ibid. On the presence of St. Regis Native Americans in Saratoga Springs, see Jean McGregor, "Unique Memorials Mark Graves of Indians in Greenridge Cemetery," *Saratogian,* April 27, 1945.

27. Samuel Kirkland, *Journal of Samuel Kirkland,* ed. Walter Pilkington (Clinton, N.Y., 1980), 197.

28. Cooper, *The Last of the Mohicans,* 269–317.

29. John MacMullen, "The Adirondacks in 1843," *New York Evening Post,* July 23, 1881.

30. On Shepherd, see Sylvester, *History of Saratoga County,* 87, 95, 102, 146, 160.

31. Daniel Shepherd, *Saratoga: An Indian Tale of Frontier Life. A True Story of 1787* (Philadelphia, 1856), 68–69, 103, 109, 128, 213, 224.

32. Ibid., Preface, 56.

33. Northup, *Twelve Years a Slave,* 6–7.

34. Stone, *Reminiscences,* 121–128.

35. Ibid., 213–218.

36. Holley, *Samantha at Saratoga,* 323–343, 532–535.

CHAPTER 11: *Wickedness versus Pleasure*

1. For background, see the Bowles & Carver print found in Diana Donald, *The Age of Caricature: Satirical Prints in the Reign of George III* (New Haven, Conn., 1996), 76–77.

2. This concept was introduced by Rhys Isaac, *The Transformation of Virginia 1740–1790* (Chapel Hill, N.C., 1982); it has been expanded in Richard Bushman, *The Refinement of America, Persons, Houses, Cities* (New York, 1992), 313–352.

3. Clifford Morehouse, *Matters of Churches: An Informal History of Trinity Parish in the City of New York* (New York, 1973), 87–89.

4. Sylvester, *History of Saratoga County,* 235–236, 489.

5. Thomas De Laune, *A Plea for the Nonconformists, Shewing the True State of Their Case,* with a preface by Elias Lee (1683; reprint, Ballston, N.Y., 1800), v–xxxix; Sylvester, *History of Saratoga County,* 100, 211, 236, 484. On De Laune, see *Dictionary of National Biography* (London, 1937–1938), 5:221–222. On the New York edition, see Herbert Osgood, "The Society of Dissenters, Founded at New York in 1769," *American Historical Review* 6 (1900–1901): 498–507.

6. De Laune, *A Plea for the Nonconformists,* vi–vii.

7. Ibid., xi–xxii.

8. Ibid., i–xx.

9. Robert Shalhope, *The Roots of Democracy: American Thought and Cuture, 1760–1800* (Boston, 1990), 94–111.

10. Sylvester, *History of Saratoga County,* 80–82, 87, 98–99, 153, 169–171, 208, 215–217, 267, 294, 396, 448, 489.

11. Ibid., 235–236.

12. Eleanor A. Shackelford, "An Outline of the Story of Bethesda Church, Saratoga Springs, N.Y.," in *Parish Record: The Centennial Year, 1930–1931, Bethesda Episcopal Church* (Saratoga Springs, N.Y., n.d.), n.p.; Sylvester, *History of Saratoga County,* 446–447.

13. Mark Lender and James Martin, *Drinking in America* (New York, 1987), 46–58.

14. Paul Johnson, *A Shopkeeper's Millennium, Society and Revivals in Rochester, New York, 1815–1837* (New York, 1978), 6–8.

15. W. Hay, *A History of Temperance in Saratoga County* (Saratoga Springs, N.Y., 1855), 3–12.

16. Sylvester, *History of Saratoga County,* 78, 80, 86, 139, 266–268, 271, 295, 388, 403–404, 427, 430–431; Bureau of the Census, *Heads of Families,* 41.

17. Hay, *A History of Temperance in Saratoga County,* 105, 112.

18. Ibid., 73–75.

19. Ibid., 105.

20. Ibid., 73–75.

21. SSCH, Village of Saratoga Springs, Board of Trustees Minutes, April 30, 1841, 10–11; May 4, 1842, 20–21; May 5, 1844, 47–48. The Town of Saratoga Springs also sold liquor licenses; see SSCH, Town of Saratoga Springs, Commission of Excise, Minutes, 1836–1854.

22. *The Empire State,* 186.

23. Quoted in Hay, *A History of Temperance in Saratoga County,* 40–41.

24. Sylvester, *History of Saratoga County,* 167.

25. James Silk Buckingham, *America, Historical, Statistic, and Descriptive* (London, 1841), 2:418–421, 424–425.

26. Hay, *A History of Temperance in Saratoga County,* 28–31; Mann, *The Bench and Bar of Saratoga County,* 267–272.

27. SSCH, Village of Saratoga Springs, Board of Trustees Minutes, June 29, 1840. These are the earliest village minutes; those from 1838 have been lost. There is, however, a pattern of widely granting liquor licenses in the 1840s.

28. Quoted in Hay, *A History of Temperance in Saratoga County,* 30–31.

29. Clifford Clark Jr., *Henry Ward Beecher: Spokesman for a Middle Class America* (Urbana, Ill., 1978).

30. Sylvester, *History of Saratoga County,* 185–187, 193; on Granger and his enterprise, consult Harry Hall White, "New York State Glass Houses," *The Magazine Antiques,* July 1930, 40–43. Hay, *A History of Temperance in Saratoga County.*

31. Quoted in Hay, *A History of Temperance in Saratoga County,* 122–123.

32. Waller, *Saratoga,* 238.

33. Weiss, *City in the Woods,* 3–23.

34. Rev. R. Smith, *Recollections of Nettleton and the Great Revival of 1820* (Albany, N.Y., 1848), 19–22.

35. Ibid., 60–125.

36. Nathaniel Hatch, *The Democratization of American Christianity* (New Haven, Conn., 1989), 165–170.

37. Beekman Huling, *To the Legislature of the State of New York* (Saratoga Springs, N.Y., February 1862), n.p.; SR, Edmund Huling, Diary, from August 1, 1840, to March 20, 1842 (Transcript of City Historian), September 2–4, 1840; Woodworth-Barnes, *Huling Genealogy,* 291–292; Sylvester, *History of Saratoga County,* 178. It was no accident that Joel Munsell, Albany's leading printer, mechanic, and free thinker, was, like the Hulings, associated through his boarding-house roommates with that city's Universalist Church. On the connection between the evangelicals and free thinkers in Albany, see Hackett, *The Rude Hand of Innovation,* 148–152.

38. Huling, *To the Legislature.*

39. Codman Hislop, *Eliphalet Nott* (Middletown, Conn., 1971), 54–57, 381–383. On similar religious upheaval, see Clarke Garrett, *Respectable Folly, Millenarians and the French Revolution in France and England* (Baltimore, 1975), 121–143.

40. Joshua V. Himes, *Views of the Prophecies and Prophetic Chronology, Selected from Manuscripts of William Miller; with a Memoir of His Life* (Boston, 1841), 7–13; Michael Barkun, *Crucible of the Millennium: The Burned-Over District of New York in the 1840s* (Syracuse, N.Y., 1986), 31–46; David Rowe, *Thunder and Trumpets: Millerites and Dissenting Religion in Upstate New York, 1800–1850* (Chico, Calif., 1985); William Miller, *Evidence from Scripture and History of the Second Coming of Christ, about the Year 1843: Exhibited in a Course of Lectures* (Troy, N.Y., 1836), 3–11.

41. Himes, *Views of the Prophecies and Prophetic Chronology,* 12–14; Stone, *Reminiscences,* 204–205.

42. Robert Hastings Nichols, *Presbyterianism in New York State* (Philadelphia, 1963), 70–99.

43. JAM; Harriet Martineau, *Retrospective of Western Travel* (London, 1838), 3:268–269; Wade, *The Journals of Francis Parkman,* 45–47.

44. Adeline Smith, "Our Church History," *Souvenir of the 140th Anniversary (1793–1933), the First Baptist Church of Saratoga Springs, New York* (Saratoga Springs, N.Y., 1933); Adeline Smith, "Historical Sketch of First Baptist Church," *Program of the One Hundred Seventy-Fifth Anniversary, Oct. 6–13, 1968* (Saratoga Springs, N.Y., 1968); Kettlewell, *Saratoga Springs,* 16.

45. Sylvester, *History of Saratoga County,* 169–173.

46. Ibid., 173–175.

47. Karen Lystra, *Searching the Heart: Women, Men, and Romantic Love in Nineteenth-Century America* (New York, 1989).

48. Kettlewell, *Saratoga Springs,* 64, 68.

49. Shackelford, "An Outline of the Story of Bethesda Church."

50. William Pierson Jr., *American Buildings and Their Architects: Technology and the Picturesque,* *the Corporate and the Early Gothic Styles* (Garden City, N.Y., 1980), 158–168, 190–202, 433–448; Kettlewell, *Saratoga Springs,* 32.

51. Shackelford, "An Outline of the Story of Bethesda Church."

52. Mansfield T. Walworth, *Lulu: A Tale of the National Hotel Poisoning* (New York, 1863), 88–89.

CHAPTER 12: *Setting the Standards for Resort Society*

1. John J. Moorman, *A Directory of the Use of the White Sulphur* (Philadelphia, 1839), 12–13.

2. Stone, *Reminiscences, 350–351;* Reginald Wellington Walworth, *Walworth/Walsworth Genealogy 1689–1962* (Washington, D.C., 1962); "Walworth Family" (team seminar paper for Saratoga County History course, Adirondack Community College, December 7, 1995).

3. Mann, *The Bench and Bar of Saratoga County,* 270–271.

4. [Beaufoy], *Tour through Parts of the United States and Canada. By a British Subject* (London, 1828), 135. See also John Freeman and Clem Labine, "In Praise of Porches," *Old-House Journal* 9 (August 1981): 167, 182–187; Hall, *Travels in North America,* 2:23–25.

5. Downing, *The Architecture of Country Houses,* 122–123, 152–153; Evelyn Barrett Britten, "Block Long Associated with Doctors," *The Saratogian,* October 18, 1957.

6. Durkee, *Reminiscences of Saratoga,* 6; [Beaufoy], *Tour through Parts of the United States and Canada,* 135–136.

7. Allen, *Analysis,* 44–71.

8. Edith Wharton, *Old New York, "The Old Maid"* (1924; reprint, New York, 1978), 428; the latest biography of the author is Eleanor Dwight, *Edith Wharton: An Extraordinary Life* (New York, 1994). Washington Irving, *Salmagundi,* "No XVI.—Thursday, October 15, 1807, Style, at Ballston by William Wizlard, Esq.," in *Works of Washington Irving* (New York, 1897), 5:242.

9. Edith Wharton, *The Age of Innocence* (1920; reprint, New York, 1968), 13, 60–62, 138, 205–206, 214, 239; John Kasson, *Rudeness and Civility, Manners in Nineteenth-Century America* (New York, 1990), 131, 215.

10. Wharton, *Old New York,* 426–427; Margaret More, *End of the Road for Ladies Miles?* (New York, 1985).

11. Nelson Aldrich, *Old Money* (New York, 1988), 29–69.

12. David Hosack, *Memoir of De Witt Clinton* (New York, 1829), 32–33.

13. *The Diary of Philip Hone,* 410–411.

14. William Cary Duncan, *The Amazing Madame Jumel* (New York, 1935), 43, 254–255, 310–311; NYHS, Papers of Madame Jumel; SCCO, X, 138, September 13, 1832, Jose Villalase to Eliza Jumel.

15. Duncan, *The Amazing Madame Jumel,* 272–273, 304–305; Stone, *Reminiscences,* 219–220.

16. Mary Kelley, "Introduction," in *Hope Leslie,* Catharine Maria Sedgwick (New Brunswick, N.J., 1987), v–xiv; Edward Spann, *Ideas & Politics: New York Intellectuals and Liberal Democracy 1820–1880* (Albany, N.Y., 1972), 7–8, 10–12, 27–28, 85–86, 91, 250–251.

17. *Life and Letters of Catharine Maria Sedgwick,* ed. Mary Dewey (New York, 1871), 13–78, 192–193, 306–307, quotes on 193, 306; Ryan, *Cradle of the Middle Class,* 21–23, 32, 121.

18. JAM.

19. Ibid.; Corbett, "Women at the Spas," 1–8.

20. JAM.

21. Nicolai Cikovsky, *Winslow Homer* (New York, 1990), 23–25, 92–97.

22. Gallery Association of New York State, *Winslow Homer Prints from Harper's Weekly* (Hamilton, N.Y., n.d.), 7–9; David Park Curry, "Winslow Homer and Croquet," *The Magazine Antiques* 126, no. 1 (July 1984): 154–162.

23. Wharton, *Old New York,* 436–437.

24. Stone, *Reminiscences,* 340–342.

25. Quoted in ibid., 233–234.

26. Spann, *Ideas & Politics,* 15, 18, 21–22, 95; Van Wyck Brooks, *The World of Washington Irving* (New York, 1944), 192, 321, 376.

27. Sands et al., *Tales of Glauber Spa,* 15–17.

28. Barbara Weakley, "Letters Evoke Old Saratoga," *Times Union* (Albany, N.Y.), August 9, 1987, G-1, G-7.

29. James Kirke Paulding, *The New Mirror for Travelers and Guide to the Springs* (n.p., 1828), 239–277.

30. The story was attributed to Paulding; see Ralph Aderman, ed., *The Letters of James Kirke Paulding* (Madison, Wis., 1962), 126. Paulding contributed another tale, "Selim," to Sands et al., *Tales of Glauber Spa,* 155–220.

31. JAM.

32. Ibid.

33. Ellen Rothman, *Hands and Hearts: A History of Courtship in America* (Cambridge, Mass., 1987), 44–45, 70–71, 160–161.

CHAPTER 13: *The Nature of Visitors*

1. Holley, *Samantha at Saratoga,* 17–18.

2. Ibid., 156.

3. Winter, *Life with "Josiah Allen's Wife,"* 11–26, 75–76, 90–93, 104–105; Holley, "Publishers' Preface," *Samantha at Saratoga.*

4. T. H. Perkins, *The Springs of Virginia* (Boston, 1839); Moorman, *A Directory of the Use of the White Sulphur;* Abner Reed, *Six Views, in Aquatinta, Taken from Nature* (Hartford, Conn., 1810), found in the Wadsworth Atheneum, Hartford, Conn.; *The Great River, Art and Society of the Connecticut Valley, 1635–1820* (Hartford, Conn., 1985), 465–467; National Survey, *A Gazetteer of Vermont Heritage* (Chester, Vt., 1966), 47; Vermont Division for Historic Preservation, *The Historic Architecture of Rutland County* (Montpelier, Vt., 1988), 102, 108.

5. Marquis de Chastellux, *Travels in North America in the Years 1780, 1781 and 1782,* trans. and ed. Howard Rice (Chapel Hill, N.C., 1963), 1:210–214, 1:355; *The New Democracy in America, Travels of Francisco de Miranda in the United States, 1783–1784,* ed. John Ezell (Norman, Okla., 1963), 100–102.

6. James MacGregor Burns, *The Deadlock of Democracy* (New York, 1963), 26–27.

7. *Letters of Benjamin Rush, 1761–1813,* ed. L. H. Butterfield (Princeton, N.J., 1951), 2:1006–1007; Huling, "Saratoga in 1831," 26–27.

8. Irving, *Salmagundi,* 5:241–242.

9. C. D. Arfwedson, *The United States and Canada, in 1832, 1833, and 1834* (London, 1834), 2:269.

10. Irving, *Salmagundi,* 5:241–242.

11. Francis Johnson Dallam, "Documents," *New York History* 28 (July 1947): 330–332 (ed. William Hoyt Jr.). The original is found in the Dallam Papers, Maryland Historical Society, Baltimore.

12. Edward Allen Talbott, *Five Years' Residence in Canada, including a Tour of America in the Year 1823* (London, 1824), 348–349; Charles Latrobe, *The Rambler in North America* (1832; reprint, New York, 1970), 137; C. D. Arfwedson, *The United States and Canada in 1832, 1833, and 1834* (London, 1834), 2: 269–270.

13. *The Traveler's Guide for Montreal, Quebec and Saratoga Springs* (Buffalo, 1852), 26.

14. Jacob Judd, ed., *Correspondence of the Van Cortlandt Family of Cortlandt Manor 1815–1848* (Tarrytown, N.Y., 1981), 113.

15. Irving, *Salmagundi,* 5:241–242.

16. DeVeaux, *The Traveller's Own Book to Saratoga Springs, Niagara Falls and Canada,* 90.

17. Wade, *The Journals of Francis Parkman,* 45–47.

18. Hedrick, *Harriet Beecher Stowe,* 177–183.

19. Jane Donegan, *"Hydropathic Highway to Health," Women and the Water-Cure in Antebellum America* (Westport, Conn., 1986).

20. See Chapter 5.

21. Holley, *Samantha at Saratoga,* 17–18.

22. Rosenzweig and Blackmar, *The Park and the People,* 225–229.

23. Irving, *Salmagundi,* 5:241–243; SSCH, Village of Saratoga Springs, Board of Trustees Minutes, April 30, 1841, 11.

24. HCHP, Solomon Van Rensselaer to Daughters, January 7, 1821, 6/2.

25. Gilborn and Gilborn, *Museum of the Adirondacks,* 54; on Tait, see Warder Cadbury, *Arthur Fitzwilliam Tait: Artist in the Adirondacks* (Newark, Del., 1986).

26. *Currier and Ives America,* ed. Colin Simkin (New York, 1952), n.p.

27. Marjorie Peabody Waite, *Yaddo Yesterday and Today* (Saratoga Springs, N.Y., 1933), 3–23; quote from *The Diary of Philip Hone,* 586.

28. Stone, *Reminiscences,* 340–341, 344; Robert Remini, *Andrew Jackson and the Course of American Democracy 1833–1845* (New York, 1984), 3:64.

29. Stone, *Reminiscences,* 190–196; SR, Huling, Diary, August 19, 1840.

30. Holley, *Samantha at Saratoga,* 362–367; quotes on 362, 367.

31. *Saratogian,* June 17 and August 26, 1871.

32. William McFeely, *Grant* (New York, 1982), 505–517; Durkee, *Reminiscences of Saratoga,* 19; Holley, *Samantha at Saratoga,* 411–431, quote on 416.

33. See notes 40–43 below.

34. NYHS, Charles West Thomson Papers, "A Traveller's Diary being the Journal of a Tour to the Springs," July 30 and 31, 1824.

35. HCHP, Solomon Van Rensselaer to Arriet Van Rensselaer, July 16, 1796, 6/2; Margaretta Van Rensselaer to Adeline Van Rensselaer, July 16, 1829, 7/10; Ann Ludlow to Harriet Van Rensselaer, November 17, 1794, 7/10; Solomon Van Rensselaer to Adeline Van Rensselaer, July 8, 1829, 6/2.

36. Helen Morgan, ed., *A Season in New York, 1801, Letters of Harriet and Marie Trumbull* (Pittsburgh, 1969), 87–88.

37. Nancy Cott, *The Bonds of Womanhood: "Women's Sphere" in New England, 1780–1835* (New Haven, Conn., 1977), 63–100.

38. JAM.

39. Irving, *Salmagundi,* 5:269.

40. BM, Sans Souci Hotel Register, 1823–1825.

41. HS, Union Hall Register, Putnam and Hathorn and Son, 1852.

42. SR, Union Hotel Register, 1869.

43. HS, Continental Hotel Register, 1883.

44. Ida Husted Harper, *The Life and Work of Susan B. Anthony* (Indianapolis, 1898), 1:176–177.

45. Ibid., 1:120, 130–131, 143, 329, 365.

46. Hislop, *Eliphalet Nott,* 33–34, 58; Jacob Judd, ed., *Correspondence of the Van Cortlandt Family of Cortlandt Manor 1800–1814* (Tarrytown, N.Y., 1978), 122–123.

47. HS, Union Hall Register, Putnam and Hathorn and Son, 1852; SR, Union Hotel Register, 1869.

48. Albion, *The Rise of New York Port;* HSP, Cadwalder Collection, McCall Section, Family and Social Correspondence, 1823–1849, Henry McCall Jr. to Peter McCall, Saratoga, August 13, 1848.

49. *The Diary of Philip Hone,* 410–416.

50. Martineau, *Retrospective of Western Travel,* 3:268–269.

51. HSP, Cadwalder Collection, McCall Section, Family and Social Correspondence, 1823–1849, Henry McCall Jr. to Peter McCall, Saratoga, August 13, 1848.

52. Dallam, "Documents," 330–332; Davison, *The Fashionable Tour;* Franklin, *A Southern Odyssey,* 6–7, 26–29, 38–69, 143, 148, 161, 181, 206–209, 255, 272; Stuart, *Three Years in North America* 1:192–200; *Mary Chestnut's Civil War,* ed. C. Vann Woodward (New Haven, Conn., 1981), xxxiii, xxxvii, 38, 91, 100, 116, 140, 447.

53. *New York Times,* August 5, 1856; Grant Tefft, *The Story of Union Village* (Greenwich, N.Y., 1942), 1:61–64; Vermont Division for Historic Preservation, *The Historic Architecture of Rutland County,* 102; National Survey, *A Gazetteer of Vermont Heritage,* 47. Numerical estimates of southern visitors to the North are decidedly impressionistic and are colored by the political views of the estimator. By the 1850s the Union was showing serious signs of coming apart. Those who were strong on its preservation took the view that little had fundamentally changed between the North and the South, that visitors from the South were still arriving at northern resorts as they always had. In New York City there was a strong tie between the banking and financial establishment and the cotton planters, an economic interest that sought to preserve the Union. In addition, since the riots of 1834, the city had demonstrated that it was a formidable center of antiabolition sentiment and viewed abolitionists as undermining the Union. William Leete Stone, editor of the *New York Commercial Advertiser,* was blamed by abolitionists for the destructive 1834 riots, which targeted abolitionists and blacks. Neither he nor the banking establishment wished to admit that the spa was no longer attracting southerners. See Leonard Richards, *Gentlemen of Property and Standing, Anti-Abolition Mobs in Jacksonian America* (New York, 1970), 114–115, 122, 150; Howard Perkins, "The Defense of Slavery in the Northern Press on the Eve of the Civil War," *Journal of Southern History* 9 (November 1943): 501–531; Kenneth Stampp, *America in 1857, a Nation on the Brink* (New York, 1990), 229–231; for another view, see Jon Sterngass, "African American Workers, Southern Visitors, and Antebellum Saratoga Springs" (paper presented October 20, 1999, for the Saratoga Springs Urban Heritage Area).

54. Albion, *The Rise of New York Port,* 174–179, 182–184; *The Empire State,* 193.

55. Irene Neu, *Erastus Corning, Merchant and Financier, 1794–1872* (Ithaca, N.Y., 1960), 112, 192–193.

56. Arthur Vanderbilt, *Fortune's Children: The Fall of the House of Vanderbilt* (New York, 1989), 45, 57–58, 84, 214–215, 298, 328.

57. Ibid., 143–146; Aldrich, *Old Money,* 29–69; Michael Lewis, "The Rich: How They're Different . . . Than They Used to Be," *New York Times,* November 19, 1995, 65–69.

58. On the general acceptance of suburbanization by most nineteenth-century U.S. communities, see Clark, *The American Family Home;* Kenneth Jackson, *Crabgrass Frontier: The Suburbanization of the United States* (New York, 1985).

59. WCCO, Frederick B. Hubbell to Walter Price, Deed Book 20, 337, July 19, 1869; WCCO, John H. Smith to Walter Price, Deed Book 20, 344, July 19, 1869; WCCO, Pierre Van Cortlandt and Catherine E. Van Cortlandt to Isaac H. Tuttle, Deed Book 15, 70, September 29, 1866; WCCO, Pierre Van Cortlandt and Catherine E. Van Cortlandt to Isaac H. Tuttle, Deed Book 18, 41, December 4, 1867; O'Brien, *The Great and the Gracious,* 29–33, 73–82. Price's and Tuttle's cottages predated William Durant's Camp Pine Knot, which was begun on Raquette Lake in 1879. In 1881, the Lake House still had two cottages on its grounds for private parties.

60. While North Broadway and Union Avenue, exclusive residential developments, are well known, Grand Avenue is neglected, probably because it is not in that category today; Kettlewell, *Saratoga Springs,* 59–60, 81–87.

EPILOGUE: *Why Do Resorts Succeed?*

1. Chemung County Historical Society Collections, Elmira, N.Y., "Breesport," *Buffalo Express* (Buffalo, N.Y.), November 14, 1886.

2. Britten, *Chronicles of Saratoga,* 58–59.

3. William Gaberson, "Fun and Profit vs. Peace and Quiet on Lake George," *New York Times,* July 28, 1991, 37.

4. Britten, *Chronicles of Saratoga,* 71–72.

5. Arfwedson, *The United States and Canada in 1832, 1833, and 1834,* 270.

6. Betsy Wade, "Plenty of Room for One," *New York Times,* July 20, 1997, 12, 22.

Index

Note: Page numbers in boldface refer to illustrations.

About the Author

*T*heodore Corbett earned his Ph.D. from the University of Southern California. He is a former director of the Saratoga Springs Preservation Foundation and taught history at Florida State University and Columbia-Greene Community College; he currently teaches at Adirondack Community College. His latest projects include an exhibit for the Saratoga Springs Urban Heritage Area entitled "Reclaiming African-American and Irish-American Heritage" and a new account of the "Warpath of Nations" in the Hudson-Champlain Valley.